FABULAE GRAECAE

A REVISED EDITION OF

RITCHIE'S

FABULAE FACILES

EDITED BY

GILBERT LAWALL
STANLEY IVERSON
ALLAN WOOLEY

Longman

New York

Fabulae Graecae: A Revised Edition of Ritchie's *Fabulae Faciles*

Longman, 10 Bank Street, White Plains, N.Y. 10606

Associated companies:
Longman Group Ltd., London
Longman Cheshire Pty., Melbourne
Longman Paul Pty., Auckland
Copp Clark Pitman, Toronto

Executive editor: Lyn McLean

ISBN 0-8013-0756-2

8 9 10-DOC-99 98 97 96

Photo Credit

Page 1: Alinari/Art Resource, NY.

Preface
for Students

This book contains the stories of Perseus, Hercules, the Argonauts, and Ulysses as told in Ritchie's *Fabulae Faciles*, a book that generations of students have enjoyed as an intermediate Latin reader. The present edition contains many features that will help you read and understand the Latin stories themselves and that will at the same time enrich your knowledge of Latin vocabulary and grammar and enhance your skill in reading Latin at sight. These features include the following:

1. Facing running vocabularies with each paragraph of the Latin text
2. Grammatical notes incorporated in the running vocabularies
3. Fuller descriptions of selected elements of grammar, illustrated by phrases, clauses, or sentences taken from the Latin readings; these are contained in boxes, and they often deal with the process of translating from Latin to English (these grammar boxes are usually placed at the bottom of the left-hand pages and occasionally on the right-hand pages)
4. Sets of five English sentences accompanying each paragraph of the Latin and based closely on the Latin of the stories themselves; these English sentences are for you to translate into Latin; they are usually placed at the bottom of the right-hand pages, and they are often accompanied by Helpful Hints dealing with the process of translating from English into Latin

The exercises in English to Latin translation will help you consolidate your knowledge of forms, syntax, and vocabulary and will thus reinforce the knowledge and the skills that you will need to read new Latin at sight.

At the end of the book you will find:

1. Lists of the grammatical topics covered in the boxed descriptions of selected elements of grammar that accompany the reading passages
2. A complete Latin to English vocabulary list with all the information you need about individual words
3. A list of selected idioms and special grammatical and verbal items that recur in the readings

4. A complete English to Latin vocabulary list to help you locate the right Latin word when translating the sentences from English to Latin

Asterisks in the vocabularies facing the paragraphs of the Latin stories indicate that the words so marked should be thoroughly learned when they are first met in reading.

The elements of compound words are frequently given in parentheses in the vocabulary entries; attention to the way in which words are put together in Latin will help you deduce the meaning of new compound words as you meet them.

In the vocabulary notes that face the Latin passages you will also find idioms that are used in the Latin stories, and we will frequently call your attention to pairs or groups of words that are similar in spelling and often confused. Careful attention should be paid to the idioms and to the differences in spelling that will help you avoid confusing words as you meet them in your reading.

In the final section containing the stories of Ulysses, there are Review Questions to consolidate your knowledge of forms and syntax and Content Questions to test your comprehension of the Latin without recourse to translation.

Upon completion of this book, you will be ready to read any of a variety of Latin authors as they are presented in the standard school and college textbooks. This in itself is well worth the effort that you will put into reading the stories and doing the English to Latin exercises contained in this book, but above all we urge that you enjoy the stories themselves as they are told in this book with simple elegance and enduring human interest.

Contents

Perseus

Perseus holding the head of Medusa

Acrisius, an ancient king of Argos, had been warned by an oracle that he would perish by the hand of his grandson. On discovering, therefore, that his daughter Danaë had given birth to a son, Acrisius endeavored to escape his fate by setting both mother and child adrift on the sea. They were saved, however, by the help of Jupiter, and Perseus, the child, grew up at the court of Polydectes, king of Seriphos, an island in the Aegean Sea.

When he reached manhood, Perseus was sent by Polydectes to fetch the head of Medusa, one of the Gorgons. This dangerous task he accomplished with the help of Apollo and Minerva, and on his way home he rescued Andromeda, daughter of Cepheus, from a sea monster. Perseus married Andromeda and lived some time in the country of Cepheus.

At length Perseus returned to Seriphos and turned Polydectes to stone by showing him the Gorgon's head. He then went to the court of Acrisius, who fled in terror at the news of his grandson's return. The oracle was duly fulfilled, for Acrisius was accidentally killed by a discus thrown by Perseus.

1   **Haec:** "The following things"; this is a common use of **haec.**
     ā poētīs: *ablative of agent* with the *passive verb* **nārrantur.**
     ***Perseus, -ī** (m),* Perseus.
2   ***Iuppiter, Iovis** (m),* Jupiter.
     maximī: in *apposition* to **Iovis.**
     ***avus, -ī** (m),* grandfather.
     ***Acrisius, -ī** (m),* Acrisius.
     ***appellō** (1),* to call, name.
3   **volēbat:** from **volō, velle** *(irreg.),* **voluī,** to be willing, wish.
         Distinguish this verb carefully from **volō** (1), to fly.
     ***nepōs, nepōtis** (m),* grandson.
     necāre: *complementary infinitive* with **volēbat.**
4   ***ōrāculum, -ī** (n),* oracle. It was believed in antiquity that the will of the
         gods and the course of future events could be learned at certain shrines.
         Both the prophecy and the shrine were called **ōrāculum.**
     Perseum: *direct object* of **comprehendit** and **inclūsit.**
     etiam tum īnfantem: translate with a relative clause.
5   ***comprehendō, comprehendere** (3),* **comprehendī, comprehēn-**
     sum, to seize, catch.
     ***arca, -ae** (f),* chest, box, ark.
     ligneus, -a, -um, of wood, wooden.
     ***inclūdō** (in- + claudō), **inclūdere** (3), **inclūsī, inclūsum,** to shut up,
         enclose, imprison.
6   ***Danaē** (three syllables),* **Danaēs,** *(f),* Danaē. Many proper nouns in this
         book are Greek and have forms different from the regular Latin declen-
         sions. It will not be necessary to learn these Greek forms; the notes will
         provide all needed help.
     Perseī: *three syllables.*
7   **territa est:** *perfect passive indicative.*
8   ***turbō** (1),* to confuse, throw into disorder, disturb, trouble.
     ***autem,** moreover, but, however, now, and indeed.
     sinus, -ūs (m), bosom, lap.

Ablative of Agent

If the action of a passive verb is carried out by a person, we say in English that the action is done *by* someone, e.g., "The story is told by the poet." Latin uses the preposition **ab (ā)** with the ablative case, e.g., **Haec ā poētīs nārrantur,** "The following things are told by poets." This is called the *ablative of agent.*

Complementary Infinitive

An infinitive may be used to complete the meaning of Latin verbs such as **volō,** "I wish," and **cōnstituō,** "I decide," e.g., **Acrisius volēbat Perseum necāre,** "Acrisius wished to kill Perseus." This is called the *complementary infinitive.*

1. THE ARK

Haec ā poētīs dē Perseō nārrantur. Perseus fīlius erat 1
Iovis, maximī deōrum; avus eius Acrisius appellābātur. 2
Acrisius volēbat Perseum nepōtem suum necāre; nam 3
propter ōrāculum puerum timēbat. Perseum etiam tum 4
īnfantem comprehendit, et cum mātre in arcā līgneā in- 5
clūsit. Tum arcam ipsam in mare coniēcit. Danaē, Perseī 6
māter, magnopere territa est; tempestās enim magna 7
mare turbābat. Perseus autem in sinū mātris dormiēbat. 8

1. Danaë was the mother of Perseus.
2. She had been seized by Acrisius.
3. He cast mother and son into the sea.
4. For he feared the boy and wished to kill him.
5. Perseus, however, was not frightened.

Helpful Hints
1. Use the same case after as before any form of the verb **esse**.
2. "Had been seized" = pluperfect passive; be sure that the participle you use in writing the Latin verb agrees with the subject of the sentence in gender and number.
The subject need not be expressed with a separate word in Latin.
3. "And" can be **et**, **atque**, or **-que**.
4. **Nam** "for" comes first in its clause; **enim** "for" comes second.
5. **Sed** "but" comes first in its clause; **autem** "however" comes second.

2 cōnstituō (con- + statuō), cōnstituere (3), cōnstituī, cōnstitūtum, to
   set up, appoint, determine, decide. Distinguish this verb carefully from
   cōnstō, cōnstāre (1), cōnstitī, cōnstātum, to stand together, agree,
   consist, and from cōnsistō, cōnsistere (3), cōnstitī, to station oneself, take one's stand, consist.
   tranquillus, -a, -um, calm.
   tranquillum: *double or predicate accusative*, "made the sea calm."
   scēptrum, -ī (*n*), scepter, staff.
   scēptrō: *ablative of means or instrument*, "with his scepter."
3 Serīphus, -ī (*f*), Seriphos.
   Serīphum: in *apposition* to īnsulam, but we say in English "the island
   of Seriphos."
   perdūcō, perdūcere (3), perdūxī, perductum, to lead *or* bring
   through, lead, bring.
   *Polydectēs, Polydectis (*m*), Polydectes.
4 *appellō (ad- + pellō), appellere (3), appulī, appulsum, to drive to,
   bring to. Distinguish this verb carefully from appellō (1), to call, name.
   appulsa est: *perfect indicative* with postquam, denoting an action
   completed before the action of the main verb; translate with English
   pluperfect, "had been driven."
5 harēna, -ae (*f*), sand, shore.
   Brevī tempore: *ablative of time when* or *within which*, "In a short time,"
   "Soon."
   quiētem capere, *idiom*, to rest.
   piscātor, piscātōris (*m*), fisherman.
6 quōdam: from quīdam, quaedam, quiddam, "a certain," "certain," declined like quī, quae, quod + -dam.
   *reperiō, reperīre (4), repperī, repertum, to find, discover.
7 Ille: "He," i.e., Polydectes.
   *benignē (*adv.*), kindly.
   *sēdēs, sēdis, sēdum *or* sēdium (*f*), seat, abode, home.
8 *tūtus, -a, -um, safe.
   *fīnis, fīnis, fīnium (*m*), end, boundary; (*pl.*) borders, territory, country.
   *dōnum, -ī (*n*), gift.
9 *prō (+ *abl.*), before, in front of, for, in behalf of, as, in return for.
   *beneficium, -ī (*n*), well-doing, kindness, service, benefit. Note the
   derivation of this word from bene and faciō; the meaning of a word
   may often be seen most clearly and remembered best by noticing its
   derivation.
   *grātia, -ae (*f*), favor, gratitude, thanks; (*pl.*) thanks.
   grātiās agere (+ *dat.*), *idiom*, to give thanks, thank.

Double or Predicate Accusative

Verbs of naming, electing, making, and asking often
take two accusatives, the first the direct object and the
second a predicate to that object, e.g., **Tranquillum
mare fēcit**, "He made the sea (*direct object*) calm
(*predicate*)." The second accusative may also be a
noun, e.g., "They elected Cicero consul."

2. JUPITER SAVES HIS SON

Iuppiter tamen haec omnia vīdit, et fīlium suum servāre 1
cōnstituit. Itaque tranquillum mare scēptrō fēcit, et arcam 2
ad īnsulam Serīphum perdūxit. Huius īnsulae Polydectēs 3
tum rēx erat. Postquam arca ad lītus appulsa est, Danaē 4
in harēnā quiētem capiēbat. Brevī tempore ā piscātōre 5
quōdam reperta est, et ad domum rēgis Polydectis adducta 6
est. Ille mātrem et puerum benignē excēpit, et eīs sēdem 7
tūtam in fīnibus suīs dedit. Danaē hoc dōnum libenter ac- 8
cēpit, et prō tantō beneficiō rēgī grātiās ēgit. 9

Ablative of Means, Instrument, or Cause with Verbs

Both active and passive verbs may be accompanied by a noun or phrase in the ablative case without a preposition to express the *means* by which, the *instrument* with which, or the *cause* on account of which the action takes place, e.g., **tranquillum mare scēptrō fēcit,** "he made the sea calm <u>with (by means of) his scepter.</u>"

Ablative of Time When or Within Which

The ablative case without a preposition may express the *time when* or *within which* an action takes place, e.g., **Brevī tempore reperta est,** "<u>In a short time (Soon)</u> she was found."

---

1. In a short time they were brought by the waves to the island (of) Seriphos.
2. At that time the king of this island was called Polydectes.
3. After they had been found on the shore, they were taken to the king.
4. He decided to give them a home.
5. For he wished to make them (his) friends.

Helpful Hints
3. **Postquam** with the perfect translates an English pluperfect. Put the subordinating conjunction first in its clause here, and do not translate "they" with a separate word.
4. Verbs of giving, showing, and telling take an indirect object in the dative case, which usually precedes the direct object.

1   **multōs annōs**: *accusative of duration of time.*
2   *****vīta, -ae** (*f*), life.
      vītam agere, *idiom,* to live.
    *****beātus, -a, -um**, happy, blest.
      Danaēn: *Greek accusative singular.*
3   *****mātrimōnium, -ī** (*n*), marriage.
      in mātrimōnium dūcere, *idiom,* to lead into marrriage, to marry.
4   *****cōnsilium, -ī** (*n*), advice, plan, design, purpose.
      Perseō: *dative* with the *adjective* **grātum**.
      grātus, -a, -um (+ *dat.*), pleasing (to).
5   *****dīmittō, dīmittere** (3), **dīmīsī, dīmissum**, to send different ways,
      send forth *or* away, dispatch.
6   *****iuvenis, -is** (*m*), young man.
      turpis, -is, -e, disgraceful.
7   **agere**: the *infinitive* is the *subject* of the sentence; infinitives used as
      subjects are *neuter,* hence the neuter *predicate adjective* here, **turpe**.
      iam diū . . . es: **iam diū** + *present indicative* to represent an action or
      state that began at some past time and is still continuing; translate with a
      perfect tense in English, "you have been . . . for a long time now."
      quō ūsque, till when? how long?
8   **Tempus est**: "It is time," with the *infinitives* **capere** and **praestāre** as
      predicate nominatives.
    *****virtūs, virtūtis** (*f*), manliness, courage, bravery.
9   *****praestō, praestāre** (1), **praestitī, praestitum**, to show.
      hinc (*adv.*), from this place, hence.
    *****Medūsa, -ae** (*f*), Medusa.
    *****referō, referre** (*irreg.*), **rettulī, relātum**, to bring *or* carry back, re-
      turn, fetch.
        refer: *irregular imperative* of **re-ferō** (compare **dīc, dūc,** and
        fac). Review the principal parts of **ferō**: **ferō, ferre** (*irreg.*),
        tulī, lātum.

Accusative of Duration of Time

The *accusative case* without a preposition may express
time *how long* or *duration of time*, e.g., **Perseus
multōs annōs ibi habitābat**, "Perseus lived there
(for) many years." Compare the *ablative of time when,*
e.g., **brevī tempore**, "in a short time," "soon" (see
grammar note with paragraph 2).

Dative with Adjectives

Many Latin *adjectives* are accompanied by a word or
phrase in the *dative* case, e.g., **Perseō grātum erat**,
"It was pleasing to Perseus." You may wish to make a
list of such adjectives as you meet them in your
reading.

3. PERSEUS IS SENT ON HIS TRAVELS

Perseus igitur multōs annōs ibi habitābat, et cum 1
mātre suā vītam beātam agēbat. At Polydectēs Danaēn 2
magnopere amābat, atque eam in mātrimōnium dūcere 3
volēbat. Hoc tamen cōnsilium Perseō minimē grātum 4
erat. Itaque Polydectēs Perseum dīmittere cōnstituit. 5
Tum iuvenem ad sē vocāvit et haec dīxit: "Turpe est hanc 6
ignāvam vītam agere; iam diū tū adulēscēns es. Quō 7
ūsque hīc manēbis? Tempus est arma capere et virtūtem 8
praestāre. Hinc abī, et caput Medūsae ad mē refer." 9

Infinitive as Subject or Predicate Nominative

The infinitive may be used as the *subject* of a Latin
sentence; it is regarded as neuter in gender, and a
predicate adjective used with it will be neuter, e.g.,
Turpe est hanc ignāvam vītam agere, "To lead
this lazy life is disgraceful." The infinitive may also be
used as a *predicate nominative*, e.g., **Tempus est
arma capere**, "It is time to take up arms."

Iam diū + Present Indicative

Iam diū is used with the *present indicative* to represent an action or state that began at some past time
and is still continuing; it should be translated with a
perfect tense in English, e.g., **iam diū tū
adulēscēns es**, "you have been a young man for a
long time now (and you still are a young man)."

---

1. Perseus remained many years in the country of the king.
2. Polydectes, however, wished to send him away.
3. He said the following things: "To live without dangers is
   disgraceful."
4. "Take up arms, young man, and show your courage."
5. For a long time it has not been pleasing to this woman to see Polydectes.

Helpful Hints
1. When something occurs at one point of time or off and on in a period of time,
   use the ablative of time when, but when it occurs throughout or continuously,
   use the accusative of duration of time.
4. The imperative is the mood of command; it usually has no separately stated
   subject, but there may be a vocative in the sentence, although it should not
   come first.
   In paragraph 3 above, find the idiom for "take up arms."

1   **Perseus ubi**: if a Latin sentence begins with a subordinate clause the subject of which is also the subject of the main clause, this word is usually put first, before the subordinating conjunction; translate, "When Perseus. . . . "

2   *__continēns, continentis__ (*f*), mainland, continent.

4   *__Apollō, Apollinis__ (*m*), Apollo.

    *__Minerva, -ae__ (*f*), Minerva.

5   **Graeae, -ārum** (*f pl*), the Graeae (three old women, who had one eye and one tooth in common and took turns using them; Perseus seized the eye and tooth and so compelled the Graeae to tell him how to obtain help for his undertaking).

    Ab hīs: "From these (them)." Note that **ab** can mean "from" as well as "by."

    *__tālāria, tālārium__ (*n pl*), winged shoes.

6   *__galea, -ae__ (*f*), helmet.

    *__magicus, -a, -um__, of magic, magic.

    galeam magicam: this helmet made its wearer invisible.

    eī: *dative singular* of **is**.

    *__falx, falcis, falcium__ (*f*), sickle, curved sword.

7   **pedibus**: *dative indirect object* with **induit**; translate "on his feet," and note that the possessive adjective "his" is not given in Latin unless for emphasis or to avoid ambiguity.

8   *__āēr, āeris__, (*Greek accusative*) **āera** (*m*), air. Compare **aere** (from **aes, aeris**, *n*, bronze) in the last line of this paragraph.

    *__volō__ (1), to fly. Do not confuse with **volō, velle** (*irreg.*), **voluī**, to be willing, wish.

9   **eum**: "that," modifying **locum**. Remember that **is, ea, id** can be used as an adjective or as a pronoun.

10   *__Gorgōn, Gorgonis__ (*f*), Gorgon.

    *__mōnstrum, -ī__ (*n*), wonder, monster.

11   *__speciēs, -ēī__ (*f*), sight, appearance, shape.

    *__horribilis, -is, -e__, dreadful, terrible, horrible.

    speciē horribilī: *ablative of description*; the noun and its adjective in the ablative case modify the noun **mōnstra**, "monsters of horrible appearance."

    anguis, anguis, anguium (*m/f*), serpent, snake.

    anguibus: *ablative of means* without a preposition, "with snakes," modifying **contēcta**.

    *__omnīnō__ (*adv.*), altogether, wholly, entirely, at all.

12   **contegō, contegere** (3), **contēxī, contēctum**, to cover.

    contēcta erant: *pluperfect passive indicative*, literally, "had been covered," describing a state or condition completed prior to some time in the past; translate "were covered."

    factae erant: *pluperfect passive indicative* of the irregular verb **fīō, fierī, factus sum**; see note on **contēcta erant** above; translate "were made."

4. PERSEUS GETS HIS OUTFIT

Perseus ubi haec audīvit, ex īnsulā discessit; et 1
postquam ad continentem vēnit, Medūsam quaesīvit. Diū 2
frūstrā quaerēbat, nam nātūram locī ignōrābat. Tandem 3
Apollō et Minerva viam dēmōnstrāvērunt. Prīmum ad 4
Graeās, sorōrēs Medūsae, pervēnit. Ab hīs tālāria et 5
galeam magicam accēpit. Apollō autem et Minerva eī fal- 6
cem et speculum dedērunt. Tum, postquam tālāria pe- 7
dibus induit, in āera ascendit. Diū per āera volāvit; 8
tandem tamen ad eum locum vēnit ubi Medūsa cum cēterīs 9
Gorgonibus habitābat. Gorgonēs autem mōnstra erant 10
speciē horribilī; capita enim eārum anguibus omnīnō 11
contēcta erant. Manūs etiam ex aere factae erant. 12

Ablative of Description

A noun and adjective in the ablative case without a
preposition may describe another noun, e.g., **Gorgonēs
mōnstra erant speciē horribilī**, "The Gorgons
were monsters of horrible appearance." The word "of"
is usually used in English translation of the ablative of
description.

**Ablative of Means, Instrument, or Cause with
Adjectives or Participles**

Certain adjectives or participles may be accompanied
by an *ablative of means, instrument, or cause* without
a preposition, e.g., **capita anguibus contēcta**,
"heads covered with snakes."

---

1. Perseus was a young man of great bravery.
2. And so he decided to go away and seek Medusa.
3. In a short time Perseus was miserable because of his great labor.
4. After he had departed from the island, he came to the abode of Medusa.
5. Perseus was armed with a curved sword and a mirror.

Helpful Hints

3. With the adjective used to translate "miserable," use an ablative without a preposition to express the cause of the feeling or emotion.

1   **difficillima**: some adjectives ending in **-lis**, such as **difficilis**, have
     superlatives in **-limus, -a, -um** (see paragraph 40).
     *abscīdō (abs- = ab- + caedō), **abscīdere** (3), **abscīdī, abscīsum**, to cut
     away, cut off.
           abscīdere: the infinitive is *subject*; **rēs difficillima** is *predicate
           nominative*.
2   ***cōnspectus, -ūs** (*m*), sight.
     *vertō, vertere (3), **vertī, versum**, to turn.
           vertēbantur: the *imperfect tense* here represents the action as
           customary or *habitual*, one of its regular uses.
4   **in speculum īnspiciēbat**: the *imperfect tense* here represents the
     action as *repeated*, another of its regular uses, "kept looking."
     hōc modō: *ablative of manner*.
5   **suā** and **eius**: distinguish carefully between these words, both meaning
     "his"; the former is *reflexive* and used to describe something that
     belongs to the subject, while the latter is used of that which belongs to
     some other person or thing just mentioned.
6   ***ictus, -ūs** (*m*), blow.
           ūnō ictū: *ablative of manner* (**cum** is optional when the noun is
           accompanied by an adjective).
8   ***occīdō** (ob- + caedō), **occīdere** (3), **occīdī, occīsum**, to cut down, kill.
     Ille . . . dum fugit, galeam . . . induit: note that the subject (**Ille**) of
     the subordinate clause precedes the subordinating conjunction (**dum**)
     when it is the same as the subject of the main clause.
     dum fugit . . . induit: **dum** with *present indicative* in the subordinate
     clause followed by the *perfect tense* in the main clause = "while," "while
     he was fleeing, he put on. . . . "
9   **ubi . . . fēcit**: *perfect indicative* with **ubi**, "when," as with **postquam**
     (see note with line 4 of paragraph 2), to be translated with *pluperfect* in
     English, "when he had done this."

Ablative of Manner

A noun and adjective in the ablative case may describe
how (i.e., the *manner* in which) an action is carried out,
e.g. **Hōc modō ad locum vēnit**, "In this way he
came to the place." The preposition **cum** is optional;
when used it often appears between the adjective and
the noun, e.g., **Caput ūnō ictū abscīdit** or **ūnō
cum ictū**, "He cut off her head with one blow."

Dum + Present Indicative = "while"

Dum means "while" when it introduces a subordinate
clause with its verb in the *present indicative* in a sentence with a main verb in the *perfect tense*, e.g., **Dum
fugit** (present tense), **galeam magicam induit**
(perfect tense), "While he was fleeing, he put on the
magic helmet."

5. THE GORGON'S HEAD

Rēs difficillima erat caput Gorgonis abscīdere; eius enim   1
cōnspectū hominēs in saxum vertēbantur. Propter hanc   2
causam Minerva speculum Perseō dederat. Ille igitur ter-   3
gum vertit et in speculum īnspiciēbat; hōc modō ad locum   4
vēnit ubi Medūsa dormiēbat. Tum falce suā caput eius ūnō   5
ictū abscīdit. Cēterae Gorgonēs statim ē somnō excitātae   6
sunt; et ubi rem vīdērunt, īrā commōtae sunt. Arma   7
cēpērunt; nam Perseum occīdere volēbant. Ille autem dum   8
fugit, galeam magicam induit; et ubi hoc fēcit, statim ē cōn-   9
spectū eārum ēvāsit.   10

> **Dum = "while"** (continued)
>
> The present indicative in the **dum** clause is a
> special use of the *vivid* or *historic present*, i.e., the use
> of the present tense to describe a past action. The
> clause with **dum** and the present indicative describes
> what was happening at the moment when the action of
> the main clause took place; we thus translate "While
> he <u>was</u> fleeing."

1. When Perseus had come, he immediately killed Medusa with one blow of his curved sword.
2. He wished to carry her head back to (his) king.
3. The sight of this head used to turn men into stone.
4. After Medusa had been killed by Perseus, the other Gorgons took up arms.
5. While they were doing this, Perseus fled with great speed.

Helpful Hints
1. Put the subject of the subordinate clause before the subordinating conjunction when it is the same as the subject of the main clause.

   Many English words need not be represented with separate words in Latin, because they are understood from context or the endings of words, e.g., "had," "he," "with," and "of" in this sentence. The word "his" or "her" is also often not translated if it refers to the same person as the subject of the clause in which it appears, as here.
2. "Her" in this sentence must be translated; use the genitive of **is, ea, id**. "His" refers to the subject of its own clause (i.e., it is reflexive) and may be omitted in Latin; if expressed, it must be a form of **suus, -a, -um**.
3. Several English expressions can be translated by using the Latin imperfect tense, e.g., "was turning" (progressive), "used to turn" (customary or habitual), "kept turning" (repeated), or "tried to turn" (conative).
4. "The other" = "the rest of" = **cēterī, -ae, -a** or **reliquī, -ae, -a**, not **aliī, -ae, -a** = "other" or **alterī, -ae, -a** = "the others" of two groups.

1   **Posteā**: note that **posteā** is an *adverb*, "after this," "afterwards"; distin-
     guish it carefully from **post**, which may be either an adverb, "after,"
     "later," or a preposition, "after," "behind," taking the accusative case; also
     compare **postquam**, the conjunction, which introduces a subordinate
     clause and means "after" or "when."
     *Aethiopēs, -um (*m pl*), Ethiopians.
     *Cēpheus, -ī (*m*), Cepheus.
2   *rēgnō (1), to reign, rule.
     *Neptūnus, -ī (*m*), Neptune.
3   *quondam (*adv.*), once upon a time, formerly, once.
     offendō, offendere (3), offendī, offēnsum, to offend.
4   *saevus, -a, -um, fierce, savage.
     saevissimum: *superlative* used to denote a very high degree, "most
     fierce" or "very fierce," not "fiercest."
     *cotīdiē (*adv.*), daily, every day.
     marī: *3rd declension neuter i-stem nouns* have ablative singular in -*ī*.
5   pavor, pavōris (*m*), terror, panic.
6   *Hammōn, Hammōnis (*m*), Amen *or* Amon (an Egyptian god, often
     represented with the horns of a ram; his oracle, shared with the Greek
     god Zeus, was in an oasis of the Libyan desert in northern Africa; our
     word *ammonia* is related to the name of this shrine).
7   iussus est . . . trādere: *perfect passive + infinitive*. The form with an
     active verb would be, **Deus iussit Cēpheum fīliam mōnstrō
     trādere**. The passive verb avoids the possible confusion of the two
     accusatives.
8   nōmine: *ablative of respect*, "by name."
     *Andromeda, -ae (*f*), Andromeda.
     *virgō, virginis (*f*), maiden.
     *fōrmōsus, -a, -um, beautiful.
9   dolōrem capere, *idiom*, to suffer grief.
11   *iussum, -ī (*n*), order, command.

Third Declension I-stem Nouns

Some third declension nouns are called *i-stem nouns*;
all such nouns have their genitive plural in -*ium* rather
than -*um*. The ablative singular of some masculine
and feminine i-stem nouns may end in either -*e* or -*ī*,
as does **ignis**; other masculine and feminine i-stem
nouns always have -**e** in the ablative singular, e.g.:

Singular	Plural	Singular	Plural
ignis	ignēs	urbs	urbēs
ignis	ignium	urbis	urbium
ignī	ignibus	urbī	urbibus
ignem	ignēs	urbem	urbēs
igne (-ī)	ignibus	urbe	urbibus

6. THE SEA-SERPENT

Posteā Perseus in fīnēs Aethiopum vēnit. Ibi Cēpheus 1
quīdam illō tempore rēgnābat. Hic Neptūnum, maris 2
deum, quondam offenderat. Neptūnus autem mōnstrum 3
saevissimum mīserat. Hoc cotīdiē ē marī veniēbat et ho- 4
minēs dēvorābat. Ob hanc causam pavor animōs omnium 5
occupāverat. Itaque Cēpheus ōrāculum deī Hammōnis 6
cōnsuluit, atque ā deō iussus est fīliam mōnstrō trādere. 7
Eius autem fīlia, nōmine Andromeda, virgō fōrmōsissima 8
erat. Cēpheus ubi haec audīvit, magnum dolōrem cēpit. 9
Volēbat tamen cīvēs suōs ē tantō perīculō extrahere, atque 10
ob eam causam iussa Hammōnis facere cōnstituit. 11

Neuter I-stem Nouns *(see page 15)*

Third Declension Adjectives *(see Forms, page 215)*

Ablative of Respect

A word in the ablative case without a preposition may indicate that *with respect to which* something is or is done, e.g., **fīlia, nōmine Andromeda**, literally, "the daughter, Andromeda <u>with respect to name</u>," better English, "Andromache <u>by name</u>" or "<u>named</u> Andromeda."

---

1. While Perseus was in the country of Cepheus, he rescued Andromeda from the greatest danger.
2. At this time Cepheus was king both in name and in deed.
3. He had been ordered to give up (his) daughter to a horrible monster, the most savage of animals that lived in the sea.
4. For this reason all men were moved with grief.
5. When Perseus had seen Andromeda, he decided to save her.

Helpful Hints
1. For translation of "while . . . ," see grammar note with paragraph 5.
   For "from the greatest danger," find a model in paragraph 6 above.
4. Verbs of feeling or emotion often have an ablative of cause without a preposition (see grammar note with paragraph 2).

1   *diem dīcere, *idiom*, to appoint *or* set a day. Note that when diēs denotes an appointed day, as it does here, it is feminine.
     diem certam: "certain" in the sense of "definite."

2   *dēdūcō, dēdūcere (3), dēdūxī, dēductum, to lead down *or* away, bring.

3   rūpēs, rūpis (*f*), rock, cliff.
     *alligō (ad- + ligō) (1), to bind to, bind.
     *fātum, -ī (*n*), destiny, fate.
     dēplōrō (1), to lament.

4   nec, and . . . not.
     *lacrima, -ae (*f*), tear.

6   quaerit: *vivid or historic present*, used of a past action, to represent it vividly, as if it were now going on.
     Illī: the pronoun ille often indicates a change of subject.
     *expōnō, expōnere (3), exposuī, expositum, to set forth, explain.

7   *fremitus, -ūs (*m*), roaring, roar.

9   omnibus: *dative* with the *compound verb* iniēcit (not all compound verbs take the dative, nor even all verbs compounded with one preposition; compare in speculum īnspiciēbat, paragraph 5).
     iniciō (in- + iaciō), inicere (3), iniēcī, iniectum, to throw in *or* upon, cause, inspire.

10   *contendō, contendere (3), contendī, contentum to stretch, exert oneself, hurry, rush.
     locō: *dative* with the *compound verb* appropinquābat.

Vivid or Historic Present

When describing past actions Latin writers often switched to the present tense to make the narrative more vivid and to make the reader feel personally involved in it. This is called the *vivid* or *historic present*. We often do this in English as well. In paragraph 7 all of the verbs from quaerit to cōnspicitur are in the vivid or historic present. The perfect tense resumes with iniēcit (note that contendit is perfect tense).

Dative with Compound Verbs

Many verbs that are compounded with prepositional prefixes are used with the dative case, e.g., Timōrem omnibus iniēcit, "It threw fear into all," and Locō appropinquābat, "It was approaching the place." You should make a list of such verbs as you meet them in your reading.

7. A HUMAN SACRIFICE

Tum rēx diem certam dīxit et omnia parāvit. Ubi ea diēs 1
vēnit, Andromeda ad lītus dēducta est, et in cōnspectū om- 2
nium ad rūpem alligāta est. Omnēs fātum eius dē- 3
plōrābant, nec lacrimās tenēbant. At subitō, dum mōn- 4
strum exspectant, Perseus accurrit; et ubi lacrimās vīdit, 5
causam dolōris quaerit. Illī rem tōtam expōnunt et puel- 6
lam dēmōnstrant. Dum haec geruntur, fremitus terribilis 7
audītur; simul mōnstrum horribilī speciē procul cōnspicitur. 8
Eius cōnspectus timōrem maximum omnibus iniēcit. Mōn- 9
strum magnā celeritāte ad lītus contendit, iamque locō ap- 10
propinquābat ubi puella stābat. 11

Neuter I-stem Nouns of the Third Declension

Neuter i-stem nouns have **-ia** instead of **-a** in the nominative and accusative plural and always have **-ī** instead of **-e** in the ablative singular, e.g.:

Singular	*Plural*
animal	animālia
animālis	animālium
animālī	animālibus
animal	animālia
animālī	animālibus

I-stem nouns are identified in the vocabularies in this book by inclusion of the genitive plural ending, **-ium**, thus: **nox, noctis, noctium** (*f*), night.

---

1. All things had been made ready, and a definite day had been set.
2. On that day a certain man met Andromeda, and he led her down to the sea.
3. While all were waiting on the shore, Perseus approached the place with the greatest swiftness.
4. He was hurrying to his mother with the head of Medusa.
5. After he had asked the cause of (their) grief, they explained the whole situation.

Helpful Hints
2. For the gender of **diēs** here, see the vocabulary note on page 14.
3. When the ablative of manner is accompanied by an adjective, **cum** is optional (see grammar note with paragraph 5).
5. Find a model for translating "the whole situation" in paragraph 7 above.

2   *tollō, tollere, (3), sustulī, sublātum to lift, raise.
    *dēsuper (adv.), down from above.
3   *impetus, -ūs (m), attack.
    impetum facere, idiom, to make an attack, charge.
    *collum, -ī (n), neck.
4   *sentiō, sentīre (4), sēnsī, sēnsum, to perceive, feel.
5   *ēdō, ēdere (3), ēdidī, ēditum, to put forth, give out, utter. Note that
        when compounded with a monosyllabic prepositional prefix as here, dō,
        dare becomes 3rd conjugation.
    *mora, -ae (f), delay.
6   *mergō, mergere (3), mersī, mersum, to dip, plunge, sink.
    dum . . . volābat, . . . exspectābat: dum with the imperfect in the
        subordinate clause followed by the imperfect in the main clause = "as
        long as."
8   *īnficiō (in- + faciō), īnficere, īnfēcī, īnfectum, to stain, dye.
    Post: adverb.
    bēlua, -ae (f), beast, monster.
9   ictū graviōre: ablative of manner or means, "with a heavier/severer
        blow."
    graviōre: comparative of gravis; note that while 3rd declension ad-
        jectives are i-stems and have -ī in the ablative singular (e.g., brevī),
        comparative adjectives are not i-stems and have -e in the ablative
        singular.
    vulnerāta est: this is feminine because the subject has changed from
        mōnstrum (n) to bēlua (f).
    sē: this reflexive pronoun is grammatically accusative, singular, and
        feminine, but it should be translated "itself," or the phrase sē . . .
        mersit may be translated "it plunged." Like cēlō, cēlāre, "I hide," the
        verb mergō, mergere is transitive and must have a direct object, but
        when used with the reflexive pronoun it may be translated
        intransitively, "it plunged."
10 neque, and . . . not.

> ## Dum + Imperfect Indicative = "while," "as long as"
>
> Dum with the imperfect indicative means "while" in the sense of "as long as" and indicates an action that was taking place simultaneously with another action over a period of time in the past, e.g., Perseus dum circum lītus volābat, reditum eius exspectābat, "As long as Perseus was flying around the shore, he was awaiting its (the monster's) return." Compare this with the use of dum with the present tense ("while") in a sentence with the perfect tense in the main clause (see grammar note with paragraph 5). For dum with the future indicative, see the grammar note with paragraph 76.

8. THE RESCUE

At Perseus ubi haec vīdit, gladium suum ēdūxit; et 1
postquam tālāria induit, in āera sublātus est. Tum dēsu- 2
per in mōnstrum impetum subitō fēcit, et gladiō suō collum 3
eius graviter vulnerāvit. Mōnstrum ubi sēnsit vulnus, 4
fremitum horribilem ēdidit, et sine morā tōtum corpus in 5
aquam mersit. Perseus dum circum lītus volābat, reditum 6
eius exspectābat. Mare autem intereā undique sanguine 7
īnficitur. Post bēlua rūrsus caput sustulit; brevī tempore 8
tamen ā Perseō ictū graviōre vulnerāta est. Tum iterum sē 9
in undās mersit, neque posteā vīsa est. 10

1. In a short time the monster came to the place where Andromeda was standing.
2. Perseus made an attack upon the monster with great bravery.
3. He wounded the monster's body severely with (his) sword.
4. As long as the monster kept attacking, Perseus kept wounding it.
5. Then the monster fled, and Perseus awaited its return for a long time in vain.

Helpful Hints

2. "Made an attack" is a verbal idea that implies motion, and so it takes an accusative with an appropriate preposition. Find a model for this idiom in paragraph 8 above.
3. Note the difference between "with great bravery" (no. 2: abstract noun = *manner*) and "with his sword" (no. 3: concrete thing = *instrument*); the second phrase requires no preposition in Latin (see grammar note with paragraph 2).
5. Think of a better way to express "for a long time" than **longum tempus.** Latin usually prefers adverbs to accusative phrases.

   In Latin an adverb generally precedes the word it modifies; here two adverbs will precede the verb.

2   **exuō, exuere** (3), **exuī, exūtum**, to put *or* take off.
    Compare **induit**, paragraph 8, line 2.
    alligāta erat: see note with line 12 of paragraph 4; translate "was
    bound."

3   *__spēs, speī__ (*f*), hope.
    *__salūs, salūtis__ (*f*), safety, deliverance, escape.
    dēpōnō, dēpōnere (3), **dēposuī, dēpositum**, to put down, deposit, lay
    aside, give up.

4   *__adeō, adīre__ (*irreg.*), **adiī, aditum**, to go to, approach.
    terrōre: *ablative of cause* with **examimāta**.
    *__exanimō__ (ex- + anima) (1), to put out of breath, exhaust, stupefy, kill.
    exanimāta erat: see note with line 12 of paragraph 4; translate "was
    stupefied," "lifeless."

5   **maximī perīculī**: *predicate genitive of description*, "(a mattter) of the
    greatest danger"; this form of the genitive of description is called the
    predicate genitive of description because it forms part of what is said
    about the subject.
    *__vinculum, -ī__ (*n*), bond, chain.
    *__solvō, solvere__ (3), **solvī, solūtum**, to loosen, unbind.

6   *__afficiō__ (ad- + faciō), **afficere** (3), **affēcī, affectum**, to do to, move, af-
    fect, visit, afflict.

7   *__meritus, -a, -um__, deserved, due, just.
    *__grātia, -ae__ (*f*), favor, gratitude, thanks; (*pl.*) thanks.
    grātiās agere (+ *dat.*), *idiom*, to give thanks, thank.

9   **dūxit**: i.e., **in mātrimōnium**; the Roman bridegroom "led" his wife to his
    own home in a wedding procession.
    Paucōs annōs: what kind of accusative phrase is this?

10 *__regiō, regiōnis__ (*f*), direction, country, region.
    *__honor, honōris__ (*m*), honor.

13 **discēdō, discēdere** (3), **discessī, discessum**, to go apart, withdraw,
    depart, wander.

Genitive of Description

We have already seen that a noun and adjective phrase
in the ablative can be used to describe a noun (see
grammar note with paragraph 4). Such descriptive
phrases may also appear in the *genitive*, e.g., **Perseus
erat vir __magnī virtūtis__**, "Perseus was a man _of
great courage_." Sometimes the genitive phrase stands
alone in the *predicate* without a noun to modify, e.g.,
rēs . . . erat __maximī perīculī__, "the undertaking
(**rēs**) was (a matter/one) _of the greatest danger_" i.e., "(a
matter) of greatest danger." With the predicate
genitive of description it is often convenient to supply
words such as "a matter" or "one" in the predicate for
the genitive phrase to depend on.

9. THE REWARD OF VALOR

Perseus postquam ad lītus dēscendit, prīmum tālāria 1
exuit; tum ad rūpem vēnit ad quam Andromeda alligāta 2
erat. Ea autem omnem spem salūtis dēposuerat; et ubi 3
Perseus adiit, terrōre paene exanimāta erat, rēs enim erat 4
maximī perīculī. Ille vincula statim solvit, et puellam patrī 5
reddidit. Cēpheus ob hanc rem maximō gaudiō affectus est. 6
Perseō meritās grātiās prō tantō beneficiō ēgit; praetereā 7
Andromedam ipsam eī in mātrimōnium dedit. Ille libenter 8
hoc dōnum accēpit et puellam dūxit. Paucōs annōs cum 9
uxōre suā in eā regiōne habitābat, et in magnō honōre erat 10
apud omnēs Aethiopēs. Magnopere tamen mātrem suam 11
rūrsus vidēre cupiēbat. Tandem cum uxōre suā ē rēgnō 12
Cēpheī discessit. 13

1. As long as these things were being done in this way, all were
   stupefied with fright.
2. Andromeda was (a person) of great courage, but she had almost
   given up all hope of deliverance.
3. When she had been returned to (her) father, she desired to thank
   Perseus.
4. After Perseus had married her, they remained a few years in the
   kingdom of Cepheus.
5. Afterwards they decided to depart from that kingdom.

Helpful Hints

1. For "were being done," find a model in paragraph 7, line 7.
   In paragraph 9 above, locate the idiom for "were stupefied with fright"
   and use it in your translation here.
2. For "give up all hope of deliverance," find a model in paragraph 9 above.
3. In paragraph 9 above, locate the idiom for "to thank" and its syntax and use it
   in your translation here.
4. The subordinating conjunction here will stand first in its clause. Why? (See
   Helpful Hints note 1 with paragraph 5.)
   In the vocabulary list on page 18, locate the full idiom for "to marry
   (someone)." What, literally, does the Latin idiom say?

1 **nāvem appellere**, *idiom*, to put in.
2 ****cōnferō, cōnferre** (*irreg.*), **contulī, collātum**, to bring together.
  sē cōnferre, *idiom*, to betake oneself, make one's way, go.
3 **vacuus, -a, -um**, empty. Why is the adjective feminine here?
  dēsertus, -a, -um, deserted.
  Trēs diēs: *accusative of duration of time*, "for three days."
4 **quārtō diē**: *ablative of time when.*
5 **Diāna, -ae** (*f*), Diana.
  ****refugiō, refugere** (3), **refūgī**, to flee back, run away, retreat.
  quod: not the relative pronoun, but the *conjunction* (you must always be
    careful to distinguish the one from the other).
6 ****cognōscō, cognōscere** (3), **cognōvī, cognitum**, to find out, learn of,
    learn; (*perfect*) to have found out, have learned of, be aware of, know.
7 ****rēgia, -ae** (*f*), palace.
8 **eō** (*adv.*), to that place, there.
  ****irrumpō** (in- + rumpō), **irrumpere** (3), **irrūpī, irruptum**, to burst in *or*
    into.
10 ****ostendō, ostendere** (3), **ostendī, ostentum**, to stretch out before,
    show.
  ****simul atque**, as soon as.
    simul atque . . . vīdit: *perfect indicative* with **simul atque**, "as
      soon as," as with **postquam** and **ubi** (see notes with line 4 of
      paragraph 2 and line 9 of paragraph 5), often to be translated with
      pluperfect in English, "as soon as he had seen."

Adverbs of Place

The adverbs **hūc**, **hīc**, and **hinc** are closely related to
the adjective **hic, haec, hoc**:

> **hūc = ad hunc locum**, e.g., **Hūc venī**, "Come
>   here!"
> **hīc = in hōc locō**, e.g., **Hīc stā**, "Stand here!"
> **hinc = ab/ex hōc locō**, e.g., **Hinc abī**, "Go away
>   from here!"

Correspondingly, the adverbs **illūc**, **illīc**, and **illinc**
are closely related to the adjective **ille, illa, illud**:

> **illūc = ad illum locum**, e.g., **Illūc ī**, "Go there!"
> **illīc = in illō locō**, e.g., **Illīc stā**, "Stand there!"
> **illinc = ab/ex illō locō**, e.g., **Illinc abī**, "Go
>   away from there!"

Latin also has:

> **eō** = to that place, there

10. POLYDECTES IS TURNED TO STONE

Postquam Perseus ad īnsulam nāvem appulit, sē ad 1
locum contulit ubi māter quondam habitāverat; sed domum 2
invēnit vacuam et omnīnō dēsertam. Trēs diēs per tōtam 3
īnsulam mātrem quaerēbat; tandem quārtō diē ad tem- 4
plum Diānae pervēnit. Hūc Danaē refūgerat, quod Poly- 5
dectem timēbat. Perseus ubi haec cognōvit, īrā magnā 6
commōtus est, atque ad rēgiam Polydectis sine morā con- 7
tendit. Ubi eō vēnit, statim in ātrium irrūpit. Polydectēs 8
magnō timōre affectus est et effugere volēbat. Dum tamen 9
ille fugit, Perseus caput Medūsae ostendit; ille autem simul 10
atque hoc vīdit, in saxum versus est. 11

1. When Perseus had gone to his mother's house, fear seized his
   heart.
2. For the place had been deserted for a long time.
3. Danaë had gone away from this place, because Polydectes wished
   to marry her.
4. On the fourth day Perseus found his mother.
5. He turned the king into stone with the head of Medusa.

Helpful Hints

1. In paragraph 10 above, find an idiomatic expression for "go."
   No preposition is used with expressions of place involving the names of
   cities, towns, small islands, peninsulas, and the words **domus** (meaning
   "home") and **rūs** (see grammar note with paragraph 16). The word *house*,
   however, when it refers to the physical entity is translated with **domus** and
   preceded by the preposition **ad** in place expressions (see paragraph 2, line
   6).
2. See grammar note with paragraph 3 on **iam diū**. Use the imperfect with
   iam diū here = "had been (and still was)."

3   **ōrāculum istud**: the one mentioned in paragraph 1.
     *__iste, ista, istud__, that of yours, that.
4   *__Thessalia, -ae__ (_f_), Thessaly.
     *__Lārīsa, -ae__ (_f_), Larissa.
5   **neque enim**: "for . . . not," as if it were **nōn enim**.
9   *__certāmen, certāminis__ (_n_), struggle, contest; direct object of **iniit**
     discus, -ī (_m_), discus (a round, flat piece of stone or metal; as now, the
     athlete who threw it farthest won the contest).
     iniit: _intransitive_ verbs such as **eō** may become _transitive_ when com-
     pounded with prepositional prefixes; they may then take direct objects.
10   *__cāsus, -ūs__ (_m_), fall, chance, accident.
     cāsū: _ablative of manner_ (without **cum** or accompanying adjective).
     eius: modifying **certāminis**.
11   *__forte stābat__: "he happened to be standing."

Ablative of Manner

You have seen an example of the _ablative of manner_
consisting of a noun and an adjective: **ūnō ictū**, "with
one blow" (paragraph 5); the preposition **cum** may be
used with such expressions, e.g., **ūnō cum ictū**. If the
noun is not accompanied by an adjective, **cum** is generally required, e.g., **cum ictū**, "with a blow." With
some common expressions of manner such as **vī** "with
force," **viā** "by way of," and **cāsū** "by chance," "by accident," the preposition is not used; the ablative stands
alone and functions as an adverb.

11. THE ORACLE IS FULFILLED

Posteā Perseus cum uxōre suā ad urbem Acrisī rediit. 1
Ille autem ubi Perseum vīdit, magnō terrōre affectus est; 2
nam propter ōrāculum istud nepōtem suum timēbat. 3
Itaque in Thessaliam ad urbem Lārīsam statim refūgit, 4
frustrā tamen; neque enim fātum suum vītāvit. Post 5
paucōs annōs rēx Lārīsae lūdōs magnōs fēcit; nūntiōs in 6
omnēs partēs dīmīserat et diem dīxerat. Multī ex omnibus 7
urbibus Graeciae ad lūdōs convēnērunt. Ipse Perseus 8
certāmen discī iniit. At dum discum conicit, avum suum 9
cāsū occīdit; Acrisius enim inter spectātōrēs eius certāmi- 10
nis forte stābat. 11

1. Afterwards the head was given by Perseus to Minerva.
2. In that year he returned to the city of Acrisius with Andromeda and his mother.
3. The king at once fled to the city of Larissa, because he feared Perseus.
4. When messengers had been sent forth in all directions, Perseus himself came to that place.
5. In a short time Acrisius was accidentally killed by him.

Helpful Hints

1. A passive verb does not have a direct object, but it may still have an indirect object, which will be expressed with the dative case in Latin.
2. Ablative of time when does not have a preposition in Latin.
   "His" is often not expressed with a separate word in Latin, cf. **Helpful Hints** notes 1 and 2 with paragraph 5.
3. "Larissa" refers to the same thing as "city," and so in Latin it is an appositive in the same case, while in English we use the phrase "of Larissa." Find an example in paragraph 11 above. Note that the word **Larīsa** has one s in Latin while the English word has two.
4. Look for a word in paragraph 11 above that can mean "direction." Latin has many fewer words than English because Latin words have wider, more general fields of reference that are then narrowed down by the context in which they are used.

Hercules

Hercules, Nessus, and Dejanira

Hercules, a Greek hero celebrated for his great strength, was pursued throughout his life by the hatred of Juno. While yet an infant, he strangled the serpents sent by the goddess to destroy him. During his boyhood and youth, he did various marvelous feats, and on reaching manhood he succeeded in delivering the Thebans from the oppression of the Minyae.

In a fit of madness sent upon him by Juno, he slew his own children. When he inquired of the Delphic oracle how he should cleanse himself from this crime, he was ordered to submit himself for twelve years to Eurystheus, king of Tiryns, and to perform whatever tasks were appointed him. Hercules obeyed the oracle, and during the twelve years of his servitude accomplished twelve extraordinary feats known as the Labors of Hercules.

His death was caused unintentionally by his wife Dejanira. Hercules had shot with a poisoned arrow a centaur named Nessus, who, before he died, gave some of his blood to Dejanira, and told her it would act as a charm to secure her husband's love. Some time after, wishing to try the charm, Dejanira soaked one of her husband's garments in the blood, not knowing that it was poisoned. Hercules put on the robe, and after suffering terrible torments he died or, as some say, he was carried off by his father, Jupiter.

1   *Herculēs, Herculis (m), Hercules.
    *Alcmēna, -ae (f), Alcmena.
2   omnium hominum: *partitive genitive* with *superlative adjective*.
    validus, -a, -um, strong.
    fuisse: *perfect active infinitive* of sum, "to have been."
3   *Iūnō, Iūnōnis (f), Juno.
    ōdī, ōdisse, ōsūrus (*used in perfect with the force of the present*), to
      hate.
        ōderat: *pluperfect* in form, *imperfect* in meaning, "hated."
    etiam tum īnfantem: translate with a relative clause.
4   *serpēns, serpentis, serpentium (f), serpent.
5   mediā nocte: mediā is an *adjective used to denote a part*, "in the middle
      (part) of the night."
    cubiculum: see cubō below.
7   cūnae, -ārum (f pl), cradle.
    *scūtum, -ī (n), shield.
    cubō, cubāre (1), cubuī, cubitum, to lie down, lie, recline.
    Compare the noun cubiculum, -ī (n), bedroom.

Perfect Infinitives, Active and Passive

The *perfect active infinitive* is formed by adding the
ending -isse to the perfect stem (formed from the *third*
principal part of the verb).

The *perfect passive infinitive* is formed by combining
the perfect passive participle (the *fourth* principal part
of the verb) with the present infinitive of sum, namely
esse.

The *perfect infinitives* of *deponent verbs* are exactly
the same in form as the perfect passive infinitives of
regular verbs in their respective conjugations, but they
have active meanings, e.g.:

Active	*Passive*	*Deponent*
portāvisse	portātus* esse	cōnātus esse
to have carried	to have been carried	to have tried
mōvisse	mōtus esse	veritus esse
to have moved	to have been moved	to have feared
mīsisse	missus esse	profectus esse
to have sent	to have been sent	to have set out
iēcisse	iactus esse	regressus esse
to have thrown	to have been thrown	to have returned
audīvisse	audītus esse	exortus esse
to have heard	to have been heard	to have arisen

*Note that all the forms ending in -us may be fully de-
clined as first and second declension adjectives, as
needed in the clauses in which they are used.

The perfect active infinitive of sum is fuisse (see
paragraph 12, line 2).

12. THE HATRED OF JUNO

Herculēs, Alcmēnae fīlius, quondam in Graeciā habitā- 1
bat. Hic omnium hominum validissimus fuisse dīcitur. At 2
Iūnō, rēgīna deōrum, Alcmēnam ōderat et Herculem etiam 3
tum īnfantem necāre voluit. Itaque duās serpentēs saevis- 4
simās mīsit; hae mediā nocte in cubiculum Alcmēnae 5
vēnērunt, ubi Herculēs cum frātre suō dormiēbat. Nec ta- 6
men in cūnīs, sed in scūtō magnō cubābant. Serpentēs iam 7
appropinquāvērunt et scūtum movēbant; ita puerī ē somnō 8
excitātī sunt. 9

Partitive Genitive with Superlative Adjectives

A noun or phrase in the *genitive case* often accompanies
a *superlative adjective* to express the whole or the
group within which a comparison is being made, e.g.,
omnium hominum validissimus, "the strongest of
all men."

---

1. Hercules is said to have been the greatest of all men.
2. He even used to be called a god.
3. Juno, however, desired to kill him, because Alcmena was his
   mother.
4. Hercules, who was still a boy, escaped the peril.
5. He saved his life at midnight by his bravery.

Helpful Hints
1. Find a model for translation of this sentence in paragraph 12 above.
2. Remember that "used to be called" is equivalent to "was called" and is translated by the imperfect tense.
4. In lines 3–4 of paragraph 12 above, find a way to translate this sentence
   without using a relative pronoun.
5. "Midnight" is expressed in Latin as "the middle (part of the) night" and requires the partitive adjective **medius**, not a partitive genitive.
   For "by his bravery," use ablative of means.

1   Īphiclēs, Īphiclis (*m*), Iphicles.
2   nūllō modō: *ablative of manner.*
3   Parvīs manibus: *ablative of means.*
    *prehendō, prehendere (3), prehendī, prehēnsum, to seize.
4   magnā vī: *ablative of manner.*
    *vīs, vīs (*f*), violence, force, virtue, potency, efficacy; (*pl.*) vīrēs, vīrium,
      strength. Note that the plural has a different meaning from the singular.
      Be sure to distinguish virīs (*dative/ablative plural* of vir, "man") from
      the plural forms of vīs: vīrēs (*nominative and accusative plural*) and
      vīribus (*dative and ablative plural*), "strength."
    *comprimō (con- + premō), comprimere, (3), compressī, compres-
      sum, to press together, squeeze, compress.
    *interficiō (inter- + faciō), interficere (3), interfēcī, interfectum, to
      put out of the way, kill. This is the most general of the verbs meaning "to
      kill"; necāre implies wickedness and cruelty; and occīdere commonly
      is used of cutting down an enemy in battle.
6   *marītus, -ī (*m*), husband.
    *lūmen, lūminis (*n*), light.
7   *accendō, accendere (3), accendī, accēnsum, to kindle, light.
      Distinguish this verb carefully from ascendō, ascendere (3), as-
      cendī, ascēnsum, to climb to, ascend, mount.
8   properō (1), to hurry.

13. HERCULES AND THE SERPENTS

Īphiclēs, frāter Herculis, magnā vōce exclāmāvit; sed 1
Herculēs ipse, fortissimus puer, nūllō modō territus est. 2
Parvīs manibus serpentēs statim prehendit, et colla eārum 3
magnā vī compressit. Tālī modō serpentēs ā puerō inter- 4
fectae sunt. Alcmēna autem, māter puerōrum, clāmōrem 5
audīverat et marītum suum ē somnō excitāverat. Ille lū- 6
men accendit et gladium suum arripuit; tum ad puerōs 7
properāvit. Sed ubi ad locum vēnit, rem mīram vīdit; Her- 8
culēs enim rīdēbat et serpentēs mortuās dēmōnstrābat. 9

1. His brother, Iphicles by name, had been frightened by the danger.
2. He was saved, however, by the brave boy.
3. Iphicles is said to have cried out in a loud voice.
4. When this cry had been heard, his father ran to the place with great swiftness.
5. There he found the boys safe.

1 **ā puerō**: literally, "from a boy," better English, "from boyhood." Cf. **ā puerō** in paragraph 13.
exerceō (2) (*trans.*), to exercise.

2 **diēī**: *partitive genitive.*
palaestra, -ae (*f*), palestra, wrestling-place.
*****cōnsūmō, cōnsūmere** (3), **cōnsūmpsī, cōnsūmptum**, to take completely, use up, consume, spend.
Didicit: discō + *infinitive* means "to learn how to."

3 *****arcus, -ūs** (*m*), bow.
*****intendō, intendere** (3), **intendī, intentum**, to stretch out, stretch, draw, aim.
*****tēlum, -ī** (*n*), missile, spear, weapon.
exercitātiō, exercitātiōnis (*f*), exercise.
vīrēs: see vocabulary note with line 4 of paragraph 13.

4 *****cōnfīrmō** (1), to strengthen, establish.
mūsica, -ae (*f*), music.
*****Linus, -ī** (*m*), Linus.

5 **ērudiō** (4), to instruct.
huic . . . artī: *dative* with the *intransitive verb* **studēbat**.
studeō (2) (+ *dat.*), to be eager, give attention, apply oneself.

6 *****obiūrgō** (1), to chide, scold, reproach.
studiōsus, -a, -um, eager, diligent, studious.

7 **cithara, -ae** (*f*), cithara, lyre.
omnibus vīribus: what kind of ablative? For **vīribus**, see vocabulary note with line 4 of paragraph 13.

8 *****īnfēlīx, īnfēlīcis**, unhappy, unfortunate.
ictū: *ablative of means.*
*****prōsternō, prōsternere** (3), **prōstrāvī, prōstrātum**, to strew *or* spread before, throw *or* knock down.

9 *****paulō post**: literally, "later by a little," better English, "a little later."
paulō: *ablative of degree of difference* with the *adverb* **post**.
*****excēdō, excēdere** (3), **excessī, excessum**, to go out *or* forth, depart.
ē vītā excēdere, *idiom*, to die.
neque quisquam: literally, "and not anyone," better English, "and no one"; **quisquam/quicquam** "anyone/anything" is used instead of **aliquis/aliquid** "anyone/anything" when expressing a negative idea.

10 *****officium, -ī** (*n*), service, duty.
*****suscipiō** (sub- + capiō), **suscipere** (3), **suscēpī, susceptum**, to undertake.

Partitive Genitive

A word or phrase in the *genitive case* may express the whole of which the word on which the genitive depends is a part, e.g., **magnam partem diēī**, "a large part of the day."

14. THE MUSIC-LESSON

Herculēs ā puerō corpus suum dīligenter exercēbat; mag- 1
nam partem diēī in palaestrā cōnsūmēbat. Didicit etiam 2
arcum intendere et tēla conicere. Hīs exercitātiōnibus vīrēs 3
eius cōnfīrmātae sunt. In mūsicā etiam ā Linō quōdam 4
ērudiēbātur; huic tamen artī minus dīligenter studēbat. 5
Linus Herculem quondam obiūrgābat, quod nōn studiōsus 6
erat; puer īrātus citharam subitō arripuit, et omnibus 7
vīribus caput magistrī īnfēlīcis percussit. Ille ictū prōstrā- 8
tus est, et paulō post ē vītā excessit; neque quisquam 9
posteā id officium suscipere voluit. 10

Dative with Special Intransitive Verbs

The meaning of many intransitive verbs such as
studeō, studēre is completed by a word or phrase in
the dative case, e.g., **Huic artī minus dīligenter
studēbat**, "He was applying himself less diligently to
this art." Make a list of such verbs as you meet them
in your reading.

Ablative of Degree of Difference

A noun, adjective, or phrase in the ablative may indicate the degree of difference with comparative adjectives, e.g., "The woman was taller than the man by a
foot," or with adverbs, e.g., **paulō post**, "later by a little," "a little later."

---

1. A little later Hercules killed a certain Linus, because he had
   scolded him.
2. For the boy used to apply himself to exercise of his body.
3. And he did not undertake anything without a reason.
4. He wished to establish his strength in this way.
5. His plan was by no means pleasing to Linus.

Helpful Hints
1. For "he," use **ille** to indicate a change of subject.
2. For "apply himself to," use **studeō** + *dat.*
3. Find models for "and . . . not" and "anything" in paragraph 14, line 9, above
   and the vocabulary note before translating this sentence.
5. Often a single Latin adverb will best translate an English phrase such as "by
   no means."

2   **Aegyptiī, -ōrum** (*m pl*), Egyptians.
3   **Būsīris, Būsīridis** (*m*), Busiris.
4   **hominēs**: "human beings," both men and women (**vir** generally denotes a
     man as distinguished from a woman).
     immolō (in- + mola) (1), to sacrifice.
     *****cōnsuēscō, cōnsuēscere** (3), **cōnsuēvī, consuētum**, to become ac-
     customed; (*perfect*) to have become accustomed, be accustomed.
     cōnsuēverat: "had become accustomed," "was accustomed."
5   *****sacrificium, -ī** (*n*), sacrifice.
     sacrificiō: *dative of purpose.*
6   *****appetō** (ad- + petō), **appetere** (3), **appetīvī, appetītum**, to draw near.
     rīte, duly, fitly, properly.
7   *****catēna, -ae** (*f*), chain.
     ferreus, -a, -um, of iron, iron.
     *****vinciō, vincīre** (4), **vīnxī, vīnctum**, to bind.
     Distinguish this verb carefully from **vincō, vincere** (3), **vīcī, victum**,
     to conquer, and from **vīvō, vīvere** (3), **vīxī, vīctum**, to live.
     mola, -ae (*f*), meal.
     salsus, -a, -um, salted, salt.
8   *****impōnō** (in- + pōnō), **impōnere** (3), **imposuī, impositum**, to place *or*
     lay upon.
     *****mōs, mōris** (*m*), way, manner, habit, custom.
     Note the use of the phrase **mōs erat** with the *infinitive.*
9   **sāl, salis** (*m*), salt.
     far, farris (*n*), spelt, wheat, meal.
     *****victima, -ae** (*f*), victim.
     Iam . . . iam: the omission of the conjunction (*asyndeton*) that would
     normally connect the two clauses introduced by these words and the em-
     phatic repetition of the word at the beginning of the clauses (*anaphora*)
     reflect the imminence of the danger; the tenses of the verbs contribute to
     the vividness of the picture. We see Hercules standing at the altar and
     the priest with the knife in his hand.
10   *****āra, -ae** (*f*), altar.
     *****sacerdōs, sacerdōtis**, (*m/f*) priest, priestess.
     culter, cultrī (*m*), knife.
11   *****cōnātus, -ūs** (*m*), attempt, effort.
     Compare the related verb **cōnor, cōnārī** (1), **cōnātus sum**, to try.
     *****perrumpō, perrumpere** (3), **perrūpī, perruptum**, to burst *or* break
     through, break.

15. HERCULES ESCAPES SACRIFICE

Dē Hercule haec etiam nārrantur. Quondam dum iter 1
facit, in fīnēs Aegyptiōrum vēnit. Ibi rēx quīdam, nōmine 2
Būsīris, illō tempore rēgnābat; hic autem vir crūdēlissimus 3
hominēs immolāre cōnsuēverat. Herculem igitur corripuit 4
et in vincula coniēcit. Tum nūntiōs dīmīsit et diem sacrifi- 5
ciō dīxit. Iam ea diēs appetēbat, et omnia rīte parāta sunt. 6
Manūs Herculis catēnīs ferreīs vīnctae sunt, et mola salsa 7
in caput eius imposita est. Mōs enim erat apud antīquōs 8
salem et far in caput victimārum impōnere. Iam victima ad 9
āram stābat; iam sacerdōs cultrum sūmpserat. Subitō ta- 10
men Herculēs magnō cōnātū vincula perrūpit. Tum ictū 11
sacerdōtem prōstrāvit; alterō rēgem ipsum occīdit. 12

Dative of Purpose

A word or phrase in the dative case may indicate the
purpose for which an action is carried out or the end
that it has in view, e.g., **Diem sacrificiō dīxit**, "He
set a day for the (purpose of the) sacrifice."

---

1. Hercules was accustomed to making journeys in all directions
   without fear.
2. And no one undertook greater services.
3. Now it was the custom of a certain king to seize human beings and
   kill (them).
4. A definite day was set for this thing, and men gathered from all
   sides.
5. When Hercules had been seized by this king, he saved himself
   with great effort.

Helpful Hints
1. In paragraph 15 above, find a model for "was accustomed" + complementary
   infinitive. Study the vocabulary note on page 32 carefully for the proper
   tense of the verb to use here.
2. For "and no one," see paragraph 14, line 9.
3. Find a model in paragraph 15 above for "it was the custom."
   The adjective **quīdam** may either precede or follow the noun it modifies
   (find an example in paragraph 15 above).
4. Find a model for the first half of this sentence in paragraph 15 above and the
   grammar note on this page.
5. Be sure to use a reflexive pronoun to translate "himself," since the pronoun
   refers to the subject of its own clause.

1 *Thēbae, -ārum (*f pl*), Thebes.
     Thēbīs: *locative case* (same as ablative plural).
2 *Creōn, Creontis (*m*), Creon.
     *Minyae, -ārum (*m pl*), Minyae.
     *gēns, gentis, gentium (*f*), race, nation, people.
3 *bellicōsus, -a, -um, warlike.
     *Thēbānī, -ōrum (*m pl*), Thebans.
     Thēbānīs: *dative* with the *adjective* fīnitimī, literally, "adjacent to
       the Thebans," better English, "neighbors of the Thebans."
     *fīnitimus, -a, -um (+ *dat.*), neighboring, adjoining, adjacent.
4 quotannīs (*adv.*), every year, yearly, annually.
     mittēbantur: *imperfect passive.*
     Thēbās: *accusative* of name of town or city used without a preposition to
       express the *place to which.*
5 veniēbant, postulābant, and pendēbant (line 7): *imperfects* used to
       show *habitual action* in past time.
     *postulō (1), to request, demand.
6 *tribūtum, -ī (*n*), contribution, tribute.
7 pendō, pendere (3), pependī, pēnsum, to weigh out, pay.
     hōc tribūtō: *ablative of separation* with līberāre, "to set free from."
8 *līberō (1) (+ *abl.* or ab or ex + *abl.*), to set free, free, liberate, release.
     atque: this word regularly introduces something of greater importance
       than that which precedes it.
     *auris, auris, aurium (*f*), ear.
10 sānctus, -a, -um, consecrated, sacred.
     sānctī: *predicate adjective.*
     habeō (2), to have, hold, consider.

Locative Case

The *locative case* without a preposition expresses *place
in which* for names of cities, towns, and small islands,
e.g., Thēbīs habitābat, "he lived in Thebes." For
nouns of the 1st and 2nd declensions, the locative case
is the same as the genitive singular, e.g., Rōmae,
Brundisī. For singular nouns of the 3rd declension it
is the same as the ablative (sometimes dative) singular, e.g., Carthāgine or Carthāginī. For all plural
nouns it is the same as the ablative plural, e.g,
Thēbīs.

16. A CRUEL DEED

Herculēs iam adulēscēns Thēbīs habitābat. Rēx 1
Thēbārum, vir ignāvus, Creōn appellābātur. Minyae, gēns 2
bellicōsissima, Thēbānīs fīnitimī erant. Lēgātī autem ā 3
Minyīs ad Thēbānōs quotannīs mittēbantur; hī Thēbās 4
veniēbant et centum bovēs postulābant. Thēbānī enim, 5
quoniam ā Minyīs superātī erant, tribūtum rēgī Minyārum 6
quotannīs pendēbant. At Herculēs cīvēs suōs hōc tribūtō 7
līberāre cōnstituit; itaque lēgātōs comprehendit atque au- 8
rēs eōrum abscīdit. Lēgātī autem apud omnēs gentēs 9
sānctī habentur. 10

Accusative of Place to Which

The *accusative case* without a preposition may express the idea of *place to which* with names of cities, towns, small islands, peninsulas, and the words **domus** (meaning "home") and **rūs**, e.g., **Hī Thēbās veni-ēbant**, "They used to come to Thebes."

Ablative of Separation

Verbs or adjectives implying *separation* are often accompanied by words or phrases in the *ablative*, sometimes with **ab** or **ex** and sometimes without a preposition, to express the thing from which something is separated or set free, e.g., **Herculēs cīvēs suōs hōc tribūtō līberāre cōnstituit**, "Hercules decided to free his citizens from this tribute."

---

1. Hercules had been sent away from the city (of) Thebes because he had killed Linus.
2. A little later the youth returned to Thebes.
3. While he was in Thebes, he freed his fellow citizens from a great danger.
4. They were neighbors of a very brave race and had been conquered by it.
5. For this reason all were affected with great fear.

Helpful Hints
3. For "from a great danger," find a model in paragraph 16 above.
4. In paragraph 16 above, find the correct case to use with the Latin word for "neighbors."
5. To translate "for this reason," see paragraph 6, lines 5 and 10–11.
   For "affected with great fear," see paragraph 10, line 9.

1   **Ergīnus,** -ī (*m*), Erginus.

2   ***cōpia, -ae** (*f*), supply, abundance; (*pl.*) forces, troops.
      cum omnibus cōpiīs: *ablative of accompaniment.*
      fīnēs: remember that **fīnis, fīnis, fīnium,** "end," "boundary," means
      "territory," "country" in the plural (see paragraph 2, line 8).

3   **adventus, -ūs** (*m*), approach, arrival.
      ***explōrātor, explōrātōris** (*m*), explorer, scout, spy.
      ***cognōscō, cognōscere** (3), **cognōvī, cognitum,** to find out, learn of,
      learn; (*perfect*) to have found out, have learned of, be aware of, know.

4   ***pugnō** (1), to fight.

5   **imperātor, imperātōris** (*m*), commander, general.
      imperātōrem: *predicate accusative* with **Herculem.**

6   ***cōgō** (co- + agō), **cōgere** (3), **coēgī, coāctum,** to drive together, collect,
      compel.
      ***proximus, -a, -um,** nearest, next.

7   ***exercitus, -ūs** (*m*), army.
      cum magnō exercitū: what kind of ablative?
      proficīscor, proficīscī (3), **profectus sum,** to set out, depart. A *de-*
      ponent verb, passive in form but active in meaning.
      ***idōneus, -a, -um,** suitable, fit, favorable.
      ***dēligō** (dē- + legō), **dēligere** (3), **dēlēgī, dēlēctum,** to choose out,
      choose, select.

8   ***aciēs, -ēī** (*f*), line of battle.
      impetum facere, *idiom,* to charge (against *or* upon + **in** + *acc.*)

10   **pellō, pellere** (3), **pepulī, pulsum,** to drive, drive away, beat, rout.
      pulsa: *perfect passive indicative;* the **est** goes with **pulsa** as well as
      conversa.
      ***fuga, -ae** (*f*), flight.
      Compare the related verbs **fūgō** (1), to put to flight, and **fugiō, fugere**
      (3), **fūgī, fugitum,** to flee.
      ***convertō, convertere** (3), **convertī, conversum,** to turn around,
      turn, change.
      in fugam convertere, *idiom,* to put to flight.

Ablative of Accompaniment

The preposition **cum** with the *ablative case* often expresses the idea of *accompaniment*, e.g., **Ergīnus <u>cum
omnibus cōpiīs</u> in fīnēs Thēbānōrum contendit,** "Erginus hurried into the territory of the
Thebans <u>with all his forces</u>." With military terms such
as **omnibus cōpiīs,** however, the preposition may be
omitted.

17. THE DEFEAT OF THE MINYAE

Ergīnus, rēx Minyārum, ob haec vehementer īrātus sta- 1
tim cum omnibus cōpiīs in fīnēs Thēbānōrum contendit. 2
Creōn adventum eius per explōrātōrēs cognōvit. Ipse tamen 3
pugnāre nōluit; nam magnō timōre affectus erat. Itaque 4
Thēbānī Herculem imperātōrem creāvērunt. Ille nūntiōs in 5
omnēs partēs dīmīsit et cōpiās coēgit; tum proximō diē cum 6
magnō exercitū profectus est. Locum idōneum dēlēgit et 7
aciem īnstrūxit. Tum Thēbānī ē superiōre locō impetum in 8
hostēs fēcērunt. Illī autem impetum sustinēre nōn po- 9
tuērunt; ita aciēs hostium pulsa atque in fugam conversa 10
est. 11

Deponent Verbs

You will encounter many Latin verbs that are *passive in form but active in meaning*; they have, so to speak, "put aside" (**dēpōnere**) their active forms and appear only in the passive (with active meanings), e.g., **cōnor, cōnārī, cōnātus sum**, to try; **vereor, verērī, veritus sum**, to be afraid; **proficīscor, proficīscī, profectus sum**, to set out; **regredior, regredī, regressus sum**, to go back; and **experior, experīrī, expertus sum**, to test. Thus **profectus est** means "he set out."

---

1. Creon, their king, a man of no courage, was unwilling to fight.
2. And so Hercules was made commander.
3. After the scouts had learned of the approach of the foe, messengers were ordered to set out in the middle of the night.
4. The next day the army was collected and drawn up.
5. When Hercules had arrived with all his forces, he charged upon the line of battle of the enemy and put them to flight.

Helpful Hints

1. To translate "man of no courage," use the phrase **speciē horribilī** (paragraph 4, lines 10–11) as a model, and see the grammar note with paragraph 4.
3. In paragraph 17 above, find the verb for "to learn of." Note that it takes a direct object in the accusative case. Study the vocabulary entry on the facing page and note the meaning of the present and the perfect tenses.
   Remember that **ubi** or **postquam** with the perfect tense translates an English pluperfect (see **Helpful Hints** note 3 with paragraph 2).
4. In paragraph 17 above, find a verb meaning "collect."
5. In paragraph 17 above, find the Latin idioms for "charged" and "put to flight."

1   **proelium, -ī** (*n*), battle, combat.
2   **hāc victōriā**: *ablative of cause* with **gaudēbant**.
3   ***decorō** (1), to adorn, distinguish.
4   **cum uxōre suā**: note the *reflexive adjective*, "his own."
5   **vītam agere**, *idiom*, to live a . . . life.
    ***furor, furōris** (*m*), rage, fury, frenzy, madness.
    ***incidō** (in- + cadō), **incidere** (3), **incidī**, to fall into *or* upon.
6   **līberōs suōs . . . suā manū**: note the *reflexive adjectives*, "his own."
    ipse: note the *intensive adjective*, (he) "himself"; **suōs ipse suā**: the
      enormity of the crime is emphasized by the use of all of these words re-
      peating the same idea; the position of **suā** before **manū** is itself em-
      phatic.
7   **sānitās, sānitātis** (*f*), soundness, right reason, sanity.
    facinus, facinoris (*n*), deed, crime.
9   ***recipiō** (re- + capiō), **recipere** (3), **recēpī**, **receptum**, to take *or* get
      back, recover.
    sē recipere, *idiom*, to betake oneself, withdraw.
    ***sermō, sermōnis** (*m*), conversation, talk, speech.
    sermōnem . . . habēre, *idiom*, to converse (with), have dealings
      (with), talk (with).

Reflexive Adjective

The 3rd person *reflexive adjective* **suus, -a, -um**
stands in the predicate of a sentence and refers to
(reflects) the subject, e.g., **Herculēs cum uxōre suā**
beātam vītam agēbat, "Hercules was leading a
happy life with his own wife."

Intensive Adjective

The *intensive adjective* **ipse, ipsa, ipsum** calls par-
ticular attention to (i.e., intensifies) the word it modifies. It often intensifies the implied subject of the verb,
e.g., **Līberōs ipse occīdit**, "He himself killed his children."

18. MADNESS AND MURDER

Post hoc proelium Herculēs cōpiās suās ad urbem 1
redūxit. Omnēs Thēbānī hāc victōriā maximē gaudēbant; 2
Creōn autem magnīs honōribus Herculem decorāvit, atque 3
eī fīliam suam in mātrimōnium dedit. Herculēs cum uxōre 4
suā beātam vītam agēbat; sed subitō in furōrem incidit, 5
atque līberōs suōs ipse suā manū occīdit. Paulō post ad 6
sānitātem reductus est, et propter hoc facinus magnō dolōre 7
affectus est. Brevī tempore ex urbe fūgit et in silvās sē 8
recēpit; cīvēs enim sermōnem cum eō habēre nōlēbant. 9

1. They had fought for the greater part of the day.
2. Nevertheless the army was led back to Thebes that very day.
3. When Hercules had arrived at the city, he was received with great honor because of his bravery.
4. For the whole region had been freed from fear by him.
5. A little later he fled into the woods, because he did not wish to remain in Thebes.

Helpful Hints
1. Use accusative of duration of time (no preposition).
2. **Tamen** may come first in its clause, or it may come in second position or later (postpositive).
   For "very," use the intensive adjective **ipse, ipsa, ipsum.**
3. For "at," use **ad** + *acc.*

1   *scelus, sceleris (*n*), wickedness, crime.
    *expiō (1), to expiate.
2   Delphicus, -a, -um, of Delphi, Delphic, Delphian.
3   omnium ōrāculōrum: *partitive genitive* with the *superlative adjective*
    nōtissimum.
4   ornō (1), to equip, adorn.
    Hōc in templō: a *monosyllabic preposition* often stands between an
    adjective and the noun that it modifies.
    *fēmina, -ae (*f*), woman.
5   *Pȳthia, -ae (*f*), Pythia.
7   voluntās, voluntātis (*f*), wish, will.
    ēnūntiō (1), to speak out, announce, make known.
8   *praecipuē, especially.

Relative Pronouns

As their name indicates, relative pronouns are words
that stand in the place of nouns and are "related" to
some other word in the sentence. They introduce relative clauses, e.g., **Herculēs igitur, quī Apollinem
colēbat, hūc vēnit**, "Hercules, therefore, <u>who</u> especially worshiped Apollo, came to this place." Here the
word **quī** is related to the word **Herculēs**, which is
called its *antecedent*. The gender and number of the
relative pronoun are detemined by its antecedent, but
its case is determined by its use in its own clause (here
nominative, as its subject).

The forms of the relative pronoun are as follows:

Singular   *Plural*

M.	F.	N.	M.	F.	N.
quī	quae	quod	quī	quae	quae
cuius	cuius	cuius	quōrum	quārum	quōrum
cui	cui	cui	quibus	quibus	quibus
quem	quam	quod	quōs	quās	quae
quō	quā	quō	quibus	quibus	quibus

19. HERCULES CONSULTS THE ORACLES

Herculēs tantum scelus expiāre magnopere cupiēbat, 1
atque ad ōrāculum Delphicum īre cōnstituit; hoc enim erat 2
omnium ōrāculōrum nōtissimum. Ibi templum erat Apolli- 3
nis plūrimīs dōnīs ōrnātum. Hōc in templō sedēbat fēmina 4
quaedam, nōmine Pȳthia, et cōnsilium dabat eīs quī ad 5
ōrāculum vēnerant. Haec autem fēmina ab ipsō Apolline 6
docēbātur, et voluntātem deī hominibus ēnūntiābat. Her- 7
culēs igitur, quī Apollinem praecipuē colēbat, hūc vēnit. 8
Tum rem tōtam exposuit, neque scelus cēlāvit. 9

Past General

A complex sentence that refers to a general truth or makes a general statement about something that happened in past time takes the *imperfect indicative* in the *main clause* and the *pluperfect indicative* in the *subordinate clause*, e.g., **Pȳthia cōnsilium dabat eīs quī ad ōrāculum vēnerant**, literally, "Pythia used to give advice to those who had come to the oracle," better translation, "Pythia (always) gave advice to whoever came to the oracle." The latter translation with the insertion of "always" and "ever" emphasizes the generality of the statement that is being made.

---

1. He could not bring back to life the children whom he had killed with his own hand.
2. Yet he desired to learn the will of Apollo, who gave advice to men through Pythia.
3. He was eager for this thing because of (his) hope for safety.
4. And so he hastened from the woods to the place that the god had chosen.
5. Then he explained to Pythia everything that he had done.

Helpful Hints

1. To translate "bring back to life," find a model in paragraph 18, lines 6–7.
   For "his own," use the reflexive adjective (see grammar note with paragraph 18).
3. "Eager for" may be translated with **studeō** (+ *dat.*) or **cupidus** (+ *gen.*).
4. Place the main verb at the end of the main clause, and then add the relative clause.
5. Be sure to put the indirect object before the direct.
   In line 9 of paragraph 19 above, find a simple way to express in Latin the idea expressed in the English words "everything that he had done."

2 **Tīrȳns, Tīrynthis,** (*Greek accusative*) **Tīryntha** (*f*), Tiryns.
   *Eurystheus, -ī (*m*), Eurystheus.
4 ***servitūs, servitūtis** (*f*), slavery, servitude, service.
5 **crūdēlissimō Eurystheō:** *dative* with the *special verb* **servīvit,** literally, "was subject to very cruel Eurystheus," more freely, "served very
   cruel Eurystheus."
6 ***imperō** (1) (+ *dat.*), to command, order, enjoin upon.
7 **tantum scelus,** *nominative singular neuter.* Cf. paragraph 19, line 1,
   where **tantum scelus** is *accusative singular.*
   expiārī: *present passive infinitive.*
   With **tantum scelus expiārī potuit,** using the *passive infinitive,*
   compare **Herculēs tantum scelus expiāre . . . cupiēbat**
   (paragraph 19, line 1), using the *active infinitive.*
8 **quae:** what case? Why?
9 **crēdibilis, -is, -e,** believable, credible.

Present Active and Passive Infinitives

Note the forms of the *present active* and *passive infini-tives*:

Active	*Passive*
portāre "to carry"	**portārī** "to be carried"
movēre "to move"	**movērī** "to be moved"
mittere "to send"	**mittī** "to be sent"
iacere "to throw"	**iacī** "to be thrown"
audīre "to hear"	**audīrī** "to be heard"

20. THE ORACLE'S REPLY

Ubi Herculēs fīnem fēcit, Pȳthia prīmō tacēbat; tandem
tamen iussit eum ad urbem Tīryntha īre, et Eurystheī rēgis
omnia iussa facere. Herculēs ubi haec audīvit, ad urbem il-
lam contendit, et Eurystheō rēgī sē in servitūtem trādidit.
Duodecim annōs crūdēlissimō Eurystheō servīvit, et
duodecim labōrēs, quōs ille imperāverat, cōnfēcit; hōc enim
ūnō modō tantum scelus expiārī potuit. Dē hīs labōribus
plūrima ā poētīs scrīpta sunt. Multa tamen quae poētae
nārrant crēdibilia nōn sunt.

1. Apollo ordered Hercules to hand himself over to Eurystheus.
2. Much can be written concerning the labors that he accomplished.
3. Now this man of great strength undertook twelve labors.
4. Those things that the king had commanded could not be done
   without danger.
5. From boyhood, however, he was accustomed to be eager for danger.

Helpful Hints
1. Find models for the vocabulary and structure of this sentence in paragraph
   20 above.
2. Translate "much" into Latin with a neuter plural, "many things."
   When determining the form of the relative pronoun, keep in mind that
   labor, labōris is masculine.
3. For "now," use **autem**.
4. Begin your translation with **nec** in order to relate the thought of this sentence to that of the previous one.
   You will need to use a present passive infinitive in this sentence.
5. In paragraph 14, locate an expression for "from boyhood." Latin prefers concrete expressions to abstract ones, even when the abstract seems more natu-
   ral to us.
   For "was accustomed," see paragraph 15, line 4, and vocabulary note.
   To translate "eager for," see **Helpful Hints** note 3 with paragraph 19.

1   *leō, leōnis (*m*), lion.
2   illō tempore: what kind of an ablative is this?
    *vallēs, vallis, vallium (*f*), valley.
    Nemeaeus, -a, -um, of Nemea, Nemean.
    īnfestus, -a, -um, unsafe, dangerous.
4   fera, -ae (*f*), wild animal, beast.
    sēcum: = cum sē; the *preposition* cum follows and is joined to a *personal, reflexive,* or *relative* pronoun.
5   *pellis, pellis, pellium (*f*), hide, skin, pelt.
    *dēnsus, -a, -um, thick.
    trāiciō (trāns- + iaciō), trāicere (3), trāiēcī, trāiectum, to throw across, strike through, pierce.
6   *clāva, -ae (*f*), stick, club.
7   neque enim, for . . . not.
8   *dēmum, at last.
    *bracchium, -ī, (*n*), arm.
    *complector, complectī (3), complexus sum, to embrace, grasp.
9   *faucēs, faucium (*f pl*), throat, jaws, mouth.
10 *respīrō (1), to breathe back *or* out, breathe.
    respīrandī: *gerund* or *verbal noun* in the *genitive case,* "of breathing"; the *gerund* is a form of the verb, but it has the construction of a noun. In English the *gerund* ends in *-ing,* and so is identical in form with the English present participle.
    respīrandī facultās: "means of breathing."
11 *facultās, facultātis (*f*), possibility, opportunity, chance, means.
    *cadāver, cadāveris (*n*), dead body, corpse, carcass.
12 *umerus, -ī (*m*), shoulder.
    umerīs: *ablative of means,* but translate "on his shoulders."
    *dētrahō, dētrahere (3), dētrāxī, dētractum, to draw *or* pull off.
13 *incolō, incolere (3), incoluī, to inhabit.
14 *fāma, -ae (*f*), report, rumor.

Gerund or Verbal Noun

The *gerund* is a neuter *verbal noun* that appears in the genitive, dative, accusative, and ablative singular only:

parandī	habendī	mittendī	iaciendī	audiendī
parandō	habendō	mittendō	iaciendō	audiendō
parandum	habendum	mittendum	iaciendum	audiendum
parandō	habendō	mittendō	iaciendō	audiendō

Note the letters -nd- in all the forms.

Gerunds are translated as verbal nouns in English, e.g., "of preparing," "to or for preparing," etc. In paragraph 21 a gerund is used in the genitive case to make it dependent on another noun: **respīrandī facultās,** "means of breathing." Gerunds of deponent verbs are the same in form as those of regular verbs, e.g., **complectendī,** "of grasping."

21. FIRST LABOR: THE NEMEAN LION

Prīmum ab Eurystheō iussus est Herculēs leōnem inter- 1
ficere quī illō tempore vallem Nemeaeam reddēbat īnfes- 2
tam. Itaque in silvās in quibus leō habitābat statim sē 3
contulit. Ubi feram vīdit, arcum quem sēcum attulerat in- 4
tendit; eius tamen pellem, quae dēnsissima erat, trāicere 5
nōn potuit. Tum clāvā magnā quam semper gerēbat leōnem 6
frūstrā percussit; neque enim hōc modō eum interficere po- 7
tuit. Tum dēmum collum mōnstrī bracchiīs suīs complexus 8
est, et faucēs eius omnibus vīribus compressit. Hōc modō 9
leō brevī tempore exanimātus est; nūlla enim respīrandī 10
facultās eī dabātur. Tum Herculēs cadāver ad oppidum 11
umerīs rettulit; et pellem, quam dētrāxerat, posteā prō 12
veste gerēbat. Omnēs autem quī eam regiōnem incolēbant, 13
ubi fāma dē morte leōnis ad aurēs eōrum pervēnit, vehe- 14
menter gaudēbant et Herculem magnō in honōre habēbant. 15

1. The king had heard of a lion that men were accustomed to avoid from fear.
2. He ordered Hercules to kill this lion.
3. The lion could not be killed with the weapons that Hercules had with him.
4. It had, however, no means of fleeing and was overcome by the man's strength.
5. And so those who inhabited the places adjacent to the forest were freed from danger.

Helpful Hints
1. For "heard of," use the verb **audiō** + **dē** + *abl.*
   To choose the correct tense of **cōnsuēscō**, see the vocabulary with paragraph 15.
   The English phrase "from fear" will be translated by a Latin ablative of cause without a preposition.
2. For "he ordered," use the verb **iubeō** + *acc.* + *infinitive.*
3. In paragraph 21 above, find a model for translating "with him" into Latin.
5. For "adjacent," use **fīnitimus, -a, -um** + *dat.*
   Be careful about the gender of the word for "places."

1 *Hydra, -ae (f), the Hyrdra, a many-headed water snake.
2 Hoc: agreeing with mōnstrum, not Hydram; a demonstrative or relative pronoun is commonly attracted into the gender of a predicate noun.
   cui . . . erant: dative of possession, literally, "to which were," better
   English, "that had."
3 Iolāus, -ī (m), Iolaus.
   *palūs, palūdis (f), swamp, marsh.
   Lernaeus, -a, -um, of Lerna, Lernean.
5 rēs: "undertaking"; in translating this word always choose the most
   suitable English word.
   magnī periculī: predicate genitive of description, (see grammar note
   with paragraph 9).
   sinistra, -ae (f), left hand.
   sinistrā: ablative of means.
6 dextra, -ae (f), right hand.
   *coepī, coepisse, coeptum (used in forms of the perfect system), have
   begun, began. coepit: "he began."
7 *quotiēns, as often as.
   quotiēns . . . hoc fēcerat, . . . exoriēbantur: past general (see
   grammar note with paragraph 19), "as often as he (ever) did this . . .
   (always) sprang up."
   *exorior, exorīrī (4), exortus sum, to arise from, spring up, rise.
8 hōc cōnātū: ablative of separation with dēstitit, "he ceased (from)."
   *dēsistō, dēsistere (3), dēstitī, dēstitum (+ abl. or ab + abl.), to leave
   off, desist, cease, stop.
9 succīdō (sub- + caedō), succīdere (3), succīdī, succīsum, to cut below
   or down, fell.
   *ignis, ignis, ignium (m), fire.
10 *ligna, -ōrum (n pl), wood.
   *fax, facis (f), torch, firebrand.
   *ārdeō, ārdēre (2), ārsī, ārsūrus, to be on fire, burn.
   face ārdente: ablative of means, "with a burning torch"; for the
   participle, see pages 54–55.
11 adūrō, adūrere (3), adussī, adustum, to set fire to, burn, scorch, sear.
   *unde, whence, from where (here equivalent to ex quibus).
12 cancer, cancrī (m), crab.
   auxiliō Hydrae: double dative construction, literally, "for the purpose of
   aid with reference to the Hydra," better English, "to aid the Hydra"; auxiliō is dative of purpose, and Hydrae is dative of reference, denoting
   the person or thing concerned.
13 crūs, crūris (n), leg.
14 mordeō, mordēre (2), momordī, morsum, to bite.
   mordēbat: imperfect denoting repeated action, "kept biting."
15 *sagitta, -ae (f), arrow.
   *imbuō, imbuere (3), imbuī, imbūtum, to wet, soak, dip.
   itaque: "and thus"; not the conjunction itaque but the adverb ita with the
   enclitic conjunction -que.
   mortifer, mortifera, mortiferum, death-bringing, deadly.
   reddidit: sagittās suās is object of this verb as well as of imbuit.

22. SECOND LABOR: THE LERNEAN HYDRA

Paulō post ab Eurystheō Hydram interficere iussus est. 1
Hoc autem erat mōnstrum cui novem erant capita. Her- 2
culēs igitur cum amīcō Iolāō profectus est ad palūdem Ler- 3
naeam, in quā Hydra habitābat. Brevī tempore mōnstrum 4
invēnit; et quamquam rēs erat magnī perīculī, id sinistrā 5
prehendit. Tum dextrā capita novem abscīdere coepit; 6
quotiēns tamen hoc fēcerat, nova capita exoriēbantur. Diū 7
frūstrā labōrābat; tandem hōc cōnātū dēstitit. Deinde ar- 8
borēs succīdere et ignem accendere cōnstituit. Hoc celeriter 9
fēcit; et postquam ligna ignem comprehendērunt, face ār- 10
dente colla adussit, unde capita exoriēbantur. Nec tamen 11
sine magnō labōre haec fēcit; cancer enim ingēns auxiliō 12
Hydrae vēnit, quī, dum Herculēs capita abscindēbat, crūra 13
eius mordēbat. Postquam mōnstrum tālī modō interfēcit, 14
sagittās suās sanguine eius imbuit, itaque mortiferās red- 15
didit. 16

> **Dative of Possession**
>
> A noun or pronoun in the *dative case* may appear with the verb **sum** to indicate *possession*; the thing possessed is the subject of the verb, and the person or thing that possesses it is in the dative case, e.g., <u>cui</u> **novem erant capita**, literally, "<u>to which</u> there were nine heads," better English, "<u>which had</u> nine heads."

> **Double Dative**
>
> Two datives may be found together in what is called the *double dative construction*. One of the datives is a *dative of purpose* (see grammar note with paragraph 15), and the other is a *dative of reference*, denoting the person or thing concerned, e.g., **cancer ingēns <u>aux-iliō</u> Hydrae vēnit**, literally, "a huge crab came <u>for the purpose of aid</u> <u>with reference to the Hydra</u>," better English, "to aid the Hydra."

1. While Hercules was in servitude, he came upon the Hydra in a swamp.
2. This Hydra had nine heads.
3. To kill it was a most difficult matter, but Hercules did not cease from the attempt.
4. A friend, moreover, came to his aid.
5. When the Hydra had been overcome, Hercules set out for the city.

1   **caedēs, caedis, caedium** (*f*), cutting down, killing, slaughter.
     ***nūntiō** (1), to report, announce.
2   **Herculem**: *direct object* of iussit (with **referre**).
     ***cervus, -ī** (*m*), stag.
3   ***audācia, -ae** (*f*), daring, boldness, audacity.
     tantae audāciae: *genitive of description* with **virum**, "a man of such
          great boldness."
4   ***cornū, -ūs** (*n*), horn.
5   ***incrēdibilis, -is, -e**, unbelievable, incredible.
     incrēdibilī . . . celeritāte: *ablative of description*, in the predicate
          after **hic . . . cervus . . . fuit**, "this stag was of incredible
          swiftness."
6   **persequor, persequī** (3), **persecūtus sum**, to follow up, pursue.
7   **ipsum**: *intensive adjective* contrasting **cervum** with **vēstīgiīs**; up to
          this time Hercules had seen only the stag's tracks.
8   **ad quiētem**: ad with the *accusative* to express *purpose*, "to rest."
12   ***cursus, -ūs** (*m*), running, course.
     exanimātum: *participle*; translate as a relative clause.
     ***vīvus, -a, -um**, alive, living.
     vīvum: *predicate adjective*.

Subjunctive Mood

The *indicative mood* is used for direct statements and
for simple questions; the *imperative mood* is used for
direct commands. In paragraph 25 you will find your
first verb in the *subjunctive mood*. This mood is used
in many subordinate clauses introduced by subordinating conjunctions, in indirect questions, indirect commands, and in a few independent clauses. The subjunctive mood has only the following tenses: present,
imperfect, perfect, and pluperfect; there are no future or
future perfect subjunctives. The personal endings are
the same as for indicative verbs.

Ad + Noun in the Accusative to Express Purpose

Ad with a noun or noun phrase may express *purpose*,
e.g., **Neque nocturnum tempus sibi ad quiētem
relinquēbat**, "Nor did he leave the night time for himself for the purpose of rest," better English, "to rest."

23. THIRD LABOR: THE CERYNEAN STAG

Postquam Eurystheō caedēs Hydrae nūntiāta est, mag- 1
nus timor animum eius occupāvit. Itaque Herculem cervum 2
quendam ad sē referre iussit; virum enim tantae audāciae 3
in urbe retinēre nōlēbat. Hic autem cervus, cuius cornua au- 4
rea fuisse trāduntur, incrēdibilī fuit celeritāte. Herculēs igi- 5
tur prīmō vēstīgiīs eum in silvā persequēbatur; deinde, ubi 6
cervum ipsum vīdit, omnibus vīribus currere coepit. Ūsque 7
ad vesperum currēbat, neque nocturnum tempus sibi ad 8
quiētem relinquēbat. Frūstrā tamen tantum labōrem 9
suscēpit; nūllō enim modō cervum cōnsequī poterat. Tan- 10
dem, postquam tōtum annum cucurrit (ita trāditur), cervum 11
cursū exanimātum cēpit, et vīvum ad Eurystheum rettulit. 12

1. Hercules, who had been ordered to catch a certain stag, immediately undertook the labor.
2. This stag had golden horns.
3. Furthermore, it was able to run many days with great swiftness.
4. But nevertheless, Hercules made no end of pursuing.
5. A year later he brought the stag back with him.

Helpful Hints

1. Find a model for part of this sentence in paragraph 22, line 1.
2. The English verb "had" can be translated either with the Latin verb **habeō**
   or by using the dative of possession with the verb **sum** (see grammar note
   with paragraph 22).
3. Since "run" is intransitive, "days" cannot be its direct object; rather, it tells
   how long the stag could run (accusative of duration of time). Find an example in paragraph 23 above.
4. For "of pursuing," use a gerund (see grammar note with paragraph 21);
   gerunds of deponent verbs have the same forms as those of regular verbs.
5. For "a year later," translate as if the expression were "later by a year"; for
   the grammar and the order of the words, see paragraph 22, line 1.

1   **iussus est: Herculēs** is the subject. Compare **Herculem . . . iussit**
     in the second sentence of paragraph 23.
     *__aper, aprī__ (*m*), wild boar.
2   **Erymanthius, -a, -um,** of Erymanthus, Erymanthian.
     *__vāstō__ (1), to lay waste.
4   *__Arcadia, -ae__ (*f*), Arcadia (a country).
5   **aprō:** *dative* with the *compound verb* **occurrit.**
     Ille: here and in line 9 below the pronoun at the beginning of the sentence
     signals a change of subject from the previous sentence.
6   **timōre perterritus:** the Latin is redundant here, and it is not necessary
     to translate both words; "in its fear" or "since it was terrified" will do.
     Always try first to discover the exact meaning of the Latin and then to
     express this meaning in idiomatic English.
     altus, -a, -um, deep, high.
7   *__prōiciō__ (prō- + iaciō), **prōicere** (3), **prōiēcī, prōiectum,** to throw
     forth *or* down, throw.
     laqueus, -ī (*m*), noose.
     aprō laqueum . . . iniēcit: *dative* and *accusative* with the *compound
     verb* **iniēcit.** The same idea could have been expressed with **in
     aprum laqueum iēcit.**
8   **summā cum difficultāte:** *ablative of manner* with **cum,** which may be
     used when the noun is modified by an adjective (see grammar note with
     paragraph 5).
9   *__etsī:__ even if, although.
     *__repugnō__ (1), to fight against, struggle, resist.
10   **ad Eurystheum:** we are told that Eurystheus was so frightened that he
     hid in a great jar.
     vīvus: why is the nominative used here and the accusative at the end of
     paragraph 23?

Sequence of Tenses with the Subjunctive		
	Main Clause Indicative or Imperative	*Subordinate Clause* Tense of Subjunctive *Type of Action*
Primary *Sequence*	Present Future Future Perfect	Present = *Simultaneous or subse-* *quent, incomplete* Perfect = *Prior, completed*
Secondary *Sequence*	Imperfect Perfect Pluperfect	Imperfect = *Simultaneous or subse-* *quent, incomplete* Pluperfect = *Prior, completed*

24. FOURTH LABOR: THE ERYMANTHIAN BOAR

Tum vērō iussus est Herculēs aprum quendam capere, 1
quī illō tempore agrōs Erymanthiōs vāstābat, et incolās 2
huius regiōnis magnopere terrēbat. Herculēs rem suscēpit, 3
et in Arcadiam profectus est. Postquam in silvam paulum 4
prōgressus est, aprō occurrit. Ille autem simul atque Her- 5
culem vīdit, statim refūgit, et timōre perterritus in altam 6
fossam sē prōiēcit. Herculēs aprō laqueum quem attulerat 7
iniēcit, et summā cum difficultāte eum ē fossā extrāxit. 8
Ille etsī fortiter repugnābat, tamen nūllō modō sē līberāre 9
potuit, atque ab Hercule ad Eurystheum vīvus relātus est. 10

1. Hercules was always eager for labor, and danger was pleasing to
   him.
2. Because of his boldness, he was able to accomplish everything that
   the king had demanded.
3. After he had brought the stag back alive, a boar was also brought
   back alive by him.
4. This boar he had met in a forest.
5. Although the undertaking was one of great danger, nevertheless
   Hercules dragged the boar out of a ditch.

Helpful Hints

1. Be sure to use the appropriate cases of the nouns that accompany **cupidus**
   and **grātus**.
     "Him" is not reflexive here because it does not refer to the subject of its
   own clause.
2. For "because of his boldness," use **ob** or **propter** + *acc.*
3. Models for translating the predicate accusative ("brought the stag back *alive*)
   and the predicate nominative ("was also brought back *alive*") can be found in
   paragraph 23, lines 11–12 and paragraph 24, line 10.
4. Be sure to use the dative with the intransitive compound verb **occurrō**.
5. Find a model for the structure ("Although . . . nevertheless") of this sentence
   in paragraph 24 above.

---

1 **nārrāvimus**: in Latin, as in English, writers sometimes use the first person plural in speaking of themselves instead of the first person singular.

3 *****centaurus, -ī** (*m*), centaur.

4 **Cum . . . appeteret**: **cum** *causal clause* with *imperfect subjunctive* in *secondary sequence*, "Since . . . was approaching." Note that the imperfect subjunctive is here translated as one would translate an imperfect indicative.

5 *****spēlunca, -ae** (*f*), cave, cavern.
 *****Pholus, -ī** (*m*), Pholus.

8 *****amphora, -ae** (*f*), jar, bottle.

9 **quod**: "because" (not the relative).

10 *****reliquus, -a, -um**, left, the remaining, the other, the rest of (denoting a part).

11 **inquit**: *vivid or historic present* (this verb is postpositive, i.e., it always follows one or more words of the direct quotation that it introduces; it never comes before the quotation).
 *****committō, committere** (3), **commīsī, commissum**, to send together, commit, entrust.

12 **sī id dederō, . . . interficient**: *future more vivid condition* (future perfect in the if-clause and future in the main clause; translate the if-clause with a present tense in English).

13 **irrīdeō** (in- + rīdeō), **irrīdēre** (2), **irrīsī, irrīsum**, to laugh at, mock.

Cum Causal Clauses

Cum may introduce a clause that states a *reason* or gives a *cause*. If the verb of the main clause is in the present or future tense (primary sequence), the present or perfect subjunctive is used in the causal clause; if the main verb is in a past tense (secondary sequence), the imperfect or pluperfect subjunctive is used in the causal clause, e.g., <u>Cum</u> nox iam **appeteret, ad spēluncam dēvertit**, "<u>Since</u> night <u>was</u> already <u>approaching</u>, he turned aside to a cave."

Future More Vivid Conditions

Future more vivid conditions express strong probabilities or certainties with reference to future time. The if-clause has a future or future perfect indicative, and the main clause has a future indicative; the if-clause should always be translated with a present tense in English, e.g., **Sī id <u>dederō</u>, centaurī mē interficient**, "If I <u>give</u> it (away), the centaurs will kill me." The future perfect must be used in the if-clause when the action of that clause, as here, is thought of as having been completed prior to the action of the main clause.

25. HERCULES AT THE CENTAUR'S CAVE

Dē quārtō labōre, quem suprā nārrāvimus, haec etiam 1
trāduntur. Herculēs dum iter in Arcadiam facit, ad eam 2
regiōnem vēnit quam centaurī incolēbant, quī erant equī, 3
sed hominis caput habēbant. Cum nox iam appeteret, ad 4
spēluncam dēvertit in quā centaurus quīdam, nōmine Pho- 5
lus, habitābat. Ille Herculem benignē excēpit et cēnam 6
parāvit. At Herculēs postquam cēnāvit, vīnum ā Pholō pos- 7
tulāvit. Erat autem in spēluncā magna amphora vīnī, quam 8
centaurī ibi dēposuerant. Pholus id dare nōlēbat, quod 9
reliquōs centaurōs timēbat; nūllum tamen vīnum praeter 10
hoc in spēluncā habēbat. "Hoc vīnum," inquit, "mihi com- 11
missum est. Sī id dederō, centaurī mē interficient." Her- 12
culēs tamen eum irrīsit, et ipse pōculum vīnī ex amphorā 13
hausit. 14

Imperfect Subjunctive

The *imperfect subjunctive* is formed by adding personal
endings to the *present active infinitive*; for the deponent
verbs a corresponding *present active infinitive* must be
formed before adding the passive endings.

Active	*Passive*	*Deponent*
portārem	portārer	cōnārer
portārēs	portārēris	cōnārēris (-re)
portāret	portārētur	cōnārētur
etc.	etc.	etc.
movērem	movērer	verērer
mitteret	mitterētur	proficīscerētur
iacerēmus	iacerēmur	regrederēmur
audīrent	audīrentur	exorīrentur

---

1. If there are centaurs in the region, a traveler will meet them.
2. While Hercules was going through their country, he met Pholus.
3. Since he wished to give himself to rest, he decided to spend the night there.
4. The other centaurs had not learned of the arrival of Hercules.
5. Pholus himself entertained him, but he was unwilling to give him everything that he requested.

Helpful Hints
1. Use the future tense in both clauses of this future more vivid condition.

1   **vīnī optimī**: *genitive* with the *adjective* **plēna**.
      plēnus, -a, -um (+ *gen.*), full (of).
      *****odor, odōris** (*m*), smell, odor.
2   **iūcundus, -a, -um**, pleasant, sweet.
      diffundō (dis- + fundō), **diffundere** (3), **diffūdī, diffūsum**, to pour
        forth, spread *or* shed abroad, diffuse.
5   **bibentem**: *present participle.*
6   *****aditus, -ūs** (*m*), approach, entrance.
7   *****cōnsistō, cōnsistere** (3), **cōnstitī**, to station oneself, take one's stand,
        consist.
      *****sustineō** (subs- = sub- + teneō) (2), to hold *or* bear up, sustain, withstand.
8   **fax, facis** (*f*), torch.
11   *****venēnum, -ī** (*n*), poison.
      absūmō, absūmere (3), **absūmpsī, absūmptum**, to take away, con-
        sume, destroy.
12   **fugā**: *ablative of means*, but the English idiom is "in flight."

Present Active Participle

The letters **-nt-** added to the present stem of a verb and followed by third declension case endings make the *present active participle*. The nominative singular has **-ns** added to the verb stem.

See below for sample nominative and genitive forms, and see page 55 for the full declension of present active participles.

The present active participle (there is no present passive participle) is an *adjective* in that it modifies a noun or pronoun and is a *verb* in that it can take a direct object. The participle **bibentem** in the clause **Herculem bibentem vīdērunt**, "they saw Hercules drinking," modifies the noun **Herculem** and could have a direct object such as **vīnum**, e.g.: **Herculem vīnum bibentem vīdērunt**, "they saw Hercules drinking wine."

The present participle, like the present infinitive, shows the *same time* as the main verb; i.e., they saw Hercules at the same time that he was drinking.

parāns	habēns	mittēns	iaciēns	audiēns
parantis	habentis	mittentis	iacientis	audientis

Genitive with Adjectives

The meaning of some adjectives, especially those denoting fullness, may be completed with a word in the genitive case, e.g., **amphora vīnī optimī plēna**, "a jar full of very good wine."

26. THE FIGHT WITH THE CENTAURS

Simul atque amphora vīnī optimī plēna aperta est, odor 1
iūcundissimus undique diffūsus est; vīnum enim suāvissi- 2
mum erat. Centaurī nōtum odōrem sēnsērunt, atque omnēs 3
ad locum convēnērunt. Ubi ad spēluncam pervēnērunt, 4
magnopere īrātī erant, quod Herculem bibentem vīdērunt, 5
ac Pholum interficere volēbant. Herculēs tamen in aditū 6
spēluncae cōnstitit et impetum eōrum fortissimē sustinē- 7
bat. Facēs ārdentēs in eōs coniēcit; multōs etiam sagittīs 8
suīs vulnerāvit. Hae autem sagittae eaedem erant quae 9
sanguine Hydrae imbūtae erant. Omnēs igitur quōs ille 10
sagittīs vulnerāverat venēnō statim absūmptī sunt; reliquī 11
autem ubi hoc vīdērunt, terga vertērunt et fugā salūtem 12
petiērunt. 13

Declension of Present Active Participles	
Singular	*Plural*
M., F., N.	M., F., N.
parāns	parantēs, parantia (*n.*)
parantis	parantium
parantī	parantibus
parantem, parāns (*n.*)	parantēs, parantia (*n.*)
parante (-ī)	parantibus

1. When an attack had been made upon Pholus by the other centaurs, Hercules came to his aid.
2. For he was unwilling to seek safety in flight.
3. Sustaining the attack of the enemy long and bravely, he never lacked hope.
4. When many centaurs had been wounded by his arrows, the rest fled in all directions.
5. Desiring rest, they desisted from flight at midnight.

Helpful Hints
1. To translate "to his aid," use the double dative construction (for a model, see paragraph 22, lines 12–13, and see the grammar note there).
2. For "in flight," use the ablative of means.
3. For "sustaining," use a present participle.
5. For "desiring," use either a participle or the adjective **cupidus**.
   For "from flight," use the ablative of separation.

1   **Cum reliquī fūgissent**: "When (after) the others had fled. . . . "; for grammar, see below.

3   **mīror, mīrārī* (1), *mīrātus sum*, to wonder, wonder at.
     levis, -is, -e, light, slight.

5   **locum**: *direct object* of **adiit**, which is here transitive, "approached."
     *iaceō, iacēre (2), *iacuī*, to lie, be prostrate. Distinguish this verb carefully from **iaciō, iacere** (3), **iēcī, iactum**, to throw, cast, hurl.

6   **sīve or seu*, or if.
     sīve . . . sīve, whether . . . or.
     cāsū . . . cōnsiliō: *ablative of manner* without **cum** or accompanying adjectives (see grammar note with paragraph 11).
     sīve cāsū sīve cōnsiliō deōrum: a commonplace idea, "whether by chance or a plan of the gods." You will see this again.

7   **ēlābor, ēlābī** (3), **ēlāpsus sum**, to slip out, slip. This verb is a compound of **ē- (ex-)** + **lābor, lābī** (3), **lāpsus sum**, to slip.
     leviter, slightly.

12 ***exhauriō, exhaurīre** (4), **exhausī, exhaustum**, to drink up *or* off, drain.

Cum Circumstantial Clauses

In addition to introducing a clause that states a reason or gives a cause (**cum** causal; see grammar note with paragraph 25), **cum** may introduce a clause that describes the *circumstances* or the *situation* prior to or simultaneous with the action of the main clause. When the verb of the main clause is in a past tense (secondary sequence), the verb of the **cum** circumstantial clause is in the pluperfect subjunctive if it describes circumstances prior to the action of the main verb and in the imperfect subjunctive if it describes circumstances simultaneous with the action of the main verb, e.g., **Cum reliquī fūgissent, Pholus ex spēluncā ēgressus est**, "When (After) the others had fled, Pholus went out of the cave."

---

1. When the centaurs had made an end of fleeing, Hercules was able to overtake them.
2. In the meantime Pholus remained in that place where Hercules had met him.
3. He felt grief at the death of his friends.
4. He wondered, moreover, that they had departed from life so quickly.
5. While he was seeking the cause of this thing, he himself was accidentally killed.

27. THE FATE OF PHOLUS

Cum reliquī fūgissent, Pholus ex spēluncā ēgressus est, 1
et corpora spectābat eōrum quī sagittīs interfectī erant. 2
Magnopere autem mīrābātur quod tam levī vulnere ex- 3
animātī erant, et causam eius reī quaerēbat. Itaque adiit 4
locum ubi cadāver cuiusdam centaurī iacēbat, ac sagittam ē 5
vulnere extrāxit. Haec tamen, sīve cāsū sīve cōnsiliō 6
deōrum, dē manibus eius ēlāpsa est et pedem leviter vul- 7
nerāvit. Ille statim gravem dolōrem sēnsit, et brevī tem- 8
pore vī venēnī exanimātus est. Ubi Herculēs, quī reliquōs 9
centaurōs secūtus erat, ad spēluncam rediit, magnō cum 10
dolōre Pholum mortuum vīdit. Multīs cum lacrimīs 11
amīcum sepelīvit; tum, postquam alterum pōculum vīnī ex- 12
hausit, somnō sē dedit. 13

Pluperfect (Past Perfect) Subjunctive

While the imperfect subjunctive is formed by adding personal endings to the present infinitive (see page 53), the *pluperfect subjunctive* is formed by adding personal endings to the *perfect infinitive* (see page 26), e.g.:

Active	*Passive*	*Deponent*
portāvissem	portātus essem	conātus essem
portāvissēs	portātus essēs	conātus essēs
portāvisset	portātus esset	conātus esset
portāvissēmus	portātī essēmus	conātī essēmus
portāvissētis	portātī essētis	conātī essētis
portāvissent	portātī essent	conātī essent
mōvissem	mōtus essem	veritus essem
mīsisset	missus esset	profectus esset
iēcissēmus	iactī essēmus	regressī essēmus
audīvissent	audītī essent	exortī essent

Note that all the forms ending in **-us** and **-ī** may also have **-a** and **-um** and **-ae** and **-a** endings respectively because the participial (adjectival) part of the verb must agree in gender and number with the subject.

Helpful Hints
3. To translate "felt grief," find a model in paragraph 27 above.
    For "at the death," use an ablative of cause.
4. For "he wondered that," find a model in paragraph 27 above.

1 ut . . . cōnficeret: *indirect command* with *imperfect subjunctive,* "that he accomplish," better English, "to accomplish.

2 Augēās, Augēae (*m*), Augeas.

3 Ēlis, Ēlidis (*f*), Elis.

*obtineō (ob- + teneō) (2), to hold against, hold.

mīlle (*indecl. adj.*), a thousand; mīlia, -ium (*n pl*), thousands.

tria mīlia boum: literally, "three thousands of oxen," better English, "three thousand oxen." The singular mīlle is commonly used as an *indeclinable adjective,* like English "thousand," but the plural mīlia is used as a *substantive* (i.e., a *noun*) and is accompanied by a *partitive genitive.*

bōs, bovis, (*gen. pl.*) boum, (*dat.* and *abl. pl.*) būbus (*m/f*), ox, bull, cow.

4 *stabulum, -ī (*n*), standing-place, stall, stable, enclosure.

ingentis magnitūdinis: *genitive of description* with stabulō.

*magnitūdō, magnitūdinis (*f*), greatness, size.

5 squālor, squālōris (*m*), dirt, filth.

obserō, obserere (3), obsēvī, obsitum, to sow, plant, cover, fill.

obsitum: *predicate adjective.*

neque enim . . . umquam: "for . . . never."

6 ūnō diē: *ablative of time when.*

*pūrgō (1), to make clean, clean, cleanse.

7 opera, -ae (*f*), work, effort, labor.

multae operae: *predicate genitive of description.*

*negōtium, -ī (*n*), business, matter, task, trouble, difficulty.

8 fossam . . . dūxit: "dug a ditch"; the verb is here used with reference to the progress of work on a wall or ditch, from one end to the other.

duodēvīgintī (*indecl. adj.*), eighteen.

duodēvīgintī pedum: *genitive of description* used to define the width of the ditch, "eighteen feet wide."

9 *flūmen, flūminis (*n*), river.

11 *immittō (in- + mittō), immittere (3), immīsī, immissum, to send *or* let in.

*contrā (+ *acc.*), against, contrary to.

*opīniō, opīniōnis, (*f*), opinion, expectation, reputation.

12 *opus, operis (*n*), work, task.

opus: compare this word with operae (line 7) and labōre (line 8); labor is used of heavy or exhausting labor, opera of voluntary exertion or effort, and opus of that upon which one works or of the completed work.

1. Then the king ordered him to clean the stable.
2. Two thousand men could not accomplish that labor.
3. Hercules, however, hurried to the place and began at once to dig a ditch.
4. Hercules is said to have completed this work in one day.
5. He was making life safer by his labors and was not seeking honors.

28. FIFTH LABOR: THE AUGEAN STABLES

Deinde Eurystheus Herculī imperāvit ut hunc labōrem 1
graviōrem cōnficeret. Augēās quīdam, quī illō tempore 2
rēgnum in Ēlide obtinēbat, tria mīlia boum habēbat. Hī in 3
stabulō ingentis magnitūdinis inclūsī erant. Stabulum 4
autem squālōre erat obsitum; neque enim ad id tempus 5
umquam pūrgātum erat. Hoc Herculēs ūnō diē pūrgāre 6
iussus est. Ille, etsī rēs erat multae operae, negōtium 7
suscēpit. Prīmum magnō labōre fossam duodēvīgintī pe- 8
dum dūxit, per quam flūminis aquam dē montibus ad 9
mūrum stabulī dūxit. Tum, postquam mūrum perrūpit, 10
aquam in stabulum immīsit; et tālī modō contrā opīniōnem 11
omnium opus cōnfēcit. 12

Indirect Commands

Direct commands such as **Labōrem cōnfice**, "Accomplish the labor!" may be stated indirectly in clauses introduced by **ut** for a positive command or **nē** for a negative command, with the verb in the subjunctive (present in primary sequence and imperfect in secondary sequence), e.g., **Eurystheus Herculī imperāvit ut hunc labōrem graviōrem cōnficeret**, literally, "Eurystheus ordered Hercules <u>that he accomplish this heavier labor</u>," better English, "Eurystheus ordered Hercules <u>to accomplish this heavier labor</u>."

Note that the verb **imperāre** is one of the *special intransitive verbs* (see grammar note with paragraph 14) that are accompanied by the dative case. You can think of it as meaning to give a command to someone, with the content of the command expressed in the **ut** clause. Compare this use of **imperāre** + *dative* + **ut** + *subjunctive* with the construction of the other common verb of commanding, **iubēre** + *accusative* + *infinitive*, e.g., **Itaque Herculem cervum quendam ad sē referre iussit** (paragraph 23, lines 2–3).

Helpful Hints

1. Translate this sentence twice, first using **imperō** and then using **iubeō**.
2. For "two thousand men," use the neuter plural substantive **mīlia** ("thousands") + a partitive genitive ("of men").
3. To translate "dig a ditch," find a model in pararaph 28 above.
4. For "in one day," use ablative of time within which, not accusative of duration of time.

1   ***Stymphālus, -ī** (*f*), Stymphalus.
2   ***avis, avis, avium** (*f*), bird.
3   **rōstrum, -ī** (*n*) beak.
    *aēneus, -a, -um, of copper *or* bronze.
4   **carne**: *ablative* with the *deponent verb* **vēscēbantur**.
    *vēscor, vēscī (3) (+ *abl.*), to feed on, eat.
5   ***lacus, -ūs** (*m*), lake.
6   **appropinquandī**: *gerund* in the *genitive case* with **facultās**, "means of approaching" (see grammar note with paragraph 21).
7   **līmus, -ī** (*m*), mud.
    *constō, cōnstāre (1), **cōnstitī**, to stand together, agree, consist.
      cōnstitit: compare this with **cōnstitit** in paragraph 26, line 7, which is from a different verb.
8   **pedibus**: *ablative of means,* "on foot."
    *linter, lintris (*f*), boat, skiff.
10 **hōc cōnātū**: *ablative of separation* with **dēstitit**, "he left off, stopped from."
    ut . . . peteret: *purpose clause* with the *imperfect subjunctive in secondary sequence*, "to seek,"
11 **crotalum, -ī** (*n*), clapper, rattle.
    *Volcānus, -ī (*m*), Vulcan.
12 ***faber, fabrī** (*m*), smith.
    *colō, colere (3), **coluī, cultum**, to till, cultivate, inhabit, worship.
    aes, aeris (*n*), copper, bronze.
13 **crepitus, -ūs** (*m*), rattle, clatter, noise.
    *ācer, ācris, ācre, sharp, shrill. All adjectives (1st/2nd declension and 3rd declension) ending in **-er** form the superlative by adding **-rimus, -a, -um** to the positive nominative singular masculine, thus, **pulcherrimus, -a, -um** and **ācerrimus, -a, -um**.
14 **āvolō** (1), to fly away.
15 ***trānsfīgō, trānsfīgere** (3), **trānsfīxī, trānsfīxum**, to thrust *or* pierce through, transfix.

Ablative with Deponent Verbs

The meaning of several deponent verbs such as **ūtor** and **vēscor** is completed by a word or phrase in the ablative case, e.g., **Hae avēs carne hominum vēscēbantur**, "These birds were accustomed to eating the flesh of men." Make a list of such verbs as you meet them in your reading.

29. SIXTH LABOR: THE STYMPHALIAN BIRDS

Post paucōs diēs Herculēs ad oppidum Stymphālum iter 1
fēcit; imperāverat enim eī Eurystheus ut avēs Stym- 2
phālidēs interficeret. Hae avēs rōstra aēnea habēbant, et 3
carne hominum vēscēbantur. Ille postquam ad locum per- 4
vēnit, lacum vīdit; in hōc autem lacū, quī nōn procul erat ab 5
oppidō, avēs habitābant. Nūlla tamen appropinquandī 6
facultās dabātur; lacus enim nōn ex aquā, sed ē līmō cōn- 7
stitit. Herculēs igitur neque pedibus neque lintre prōgredī 8
potuit. Cum magnam partem diēī frūstrā cōnsūmpsisset, 9
hōc cōnātū dēstitit et ad Minervam sē contulit, ut auxilium 10
ab eā peteret. Illa eī crotala dedit quae ipse Volcānus (quī 11
ab fabrīs maximē colēbātur) ex aere fēcerat. Cum Herculēs 12
hīs crotalīs crepitum ācerrimum fēcisset, avēs perterritae 13
āvolāvērunt. Ille autem, dum āvolant, magnum numerum 14
eārum sagittīs trānsfīxit. 15

> ### Purpose Clauses
> The purpose for which the action described in the main clause of a sentence is undertaken is often expressed by a subordinate clause introduced by **ut** (positive) or **nē** (negative); the present subjunctive is used in primary sequence and the imperfect subjunctive in secondary sequence, e.g., **ad Minervam sē contulit, ut auxilium ab eā peteret**, literally, "he went to Minerva, so that he might seek aid from her," better English, "to seek aid from her." Note that in English an infinitive is often used to express purpose; Latin prose uses **ut** or **nē** with the subjunctive instead.

1. Next Hercules came to Stymphalus, that he might kill certain birds.
2. For Eurystheus had commanded him to do this.
3. The difficulty of approaching was great, and Hercules desisted from the attempt.
4. When a god had given him help, the birds sought safety in flight.
5. Hercules used new weapons to force the birds to depart.

Helpful Hints
4. For "in flight," use an ablative of means.
5. For "used," remember to use **ūtor** + *abl.*
   Use a purpose clause, not an infinitive, to translate "to force." For "to depart," use an infinitive.

1   **Eurystheus Herculī imperāvit ut . . . referret**: *indirect command.*
    ***taurus, -ī** (m)*, bull.
2   **ex**: compare **ab** (paragraph 29, line 5) and **dē** (paragraph 28, line 9); we
    commonly translate all three "from," but the strict meanings are "out of,"
    "away from," and "down from."
    ***Crēta, -ae** (f)*, Crete.
3   ***cōnscendō** (con- + scandō),* **cōnscendere** (3), **cōnscendī, cōnscēn-
    sum**, to climb; (*with or without* **nāvem**) to go on board, embark.
    cum . . . esset: **cum** *circumstantial clause.*
    ***solvō, solvere** (3), **solvī, solūtum**, to loosen; (*with or without* **nāvem**)
    to cast off, set sail, put to sea.
4   **īnsulae**: *dative* with *compound verb.*
    tanta tempestās . . . coorta est ut nāvis. . . nōn posset: *result
    clause* with *imperfect subjunctive* in *secondary sequence*, introduced by
    tanta tempestās coorta est, "such a great storm arose that (as a re-
    sult) the ship was not able. . . ."
6   **nauta, -ae** (*m*), sailor.
7   **nāvigandī**: *gerund* in the *genitive* with the *adjective* **imperītus**; we say
    "inexperienced in."
8   **imperītus, -a, -um** (+ *gen.*), inexperienced, unskilled, ignorant.
9   ***tranquillitās, tranquillitātis** (f)*, calm.
10 ***recipiō, recipere** (3), **recēpī, receptum**, to take back.
    sē recipere, *idiom,* to betake oneself, withdraw, collect oneself,
    recover.
12 **veniendī**: what form?
16 **cum . . . trāxisset**: **cum** *circumstantial clause.*
17 ***praeda, -ae** (f)*, booty, spoil, plunder.

Result Clauses

The result of an action described in the main clause of a
sentence may be expressed by a subordinate clause introduced by **ut** (positive) or **ut nōn** (negative); the present subjunctive is used in primary sequence and the
imperfect subjunctive (or sometimes the perfect subjunctive) in secondary sequence, e.g., **tanta tempestās subitō coorta est ut nāvis cursum
tenēre nōn posset**, "such a great storm arose that
the ship was not able to hold its course." Note that result clauses are usually anticipated in the main clause
by a word such as **tanta** "such a great," e.g., "such a
great storm arose that (as a result) the ship. . . ."

30. SEVENTH LABOR: THE CRETAN BULL

Tum Eurystheus Herculī imperāvit ut taurum quendam 1
ferōcissimum ex īnsulā Crētā vīvum referret. Ille nāvem 2
cōnscendit, et cum ventus idōneus esset, statim solvit. 3
Cum tamen īnsulae iam appropinquāret, tanta tempestās 4
subitō coorta est ut nāvis cursum tenēre nōn posset. Tan- 5
tus autem timor animōs nautārum occupāvit ut paene 6
omnem spem salūtis dēpōnerent. Herculēs etsī nāvigandī 7
imperītus erat, tamen nūllō modō territus est. Paulō post 8
summa tranquillitās cōnsecūta est, et nautae, quī sē ex 9
timōre iam recēperant, nāvem incolumem ad terram ap- 10
pulērunt. Herculēs ē nāvī ēgressus est; et cum ad rēgem 11
Crētae vēnisset, causam veniendī docuit. Deinde, 12
postquam omnia parāta sunt, ad eam regiōnem contendit 13
quam taurus vāstābat. Brevī tempore taurum vīdit; et 14
quamquam rēs erat magnī perīculī, cornua eius prehendit. 15
Tum, cum mōnstrum ad nāvem ingentī labōre trāxisset, 16
cum praedā in Graeciam rediit. 17

1. When Hercules was sailing to the island of Crete, a great storm arose.
2. He had been sent there by the king to catch a certain bull.
3. Hercules himself was so brave that he was not frightened.
4. When the rest had recovered from their fear, he commanded them to hurry to the shore.
5. In a short time the ship came safe(ly) to land.

Helpful Hints

5. Use an adjective instead of an adverb in this sentence. When English has an adverb describing the activity of the subject of a sentence, Latin prefers an adjective, which is sometimes predicate in sense. It is as if the Latin were saying, "The ship came to land (and the ship was) safe."

2   ut . . . redūceret: *purpose clause.*
     Diomēdēs, Diomēdis (*m*), Diomedes.
3   **carne:** *ablative* with the *deponent verb* **vēscēbantur.**
4   **obiciō* (ob- + iaciō), **obicere** (3), **obiēcī, obiectum,** to throw in the way
     or to.
            obiciēbat . . . vēnerant: *past general* (see grammar note with
              paragraph 19), "he used (always) to throw . . . who(ever) came."
     peregrīnus, -ī (*m*), stranger, foreigner.
6   ut . . . **trāderentur:** *indirect command,* "that they be handed over."
     sibi: *indirect reflexive,* referring not to the subject of its own clause, **equī,**
       but to that of the main clause, **Herculēs.**
7   **Cum . . . nōllet:** *causal clause* with *imperfect subjunctive* of **nōlō.**
8   **cadāver:** *accusative neuter subject* of the *infinitive* **obicī.**
     obicī: *present passive infinitive.*
9   **mīra rērum commūtātiō:** when an adjective and a genitive modify the
       same noun, the words are often in this order.
     *commūtātiō, commūtātiōnis (*f*), change.
10   **cruciātus, -ūs* (*m*), torture.
     necāverat: see note on **interficiō** (paragraph 13, line 4).
     *supplicium, -ī (*n*), punishment, torture.
12   **laetitia, -ae* (*f*), joy.
13   **grātiam referre* (+ *dat.*), *idiom,* to return a favor, show gratitude.
     nōn modo . . . sed etiam, not only . . . but also.
14   **praemium, -ī* (*n*), reward.
     *ōrō (1), to beg, pray.
15   ut . . . **susciperet:** *indirect command* (note that indirect commands can
       follow not only verbs of commanding but also many others such as verbs
       of asking, begging, persuading, urging, and wishing).
16   **redīsset:** *syncopated pluperfect subjunctive* = **rediisset** *or* **redīvisset,**
       from **redeō, redīre** (*irreg.*), **rediī** *or* **redīvī, reditum.** Shortened
       or syncopated forms of the *perfect infinitive* and the *pluperfect subjunc-*
       tive are common in the verb **eō** and its compounds and in other verbs
       that end in **-vī** in the perfect tense.
     ad nāvigandum: *gerund* in *accusative case* with **ad** to express *purpose.*
17   **collocō** (con- + locō) (1), to put, place.
18   **tempestās, tempestātis* (*f*), weather, storm, tempest.
     *nancīscor, nancīscī (3), **nactus sum,** to get, obtain, find.
     *portus, -ūs (*m*), harbor, haven, port.
19   **equōs:** *direct object* of **exposuit,** not object of **post** (*adverb*).
     Argolicus, -a, -um, of Argolis, Argolic (Tiryns was in Argolis).

Indirect Reflexives

The reflexive in a subordinate clause may refer to the
subject of the main clause, if the subordinate clause expresses the thought of that subject, e.g., **Herculēs ab**
Diomēde postulāvit ut equī <u>sibi</u> trāderentur,
"Hercules demanded of Diomedes that the horses be
handed over <u>to himself</u> (i.e., to Hercules)."

31. EIGHTH LABOR: THE HORSES OF DIOMEDES

Postquam ex īnsulā Crētā rediit, Herculēs ab Eurystheō ¹
in Thrāciam missus est, ut equōs Diomēdis redūceret. Hī ²
equī carne hominum vēscēbantur; Diomēdēs autem, vir ³
crūdēlissimus, eīs obiciēbat peregrīnōs omnēs quī in eam ⁴
regiōnem vēnerant. Herculēs igitur magnā celeritāte in ⁵
Thrāciam contendit, et ab Diomēde postulāvit ut equī sibi ⁶
trāderentur. Cum tamen rēx hoc facere nōllet, Herculēs īrā ⁷
commōtus eum interfēcit, et cadāver eius equīs obicī iussit. ⁸
Ita mīra rērum commūtātiō facta est; is enim quī anteā ⁹
multōs cum cruciātū necāverat ipse eōdem suppliciō necā- ¹⁰
tus est. Cum haec nūntiāta essent, omnēs quī eam ¹¹
regiōnem incolēbant maximā laetitiā affectī sunt, et Her- ¹²
culī meritam grātiam rettulērunt. Nōn modo maximīs ¹³
honōribus et praemiīs eum decorāvērunt, sed etiam ōrābant ¹⁴
ut rēgnum ipse susciperet. Ille tamen hoc facere nōlēbat; et ¹⁵
cum ad mare redīsset, nāvem occupāvit. Ubi omnia ad ¹⁶
nāvigandum parāta sunt, equōs in nāvī collocāvit; deinde, ¹⁷
cum idōneam tempestātem nactus esset, sine morā ē portū ¹⁸
solvit, et paulō post equōs in lītus Argolicum exposuit. ¹⁹

Gerund with ad to Express Purpose

The preposition **ad** followed by the *gerund* in the accusative case is often used to express *purpose*, e.g., **Ubi omnia ad nāvigandum parāta sunt. . . . ,** "When everything had been prepared for sailing. . . ." For the forms of the gerund, see grammar note with paragraph 21.

---

1. Afterwards Eurystheus demanded that the horses of Diomedes be seized and be brought back to him.
2. Hercules prepared everything for setting out, so that he might avoid danger.
3. Certain friends begged that they might make the journey with him.
4. They went so swiftly that they finished the journey in a few days.
5. When he had seized the horses, Hercules hurried to return.

Helpful Hints
4. You may use either the imperfect or the perfect subjunctive in the result clause (see grammar note with paragraph 30). The perfect subjunctive would stress the actuality of the result.

1 ***Amāzonēs, -um** (*f pl*), Amazons.
    dīcitur: note that the Latin construction is personal, "the race is said to have consisted"; English often has the impersonal construction, "it is said that the race consisted."
2 ***scientia, -ae** (*f*), knowledge, skill.
    ***mīlitāris, -is, -e**, military, warlike.
      rēs mīlitāris, *idiom*, art of war, warfare.
3 ***adhibeō** (ad- + habeō), **adhibēre** (2), **adhibuī, adhibitum**, to hold to, employ, show.
    ut . . . audērent: what kind of a clause?
4 ***Hippolytē, Hippolytēs**, (*acc.*) **Hippolytēn** (*f*), Hippolyte. Note the Greek endings.
    ***balteus, -ī** (*m*), belt, girdle.
5 **Mārs, Mārtis** (*m*), Mars (god of war).
    Admētē, Admētēs (*f*), Admete. Another Greek word.
6 **possideō, possidēre** (2), **possēdī, possessum**, to hold, possess.
7 ***mandō** (1) (+ *dat.* + **ut** + *subjunctive*), to put into one's hands, entrust, commit, charge, command. See grammar note with paragraph 28; you can think of the verb as meaning to give a mandate to someone, with the content of the mandate given in the **ut** clause.
8 **ut . . . cōgeret et . . . īnferret**: what kind of a clause?
    ***īnferō, īnferre** (*irreg.*), **intulī, illātum**, to bring in *or* against, wage against, inflict.
    cum . . . convēnisset: *concessive clause*, "although . . . had come together"; for the grammar, see below.
10 ***ūsus, -ūs** (*m*), use, experience.

Concessive Clauses

Concessive clauses may be introduced by **etsī**, **quamquam**, or **cum**. Clauses introduced by **etsī**, "even if," "although," and **quamquam**, "although," take the indicative and will never cause any trouble. A clause introduced by **cum** and having its verb in the subjunctive may be either causal ("since," "because") (see grammar note with paragraph 25) or circumstantial ("when," "after") (see grammar note with paragraph 27) or concessive ("although"). When cum means "although," it is said to introduce a *concessive* clause, and the main clause often contains the word **tamen**, "nevertheless," e.g., <u>Cum</u> **maxima multitūdō convēnisset, eōs** <u>tamen</u> **sōlōs dēlēgit quī maximum ūsum in rē mīlitārī habēbant**, "<u>Although</u> a very great multitude had come together, he <u>nevertheless</u> chose only those who had the greatest experience in the art of war."

32. NINTH LABOR: THE GIRDLE OF HIPPOLYTE

Gēns Amāzonum omnīnō ex mulieribus cōnstitisse dīci- 1
tur. Hae summam scientiam reī mīlitāris habēbant, et 2
tantam virtūtem adhibēbant ut cum virīs proelium com- 3
mittere audērent. Hippolytē, Amāzonum rēgīna, balteum 4
habuit nōtissimum, quem Mārs eī dederat. Admētē autem, 5
Eurysthēī fīlia, dē hōc balteō audīverat, et eum possidēre 6
vehementer cupiēbat. Eurystheus igitur Herculī mandāvit 7
ut cōpiās cōgeret et bellum Amāzonibus īnferret. Ille nūn- 8
tiōs in omnēs partēs dīmīsit; et cum maxima multitūdō 9
convēnisset, eōs tamen sōlōs dēlēgit quī maximum ūsum in 10
rē mīlitārī habēbant. 11

1. Next the king commanded Hercules to go into the region of the Amazons and to bring back to him a certain girdle.
2. His daughter had asked that this be given to her.
3. Although there were many thousands of Amazons, Hercules nevertheless dared to wage war against them.
4. He immediately prepared everything for sailing.
5. Since messengers had been sent forth in all directions, forces were quickly collected.

Helpful Hints
1. "Next" here is an adverb and not an adjective. For "commanded," use the verb **mandō** and model your syntax on the sentence in lines 7–8 of paragraph 32 above.
2. "This" must be translated in the same gender as the Latin word for the thing to which it refers.
3. Translate this sentence two ways, first using an indicative verb in the subordinate clause and then a subjunctive verb (see grammar note on page 66).
4. To translate "for sailing," see the grammar note on the gerund with paragraph 31.
5. "Directions" is a specific connotation of a more general Latin word; see line 9 of paragraph 32 above.

1   **fortissimīs virīs**: *dative* with the *special intransitive verb* **persuāsit**.
     Note that the verb **persuādeō** is related to the adjective **suāvis**
     "sweet, pleasant," and that the verb literally means "to make (something)
     pleasant (to someone)," thus the dative case. See grammar note on the
     dative with paragraph 14.

2   ***persuādeō, persuādēre** (2), **persuāsī, persuāsum** (+ *dat.* + **ut** +
     subjunctive), to persuade, prevail upon, induce (someone to do
     something)
     ut . . . facerent: *indirect command*, "he persuaded them to make the
     journey."

3   **paucīs post diēbus**: *ablative of degree of difference* with the *adverb*
     post (see grammar note on the ablative with paragraph 14); compare
     post paucōs diēs (paragraph 29, line 1); with the *ablative*, **post** is an
     adverb, but with the *accusative*, it is a *preposition*.

4   ***ōstium**, -ī (*n*), mouth, doorway, door.
     Thermōdōn, Thermōdontis (*m*), Thermodon.

5   ***appellō** (ad- + pellō), **appellere** (3), **appulī, appulsum**, to drive to;
     (*with or without* **nāvem**) to put in.

6   **quī . . . docēret et . . . posceret**: *relative clause of purpose* (with a
     relative pronoun instead of **ut**), "who might explain and ask for" or "to
     explain and ask for."

8   ***afferō** (ad- + ferō), **afferre** (*irreg.*) **attulī, allātum**, to bear to, bring.

9   **eī**: why dative?
     ***negō** (1), to say no *or* not, deny, refuse.
     ut negāret: what kind of a clause?

10   ***fortūna**, -ae (*f*), fortune.

12   ***pugna**, -ae (*f*), fighting, battle, combat.
     ēvocō (1), to call out, challenge.

13   **castra, -ōrum** (*n pl*), camp.
     ***intervāllum**, -ī, (*n*), interval, space, distance.
     magnō intervāllō: *ablative of degree of difference*.
     nōn magnō: *litotes*, the expression of an idea by negating its
     opposite, "not great" = "short."

14   ***īnstruō, īnstruere** (3), **īnstrūxī, īnstrūctum**, to build in *or* into, draw
     up, equip, furnish.

Relative Clauses of Purpose

A *relative pronoun* may introduce a clause expressing
purpose with its verb in the *subjunctive*. Compare the
use of **ut** to introduce purpose clauses (see grammar
note with paragraph 29). Relative clauses of purpose
usually occur in contexts of motion or selection, and the
relative pronoun will have a clear antecedent in the
main clause, e.g., **Nūntium ad Hippolytēn mīsit,
quī causam veniendī docēret et balteum
posceret**, "He sent a messenger to Hippolyte, who
might explain the reason for (his) coming and ask for
the girdle," or "to explain . . . and ask for. . . . "

33. THE GIRDLE IS REFUSED

Herculēs postquam causam itineris exposuit, fortissimīs 1
virīs persuāsit ut sēcum iter facerent. Tum cum eīs quibus 2
persuāserat nāvem cōnscendit; et paucīs post diēbus, cum 3
ventus idōneus esset, ad ōstium flūminis Thermōdontis 4
appulit. Postquam in fīnēs Amāzonum vēnit, nūntium ad 5
Hippolytēn mīsit, quī causam veniendī docēret et balteum 6
posceret. Ipsa Hippolytē balteum trādere volēbat, quod 7
fāma dē Herculis virtūte ad eam allāta erat; reliquae ta- 8
men Amāzonēs eī persuāsērunt ut negāret. At Herculēs, 9
cum haec nūntiāta essent, bellī fortūnam temptāre cōnsti- 10
tuit. Proximō diē cum cōpiās ēdūxisset, locum idōneum 11
dēlēgit atque hostēs ad pugnam ēvocāvit. Amāzonēs 12
quoque cōpiās suās ē castrīs ēdūxērunt, et nōn magnō in- 13
tervāllō ab Hercule aciem īnstrūxērunt. 14

1. When Hercules had chosen the bravest men, he persuaded them to embark.
2. Since they had been taught by experience, they came safely to land after a few days.
3. Then Hercules asked that the girdle be handed over to him.
4. Hippolyte wished to do this, but she could not persuade the other Amazons.
5. She sent forth forces to draw up a line of battle.

Helpful Hints

2. Where possible, Latin prefers an adjective in the nominative to an adverb, so translate the English adverb "safely" with a Latin adjective.
5. Use a relative clause of purpose to translate "to draw up." For the idiom "to draw up a line of battle," see line 14 of paragraph 33 above.

1   **nōn magna:** the effect of the position of these words may be reproduced by translating "but not a large one."

     neuter, neutra, neutrum, neither.

       neutrī: "neither side"; the plural of this word is used in speaking of two parties, the singular in speaking of two individuals.

2   **initium, -ī** (*n*), beginning.

     ****trānseō, trānīre** (*irreg.*), **trānsiī, trānsitum,** to go across *or* over, cross.

       trānseundī: what kind of word?

3   ****committō, comittere** (3), **commīsī, commissum,** to send together, commit, entrust.

       proelium committere, *idiom,* to join battle.

6   **ut . . . occīderent, . . . conicerent:** what kind of clause?

7   ****genus, generis** (*n*), kind, nature.

     ****perturbō** (1), to confuse thoroughly, throw into confusion, disturb, agitate.

9   ****dēspērō** (1), to despair.

10   ****cohortor, cohortārī** (1), **cohortātus sum,** to encourage, exhort.

     ut . . . retinērent, . . . admitterent, . . . sustinērent: what kind of clauses?

     prīstinus, -a, -um, former.

11   **neu** *or* **nēve,** or not, and that not, and not, nor.

     neu or **nēve** is used for "and not" in an indirect command.

     dēdecus, dēdecoris (*n*), dishonor, disgrace.

     admittō, admittere (3), **admīsī, admissum,** to send to, admit, allow.

12   **Quibus verbīs:** *linking* **quī,** literally, "With which words. . . .," better English, "And with these words. . . ."

13   **ita:** *adverb* modifying **cōnfirmāvit,** indicating that a *result clause* will follow.

     quī vulneribus cōnfectī essent: *subjunctive by attraction* to the mood of the surrounding *result clause,* "who had been worn out with wounds."

14   **redintegrō** (1), to make whole again, renew.

1. There was a swamp not far from the place that they had chosen for a camp.
2. Hercules persuaded his soldiers to cross this so that they might join battle with the foe.
3. The Amazons were fighting so bravely that even those soldiers who had great knowledge of the art of war sought safety in flight.
4. They had not only been thrown into confusion, but also worn out by wounds.
5. Hercules himself, although he had very little hope of victory, nevertheless exhorted his men to show courage.

34. THE BATTLE

Palūs erat nōn magna inter duōs exercitūs; neutrī tamen 1
initium trānseundī facere volēbant. Tandem Herculēs 2
signum dedit; et ubi palūdem trānsiit, proelium commīsit. 3
Amāzonēs impetum virōrum fortissimē sustinuērunt, et 4
contrā omnium opīniōnem tantam virtūtem praestitērunt 5
ut multōs eōrum occīderent, multōs etiam in fugam con- 6
icerent. Virī enim novō genere pugnae perturbābantur, nec 7
magnam virtūtem praestābant. Herculēs autem cum haec 8
vidēret, dē suīs fortunīs dēspērāre coepit. Itaque mīlitēs 9
vehementer cohortātus est ut prīstinae virtūtis memoriam 10
retinērent, neu tantum dēdecus admitterent, hostiumque 11
impetum fortiter sustinērent. Quibus verbīs animōs om- 12
nium ita cōnfirmāvit ut multī etiam quī vulneribus cōnfectī 13
essent proelium sine morā redintegrārent. 14

Subjunctive by Attraction

The verb of a subordinate clause that stands within a
clause with its verb in the *subjunctive* may be *attracted*
into the subjunctive mood when the subordinate clause
is essential to the expression of the thought, e.g.,
**Quibus verbīs animōs omnium ita cōnfirmāvit
ut multī etiam quī vulneribus cōnfectī essent
proelium sine morā redintegrārent**, "With these
words he so strengthened the hearts of all that many,
even (those) who had been worn out with wounds renewed the battle without delay." Here the relative
clause **quī . . . cōnfectī essent** has its verb attracted into the subjunctive because of its position
within the result clause **ut . . . redintegrārent** and
because it is essential to the thought of that clause. If
the relative clause were removed, the thought of the result clause would be spoiled.

Helpful Hints

1. To translate "was . . . not far from," use the verb **absum** with the adverbs
   nōn procul and the preposition **ab** + *abl.*
   To translate "for a camp," use the dative case.
2. In paragraph 34 above, find the Latin idiom to translate "join battle."
3. For "great knowledge of the art of war," see paragraph 32, line 2.
   The verb in the relative clause will be in the subjunctive by attraction
   (see grammar note above).
5. For "of victory," use **dē** + *abl.*

1   **ācriter**, sharply, fiercely.

    pugnātum est: *impersonal passive*, with the *implied subject* "it," literally, "it was fought," better English "the battle was fought" or "they fought."

    *__sōl, sōlis__ (*m*), sun, the sun-god.

        Distinguish this noun carefully from the noun **solium, -ī** (*n*), seat, throne, and from the adjective **sōlus, -a, -um**, alone.

    *__occāsus, -ūs__ (*m*), setting.

2   **tanta commūtātiō rērum facta est**: "so great a change of affairs came about."

    facta est: from **fīō**.

4   **in quō numerō**: "and in this number."

5   **clēmentia, -ae** (*f*), mercy, kindness.

6   **lībertās, lībertātis** (*f*), freedom, liberty.

7   *__socius, -ī__ (*m*), companion, comrade, ally.

8   **aestātis**: *partitive genitive*.

        Distinguish this noun carefully from **aetās, aetātis** (*f*), age.

    supersum, superesse (*irreg.*), **superfuī, superfutūrus**, to be over *or* left, remain.

        Distinguish this verb carefully from **superō** (1), to overcome, defeat, conquer.

    *__mātūrō__ (1), to hurry.

9   **nactus**: perfect participle of what verb? Note that the perfect participle of deponent verbs is often best translated into English with a present participle, "finding," "getting," even though the Latin perfect participle shows time before the main verb.

10   *__priusquam__, before than, sooner than, before.

11   *__frūmentum, -ī__ (*n*), grain.

12   *__dēficiō__ (dē- + faciō), **dēficere** (3), **dēfēcī, dēfectum**, to fail.

    coeperat, from **coepī, coepisse**, have begun, began (a *defective verb*, like **ōdī, ōdisse**, to hate).

> ### *Impersonal Passives*
>
> You will find Latin verbs used *impersonally* in the passive, with an implied subject "it," to place emphasis on the action itself rather than on any of the participants in it, e.g., **Diū et ācriter <u>pugnātum est</u>**, literally, "<u>It was fought</u> long and fiercely," better English, "The battle was long and fierce." Note the neuter gender of the participle.

35. THE DEFEAT OF THE AMAZONS

Diū et ācriter pugnātum est; tandem tamen ad sōlis oc- 1
cāsum tanta commūtātiō rērum facta est ut mulierēs terga 2
verterent et fugā salūtem peterent. Multae autem vulne- 3
ribus dēfessae dum fugiunt captae sunt, in quō numerō erat 4
ipsa Hippolytē. Herculēs summam clēmentiam praestitit; 5
postquam balteum accēpit, lībertātem omnibus captīvīs 6
dedit. Tum vērō sociōs ad mare redūxit; et quod nōn mul- 7
tum aestātis supererat, in Graeciam proficīscī mātūrāvit. 8
Itaque nāvem cōnscendit, et tempestātem idōneam nactus 9
statim solvit. Priusquam tamen in Graeciam pervēnit, ad 10
urbem Troiam nāvem appellere cōnstituit; frūmentum enim 11
quod sēcum habēbat iam dēficere coeperat. 12

1. When the battle had been fought for much of the day, the women fled.
2. Hercules sent soldiers to follow them.
3. Hippolyte herself is said by others to have been caught and killed.
4. Hercules commanded that the other women who had been caught should be set free.
5. A few days later, getting a favorable wind, he set out with the girdle.

Helpful Hints

1. In paragraph 29, line 9, find a model for "much of the day."
   In paragraph 35 above, find a model for "the battle had been fought," and see the grammar note on page 72.
2. Use a relative clause of purpose.
4. Use **imperō**.
   Use the subjunctive in the relative clause "who had been caught." See the grammar note with paragraph 34.
5. Find a model for "a few days later" in paragraph 33, line 3.
   Usually the noun in an ablative of accompaniment is a person, but it may be a thing when it is something one carries by hand.

1 ***Lāomedōn, Lāomedontis** (*m*), Laomedon.
2 **superior, -ius** (*comparative* of **superus**, upper), uppermost, highest, greatest.
    superiōre annō, *idiom, ablative of time when*, in the previous (preceding) year.
3 **cum . . . habēret: cum** *causal clause* with *imperfect subjunctive* in *secondary sequence.*
    ***moenia, moenium** (*n pl*), walls.
4 ***offerō** (ob- + ferō), **offerre** (*irreg.*), **obtulī, oblātum**, to bear to, proffer, offer.
5 ***prōpōnō, prōpōnere** (3), **prōposuī, prōpositum**, to put *or* set before, offer, propose, set forth, say.
    persolvō, persolvere (3), **persolvī, persolūtum**, to pay completely, pay.
8 ***pecus, pecudis** (*f*), head of cattle, beast, sheep, goat.
    vorō (1), to swallow whole, devour.
10 **pecus, pecoris** (*n*), cattle, herd, flock.
    pecora: used of herds of cattle, while **pecudēs** (see above) is used of individual animals, especially sheep.
    ***compellō, compellere** (3), **compulī, compulsum**, to drive together, drive.
11 **eī**: *dative* with **praecēpit**.
12 ***praecipiō** (prae- + capiō), **praecipere** (3), **praecēpī, praeceptum** (+ *dat.* + **ut** + *subjunctive*), to take beforehand, anticipate, direct, order, charge.
    Distinguish this verb carefully from **percipiō, percipere** (3), **percēpī, perceptum**, to feel.
    Hēsionē, Hēsionēs, (*acc.*) **Hēsionēn** (*f*), Hesione.

36. LAOMEDON AND THE SEA-MONSTER

Lāomedōn quīdam illō tempore rēgnum Troiae obtinēbat. 1
Ad hunc Neptūnus et Apollō superiōre annō vēnerant; et 2
cum Troia nōndum moenia habēret, ad hoc opus auxilium 3
obtulerant. Postquam tamen eōrum auxiliō moenia cōn- 4
fecta sunt, Lāomedōn praemium quod prōposuerat persol- 5
vere nōlēbat. Neptūnus et Apollō ob hanc causam īrātī 6
mōnstrum quoddam mīsērunt speciē horribilī, quod cotīdiē 7
ē marī veniēbat atque hominēs pecudēsque vorābat. 8
Troiānī autem timōre perterritī in urbe continēbantur, et 9
pecora omnia ex agrīs intrā mūrōs compulerant. Lāomedōn 10
hīs rēbus commōtus ōrāculum cōnsuluit, ac deus eī 11
praecēpit ut fīliam Hēsionēn mōnstrō obiceret. 12

1. The ship, having set out from the harbor, came to Troy in a short time.
2. There was great fear at Troy then.
3. For a monster had been sent to kill those who inhabited that city.
4. Those who inhabited the city were terrified and despaired of safety.
5. As soon as they had seen the monster, they hurried out of the fields.

Helpful Hints
1. Use the perfect participle of a deponent verb to translate "having set out."
   Before translating "to Troy," review **Helpful Hints** note 1 with paragraph 10.
2. To translate "at Troy," see grammar note with paragraph 16.
3. Use a relative clause of purpose in translating this sentence (see grammar note with paragraph 33).
   The relative clause "who inhabited that city" should have its verb in the subjunctive by attraction (see grammar note with paragraph 34).
4. Before translating "despaired of safety," study line 9 of paragraph 34.
5. In paragraph 10, lines 10–11, find a model for translating "as soon as," and remember that the pluperfect in the English sentence will be translated with a perfect in Latin.

1 *renūntiō (1), to bring back word, report, announce.
2 *percipiō (per- + capiō), percipere (3), percēpī, perceptum, to feel.
   Distinguish this verb carefully from praecipiō, praecipere (3),
   praecēpī, praeceptum (+ *dat.* + ut + *subjunctive*), to take
   beforehand, anticipate, direct, order, charge.
   tantō perīculō: *ablative of separation* with līberāre (see grammar
   note with paragraph 16).
3 ōrāculō: *dative* with the special intransitive verb pārēre.
   pāreō (2) (+ *dat.*), to obey.
   sacrificiō: *dative of purpose.*
5 opportūnus, -a, -um, suitable, seasonable, convenient, opportune.
   *attingō (ad- + tangō), attingere (3), attigī, attāctum, to touch at,
   arrive at, reach.
6 pūnctum, -ī (*n*), point, instant, moment.
   vinciō, vincīre (4), vīnxī, vīnctum, to bind.
7 dē eīs rēbus . . . certior factus est: literally, "he was made more
   certain about those things that were being done," better English, "he was
   informed of. . . . " Note the idiom with certior: "to make someone more
   certain" = "to inform that person" (*active*); "to be made more certain" = "to
   be informed" (*passive*).
9 eī: *dative* with the *special intransitive verb* concessisset.
   concēdō, concēdere (3), concessī, concessum (+ *dat.* + ut +
   subjunctive), to grant, yield, permit.
10 ut . . . līberāret: *indirect command.*
   sī posset: *subjunctive by attraction*; the king said sī potes.

Certior with dē

Certior (*gen.*, certiōris) is the comparative form of
certus, -a, -um and therefore means "more certain."
With a passive verb it agrees with the subject, as in
Herculēs dē eīs rēbus . . . certior factus est,
"Hercules was made more certain (i.e., was informed)
about those things." With an active verb the comparative adjective agrees with the direct object as a predicate accusative (see grammar note with paragraph 2);
the above sentence would then appear as Troiānī
eum certiōrem dē eīs rēbus fēcērunt, "The Trojans made him more certain (i.e., informed him) about
those things." Whether the verb is active or passive,
the idiom uses dē with the ablative to complete the
thought.
   For a similar use of an adjective in the nominative
and the accusative, see vīvus and vīvum at the ends
of paragraphs 24 and 23 respectively.

37. THE RESCUE OF HESIONE

Lāomedōn, cum hoc respōnsum renūntiātum esset, mag- 1
num dolōrem percēpit; sed tamen, ut cīvēs suōs tantō 2
perīculō līberāret, ōrāculō pārēre cōnstituit, et diem sacrifi- 3
ciō dīxit. Sed, sīve cāsū sīve cōnsiliō deōrum, Herculēs tem- 4
pore opportūnissimō Troiam attigit; ipsō enim temporis 5
pūnctō quō puella catēnīs vīncta ad lītus dēdūcēbātur, 6
nāvem appulit. Ē nāvī ēgressus dē eīs rēbus quae gerēban- 7
tur certior factus est; tum īrā commōtus ad rēgem sē con- 8
tulit atque auxilium obtulit. Cum rēx libenter eī concessis- 9
set ut, sī posset, puellam līberāret, Herculēs mōnstrum in- 10
terfēcit; et puellam, quae iam omnem spem salūtis dēpo- 11
suerat, incolumem ad patrem redūxit. Lāomedōn magnō 12
cum gaudiō fīliam accēpit, et Herculī prō tantō beneficiō 13
meritam grātiam rettulit. 14

1. A god ordered that the king's daughter should save the citizens by her own death.
2. When the king had been informed of the god's response, he felt great grief.
3. Her father obeyed the god, so that the others who were in the city might be safe.
4. Hercules, however, disembarked and came to their aid.
5. When he had found the king, he did not demand that any reward be given to him, but he willingly killed the monster.

Helpful Hints

1. For "ordered," use **praecipiō**.
   "By her own death" = ablative of means. Here the reflexive adjective refers to the subject of the subordinate clause and not to that of the main clause (compare the indirect reflexive; see grammar note with paragraph 31).
3. Here "so that" introduces a purpose clause, which tells why the father obeyed the god, i.e., states his purpose in doing what he did.
   To translate "who were in the city," see grammar note with paragraph 34.
4. Translate as if the English said "Hercules, having disembarked, came to their aid." Use the perfect participle of a deponent verb for "having disembarked."
   The ablative singular of **nāvis** may end in either *-e* or *-ī* (see grammar note with paragraph 6).
   To translate "to their aid," review the grammar note on the double dative with paragraph 22.
5. For "any" in this negative clause, use **ūllus, -a, -um**.

1   **Erythēa, -ae** (*f*), Erythea.
2   ***Gēryōn, Gēryonis** (*m*), Geryon.
3   ***Eurytiōn, Eurytiōnis** (*m*), Eurytion.
     biceps, bicipitis, two-headed.
4   **Ipse:** frequently, as here, this word distinguishes a person from that which
     belongs to him or from his subordinates.
5   ***praebeō** (2), to hold forth, supply, furnish, give, show, present, exhibit.
     *coniungō, coniungere (3), **coniūnxī, coniūnctum,** to join together,
     join.
6   ***intellegō, intellegere** (3), **intellēxī, intellēctum,** to perceive, un-
     derstand.
     quantum perīculum esset: *indirect question* in *secondary sequence,*
     "how great the danger was."
7   **terra, -ae** (*f*), land, earth.
8   ***Āfrica, -ae** (*f*), Africa.
     *Eurōpa, -ae (*f*), Europe.
     Eurōpae: *dative* with the *adjective* **proximus.**
9   **uterque, utraque, utrumque,** each (of two), either, both.
     utrōque lītore: "each shore," "both shores."
     fretum, -ī (*n*), strait.
     *dīvidō, dīvidere (3), **dīvīsī, dīvīsum,** to divide, separate.
10   ***columna, -ae** (*f*), column, pillar.
     columnās: the Rock of Gibraltar was said to be the pillar set up by Her-
     cules on the European side of the strait.

Indirect Questions

When questions are stated indirectly, their verbs are
put into the subjunctive, following the usual sequence of
tenses (see grammar note with paragraph 24). The
imperfect subjunctive indicates time contemporaneous
with a main verb in the past tense, e.g., **Herculēs intellegēbat** <u>quantum</u> **perīculum** <u>esset</u>, "Hercules
understood <u>how great</u> the danger <u>was</u>." The direct
question was **Quantum est perīculum?** "How great
is the danger?" When you encounter indirect questions,
always ask yourself what the direct question was.

38. TENTH LABOR: THE OXEN OF GERYON

Tum vērō missus est Herculēs ad īnsulam Erythēam, ut   1
bovēs Gēryonis arcesseret. Rēs erat summae difficultātis,   2
quod bovēs ā quōdam Eurytiōne et ā cane bicipite cus-   3
tōdiēbantur. Ipse autem Gēryōn horribilem speciem   4
praebēbat; tria enim corpora inter sē coniūncta habēbat.   5
Herculēs etsī intellegēbat quantum perīculum esset, tamen   6
negōtium suscēpit. Postquam per multās terrās iter fēcit,   7
ad eam partem Āfricae pervēnit quae Eurōpae proxima est.   8
Ibi in utrōque lītore fretī quod Eurōpam ab Āfricā dīvidit   9
columnās cōnstituit, quae posteā Herculis Columnae ap-   10
pellābantur.   11

1. Then Eurystheus ordered Hercules to fetch oxen that were on a certain island.
2. Although he could not find out how great the size of the island was, he obeyed the king.
3. After he had accomplished a large part of the journey, he came to that shore of Africa that is nearest the island.
4. He is said to have remained in that place many days.
5. For the opportunity of advancing was not given him.

Helpful Hints

1. For "ordered," use **imperō**. Be careful in translating the relative clause (see grammar note with paragraph 34).
2. Translate two ways, first using **cum** with the subjunctive and then **etsī** or **quamquam** with the indicative.
5. Find models for this sentence in paragraph 21, lines 10–11, and in paragraph 29, lines 6–7. Keep in mind that gerunds of deponent verbs have the same forms as those of regular verbs.

1   **moror, morārī** (1), **morātus sum,** to delay, linger, stay.
     Distinguish this verb carefully from **morior, morī** (3), **mortuus sum,**
        to die, and from **mīror, mīrārī** (1), **mīrātus sum,** to wonder,
        wonder at.
     *incommodum, -ī** (n), inconvenience, harm.
2   **calor, calōris** (m), heat.
4   **tantum:** *adverb.*
     admīror, admīrārī (1), **admīrātus sum,** to wonder at, admire.
     ut . . . daret: what kind of clause?
8   **quō in locō bovēs essent:** *indirect question.*
10   **ut . . . trāderentur:** what kind of clause?
     sibi: *indirect reflexive* (see grammar note with paragraph 31).
     Cum . . . nōllet: *causal clause.*
11   **et . . . et:** "both . . . and."
12   **ingentī magnitūdine:** *ablative of description.*

Interrogative Adjective

Questions may be introduced in Latin by phrases using
interrogative adjectives, just as they may be introduced
by the *interrogative pronoun,* e.g.:

    Interrogative pronoun:
        Quis est? Who is he?
    Phrase with interrogative adjective:
        Quō in locō bovēs sunt? In what place are
    the oxen?

The interrogative adjective will always have a noun
that it modifies and with which it agrees in gender,
number, and case. The forms of the interrogative adjective are the same as those of the relative pronoun (see
grammar note with paragraph 19).

39. THE GOLDEN BOAT

Herculēs dum hīc morātur, magnum incommodum ē 1
calōre sōlis accipiēbat; tandem īrā commōtus arcum suum 2
intendit ac sōlem sagittīs petiit. Sōl tamen audāciam virī 3
tantum admīrātus est ut eī lintrem auream daret. Her- 4
culēs hoc dōnum libentissimē accēpit; nūllam enim nāvem 5
in hīs regiōnibus invenīre potuerat. Tum lintrem dēdūxit, 6
et ventum nactus idōneum paucīs post diēbus ad īnsulam 7
pervēnit. Ubi ex incolīs cognōvit quō in locō bovēs essent, in 8
eam partem statim profectus est, atque ā rēge Gēryone 9
postulāvit ut bovēs sibi trāderentur. Cum tamen ille hoc 10
facere nōllet, Herculēs et rēgem ipsum et Eurytiōnem, quī 11
erat ingentī magnitūdine corporis, interfēcit. 12

1. We were not able to understand on what island the oxen were
   found by Hercules.
2. We learned, however, by whose aid he arrived at this island.
3. Admiring the boldness of Hercules, the sun-god had come to his
   aid.
4. Hercules ordered the king to give up to him the oxen that he had.
5. Since Geryon did not obey him, he was killed.

Helpful Hints

1. Before translating "on what island," find a model for the word order in para-
    graph 39 above and see the grammar note on page 80. This interrogative
    phrase introduces an indirect question.
2. In Latin the interrogative comes first in its clause, so "by whose aid" must be
    translated as "of whom by the aid."
3. Latin is generally stricter about time and tense than English, and while
    "admiring" is a present participle in English it obviously refers to a time be-
    fore the sun-god came to Hercules' aid and should be put in the perfect tense
    in Latin.
      Begin your translation with the word for "sun-god."
      For "to his aid," use the double dative.
4. For "ordered," use **imperō**. Be careful with the verb in the relative clause.
      For the indirect reflexive "to him," see the grammar note with paragraph
    31 and find an example in line 10 of paragraph 39 above.
5. For the word order, see **Helpful Hints** note 1 with paragraph 5 and see
    line 1 of paragraph 39 above.
      Translate this sentence two ways, first using **cum** with the subjunctive
    and then using **quoniam** with the indicative.

1   **Hispānia, -ae** (*f*), Spain.
    Liguria, -ae (*f*), Liguria.
3   *****trānsportō** (1), to carry across *or* over, transport.
    *****Ligurēs, Ligurum** (*m pl*), Ligurians.
5   **longius** (*comparative adverb*), farther.
    *****prohibeō** (pro- + habeō) (2), to hold back, prevent, hinder.
       eum . . . prōgredī prohibēbant: "tried to prevent him from advanc-
       ing"; note the *accusative* and *infinitive* with **prohibēbant.**
       prohibēbant: *imperfect* of *attempted action*, "tried to prevent."
6   **barbarus, -ī** (*m*), barbarian.
       barbarī: the Greeks called all other peoples "barbarians," and the Ro-
       mans so characterized all but the Greeks and themselves.
10   *****dēmittō, dēmittere** (3), **dēmīsī, dēmissum,** to send down, let fall.
12   **ut . . . cōnsuēvit: ut** + *indicative* = "as."
       in tālibus rēbus: i.e., when a god intervenes in behalf of his favorite
       mortal.
       accidō (ad- + cadō), **accidere** (3), **accidī,** to fall to *or* upon, befall,
       happen.
13   **incommodī:** *partitive genitive.*

Adjective and Adverb Review

Positive Degree

First and Second Declension

	Adjectives	*Adverbs*
Regular:	**longus, longa, longum**	**longē**
Keep the *e:*	**miser, misera, miserum**	**miserē**
Drop the *e:*	**pulcher, pulchra, pulchrum**	**pulchrē**

Third Declension

One ending:	**audāx, audāx, audāx**	**audāciter**
Two ending:	**fortis, fortis, forte**	**fortiter**
Three ending:	**celer, celeris, celere**	**celeriter**

Comparative Degree (-er, more, rather, quite)

	longior, longius (gen., **longiōris**)	**longius**
	pulchrior, pulchrius (gen., **pulchriōris**)	**pulchrius**
	fortior, fortius (gen., **fortiōris**)	**fortius**
	celerior, celerius (gen., **celeriōris**)	**celerius**

    For the declension of comparative adjectives, see the gram-
mar note with paragraph 41.

(Continued on next page)

40. A MIRACULOUS STORM

Tum Herculēs bovēs per Hispāniam et Liguriam com- 1
pellere cōnstituit. Postquam omnia parāta sunt, bovēs ex 2
īnsulā ad continentem trānsportāvit. Ligurēs autem, gēns 3
bellicōsissima, dum ille per fīnēs eōrum iter facit, magnās 4
cōpiās coēgērunt atque eum longius prōgredī prohibēbant. 5
Haec rēs Herculī magnam difficultātem attulit; barbarī 6
enim in locīs superiōribus cōnstiterant, et lapidēs tēlaque 7
in eum coniciēbant. Ille quidem paene omnem spem 8
salūtis dēposuerat, sed tempore opportūnissimō Iuppiter 9
imbrem lapidum ingentium ē caelō dēmīsit. Hī tantā vī ce- 10
cidērunt ut magnus numerus Ligurum interficerētur; ipse 11
tamen Herculēs (ut in tālibus rēbus accidere cōnsuēvit) ni- 12
hil incommodī accēpit. 13

Superlative Degree (-est, most, very, exceedingly)

All superlative adjectives are declined as first and second declension adjectives.

Regular:	**longissimus, -a, -um**	**longissimē**
	fortissimus, -a, -um	**fortissimē**
All -*er*:	**pulcherrimus, -a, -um**	**pulcherrimē**
	celerrimus, -a, -um	**celerrimē**
Some -*lis**:	**facillimus, -a, -um**	**facillimē**

*Only **facilis**, **similis**, and **humilis** and their opposites; others are regular. (For a review of **bonus**, **malus**, **parvus**, and **magnus**, see the grammar note with paragraph 46.)

---

1. The barbarians who were nearest the sea tried to prevent Hercules from driving the oxen through their territory.
2. They kept charging upon him from the higher places.
3. For they were accustomed to fight with the greatest bravery.
4. Since Hercules had thrown all his weapons at the enemy, he gave up hope of safety.
5. A god, however, freed him from fear and peril.

Helpful Hints
1. Before translating "tried to prevent Hercules from driving," see line 5 of paragraph 40 above and the vocabulary note.
4. Find a model for "at" in line 8 of paragraph 40 above.
   For "enemy," use the plural.

2   **quam**: with *superlative*, "as swiftly as possible." **Quam** with the *superlative* indicates the highest possible degree.
     Alpēs, Alpium (*f pl*), Alps.

3   **Necesse**: *predicate nominative*; the *subject* of **erat** is the *infinitive phrase* **hās trānsīre**.

5   **Gallia, -ae** (*f*), Gaul.
     nix, nivis (*f*), snow.
     perennis, -is, -e, lasting throughout the year, perennial, perpetual.
     *__tegō, tegere__ (3), __tēxī, tēctum__, to cover, conceal.
     Dintinguish this verb carefully from **tangō, tangere** (3), **tetigī, tactum**, to touch.
     tēctī: predicate adjective.

6   *__ob__ (+ *acc.*), on account of, for.
     quam ob causam: literally, "on account of which reason"; translate, "and on account of this reason," "therefore."
     neque . . . neque, neither . . . nor.
     *__pābulum, -ī__ (*n*), food, fodder.

9   **commeātus, -ūs** (*m*), supplies, provisions.
     *__onerō__ (1), to load, burden.

10   **rēbus**: "efforts."

12   **trādūcō** (trāns- + dūcō), **trādūcere** (3), **trādūxī, trāductum**, to lead across.

Quam with Adjectives and Adverbs

Quam has various meanings with the positive, comparative, and superlative degrees of adjectives and adverbs. With the *positive* degree, it means "as" or "how"; with the *comparative* degree, it means "than"; and with the *superlative* degree it means "as possible."

Quam altus is est! "How tall he is!"

Quam celeriter currit! "How quickly he runs!"

Is tam altus quam ea est. "He is as tall as she."

Is tam celeriter quam ea currit; "He runs as quickly as she."

Is altior quam ea est. "He is taller than she."

Is celerius quam ea currit. "He runs more quickly than she."

Is quam altissimus est. "He is as tall as possible."

Is quam celerrimē currit. "He runs as quickly as possible."

41. THE PASSAGE OF THE ALPS

Postquam Ligurēs hōc modō superātī sunt, Herculēs 1
quam celerrimē prōgressus est, et brevī tempore ad Alpēs 2
pervēnit. Necesse erat hās trānsīre, ut in Italiam bovēs 3
ageret; rēs tamen summae erat difficultātis. Hī enim mon- 4
tēs, quī Galliam ab Italiā dīvidunt, nive perennī sunt tēctī; 5
quam ob causam neque frūmentum neque pābulum in hīs 6
regiōnibus invenīrī potest. Herculēs igitur priusquam as- 7
cendere coepit, magnam cōpiam frūmentī pābulīque com- 8
parāvit, et hōc commeātū bovēs onerāvit. Postquam in hīs 9
rēbus trēs diēs cōnsūmpsit, quārtō diē profectus est, et con- 10
trā omnium opīniōnem bovēs incolumēs in Italiam 11
trādūxit. 12

Declension of Comparative Adjectives			
Singular		**Plural**	
M. & F.	N.	M. & F.	N.
fortior	fortius	fortiōrēs	fortiōra
fortiōris	fortiōris	fortiōrum	fortiōrum
fortiōrī	fortiōrī	fortiōribus	fortiōribus
fortiōrem	fortius	fortiōrēs (-īs)	fortiōra
fortiōre (-ī)	fortiōre (-ī)	fortiōribus	fortiōribus
fortior = "braver," "rather brave," or "quite brave"			

1. Although Hercules fought as bravely as possible, he was not able to defeat the barbarians without the help of the god.
2. Nothing prevented him from setting out as quickly as the enemy.
3. Having advanced to the town nearest the mountains, he prepared everything for crossing.
4. He understood how great the difficulty was, but he did not desist from the attempt.
5. It was necessary to collect a rather large supply of grain.

Helpful Hints
2. To translate "prevented him from," find a model in paragraph 40, line 5.
3. "Having advanced" can be translated into Latin with a perfect participle of a deponent verb.
Be sure to use the right case with the Latin word for "nearest."
4. To translate "desist from the attempt," use the ablative of separation without a preposition.
5. See lines 8–9 of paragraph 41 above for some of the vocabulary to use in translating this sentence.

1   **Tiberis, Tiberis** (*m*), Tiber.
     Tiberim: a few nouns of the 3rd declension have this form in the ac-
       cusative singular.
2   **condō, condere** (3), **condidī, conditum**, to put together, found, build.
     Compound verbs formed from **dō, dare** (note the short *a*, an exception
       in the 1st conjugation), **dedī, datum**, appear as 3rd conjugation
       verbs when the prefix is from a monosyllabic preposition, e.g., **abdō**
       (see below), **dēdō, ēdō, reddō, subdō**, and **trādō** in this book; also
       addō, indō, and **perdō.** Compare **circumdō, circumdare** (para-
       graph 45) and **interdō, interdare**, which remain as 1st conjugation
       verbs.
3   **itinere**: *ablative of cause* with **fessus.**
     *****fessus, -a, -um**, worn out, exhausted, weary.
       fessus: the adjective may be translated as a relative or causal clause,
         "who was weary" or "since he was weary."
4   *****reficiō** (re- + faciō), **reficere** (3), **refēcī, refectum**, to make again,
       renew, repair, refresh, recruit.
     bovēs pascēbat: **bovēs** is the direct object of **pascēbat.**
5   *****Cācus, -ī** (*m*), Cacus.
7   **quod . . . quod**: "because . . . because."
8   *****ōs, ōris** (*n*), mouth.
     Distinguish this noun carefully from **os, ossis** (*n*), bone.
     *****efflō** (ex- + flō) (1), to breathe out.
     *****adventus, -ūs** (*m*), approach, arrival.
       Compare the related verb, **adveniō, advenīre** (4), **advēnī, adven-
         tum**, to come to *or* toward, approach, arrive.
9   *****noctū** (*adv.*), at *or* by night.
11   *****nē,** (*adv.*) not; (*conj.*) that not, lest.
       nē . . . posset: *negative purpose clause* (remember that negative pur-
         pose clauses are introduced by **nē** and negative result clauses by **ut
         nōn**).
     quō . . . abditī essent: what kind of a clause?
12   *****abdō, abdere** (3), **abdidī, abditum**, to put away, hide, conceal.

42. CACUS STEALS THE OXEN

Brevī tempore ad flūmen Tiberim vēnit. Tum tamen nūlla 1
erat urbs in eō locō; Rōma enim nōndum condita erat. Her- 2
culēs itinere fessus cōnstituit ibi paucōs diēs morārī, ut sē ē 3
labōre reficeret. Nōn procul ā valle ubi bovēs pāscēbat 4
spēlunca erat, in quā Cācus, horribile mōnstrum, tum 5
habitābat. Hic terribilem speciem praebēbat, nōn modo 6
quod ingentī magnitūdine corporis erat, sed quod ignem ex 7
ōre efflābat. Cācus autem, quī dē adventū Herculis fāmam 8
audīverat, noctū vēnit, et dum Herculēs dormit, quattuor 9
pulcherrimōs bovēs abripuit. Hōs caudīs in spēluncam 10
trāxit, nē Herculēs ē vēstīgiīs cognōscere posset quō in locō 11
abditī essent. 12

1. Hercules was guarding the oxen as carefully as possible so that
   they might not be carried off.
2. For many days he was trying to find a safe place for them.
3. He was so exhausted that he could not advance farther.
4. And so he wished to delay so that he might give himself to rest.
5. He did not prevent Cacus from carrying off the oxen.

Helpful Hints
2. The imperfect tense by itself can express an attempt to do something (see
   Helpful Hints note 3 with paragraph 5).
5. For "prevent . . . from carrying," find a model in paragraph 40, line 5.
   Here the Latin word for Cacus will be subject of the infinitive and
   therefore in the accusative case.

1   *posterus, -a, -um, following, next.
2   animadvertō, animadvertere (3), animadvertī, animadversum, to turn the mind to, observe, notice.
    *āmittō, āmittere (3), āmīsī, āmissum, to send away, lose.
    omnibus locīs: *ablative of place where without a preposition.*
4   *falsus, -a, -um, feigned, pretended, false.
    dēcipiō (dē- + capiō), dēcipere (3), dēcēpī, dēceptum, to catch, deceive.
6   būbus: *dat.* and *abl. pl.* of bōs, bovis.
7   ē būbus: *partitive* expressed with ē (ex) instead of *genitive* after a *cardinal number.*
8   mūgiō (4), to low, bellow.
    mūgītus, -ūs (*m*), lowing, bellowing.
    Note the relationship between the noun **mūgītus** and the fourth principal part of the verb **mūgiō, mūgīre (4), mūgīvī, mūgītum.**
9   *cognōscō, cognōscere (3), cognōvī, cognitum, to find out, learn of, learn; (*perfect*) to have found out, have learned of, be aware of, know.
12   *saxum, -ī (*n*), rock, stone.
    dēiciō (dē- + iaciō), dēicere (3), dēiēcī, dēiectum, to throw down.
    *obstruō, obstruere (3), obstrūxī, obstrūctum, to build against, block up.

Ablative of Place Where without a Preposition

The *ablative* of indefinite words such as **locus** is often used without the preposition **in** to denote *place where*, e.g., **bovēs āmissōs** <u>omnibus locīs</u> **quaerēbat**, "he sought the lost oxen <u>in all places</u> (everywhere)."

Partitive with ex or dē instead of the Partitive Genitive

With **paucī** (a few), **quīdam** (certain), **nūllus** (no, none), and cardinal numbers (**ūnus, duo, trēs,** etc.), the prepositions **ex** or **dē** with the ablative are used instead of the partitive genitive, e.g., **ūnus** <u>ē būbus</u>, "one <u>of the oxen</u>."

43. HERCULES DISCOVERS THE THEFT

Posterō diē simul atque ē somnō excitātus est, Herculēs 1
fūrtum animadvertit, et bovēs āmissōs omnibus locīs 2
quaerēbat. Hōs tamen nusquam reperīre poterat, nōn modo 3
quod locī nātūram ignōrābat, sed quod vēstīgiīs falsīs dē- 4
ceptus est. Tandem, cum magnam partem diēī frūstrā cōn- 5
sūmpsisset, cum reliquīs būbus prōgredī cōnstituit. At 6
dum proficīscī parat, ūnus ē būbus quōs sēcum habuit 7
mūgīre coepit. Subitō eī quī in spēluncā inclūsī erant mūgī- 8
tum reddidērunt, atque hōc modō Herculēs cognōvit quō in 9
locō abditī essent. Ille vehementer īrātus ad spēluncam 10
quam celerrimē sē contulit, ut praedam reciperet. At Cācus 11
saxum ingēns ita dēiēcerat ut aditus spēluncae omnīnō ob- 12
struerētur. 13

1. At first Hercules could not find out who had done this.
2. Although he looked for four of the oxen everywhere, nevertheless
   he could not find them.
3. Now the lost oxen were hidden in a very difficult place.
4. This place was adjacent to a great river.
5. Cacus had placed a stone in the entrance so that Hercules might
   not burst in.

1 *introitus, -ūs (*m*), entrance.

     Compare the related verbs **introeō, introīre** (*irreg.*), **introiī**, **introitum**, to go into, enter.

2 *āmoveō, āmovēre (2), āmōvī, āmōtum, to move away.

4 **neque quicquam**: remember that **quicquam** "anything" is used instead of **aliquid** "anything" in a negative context (see paragraph 14, line 9).

   *efficiō (ex- + faciō), **efficere** (3), **effēcī, effectum**, to make *or* work out, accomplish, effect.

5 **patefaciō, patefacere** (3), **patefēcī, patefactum**, to throw *or* lay open, open (literally, to make open).

7 **cernō, cernere** (3), **crēvī, crētum**, to discern, perceive, make out.

     Distinguish this verb carefully from **creō** (1), to elect, appoint.

   fūmī: *genitive* with the adjective **plēna**.

8 **mōre suō**: *ablative of manner*, "according to his custom."

   inūsitātus, -a, -um, unusual, extraordinary.

   turbātus: "who had been confused," "since he had been confused," or "was confused and . . . " Keep in mind these three ways of translating a perfect passive participle: by an adjectival (relative) clause, by an adverbial clause, and by a coordinate verb. In any case, the perfect passive participle shows *time before* the main verb.

9 **haesitō** (1), to hesitate.

   post: *adverb*.

44. HERCULES AND CACUS

Herculēs cum nūllum alium introitum reperīre posset, 1
hoc saxum āmovēre cōnātus est, sed propter eius mag- 2
nitūdinem rēs erat difficillima. Diū frūstrā labōrābat 3
neque quicquam efficere poterat; tandem tamen magnō 4
cōnātū saxum āmōvit ac spēluncam patefēcit. Ibi āmissōs 5
bovēs magnō cum gaudiō cōnspexit; sed Cācum ipsum vix 6
cernere potuit, quod spēlunca plēna erat fūmī, quem ille 7
mōre suō efflābat. Herculēs inūsitātā speciē turbātus 8
paulīsper haesitābat; post tamen in spēluncam irrūpit, et 9
collum mōnstrī bracchiīs complexus est. Cācus etsī mul- 10
tum repugnāvit, nūllō modō sē līberāre potuit; et cum nūlla 11
facultās respīrandī darētur, brevī tempore exanimātus est. 12

1. When Hercules had learned where the lost oxen were, he hurried to
   the place as quickly as possible.
2. The stone placed in the entrance was of such great size that it
   could not be moved away without great toil.
3. Yet Hercules undertook this task so that he might not leave the
   oxen behind, and he burst in.
4. Although Cacus was frightened, he tried to withstand his attack.
5. He had no opportunity of fleeing, and so he was seized and quickly
   killed.

Helpful Hints
2. The phrase "of such great size" will be translated with a predicate ablative of
   description.
       Remember that a negative purpose clause is introduced by **nē** and a neg-
   ative result clause by **ut nōn**.
3. Find a Latin word in line 3 of paragraph 44 above to translate the English
   word "task."
5. Use the dative of possession in translating this sentence (see grammar note
   with paragraph 22).
       Instead of translating "was seized and quickly killed," omit the conjunc-
   tion *and* and translate "seized was quickly killed."
       In paragraph 44 above find a Latin expression for "was killed."

2   **quam quōs:** for **quam eōs quōs.**

3   **eī:** *dative* with **mandāvit.**

4   *__Hesperidēs, Hesperidum__ (f pl), the Hesperides.

    *__nympha, -ae__ (f), nymph (the nymphs were minor divinities associated with the sea, springs, mountains, and trees).

5   *__fōrma, -ae__ (f), form, appearance, beauty.

    *__praestāns, praestantis__ (*participle* of **praestō**), surpassing, preeminent, remarkable.

    longinquus, -a, -um, distant, remote.

6   **quibusque:** = et quibus (not from **quisque**).

    aurea quaedam māla: *subject.*

        mālum, mālī (n), apple.

        Distinguish this noun carefully from the noun **malus, -ī** (m), mast, and from the adjective **malus, -a, -um,** bad.

7   **aurī:** *objective genitive,* "for gold."

    *__cupiditās, cupiditātis__ (f), desire, longing, eagerness.

10   **circumdō, circumdare** (1), **circumdedī, circumdatum,** to put around, surround.

        Note that this compound of **dō, dare** remains 1st conjugation (with short **a**).

    *__draco, dracōnis__ (m), dragon, serpent.

    cui centum erant capita: *dative of possession,* literally, "to whom there were a hundred heads," better English, "who had a hundred heads."

12   **Herculī:** *dative* with the *special intransitive verb* **imperāverat,** "had enjoined upon Hercules."

13   **commemorō** (1), to bring to memory, recount, mention.

15   *__situs, -a, -um,__ placed, situated.

Objective Genitive

A word in the *genitive case* may serve as the *object* of the verbal idea implied in the noun or adjective to which it is attached, e.g., **aurī** <u>**cupiditāte**</u>, "by desire <u>for gold</u>"; gold is the object of the desire.

45. ELEVENTH LABOR: THE GOLDEN APPLES

Eurystheus postquam bovēs Gēryonis accēpit, labōrem 1
ūndecimum Herculī imposuit, graviōrem quam quōs suprā 2
nārrāvimus. Mandāvit enim eī ut aurea māla ex hortō 3
Hesperidum auferret. Hesperidēs autem nymphae erant 4
quaedam fōrmā praestantissimā, quae in terrā longinquā 5
habitābant, quibusque aurea quaedam māla ā Iūnōne 6
commissa erant. Multī hominēs aurī cupiditāte inductī 7
haec māla auferre iam anteā cōnātī erant. Rēs tamen diffi- 8
cillima erat; namque hortus in quō māla erant mūrō ingentī 9
undique circumdatus erat. Praetereā dracō quīdam, cui 10
centum erant capita, portam hortī dīligenter custōdiēbat. 11
Opus igitur quod Eurystheus Herculī imperāverat erat 12
summae difficultātis, nōn modo ob causās quās commemo- 13
rāvimus, sed etiam quod Herculēs omnīnō ignōrābat quō in 14
locō hortus ille situs esset. 15

1. The Hesperides had certain apples, which were guarded by them most carefully.
2. Eurystheus, moved by a desire for plunder, sent Hercules to bring these back to him, if he could.
3. Now the apples were in a place that was surrounded by a wall, and no one could come to that place.
4. And so many (men) had been prevented from carrying off the apples.
5. Besides, Hercules himself did not know the nature of the place.

Helpful Hints

1. Use the dative of possession.
2. For "to bring," use a relative clause of purpose.
   Look at lines 9–11 of paragraph 37 before translating "if he could."
3. For "was surrounded," use the pluperfect; see line 10 of paragraph 45 above and see the notes to line 12 on page 8.
   For "and no one," see paragraph 14, line 9.
   For "to that place," use an adverb.

2 *simul ac: = simul atque. See paragraph 10, lines 10–11, and vocabulary note; simul atque/ac + *perfect indicative* is often best translated with an English *pluperfect*.

6 *subeō, subīre (*irreg.*), subiī, subitum, to go under, undergo, submit to, sustain, bear, endure.

7 *extrēmus, -a, -um, last, extreme, furthest, the end of.
orbis, orbis, orbium (*m*), circle.
orbis terrārum, circle of the lands, earth, world.
extrēmam partem orbis terrārum: the ancients, of course, had no knowledge of the greater part of the world. The early Greeks thought of the earth as a flat circle, surrounded by the river Ōceanus; this word came later to designate the Atlantic, which has its distinctive name from Atlas.

8 Ōceanus, -ī (*m*), Oceanus, the ocean.
Ōceanō: *dative* with the *adjective* proxima.

9 *Atlās, Atlantis (*m*), Atlas.

10 nē . . . dēcideret: *negative purpose clause* introduced by nē.

11 dēcidō (dē- + cadō), dēcidere (3), dēcidī, to fall down.
magnopere (*adv.* from magnus, -a, -um), greatly.
mīrātus: the *perfect participle of deponent verbs* may often best be translated with a present participle in English, although the action it describes is thought of as having taken place before that of the main verb.

12 colloquium, -ī (*n*), conversation.

13 *doceō, docēre (2), docuī, doctum, to explain, teach.

Common Irregular Adjectives and Adverbs		
	Adjectives	*Adverbs*
Positive	bonus, -a, -um	bene
	malus, -a, -um	male
	parvus, -a, -um	parum
	magnus, -a, -um	magnopere
Comparative	melior, melius (*gen.*, meliōris)	melius
	peior, peius (*gen.*, peiōris)	peius
	minor, minus (*gen.*, minōris)	minus
	maior, maius (*gen.*, maiōris)	maius
Superlative	optimus, -a, -um	optimē
	pessimus, -a, -um	pessimē
	minimus, -a, -um	minimē
	maximus, -a, -um	maximē

For regular adjectives and adverbs, see grammar note with paragraph 40.

46. HERCULES ASKS AID OF ATLAS

Herculēs quamquam quiētem vehementer cupiēbat, ta- 1
men Eurystheō pārēre cōnstituit; et simul ac iussa eius ac- 2
cēpit, proficīscī mātūrāvit. Ā multīs mercātōribus 3
quaesīverat quō in locō Hesperidēs habitārent; nihil tamen 4
certum reperīre potuerat. Frūstrā per multās terrās iter 5
fēcit et multa perīcula subiit; tandem, cum in hīs itineribus 6
tōtum annum cōnsūmpsisset, ad extrēmam partem orbis 7
terrārum, quae proxima est Ōceanō, pervēnit. Hīc stābat 8
vir quīdam, nōmine Atlās, ingentī magnitūdine corporis, quī 9
caelum (ita trāditum est) umerīs suīs sustinēbat, nē in ter- 10
ram dēcideret. Herculēs tantās vīrēs magnopere mīrātus 11
statim in colloquium cum Atlante vēnit; et cum causam 12
itineris docuisset, auxilium ab eō petiit. 13

1. Hercules was moved by a desire for rest and was unwilling to make the journey.
2. A god, however, had ordered a better man to obey a worse, as it has been reported.
3. And so, as soon as this new, greater labor had been laid upon him, Hercules prepared everything for setting out.
4. Setting out without delay, he sought the apples for a whole year.
5. The peoples that were nearest the Hesperides did not know in what place the apples were.

Helpful Hints
1. Translate as if the English said "moved by a desire for rest, he was unwilling."
    For the word order in your translation of "a desire for rest," see paragraph 45, line 7.
2. For "as," use **ut** + indicative.
3. For "as soon as," see line 2 of paragraph 46 above and the vocabulary note.
    Connect the two adjectives with **et** in Latin.
    To translate "for setting out," use **ad** + a gerund.
4. The action of setting out preceded the search, so use a perfect participle of a deponent verb.

1   **Herculī**: *dative* with the *compound verb* **prōdesse**.
     ***prōsum, prōdesse** (*irreg.*), **prōfuī** (+ *dat.*), to be of advantage, profit, avail, assist.
     cum . . . esset: what kind of clause?
3   **quam ob causam**: "why."
4   **Ipse**: *intensive adjective*; note that it modifies the 1st person singular subject in **ībō** and **persuādēbō**, "I myself. . . . "
     ībō: *future* of **eō, īre** (*irreg.*), **iī, itum**, to go.
         Eō, īre is an irregular verb of the 4th conjugation. It is, however, irregular only in the present, imperfect, and future indicative and the present subjunctive; it is regular in the perfect, pluperfect, and future perfect, although there are some syncopated or shortened forms. See page 235. Even though it is a 4th conjugation verb, note that it is not an **-iō** verb and that it uses the **-bi-** future.
     fīliābus: *dative plural* of **fīlia** (to distinguish it from the dative plural of **fīlius**).
5   **ut . . . trādant**: *indirect command* with *present subjunctive* in *primary sequence*.
     ***sponte** (*abl. sing.* with **suā**), of his (her, their) own accord, voluntarily.
6   **gaudeō, gaudēre** (2), **gāvīsus sum**, to be glad, rejoice. This is a *semi-deponent* verb.
7   **sī . . . posset**: *subjunctive in a subordinate clause within indirect statement*; Hercules' direct thought was **sī . . . potest**.
     ***aliter** (*adv.*), in another way, otherwise, differently.
     fierī: *infinitive* of **fīō**.
         The forms of **fīō, fierī** (*irreg.*), **factus sum** are used generally for the passive of **faciō, facere** (3), **fēcī, factum**. Except for the present infinitive and the imperfect subjunctive, the forms of **fīō, fierī** are those of an **-iō** verb of the 4th conjugation. One could say that this is an "anti-deponent" verb in that it has *active* forms and *passive* meanings. See page 233 for its paradigm.
8   **dum ipse abesset**: *subjunctive by attraction* to the mood of the verb in the surrounding subordinate clause; Atlas's actual words would have been **dum absum**, "as long as I am away."
11   ***pondus, ponderis** (*n*), weight.
     ***continuus, -a, -um**, continuous, successive, in succession.

Indirect Commands in Primary Sequence

Ever since paragraph 28 you have seen *indirect commands* expressed with **ut** or **nē** with the *imperfect* subjunctive in *secondary* sequence. Here in paragraph 47 you meet the first example in this book of a verb in the *present* subjunctive; it is used in an indirect command in *primary* sequence: **fīliīs meīs persuādēbō <u>ut</u> māla suā sponte <u>trādant</u>**, "I will persuade my daughters <u>to hand over</u> the apples of their own accord."

     For sequence of tenses, see the grammar note with paragraph 24.

47. HERCULES BEARS UP THE HEAVENS

Atlās autem Herculī maximē prōdesse potuit; nam cum 1
ipse esset pater Hesperidum, sciēbat quō in locō esset hor- 2
tus. Postquam igitur audīvit quam ob causam Herculēs 3
vēnisset, "Ipse," inquit, "ad hortum ībō et fīliābus meīs 4
persuādēbō ut māla suā sponte trādant." Herculēs cum 5
haec audīret, magnopere gāvīsus est; vim enim adhibēre 6
nōluit, sī rēs aliter fierī posset. Itaque auxilium oblātum 7
accipere cōnstituit. Atlās tamen postulāvit ut, dum ipse 8
abesset, Herculēs caelum umerīs sustinēret. Hoc autem 9
negōtium Herculēs libenter suscēpit. Quamquam rēs erat 10
summī labōris, tōtum pondus caelī continuōs complūrēs 11
diēs sōlus sustinuit. 12

> **Present Subjunctive** *(for forms, see pages 229, 231,
> 234, and 235).*

> **Subjunctive in Subordinate Clauses in
> Indirect Statement**
>
> Subordinate clauses within the accusative and infinitive
> construction as found in indirect statement and follow-
> ing verbs of wishing and their opposites usually have
> their verbs in the subjunctive, e.g., **Herculēs vim ad-
> hibēre nōluit, sī rēs aliter fierī posset**, "Her-
> cules did not wish to employ force, if the matter could
> be accomplished otherwise."

1. It is not necessary to inform you who Atlas was.
2. As soon as Hercules saw him, he understood who he was.
3. Atlas asked Hercules to explain the reason for the journey that he had made.
4. Then he offered help, if Hercules would undertake a heavier labor.
5. "I will be able," he said, "to persuade the Hesperides to give you the apples."

Helpful Hints
1. For the construction with **necesse est**, see paragraph 41, line 3.
   For the idiom "to inform," see the grammar note with paragraph 37.
3. The phrase "for the journey" will be translated by an objective genitive (see grammar note with paragraph 45).
4. The main clause ("he offered help") contains an implied indirect state-ment ("he said *that he would help*") and the subordinate clause ("if Her-cules would undertake . . . ") will have its verb in the subjunctive.
5. Note that **inquit** is postpositive (see line 4 of paragraph 47 above).

1   **abeō, abīre** (*irreg.*), **abiī, abitum**, to go away, depart.
     Distinguish this verb carefully from **absum, abesse** (*irreg.*), **āfuī**,
     āfutūrus, to be away, be absent.
2   ***passus, -ūs** (*m*), pace.
     mīlia passuum: *accusative of extent of space*: note the *partitive
     genitive*, thousands of paces, miles. Compare the expression **mīlle
     passūs**, a thousand paces, a mile.
4   ***hortor, hortārī** (1), **hortātus sum**, to exhort, encourage, urge.
5   **haereō, haerēre** (2), **haesī, haesūrus**, to stick, hesitate.
6   **ita ut**: "as."
     mūnus, mūneris (*n*), service, office, duty, present, gift.
7   **aliquandō** (*adv.*), at some time or other, finally, at length.
8   **plūrēs, plūra** (*comparative* of **multī, -ae, -a**), more, many, several.
11   **redeō, redīre** (*irreg.*), **rediī, reditum**, to return.
     redeuntem: modifying **Atlantem**.

Accusative of Extent of Space

Just as the *accusative case* without a preposition may
express duration of time (see grammar note with paragraph 3), so it may also express *extent of space*, e.g.,
**Ad hortum Hesperidum, quī <u>pauca mīlia</u> pas-
suum aberat, sē contulerat**, "He had betaken himself (had gone) to the garden of the Hesperides, which
was <u>a few thousands</u> of paces (miles) away," literally,
"which was away (**aberat**) <u>over the extent of a few
thousands</u> of paces (miles)."

48. THE RETURN OF ATLAS

Atlās intereā abierat, et ad hortum Hesperidum, quī 1
pauca mīlia passuum aberat, sē quam celerrimē contulerat. 2
Eō cum vēnisset, causam veniendī exposuit fīliāsque suās 3
vehementer hortātus est ut māla trāderent. Illae diū 4
haerēbant; nōlēbant enim hoc facere, quod ab ipsā Iūnōne 5
(ita ut ante dictum est) hoc mūnus accēperant. Atlās ta- 6
men aliquandō eīs persuāsit ut sibi pārērent, ac māla ad 7
Herculem rettulit. Herculēs intereā cum plūrēs diēs 8
exspectāvisset neque ūllum nūntium dē reditū Atlantis ac- 9
cēpisset, hāc morā graviter commōtus est. Tandem quīntō 10
diē Atlantem vīdit redeuntem, et brevī tempore magnō cum 11
gaudiō māla accēpit; tum, postquam grātiās prō tantō bene- 12
ficiō ēgit, ad Graeciam proficīscī mātūrāvit. 13

1. As soon as Hercules had accepted the help that had been offered, Atlas went away.
2. Going forward a few miles, he found his daughters.
3. "I ask you," he said, "to hand over the apples that have been entrusted to you."
4. When he had urged them for many days to do this, they finally obeyed him.
5. On the next day he returned to Hercules with the apples.

Helpful Hints

2. Be careful to distinguish expressions such as "go a few miles" and "wait a few days" from expressions such as "do a few deeds" and "get a few apples." The first two are accusatives of extent of space and duration of time with intransitive verbs, and the second two are direct objects of transitive verbs.
3. For "that have been entrusted" use a perfect passive participle and not a relative clause.
5. For "on the next day," use an adverb.

2   **Herculī**: why dative?

4   **aliquī, aliqua, aliquod**, some, any.

5   **unde numquam redīre posset**: *subjunctive* in a *subordinate clause* in *indirect statement* (see grammar note with paragraph 47)

    negōtium eī dedit: equivalent to a verb of *commanding* and introducing an *indirect command.*

6   *****Cerberus, -ī** (*m*), Cerberus.

    *****Orcus, -ī** (*m*), Orcus, the underworld.

9   **cingō, cingere** (3), **cīnxī, cīnctum**, to surround, gird

10   **nārrāmus**: *present indicative* with **priusquam** to represent a *future* action, as with the English *before.*

    aliēnus, -a, -um, belonging to another, out of place.

      nōn aliēnum esse vidētur: "does not seem to be out of place"; the subject is the infinitive **prōpōnere**, and the predicate adjective **aliēnum** is therefore neuter.

11   *****mentiō, mentiōnis** (*f*), mention.

49. TWELFTH LABOR: THE DOG CERBERUS

Postquam aurea māla ad Eurystheum relāta sunt, ūnus   1
modo relinquēbātur ē duodecim labōribus quōs Pȳthia Her-   2
culī praecēperat. Eurystheus autem cum Herculem   3
magnopere timēret, eum in aliquem locum mittere volēbat   4
unde numquam redīre posset. Itaque negōtium eī dedit ut   5
canem Cerberum ex Orcō in lūcem traheret. Hoc erat om-   6
nium operum difficillimum; nēmō enim umquam ex Orcō   7
redierat. Praetereā Cerberus iste mōnstrum erat horribilī   8
speciē, cui erant tria capita serpentibus saevīs cīncta. Sed   9
priusquam dē hōc labōre nārrāmus, nōn aliēnum esse vidē-   10
tur, quoniam dē Orcō mentiōnem fēcimus, pauca dē eā   11
regiōne prōpōnere.   12

1. Since only one of the labors was left, Hercules seemed to have hope
of safety.
2. Eurystheus, however, because of fear, sent him to a place that was
many miles away.
3. "The journey is so difficult," he said, "that he cannot return."
4. "Moreover, I shall order him to drag Cerberus out of that place."
5. "If he does this, he will be freed from servitude."

Helpful Hints

1. To translate "only one of the labors," find a model in paragraph 49 above.
2. For "many miles away," see grammar note with paragraph 48 and note the
idiom for "miles" = **mīlia passuum**, "thousands of paces."
3. Note that the result clause is in primary sequence (see grammar note with
paragraph 24) and will require a present subjunctive (see pages 234–235 for
the forms of the present subjunctive of irregular verbs).
4. Again, primary sequence requires the present subjunctive in the subordinate
clause.
5. This is a future more vivid condition (see grammar note with paragraph 25).
Remember that Latin is stricter with tenses than English. Hercules *will be
freed* only after he *will have done* this last labor. Latin therefore uses the future perfect indicative in the if-clause ("if he will have done this") and the future indicative ("he will be freed") in the main clause. English, however,
normally uses the present tense ("if he does this") in the if-clause in this type
of conditional sentence.

2   Ut: + *indicative* = "when."
    *quisque, quidque (*pronoun*), each.
    *dēcēdō, dēcēdere (3), dēcessī, dēcessum, to go from *or* away, depart.
        Ut . . . dēcesserat, . . . dēdūcēbantur: *past general* (see grammar
        note with paragraph 19); translate the pluperfect as a simple past.
    *mānēs, mānium (*m pl*), spirit, shade.
3   *Mercurius, -ī (*m*), Mercury.
4   *Plūtōn, Plūtōnis (*m*), Pluto.
5   *Prōserpina, -ae (*f*), Proserpina, Proserpine.
    Cerēs, Cereris (*f*), Ceres (a goddess).
6   *rīpa, -ae (*f*), bank.
    *Styx, Stygis, (*acc.*) Styga (*f*), Styx.
    quō flūmine: literally, "by which river," better English, "the river by
        which"; an antecedent that would be an appositive in English is put in the
        relative clause in Latin.
8   priusquam . . . venīre possent: in past time priusquam is used with
        the *subjunctive* to indicate *possibility, purpose, anticipation,* or
        expectancy, "before they could come."
    in hōc flūmine: we usually say "over."
9   *trānsvehō, trānsvehere (3), trānsvexī, trānsvectum, to carry
        across *or* over.
10 *Charōn, Charontis (*m*), Charon.
11 mercēs, mercēdis (*f*), pay, reward, wages.
12 *quisquam, quicquam, anyone, anything.
    nisi quī: "unless he," "except one who . . ."
13 nummus, -ī (*m*), coin.
14 mortuī: *adjective* used as a *substantive (noun).*
    eō cōnsiliō: *ablative of manner,* "in accordance with this purpose."
    ut . . . posset: *purpose clause.*
15 trāiectus, -ūs (*m*), crossing over, passage.
17 per centum annōs: note the use of the *prepositional phrase* ("during the
        whole of . . . ," "throughout . . .") instead of the *accusative of duration of
        time* without a preposition.
18 licēbat: *impersonal,* "it was permitted," "they were allowed" + *infinitive*
        (see grammar note with paragraph 53).

Substantive Use of Adjectives

Adjectives may be used as *substantives* (*nouns*), e.g.,
Dē sēde mortuōrum, "About the place of the dead."

Priusquam with the Subjunctive

Antequam and priusquam are used with the *subjunctive* in past time to indicate *possibility, purpose,
anticipation,* or *expectancy* or when the action that the
clause expresses did not take place, e.g., Hoc trānsīre
necesse erat priusquam in Orcum venīre possent, "It was necessary to cross this before they could
come into Orcus."

50. CHARON'S FERRY

Dē sēde mortuōrum, quam poētae Orcum appellant, haec ₁
trāduntur. Ut quisque dē vītā dēcesserat, mānēs eius ad ₂
Orcum ā deō Mercuriō dēdūcēbantur. Huius regiōnis, quae ₃
sub terrā fuisse dīcitur, rēx erat Plūtōn, cui uxor erat ₄
Prōserpina, Iovis et Cereris fīlia. Mānēs igitur ā Mercuriō ₅
dēductī prīmum ad rīpam veniēbant Stygis, quō flūmine ₆
rēgnum Plūtōnis continēbātur. Hoc trānsīre necesse erat ₇
priusquam in Orcum venīre possent. Cum tamen in hōc ₈
flūmine nūllus pōns factus esset, mānēs trānsvehēbantur ā ₉
Charonte quōdam, quī cum parvā lintre ad rīpam exspec- ₁₀
tābat. Charōn prō hōc officiō mercēdem postulābat, neque ₁₁
quemquam, nisi quī hanc prius dederat, trānsvehere volē- ₁₂
bat. Quam ob causam mōs erat apud antīquōs nummum in ₁₃
ōre mortuī pōnere eō cōnsiliō, ut, cum ad Styga vēnisset, ₁₄
pretium trāiectūs solvere posset. Eī autem quī post ₁₅
mortem in terrā nōn sepultī erant Styga trānsīre nōn ₁₆
poterant, sed in rīpā per centum annōs errāre cōgēbantur; ₁₇
tum dēmum Orcum intrāre licēbat. ₁₈

1. Before he should undertake this labor, Hercules inquired about the nature of the place.
2. This place was surrounded by a river, which was several feet deep.
3. Those who departed from life used to cross that river.
4. The dead did not cross by a bridge, but a certain Charon had been chosen to carry them over.
5. Without his help they could not make a beginning of crossing.

Helpful Hints
1. For translating "before he should undertake," see lines 7–8 of paragraph 50 above and the grammar note on **priusquam** on page 102.
2. For "several feet deep," use the accusative of extent of space (= "through several feet"; see grammar note with paragraph 48) with the adjective **altus, -a, -um** "deep." The Latin idiom says "deep through several feet." In writing the Latin, put the accusative of extent of space before the adjective (the same word order as in English).
3. Past general; use pluperfect and imperfect indicatives (see lines 2–3 of paragraph 50 above).
4. For "to carry them over," use a relative clause of purpose.
5. Latin stresses syntactic connections, even between sentences; here instead of **eius** for "his" use a relative pronoun and place it first in the sentence (= "of whom without the help"). This is called *linking* **quī**; find an example in line 13 of paragraph 50 above.

1   Ut . . . trānsierant, . . . veniēbant: *past general.*
2   Lēthē, Lēthēs (*f*), Lethe.
4   dēnique (*adv.*), lastly, finally.
6   vestītus, -ūs (*m*), clothing.
        nigrō vestītū: *ablative* with indūtus.
7   *solium, -ī (*n*), seat, throne.
        Distinguish this noun carefully from the noun sōl, sōlis (*m*), sun, and
            from the adjective sōlus, -a, -um, alone.
8   Mīnōs, Mīnōis (*m*), Minos.
    Rhadamanthus, -ī (*m*), Rhadamanthus.
9   Aeacus, -ī (*m*), Aeacus.
    iūdex, iūdicis (*m*), judge.
    īnferī, -ōrum (*m pl*), the inhabitants of the underworld, the dead, the
        shades.
    *iūs, iūris (*n*), right, justice, law.
        iūs dīcere, *idiom,* to pronounce judgment.
11 campus, -ī (*m*), plain, field.
    Ēlysius, -a, -um, Elysian.
    improbus, -a, -um, wicked.
12 Tartarus, -ī (*m*), Tartarus.
    multīs et variīs: an adjective is often joined by et to another adjective
        modifying the same noun.
    *varius, -a, -um, various.
13 excruciō (1), to torture.

51. THE REALM OF PLUTO

Ut autem mānēs Styga hōc modō trānsierant, ad alterum 1
flūmen veniēbant, quod Lēthē appellābātur. Ex hōc flūmine 2
aquam bibere cōgēbantur; quod cum fēcissent, rēs omnēs in 3
vītā gestās ē memoriā dēpōnēbant. Dēnique ad sēdem ip- 4
sīus Plūtōnis veniēbant, cuius introitus ā cane Cerberō 5
custōdiēbātur. Ibi Plūtōn nigrō vestītū indūtus cum uxōre 6
Prōserpinā in soliō sedēbat. Stābant etiam nōn procul ab 7
eō locō tria alia solia, in quibus sedēbant Mīnōs, Rha- 8
damanthus, Aeacusque, iūdicēs apud īnferōs. Hī iūs 9
dīcēbant et praemia poenāsque cōnstituēbant. Bonī enim 10
in campōs Ēlysiōs, sēdem beātōrum, veniēbant; improbī 11
autem in Tartarum mittēbantur, ac multīs et variīs suppli- 12
ciīs ibi excruciābantur. 13

1. There was another river, the water of which freed them from
   memory.
2. All were compelled to come to this river, before they could finish
   the journey.
3. There they laid aside the memory of those things that had been
   done in life.
4. Afterwards the good inhabited fields pleasing to the gods.
5. The bad are said to have been tortured with many heavy punishments.

Helpful Hints
2. For "before they could finish," see grammar note with paragraph 50. Do
   not use the verb **possum**.
3. Use a perfect passive participle to translate the relative clause "that had
   been done." Find a model in paragraph 51 above.
4. In translating "fields pleasing to the gods," place the dative between the
   noun and the adjective, and check the vocabulary at the end of this book
   for the dative plural of the word for "god."
5. To translate "many heavy punishments," find a model in lines 12–13 of
   paragraph 51 above. Note that Latin regularly uses **et** to connect two adjectives that simply stand side by side in English.

1   **imperium, -ī** (*n*), command, sway, rule.
     Lacōnia, -ae (*f*), Laconia (a country).
2   **Taenarus, -ī** (*f*), Taenarus (a promontory).
5   **sita**: *predicate adjective.*
     quod cum cognōvisset: "and when he had learned this," i.e., where the
     cave was located.
        cognōvisset: what tense? What kind of clause?
7   **sē . . . sociōs**: *direct object* and *predicate accusative.*
8   ***adiungō, adiungere** (3), **adiūnxī, adiūnctum**, to join to, join.
9   ***ulterior, -ius**, farther.
10   **Charōn, Charontis** (*m*), Charon.
11   **verēbātur nē linter . . . mergerētur**: *fearing clause* introduced by
     nē to express what Charon feared; *imperfect subjunctive* in *secondary*
     sequence after **verēbātur**, "was afraid his boat would sink."
     onerō (1), to load, burden.
     Compare the related noun **onus, oneris** (*n*), load, burden.
        onerāta: *conditional participle*, "if it should be loaded."
12   **mergō, mergere** (3), **mersī, mersum**, (*trans.*) to dip, plunge, sink;
     (*passive, intrans.*) to sink.
     minae, -ārum (*f pl*), threats.

Fearing Clauses

Verbs or other expressions of fearing are followed by
clauses in the subjunctive introduced by **nē** to express a
fear that something might happen (positive) and by **ut**
to express a fear that something might not happen
(negative). Note that **nē** introduces the *positive clause*
and **ut** the *negative*. Here are examples: **Charōn**
verēbātur <u>**nē**</u> **linter** <u>**mergerētur**</u>, "Charon was
afraid <u>that</u> his boat <u>would sink</u>"; here the clause introduced by **nē** expresses what Charon feared might happen (positive fear). **Charōn verēbatur** <u>**ut**</u> **linter ad**
rīpam <u>**pervenīret**</u>, "Charon was afraid <u>that</u> his boat
<u>would not arrive</u> at shore"; here the clause introduced
by **ut** expresses what Charon feared might not happen
(negative fear).

52. HERCULES CROSSES THE STYX

Herculēs postquam imperia Eurystheī accēpit, in Lacō- 1
niam ad Taenarum statim sē contulit; ibi enim spēlunca 2
erat ingentī magnitūdine, per quam, ut trāditur, hominēs 3
ad Orcum dēscendēbant. Eō cum vēnisset, ex incolīs 4
quaesīvit quō in locō spēlunca illa sita esset; quod cum 5
cognōvisset, sine morā dēscendere cōnstituit. Nec tamen 6
sōlus iter fēcit; Mercurius enim et Minerva sē eī sociōs 7
adiūnxerant. Ubi ad rīpam Stygis vēnit, Herculēs cōnscen- 8
dit, ut ad ulteriōrem rīpam trānsīret. Cum tamen Herculēs 9
esset ingentī magnitūdine corporis, Charōn solvere nōlēbat; 10
magnopere enim verēbātur nē linter sua tantō pondere one- 11
rāta in mediō flūmine mergerētur. Tandem tamen minīs 12
Herculis territus Charōn solvit, et eum incolumem ad ulte- 13
riōrem rīpam trānsvexit. 14

1. Hercules feared that he would be prevented from returning from
    this place.
2. Nevertheless, it was necessary to go to that place, before he could
    seize Cerberus.
3. He is said to have inquired of many brave men where the
    entrance was.
4. When he had reached the river, he seemed at first not to be able to
    cross it.
5. For Charon was so frightened that he did not dare to come to his
    aid.

Helpful Hints
3. "Many brave men"; Latin regularly uses a connective between two
    adjectives—"many and brave men."
       For "to have inquired of," see lines 4–5 of paragraph 52 above.
4. For "when," use **ubi**.
5. For "to his aid," use the double dative construction.

3   **licet, licēre** (2), **licuit** *or* **licitum est**, it is allowed *or* permitted.
       ut . . . sibi licēret: *impersonal verb* with *dative*, "that (it) be permit-
       ted to him," "that he be allowed"; **Cerberum auferre** "to carry off
       Cerberus" is the subject of the impersonal verb; translate freely, "that
       he be allowed to carry off Cerberus."
7   *__**polliceor, pollicērī**__ (2), **pollicitus sum**, to promise.
8   **nōn sine magnō perīculō**: *litotes*, the expression of an idea by
       negating its opposite, literally, "not without great danger," better
       English, "with great danger."

Impersonal Verbs

Latin has a number of *impersonal verbs* and *impersonal phrases* such as **licet**, "it is allowed, permitted,"
oportet, "it is proper, right," and the phrase **necesse
est**, "it is necessary"; the implied subject of such verbs
is "it," e.g., "it is permitted" "it is necessary." Often an
infinitive or a clause will serve as subject; impersonal
verbs have therefore only the forms of the third person
singular and the infinitives. In the following example
an infinitive phrase is the subject of the impersonal
verb: **petīvit ut** Cerberum   auferre **sibi** licēret,
literally, "he sought that to carry off Cerberus be allowed to him," better English, "he sought that he be allowed to carry off Cerberus." Note the use of the dative
case with **licet**; in the better English translation the
person referred to by the dative case becomes the subject of the clause.

53. THE LAST LABOR IS ACCOMPLISHED

Postquam Styga hōc modō trānsiit, Herculēs in sēdem 1
ipsīus Plūtōnis vēnit; tum causam veniendī docuit, atque ab 2
eō petīvit ut Cerberum auferre sibi licēret. Plūtōn, quī dē 3
Hercule audīverat, eum benignē excēpit, et facultātem 4
quam ille petēbat libenter dedit. Postulāvit tamen ut Her- 5
culēs ipse, cum iussa Eurysthēī fēcisset, Cerberum in Or- 6
cum rūrsus redūceret. Herculēs hoc pollicitus est, et Cer- 7
berum, quem nōn sine magnō perīculō manibus prehen- 8
derat, summō cum labōre ex Orcō in lūcem atque ad urbem 9
Eurysthēī trāxit. Eō cum vēnisset, tantus timor animum 10
Eurysthēī occupāvit ut ex ātriō statim refugeret; cum autem 11
paulum sē ex timōre recēpisset, multīs cum lacrimīs Her- 12
culem obsecrāvit ut mōnstrum sine morā in Orcum 13
redūceret. Sīc contrā omnium opīniōnem duodecim illī 14
labōrēs quōs Pȳthia praecēperat intrā duodecim annōs cōn- 15
fectī sunt; quae cum ita essent, Herculēs servitūte tandem 16
līberātus magnō cum gaudiō Thēbās rediit. 17

1. Hercules tried in vain to persuade Charon to carry him across alive.
2. And so he compelled him to do this through fear of punishment.
3. Hercules himself feared that he might lose his life before he came to the farther bank.
4. However, he was carried over unhurt and brought Cerberus back to the city of Eurystheus.
5. Since he had accomplished all the labors, he was permitted to return to Thebes.

Helpful Hints
5. For "he was permitted," use the impersonal verb **licet** (see line 3 of paragraph 53 above and the grammar note on page 108).

1 *perficiō (per- + faciō), perficere (3), perfēcī, perfectum, to make *or*
   do thoroughly, accomplish.
   quae: *direct object* of perscrībere, which is the *subject* of est.
   *perscrībō, perscrībere (3), perscrīpsī, perscrīptum, to write in
   full, describe fully, recount.
2 longum est: "would be long."
   *aetās, aetātis (f), age.
   Distinguish this noun carefully from aestās, aestātis (f), summer.
   aetāte: *ablative of respect.*
   *prōvehō, prōvehere (3), prōvexī, prōvectum, to carry forward,
   advance.
3 *Dēianīra, -ae (f), Dejanira.
   Oeneus, -ī (m), Oeneus.
4 accidit . . . ut . . . occīderet: *substantive clause of result* (ut . . . occīderet), serving as *subject* of accidit, literally, "that he killed . . . happened," better English, "it happened that he killed. . . ."
5 Eunomus, -ī (m), Eunomus.
   mōs esset ut . . . in exsilium īret: *substantive clause of result*
   (ut . . . īret), serving as *subject* of mōs esset, literally, "that he go
   into exile was the custom," better English, "it was the custom that he go
   into exile."
   sī quis, if anyone.
   After sī, nisi, num, and nē, quis is used instead of aliquis to mean
   "anyone."
6 occīdisset: *subjunctive by attraction.*
   *exsilium, -ī (n), exile.
7 *fīnis, fīnis, fīnium (m), end, boundary; (pl.) borders, territory, country.
   cīvitās, cīvitātis (f), state.
9 quō modō . . . possent: what kind of clause?
10 *Nessus, -ī (m), Nessus.
12 trānō (trāns- + nō) (1), to swim across *or* over.
13 *revertor (re- + vertō), revertī (3), revertī, reversum, to turn back,
   return.
   revertit: *perfect tense;* note that revertor is *deponent* in the
   present, imperfect, and future, but has *active* forms in the perfect,
   pluperfect, and future perfect.
15 *pectus, pectoris (n), breast.

1. When Hercules had come almost to the end of his life, it happened
   that he was driven out of the territory of the state.
2. On the bank of a certain river one of the centaurs, Nessus by
   name, met him.
3. He asked that he be permitted to carry the wife of Hercules across.
4. This plan seemed good, but Nessus had decided to flee with the
   woman.
5. Since he had the body of a horse, he was not afraid that anyone
   would overtake him.

54. THE CENTAUR NESSUS

Posteā Herculēs multa alia praeclāra perfēcit, quae per- 1
scrībere longum est. Tandem iam aetāte prōvectus 2
Dēianīram, Oeneī fīliam, in mātrimōnium dūxit. Tribus 3
post annīs accidit cāsū ut puerum quendam occīderet, cui 4
nōmen erat Eunomus. Cum autem mōs esset ut, sī quis 5
hominem cāsū occīdisset, in exsilium īret, Herculēs cum 6
uxōre suā ē fīnibus cīvitātis exīre mātūrāvit. Dum iter 7
faciunt, ad flūmen quoddam pervēnērunt in quō nūllus pōns 8
erat. Dum quaerunt quō modō flūmen trānsīre possent, ac- 9
currit centaurus Nessus, quī viātōribus auxilium obtulit. 10
Herculēs uxōrem suam in tergum eius imposuit; tum ipse 11
flūmen trānāvit. At Nessus paulum in aquam prōgressus 12
ad rīpam subitō revertit, ac Dēianīram auferre cōnātus est. 13
Quod cum animadvertisset Herculēs, graviter commōtus 14
arcum intendit et pectus Nessī sagittā trānsfīxit. 15

Substantive Clauses of Result

Result clauses may be used as the subject or object of certain verbs such as **accidit** and expressions such as **mōs est**, e.g., **accidit cāsū ut puerum quendam occīderet**, literally, "that he killed a certain boy happened by chance," better English, "it happened by chance that he killed a certain boy." Here the result clause is the subject of **accidit**. Such a clause is called a *substantive clause* because it serves the function of a substantive or a noun, e.g., it may serve as subject.

The result clauses that you have seen previously are called *adverbial clauses* because they are adverbial modifiers of the main clause, e.g., **Tanta tempestās subitō coorta est ut nāvis cursum tenēre nōn posset**, "Such a great storm arose that the ship was not able to hold its course" (paragraph 30, lines 4–5). Here the result clause stands in an adverbial relationship to the entire main clause.

Quis instead of aliquis after sī, nisi, num, and nē

The indefinite pronoun **aliquis** "someone," "anyone" appears simply as **quis** after **sī**, **nisi**, **num**, and **nē**, e.g., **sī quis hominem cāsū occīdisset**, "if anyone had killed a man by accident."

1   *humī (*locative of* **humus**), on the ground.
2   nē . . . dīmitteret: *negative purpose clause.*
    *occāsiō, occāsiōnis (*f*), chance, opportunity.
    *ulcīscor, ulcīscī (3), ultus sum, to avenge, revenge.
    occāsiōnem suī ulcīscendī: literally, "opportunity of himself about
        to be avenged," *gerundive* (verbal adjective or future passive partici-
        ple) in the genitive case agreeing with the reflexive pronoun suī "of
        himself"; better English, "opportunity of avenging himself."
3   morientis: *participle* used as a *substantive,* "of a dying man."
4   *amor, amōris (*m*), love.
    cōnservō (1), to preserve, keep.
    vīs: from volō, velle (*irreg.*), voluī, to be willing, wish.
5   effundō (ex- + fundō), effundere (3), effūdī, effūsum, to pour out.
    effunditur: *passive as intransitive,* "pours out."
    *repōnō, repōnere (3), reposuī, repositum, to put *or* set back, store up
        or away.
    sī . . . vēnerit, . . . tingue: *future more vivid condition* (see grammar
        note with paragraph 25) with future perfect indicative in the if-clause to
        indicate that the action of that clause is thought of as being completed
        before the action of the main clause is to take place. Translate the if-
        clause with the present tense in English. Here the main clause is an im-
        perative instead of a future indicative; this is common in future more
        vivid conditions.
6   suspīciō, suspīciōnis (*f*), suspicion.
    tibi: *dative of reference* (see grammar note with paragraph 56).
    vestis, vestis, vestium (*f*), clothing, dress, robe.
7   *tinguō, tinguere (3), tīnxī, tīnctum, to wet, soak, dye.
    anima, -ae (*f*), breath, soul, life.
    efflō (ex- + flō) (1), to breathe out.
8   *malum, -ī (*n*), evil, mischief.
    malī: *partitive genitive.*
    *suspicor (sub- + speciō), suspicārī (1), suspicātus sum, to suspect.
9   Eurytus, -ī (*m*), Eurytus.
    Oechalia, -ae (*f*), Oechalia.
10 *Iolē, Iolēs, (*acc.*) Iolēn (*f*), Iole.
12 Cēnaeum, -ī (*n*), Cenaeum (a promontory).
14 *Lichās, Lichae (*m*), Lichas.
    quī . . . referret: *relative clause of purpose.*
16 *albus, -a, -um, white.
    nē Herculēs . . . habēret: *fearing clause* dependent on verita "fear-
        ing" and introduced by nē to indicate what was feared, "fearing that
        Hercules had. . . . "
17 ergā (+ *acc.*), toward, for.
    vestem: *direct object* of both dedit and tinxit; the common direct object
        of a subordinate clause and a main clause may stand before the subordi-
        nate clause.

For sentences, see page 115.

55. THE POISONED ROBE

Itaque Nessus sagittā Herculis trānsfīxus moriēns humī 1
iacēbat; sed nē occāsiōnem suī ulcīscendī dīmitteret, ita 2
locūtus est: "Tū, Dēianīra, verba morientis audī. Sī 3
amōrem marītī tuī cōnservāre vīs, hunc sanguinem quī nunc 4
ē pectore meō effunditur sūme ac repōne; tum, sī Herculēs 5
umquam in suspīciōnem tibi vēnerit, vestem eius hōc san- 6
guine tingue." Haec locūtus Nessus animam efflāvit; 7
Dēianīra autem nihil malī suspicāns eius iussa fēcit. Paulō 8
post Herculēs bellum contrā Eurytum, rēgem Oechaliae, 9
suscēpit. Cum rēgem ipsum cum fīliīs interfēcisset, Iolēn 10
tamen eius fīliam sēcum redūxit. Sed priusquam domum 11
pervēnit, nāvem ad Cēnaeum appulit, et in terram ēgressus 12
āram cōnstituit, ut Iovī sacrificium faceret. Dum sacrifi- 13
cium parat, Licham comitem suum domum mīsit, quī 14
vestem albam referret; mōs enim erat apud antīquōs, cum 15
sacrificia facerent, albam vestem gerere. At Dēianīra verita 16
nē Herculēs amōrem ergā Iolēn habēret, vestem priusquam 17
Lichae dedit, sanguine Nessī tīnxit. 18

Gerundives

The *gerundive* is a *verbal adjective*, while the *gerund* (see grammar note with paragraph 21) is a *verbal noun*. The gerundive appears in all genders, numbers, and cases, just as does any other adjective; it is *future* and *passive* in meaning and is often called a future passive participle. Note the letters **-nd-** in all its forms:

parandus, -a, -um "about to be prepared"
habendus, -a, -um "about to be had"
mittendus, -a, -um "about to be sent"
iaciendus, -a, -um "about to be thrown"
audiendus, -a, -um "about to be heard"

When a gerund would have a direct object, e.g., oc-cāsiōnem s_ē_ ulcīscendī, "opportunity of avenging himself," the gerundive is commonly used instead, and the construction is turned around. Instead of s_ē_ ulcīs-cendī, "of avenging himself," we find **suī ulcīscendī**, "of himself about to be avenged" = "of avenging him-self," thus, **occāsiōnem suī ulcīscendī**, "the oppor-tunity of avenging himself."

3   **quae causa esset**: what kind of clause?
4   **exanimātus**: "exhausted."
6   *__quasi__, as if.
     *__impellō__ (in- + pellō), __impellere__ (3), __impulī__, __impulsum__, to drive *or*
         urge on, incite, urge.
     __Oeta__, -ae (*f*), Oeta.
7   *__rogus__, -ī (*m*), funeral pile, pyre.
     __exstruō__, __extruere__ (3), __extrūxī__, __extrūctum__, to pile *or* heap up, build,
         erect.
8   __circumstō__, __circumstāre__ (1), __circumstetī__, to stand around.
9   __succendō__, __succendere__ (3), __succendī__, __succēnsum__, to kindle beneath,
         set on fire.
         Distinguish this verb carefuly from __succēdō__, __succēdere__ (3), __suc-__
         __cessī__, __successum__, to go *or* come under, follow after, succeed, and
         from __succīdō__, __succīdere__ (3), __succīdī__, __succīsum__, to cut below *or*
         down, fell.
10   __recūsō__ (1), to refuse.
     *__pāstor__, __pāstōris__ (*m*), shepherd.
     __misericordia__, -ae (*f*), pity, compassion.
11   *__subdō__, __subdere__ (3), __subdidī__, __subditum__, to put under, apply.
12   __nūbēs__, __nūbis__, __nūbium__ (*f*), cloud.
     __Olympus__, -ī (*m*), Olympus (the home of the gods).

Dative of Reference

In paragraph 22, lines 12–13, we saw the *dative of reference* used in the double dative construction, e.g., **Cancer ingēns auxiliō Hydrae** vēnit, literally, "A huge crab came for the purpose of aid with reference to the Hydra," better English, "to aid the Hydra." Here the dative denotes the person or thing concerned.

This use of the dative (*dative of reference*) is common outside the double dative construction, e.g., **sī Herculēs umquam in suspīciōnem tibi vēnerit**, literally, "if Hercules ever comes into suspicion with reference to you," more freely, in better English, "if you ever come to suspect Hercules." Sometimes, as here, the expression must be changed substantially in order to be put into good English. Sometimes a dative of reference can be translated as a possessive adjective (in the first English sentence in the second set of sentences on page 115 the possessive adjective "his" may best be translated into Latin with a dative of reference, "for him").

56. THE DEATH OF HERCULES

Herculēs nihil malī suspicāns vestem quam Lichās at- 1
tulerat statim induit. Paulō post magnum dolōrem sēnsit, 2
et quae causa esset eius reī magnopere mīrābātur. Dolōre 3
paene exanimātus vestem dētrahere cōnātus est; illa tamen 4
in corpore haesit, neque ūllō modō dētrahī potuit. Tum dē- 5
mum Herculēs quasi furōre impulsus in montem Oetam sē 6
contulit, atque in rogum, quem summā celeritāte exstrūxit, 7
sē imposuit. Hoc cum fēcisset, eōs quī circumstābant ōrāvit 8
ut rogum quam celerrimē succenderent. Omnēs diū 9
recūsābant; tandem tamen pāstor quīdam ad misericor- 10
diam inductus ignem subdidit. Tum, dum omnia fūmō ob- 11
scūrantur, Herculēs dēnsā nūbe tēctus ā Iove in Olympum 12
abreptus est. 13

Sentences for Paragraph 55:

1. No opportunity of saving himself was given to Nessus.
2. For Hercules, fearing that he might escape, killed him immediately with an arrow.
3. It happened a little later that Hercules was returning home.
4. Going ashore to make a sacrifice, he sent a friend to fetch suitable
   clothing.
5. "If you do this," he said, "I will thank you."

Helpful Hint
2. The word "he" must be translated when it represents a change of subject; use ille.

Sentences for Paragraph 56:

1. It happened that this robe was the cause of his death.
2. Although he was affected with great pain, he was compelled to give
   up hope of pulling the robe off.
3. When he had returned home, he went to a certain mountain.
4. After he had departed from life, he was permitted to go away to
   the gods.
5. If anyone inquires from us what benefits men received from
   Hercules, we will be able to give a reply.

Helpful Hints
1. Translate the English possessive adjective "his" with a dative of reference, literally, "for him."
2. For "of pulling the robe off," use a gerundive (see grammar note with paragraph 55).

The Argonauts

Jason and the Golden Fleece

The celebrated voyage of the Argonauts came about in this way. Pelias had expelled his brother Aeson from his kingdom in Thessaly and had determined to take the life of Jason, the son of Aeson. Jason, however, escaped and grew up to manhood in another country. At last he returned to Thessaly. Pelias, fearing that he might attempt to recover the kingdom, sent him to fetch the Golden Fleece from Colchis, supposing this to be an impossible feat.

Jason sailed with a band of heroes in the ship Argo (called after Argus, its builder), and after many adventures reached Colchis. Here Aeetes, king of Colchis, who was unwilling to give up the Fleece, sent him to perform what seemed an impossible task. He was to plow a field with certain fire-breathing bulls, and then to sow the teeth of a dragon. Medea, the daughter of the king, assisted Jason by her skill in magic, first to perform the task appointed, and then to procure the Fleece.

Medea fled with Jason, and to delay the pursuit of her father she sacrificed her brother Absyrtus. After reaching Thessaly, Medea caused the death of Pelias and was expelled from the country with her husband. They went to Corinth, and here Medea, becoming jealous of Glauce, daughter of Creon, caused her death by means of a poisoned robe. After committing an even greater crime, she was carried off in a chariot sent by the sun-god. A little later Jason was accidentally killed.

1 **alter Aesōn, Peliās alter:** *chiasmus.* A chiasmus is an arrangement of words in which variety and emphasis are gained by reversing the position of the words in the second of two contrasted expressions. Here the two names are brought together by this arrangement.

2 ***Aesōn, Aesonis** (*m*), Aeson.
*Peliās, Peliae (*m*), Pelias.

3 **rēgnī:** *objective genitive.*

4 ***in animō habēre,** *idiom,* to have in mind, intend.

5 ***Iāsōn, Iāsonis** (*m*), Jason.
Quīdam . . . ex amīcīs Aesonis: "certain of Aeson's friends"; note that **ex** or **dē** with the *ablative* is used instead of the *partitive genitive* with **quīdam.**

6 ***sententia, -ae** (*f*), opinion, purpose.

8 ***auferō** (ab- + ferō), **auferre** (*irreg.*), **abstulī, ablātum,** to bear away, carry off.

9 **redīssent:** *syncopated* or *shortened form* of **rediissent.**
puerum mortuum esse: *indirect statement* with *present infinitive* (same tense as in the implied direct statement and indicating time contemporaneous with that of the main verb), "announced that the boy was dead."

10 ***rē vērā,** in truth, in fact, really.
*voluptās, voluptātis (*f*), pleasure.

11 **quae causa fuisset mortis:** what kind of clause?

13 **nesciō quī,** *idiom,* I don't know what = some.
nesciō quam fābulam: "some story or other."

14 **fingō, fingere** (3), **fīnxī, fictum,** to invent, make up.

Indirect Statement with Present Infinitive

Indirect statements have their *subjects* in the *accusative case* and their *verbs* in the *infinitive.* The tense of the infinitive is the same as the tense of the verb in the direct statement, e.g., **Eī renūntiāvērunt puerum mortuum esse,** "They reported to him that the boy was dead." The original statement was **Puer mortuus est,** "The boy is dead," and the present indicative **est** of the direct statement is replaced by the present infinitive **esse** in the indirect statement.

When translating into English, the present infinitive in the indirect statement will be translated with the *same* tense as that of the verb in the main clause. In the Latin sentence above, the main verb is past tense (**renūntiāvērunt**), so the past tense is to be used in translating the indirect statement: "they reported that the boy was dead."

Also note that when translating Latin indirect statements into English we often use the word *that* to introduce the indirect statement; there is no corresponding word in the indirect statement in Latin.

57. THE WICKED UNCLE

Erant quondam in Thessaliā duo frātrēs, quōrum alter 1
Aesōn, Peliās alter appellābātur. Aesōn prīmō rēgnum ob- 2
tinuit; posteā vērō Peliās rēgnī cupiditāte adductus nōn 3
modo frātrem suum expulit, sed etiam in animō habēbat 4
Iāsonem, Aesonis fīlium, interficere. Quīdam tamen ex 5
amīcīs Aesonis, ubi sententiam Peliae cognōvērunt, puerum 6
ē tantō perīculō ēripere cōnstituērunt. Itaque noctū Iā- 7
sonem ex urbe abstulērunt; et cum posterō diē ad rēgem 8
redīssent, eī renūntiāvērunt puerum mortuum esse. Peliās 9
cum hoc audīvisset, etsī rē vērā magnam voluptātem per- 10
cipiēbat, speciem tamen dolōris praebuit, et quae causa 11
fuisset mortis quaesīvit. Illī autem cum intellegerent 12
dolōrem eius falsum esse, nesciō quam fābulam dē morte 13
puerī fīnxērunt. 14

1. Because of his desire for royal power, Pelias intended to expel his brother.
2. Certain of the citizens feared that someone would kill Aeson's son, and they went away with him.
3. In a short time they returned home and said that they were suffering heavy grief.
4. The king inquired of them where Jason was.
5. They said that the boy was dead.

Helpful Hints
1. Find the Latin for "intended" in line 4 of paragraph 57 above.
2. For "certain of the citizens," see lines 5–6 of paragraph 57 above and the grammar note with paragraph 43.
3. Use an accusative and infinitive to translate the indirect statement, and do not translate the word *that* with a separate word in Latin.
4. For "inquired of," see lines 4–5 of paragraph 52.

2   **fraus, fraudis** (*f*), deception, fraud.
     *****Delphī, -ōrum** (*m pl*), Delphi (a town).
5   **praesentia, -ae** (*f*), the present.
6   **sī quis . . . venīret:** *subjunctive by attraction*; the direct form would be
     sī quis veniet.
     *****quis, quae** or **qua, quid** (*indefinite pronoun after* **sī**), any, anyone,
     anybody, anything.
     *****calceus, -ī** (*m*), shoe.
7   **accidit ut:** "it happened that."
8   **factūrus esset:** *imperfect subjunctive of the active periphrastic conjuga-
     tion,* which consists of the *future active participle* with a form of the verb
     sum, "was about to make."
9   *****conveniō, convenīre** (4), **convēnī, conventum,** to come together,
     assemble, gather.
     Diē cōnstitūtā: *ablative of time when;* note the gender.
12   **in trānseundō . . . flūmine:** *gerundive,* "in crossing a river," literally,
     "in a river about to be crossed" (see grammar note with paragraph 55).

Active Periphrastic Conjugation

The future active participle (ending in **-ūrus, -a, -um**)
can be used with any form of the verb **sum** to form an
active periphrastic; the meaning is "about to," "going
to," or "intending to":

Indicative

Present	parātūrus sum	I am about to prepare
Imperfect	parātūrus eram	I was about to prepare
Future	parātūrus erō	I will be about to pre-pare
Perfect	parātūrus fuī	I was, have been, about to prepare
Pluperfect	parātūrus fueram	I had been about to prepare
Future Perfect	parātūrus fuerō	I will have been about to prepare

Subjunctive

Present	parātūrus sim
Imperfect	parātūrus essem
Perfect	parātūrus fuerim
Pluperfect	parātūrus fuissem

Infinitive

Present	parātūrus esse	to be about to prepare
Perfect	parātūrus fuisse	to have been about to prepare

58. A FATEFUL ACCIDENT

Brevī tempore Peliās, veritus nē rēgnum tantā vī et 1
fraude occupātum āmitteret, amīcum quendam Delphōs 2
mīsit, quī Apollinem cōnsuleret. Ille quam celerrimē 3
Delphōs sē contulit, et quam ob causam vēnisset dēmōn- 4
strāvit. Respondit Pȳthia nūllum esse in praesentiā 5
perīculum; monuit tamen Peliam ut, sī quis cum ūnō calceō 6
venīret, eum cavēret. Paucīs post annīs accidit ut Peliās 7
sacrificium factūrus esset; nūntiōs in omnēs partēs 8
dīmīserat, et certam diem conveniendī dīxerat. Diē cōn- 9
stitūtā magnus hominum numerus undique ex agrīs con- 10
vēnit. In hīs autem fuit Iāsōn, quī ā puerō apud centaurum 11
quendam habitāverat. Dum iter facit, calceum alterum in 12
trānseundō nesciō quō flūmine āmīsit. 13

> **Active Periphrastic Conjugation** (continued)
>
> These periphrastic forms are often used in the sub-
> junctive when a definite reference to future time is
> needed, e.g., **accidit ut Peliās sacrificium fac-
> tūrus esset**, "it happened that Pelias was about to
> make a sacrifice." As usual, the imperfect subjunctive
> is here used in secondary sequence to indicate time con-
> temporaneous with that of the main verb ("it happened
> that he was"); the participle gives the reference to fu-
> ture time ("about to make").

1. Influenced by fear of losing the kingdom, Pelias sent one of his
   friends to Delphi.
2. It happened that a certain man was going to endanger the king.
3. "I do not understand," the friend of Pelias said, "what the man is
   intending to do."
4. "Moreover, we have no opportunity of finding out."
5. "If you suspect no evil, you will be in great danger."

Helpful Hints
1. Begin your translation with **Peliās**, followed by the participial phrase.
2. For "was going to endanger" translate as if "was going to furnish danger"; use
   an active periphrastic (see grammar note on pages 120–121).
3. For "is intending to do," use an active periphrastic and not the idiom **in animō habēre**.
4. For "we have," use the dative of possession.
5. Use the future tense in both parts of this future more vivid condition.
   For "no evil," use a partitive genitive ("nothing of evil").

2   **alterō pede nūdō**: *ablative absolute*, "with one foot bare"; since Latin
     does not have a participle of the verb **sum**, this *ablative absolute* con-
     sists only of *adjectives* and a *noun*.
     nūdus, -a, -um, naked, bare.
4   **quem ōrāculum dēmōnstrāvisset**: *subjunctive* in a *relative clause* in
     indirect statement.
5   *__Aeētēs, Aeētae__ (*m*), Aeetes.
6   *__Colchis, Colchidis__ (*f*), Colchis.
7   *__vellus, velleris__ (*n*), fleece.
     Distinguish this noun carefully from the verb **volō, velle** (*irreg.*),
     voluī, to be willing, wish.
     vellus . . . aureum: Phrixus and his sister Helle were about to be put
     to death as a sacrifice, when they were rescued and carried off through
     the air by a ram with a fleece of gold. Helle fell into the strait called
     by the ancients the Hellespont (Helle's Sea), and by us the Dard-
     anelles. Phrixus came safely to Colchis, and there he sacrificed the
     ram and gave the fleece to Aeetes.
     Phrixus, -ī (*m*), Phrixus.
8   **hōc vellere**: *ablative* with the *deponent verb* **potīrētur**.
9   **potior, potīrī** (4), **potītus sum** (+ *abl.*), to become master of, get pos-
     session of.
     eum . . . peritūrum esse: *indirect statement* with the *future active in-
     finitive* after a main verb in the past tense, "that he would perish."
10   *__pereō, perīre__ (*irreg.*), **periī, peritum**, to pass away, perish.
     *__spērō__ (1), to hope.
11   **cohortātus**: is the perfect participle of a deponent verb to be translated
     actively or passively?
     quid fierī vellet: what kind of clause?
     vellet: from **volō, velle** (*irreg.*), **voluī**.

Ablative Absolutes

A *participle* and a *noun* or *pronoun* in the *ablative case*
may form an adverbial phrase that describes the circumstances within which the action of the sentence
takes place. Since Latin does not have a participle of
the verb **sum**, an ablative absolute may consist merely
of nouns or pronouns and adjectives, e.g., **alterō pede
nūdō**, "with one foot (being) bare." In translating ablative absolutes, you should use an introductory word
such as "with," "when," "since," "if," or "although," de-
pending on the context.

The present participle shows the *same* time as that
of the main verb, and the perfect participle shows time
before that of the main verb. The future participle is
seldom used in an ablative absolute.

59. THE GOLDEN FLEECE

Iāsōn cum calceum āmissum nūllō modō recuperāre pos- 1
set, alterō pede nūdō in rēgiam pervēnit. Quem cum Peliās 2
vīdisset, summō timōre affectus est; intellēxit enim hunc 3
esse hominem quem ōrāculum dēmōnstrāvisset. Itaque hoc 4
cōnsilium iniit. Rēx erat quīdam Aeētēs, quī rēgnum 5
Colchidis illō tempore obtinēbat. Huic commissum erat 6
vellus illud aureum quod Phrixus quondam ibi relīquerat. 7
Cōnstituit igitur Peliās Iāsonī negōtium dare ut hōc vellere 8
potīrētur; cum enim rēs esset magnī perīculī, eum in itinere 9
peritūrum esse spērābat. Itaque Iāsonem ad sē arcessīvit, 10
et eum cohortātus quid fierī vellet docuit. Ille etsī intel- 11
legēbat rem esse difficillimam, tamen negōtium libenter 12
suscēpit. 13

Indirect Statement with Future Active Infinitive

The *future active infinitive* is used in an *indirect state-ment* when the original statement had its verb in the *future tense*, e.g., **Eum in itinere peritūrum esse spērābat**, "He (Pelias) hoped that he (Jason) would perish on the journey." The original hope was **In itinere perībit**, "He will perish on the journey."

   Note that if the main verb were present tense (**spērat** instead of **spērābat**) we would translate "he (Pelias) hopes that he (Jason) will perish on the journey." When the main verb is in a past tense, we use "would perish" to express the future idea.

---

1. The king found out that he would avoid danger by killing Jason.
2. After he found this out, he was intending to send him to his death.
3. Therefore he demanded that Jason should attempt to get possession of a certain fleece.
4. He gave him the task of bringing this back to him.
5. Jason's friends exhorted him not to undertake this difficult task.

Helpful Hints
1. For "by killing Jason," use a gerundive (see grammar note with paragraph 55).
2. Use an ablative absolute introduced by linking **quī** to translate the subordinate clause = "which having been found out." Use an active periphrastic or the idiom **in animō habēre** in the main clause.
3. For "get possession of a certain fleece," see lines 8–9 of paragraph 59 above and the vocabulary note on **potior**.
4. To translate "task of bringing . . . ," find a model in lines 8–9 of paragraph 59.

1   **iter**: *accusative of extent of space.*
4   ***ūsus, -ūs** (m), use, experience.
      ūsuī: *dative of purpose,* "for use," "useful."
5   **ad armandās nāvēs**: *gerundive* with **ad** to express *purpose,* literally
      "for ships about to be armed/equipped," "for arming/equipping ships."
      armō (1), to arm, equip.
      comportō (1), to carry *or* bring together, collect.
6   ***Argus, -ī** (m), Argus.
      nauticus, -a, -um, naval, nautical.
7   **circiter** (*adv.* and *prep.* + *acc.*), about.
8   **opus, operis** (n), work.
         Compare **opera, -ae** (f), work.
         operī: *dative* with the *compound verb* **praeerat**.
      ***praesum, praeesse** (*irreg.*), **praefuī** (+ *dat.*), to be before, preside
         over, be in charge of, command.
9   ***dīligentia, -ae** (f), care, diligence, industry.
      nē . . . quidem: "not even," emphasizing the word in between, "not even
         the nighttime."
10   **Ad multitūdinem hominum trānsportandam**: *gerundive* with **ad**
         to express *purpose*, "for transporting a multitude of men."
11   **paulum, -ī** (n), a little.
      paulō: *ablative of degree of difference*, "by a little," "somewhat."
      lātus, -a, -um, broad, wide.
12   **quibus**: *ablative* with **ūtī** (*infinitive* of the *deponent verb* **ūtor**), "which
         we are accustomed to use."
      nostrō marī: the Mediterranean Sea.
13   ***perferō, perferre** (*irreg.*), **pertulī, perlātum**, to bear through, bear,
         endure, weather.
      tōta: modifying **nāvis** (11), here used *adverbially*, "totally," "completely."
      rōbur, rōboris (n), oak.
      facta: supply **erat**.

Gerundive with ad to Express Purpose

We saw in paragraph 31 that the gerund may be used
with **ad** to express purpose, e.g., **Ut omnia ad
nāvigandum parāta sunt**, "When everything had
been prepared <u>for sailing</u>." When the gerund would
take a direct object, the gerundive is used instead, e.g.,
**Omnia quae sunt ūsuī ad armandās nāvēs
comportārī iussit**, "He ordered all things that were
useful <u>for equipping ships</u> to be collected." Instead of
the gerund (**ad armandum nāvēs**), where **nāvēs** is
the accusative object of **armandum**, Latin prefers the
gerundive (**ad armandās nāvēs**), where **nāvēs** is
the object of the preposition **ad**. See also **ad
<u>multitūdinem</u> hominum transportandam** and
ad <u>vim</u> tempestatum perferendam.

60. THE BUILDING OF THE GOOD SHIP ARGO

Tamen, cum Colchis multōrum diērum iter ab eō locō 1
abesset, sōlus Iāsōn proficīscī nōluit. Itaque nūntiōs in 2
omnēs partēs dīmīsit, quī causam itineris docērent, et cer- 3
tam diem conveniendī dīxit. Intereā omnia quae sunt ūsuī 4
ad armandās nāvēs comportārī iussit, ac negōtium dedit 5
Argō cuidam, quī summam scientiam nauticārum rērum 6
habēbat, ut nāvem aedificāret. In hīs rēbus diēs circiter 7
decem cōnsūmptī sunt; Argus enim, quī operī praeerat, tan- 8
tam dīligentiam adhibēbat ut nē nocturnum quidem tem- 9
pus sibi ad quiētem relinqueret. Ad multitūdinem 10
hominum trānsportandam nāvis paulō erat lātior quam 11
eae quibus in nostrō marī ūtī cōnsuēvimus, et ad vim tem- 12
pestātum perferendam tōta ex rōbore facta. 13

1. Jason, however, promised that he would do that which the king wished.
2. After a large ship had been built, he was intending to cross the sea.
3. And so he exhorted Argus to prepare everything that was useful for sailing.
4. "If we get possession of the fleece," he said, "I will give you a great reward."
5. Argus replied that he would not stop working even at night.

Helpful Hints

1. Remember that subordinate clauses within indirect statements usually have their verbs in the subjunctive (see grammar note with paragraph 47).
2. Use an ablative absolute to translate the subordinate clause. For the ablative of the word for ship, see the grammar note with paragraph 62.
   For "he was intending," use an active periphrastic.
3. For "useful," use dative of purpose = "for use."
4. Be sure to use the future perfect in the if-clause of this future more vivid condition.
5. Use an ablative of separation without a preposition with the Latin verb for "stop."
   Place **nē . . . quidem** around the single Latin word that needs most emphasis in this sentence.

1 **diēs:** *feminine* here (see paragraph 7, line 1).

3 **reī . . . glōriae:** *chiasmus* contrasting **novitās** and **spēs.**
novitās, novitātis (f), newness, novelty.

4 **Trāditum est:** *impersonal passive,* "It has been reported."
fuisse Herculem . . . , Orpheum, Theseum . . . : *indirect statement* with **trāditum est.**

5 **Orpheus, -ī (m)**, Orpheus (a mythical musician, who is said to have made such sweet music on his golden harp that wild beasts, trees, and rocks followed him).

6 **Castor, Castoris (m)**, Castor (a mythical hero, famous as a tamer of horses).

7 **quōs . . . eōs:** *relative clause* placed before its *antecedent.*
quōs . . . parātissimōs esse: *indirect statement* wth **arbitrābātur.**

8 *arbitror, **arbitrārī** (1), **arbitrātus sum**, to consider, think, judge.
numerō: *ablative of respect,* "in number," modifying **quīnquāgintā.**

9 *commoror, **commorārī** (1), **commorātus sum**, to delay, linger, stay, tarry.

10 **ad omnēs cāsūs:** *purpose* expressed by **ad** + *acc.,* "for all emergencies."
subsidium, -ī (n), support, help, reserve, reinforcement.

11 **nancīscor, nancīscī (3), nactus sum**, to get, obtain, find.

12 **plausus, -ūs (m)**, applause.

Indirect Statement with Perfect Infinitive

The *perfect infinitive* is used in an *indirect statement* when a *perfect indicative* was used in the *direct statement*, e.g., **Trāditum est . . . in hōc numerō fuisse Herculem**, "It has been reported that Hercules was in this number (of men)." The original statement would have been **Herculēs in hōc numerō fuit.**

When translating into English, keep in mind that the perfect infinitive indicates *time before* that of the main verb; thus in the sentence above we have: "It has been reported (present perfect) that Hercules was (prior to the report) in this number (of men)."

61. THE ANCHOR IS WEIGHED

Intereā ea diēs appetēbat quam Iāsōn per nūntiōs dīx- 1
erat, atque ex omnibus regiōnibus Graeciae multī, quōs aut 2
reī novitās aut spēs glōriae movēbat, undique con- 3
veniēbant. Trāditum est autem in hōc numerō fuisse Her- 4
culem, dē quō suprā multa scrīpsimus, Orpheum, Thēseum, 5
Castorem, multōsque aliōs quōrum nōmina sunt nōtis- 6
sima. Ex hīs Iāsōn quōs ad omnia perīcula subeunda 7
parātissimōs esse arbitrābātur, eōs numerō quīnquāgintā 8
dēlēgit ac sociōs sibi adiūnxit; tum paucōs diēs commorā- 9
tus, ut ad omnēs cāsūs subsidia comparāret, nāvem dē- 10
dūxit, et tempestātem ad nāvigandum idōneam nactus 11
magnō cum plausū omnium solvit. 12

1. Certain of those who gathered to make the journey knew that the king had made an ambush against Jason.
2. Jason thought that all these men would be of use.
3. You have not heard even the names of all those who came to Jason's support.
4. Those whom Jason had chosen were prepared to undergo danger.
5. When they found the wind favorable, they hastened to set out.

Helpful Hints
1. For "knew," use the pluperfect of **cognōscō** (see the vocabulary entry at the end of this book).
   Remember that the word for "ambush" in Latin is plural.
2. For "would be," use the future infinitive (**futūrus esse** or the alternative form **fore**).
   For "of use," use the dative of purpose.
3. For "to Jason's support," use the double dative construction.
4. For "to undergo danger," use **ad** + the gerundive (see grammar note with paragraph 60).
5. For "When they found," use the perfect participle of a deponent verb = "Having found" (see line 11 of paragraph 61 above).

1   *Argonautae, -ārum (*m pl*), the Argonauts.
2   nāvī: *i-stem noun of 3rd declension* with -ī in the *ablative singular*.
    *vehō, vehere (3), vexī, vectum, to carry.
    Cyzicus, -ī (*f*), Cyzicus (town on the Propontis).
3   *hospitium, -ī (*n*), hospitality.
9   agnōscō (ad- + gnōscō), agnōscere (3), agnōvī, agnitum, to
       recognize.
    obscūrus, -a, -um, dark.
10 *inimīcus, -a, -um, unfriendly, hostile.
    nāvem vēnisse: *indirect statement* after arbitrātī, "thinking."
12 dēcurrō, dēcurrere (3), dēcucurrī or dēcurrī, dēcursum, to run
       down.
13 dīlūcēscō, dīlūcēscere (3), dīlūxī, to grow light, dawn.
    errō (1), to wander, stray, be mistaken.
14 *abiciō (ab- + iaciō), abicere (3), abiēcī, abiectum, to throw away.
    occīsum esse: *perfect passive infinitive* in an *indirect statement*, ex-
       pressing time before the verb vidērent, "when they saw that the king
       had been killed."
15 dolōrem capere, *idiom*, to suffer grief.

Third Declension Parisyllabic I-stem Nouns

I-stem nouns of the 3rd declension (such as nāvis) that
end in -*is* and have the *same number of syllables* in
the genitive singular (i.e., are parisyllabic, e.g., nāvis)
may have -*ī* instead of -*e* in the ablative singular (see
the discussion of i-stem nouns in the grammar note
with paragraph 6)

Indirect Statement with Perfect Passive Infinitive

The *perfect passive infinitive* is used in an *indirect
statement* when a *perfect passive indicative* was used
in the *direct statement*, e.g., cum rēgem occīsum
esse vidērent, "when they saw that the king had
been killed." The original thought with this verb of seeing was rēx occīsus est, "the king has been killed."
   If the verb of seeing were present tense, we would
translate "when they see that the king has been killed."
When the verb of seeing is past tense, as it is above, we
translate "when they saw that the king had been
killed." In both cases the perfect infinitive in the indirect statement indicates time before that of the introductory verb (see grammar note with paragraph 61).
   The participial portion of the infinitive agrees with
the subject of the indirect statement, which is here
masculine singular; therefore the participle is occīsum.

62. A FATAL MISTAKE

Nōn multō post Argonautae (ita enim appellābantur quī 1
istā nāvī vehēbantur) īnsulam quandam, nōmine Cyzicum, 2
attigērunt; et ē nāvī ēgressī ā rēge illīus regiōnis hospitiō 3
acceptī sunt. Paucās hōrās ibi commorātī ad sōlis occāsum 4
rūrsus solvērunt; sed postquam pauca mīlia passuum prō- 5
gressī sunt, tanta tempestās subitō coorta est ut cursum 6
tenēre nōn possent, et ad eandem partem īnsulae unde 7
modo profectī erant magnō cum perīculō relātī sunt. Incolae 8
tamen, cum nox esset obscūra, Argonautās nōn ag- 9
nōscēbant, atque inimīcam nāvem vēnisse arbitrātī arma 10
cēpērunt eōsque ēgredī prohibēbant. Ācriter pugnātum est, 11
et rēx ipse, quī ad lītus dēcucurrerat, ab Argonautīs occīsus 12
est. Cum iam dīlūcēsceret, sēnsērunt incolae sē errāre 13
atque arma abiēcērunt; Argonautae autem cum rēgem occī- 14
sum esse vidērent, magnum dolōrem cēpērunt. 15

1. The Argonauts understood that they had set out so that Jason
   might get possession of the fleece.
2. They thought that everything had been given them that was useful
   for accomplishing this task.
3. When a great storm had arisen, they tried to hold their course, but
   they were prevented from advancing.
4. For this reason they determined to disembark that night so that
   they might refresh themselves.
5. As soon as they had reached land, an attack was made upon
   them.

Helpful Hints

1. For "that they had set out," use a perfect infinitive of a deponent verb, which
   has the same form as a perfect passive infinitive of a regular verb.
2. For "everything," use **omnia** "all things."
   The relative clause within the indirect statement will take the subjunctive.
   For "useful," use a dative of purpose.
3. Use an ablative absolute.
4. "For this reason": see paragraph 58, line 4 for a model.
   For "to disembark," see line 3 of paragraph 62 above.
5. To translate "had reached land," find a model in paragraph 62, lines 2–3,
   above. Use the perfect tense with **simul ac** or **simul atque** to translate
   the English pluperfect.

1 **Postrīdiē eius diēī**: note the use of the *genitive* with the *adverb*
  postrīdiē, "on the day after that day" = "on the next day." The phrase
  was used by the Romans with no real difference in meaning from the
  simple adverb **postrīdiē**.

3 **sublātīs ancorīs**: *ablative absolute*, "with the anchors having been
  weighed," "after he (Jason) had weighed anchor."
  *****ancora, -ae** (*f*), anchor.
  ancorās tollere, *idiom*, to weigh anchor.
  tollō, tollere (3), **sustulī, sublātum**, to lift, raise, take away, remove.
  Distinguish this verb carefully from **ferō, ferre** (*irreg*.), **tulī, lātum**,
  to bear, bring.

4 **Mӯsia, -ae** (*f*), Mysia (a country).

5 **in ancorīs**, *idiom*, at anchor.

6 **quam sēcum habēret**: why subjunctive?
  ob eam causam, *idiom*, on account of this reason, therefore.

8 **Quō in numerō**: "And in this number."
  *****Hylās, Hylae** (*m*), Hylas.

9 **Quī**: refers to **Hylas**, "And he."
  *****fōns, fontis, fontium** (*m*), fountain, spring.

12 **negāret**: "said . . . not."
  factūrum esse: what tense of the infinitive?

15 *****Polyphēmus, -ī** (*m*), Polyphemus.

16 **longius**: *comparative adverb*, "farther."

17 **solvisse**: **nāvem** is understood as *direct object*; the idiom may be used
   either with or without the noun.

Perfect Participles

Perfect participles that modify the *subject* of the main
verb in their clause can often best be translated as *fi-
nite verbs* parallel to the main verb, e.g., **In terram
ēgressī aquam petēbant**, "Having disembarked onto land, they were seeking water," or "They disembarked onto land and were seeking water," and **Magnō
dolōre affectī diū frūstrā quaerēbant**, "Having
been affected with great grief, they searched a long time
in vain," or "They were affected with great grief, and
they searched for a long time in vain." Note that perfect
participles show time before the main verb.

63. THE LOSS OF HYLAS

Postrīdiē eius diēī Iāsōn tempestātem satis idōneam 1
esse arbitrātus (summa enim tranquillitās iam cōnsecūta 2
erat) sublātīs ancorīs profectus est, et pauca mīlia pas- 3
suum prōgressus ante noctem Mȳsiam attigit. Ibi paucās 4
hōrās in ancorīs exspectāvit; ā nautīs enim cognōverat 5
aquae cōpiam quam sēcum habēret iam dēficere, atque ob 6
eam causam quīdam ex Argonautīs in terram ēgressī 7
aquam petēbant. Quō in numerō erat Hylās quīdam, puer 8
fōrmā praestantissimā. Quī dum fontem quaerit, ā 9
comitibus suīs paulum discessit. Nymphae autem quae 10
fontem colēbant, cum puerum vīdissent, eī persuādēre cōnā- 11
tae sunt ut apud sē manēret. Cum ille negāret sē hoc fac- 12
tūrum esse, eum vī abstulērunt. Comitēs postquam Hylam 13
āmissum esse sēnsērunt, magnō dolōre affectī diū frūstrā 14
quaerēbant. Herculēs autem et Polyphēmus, quī vēstīgia 15
puerī longius secūtī erant, ubi tandem ad lītus rediērunt, 16
Iāsonem solvisse cognōvērunt. 17

1. Drawing their swords, they withstood the attack bravely.
2. When the battle had raged for a long time, they perceived that they
   were using their swords against friends.
3. Not lingering even two days, they set out again.
4. A few hours later it happened that certain of the Argonauts went
   ashore to seek water.
5. One of them, although he had said that he would not remain there,
   was nevertheless compelled to remain.

Helpful Hints
1. The Latin idiom for "to draw a sword" is **gladium dēstringere**; use an ablative absolute here (see line 3 of paragraph 63 above). Be sure to use a
   tense of the participle in the ablative absolute that will show that the swords
   were drawn before the men withstood the attack.
2. Use **ubi** + perfect indicative.
   For "the battle had raged," find a model in line 11 of paragraph 62.
3. Use a perfect participle of a deponent verb for "lingering."
5. Use **cum** + subjunctive.

2   **Salmydēssus, -ī** (*f*), Salmydessus.

3   **quaesīssent**: = **quaesīvissent**.

4   **certiōrēs factī sunt**: see grammatical note with paragraph 37.

    Phīneum quendam tum rēgem esse: *indirect statement* after **certiōrēs factī sunt**.

    *****Phīneus, -ī** (*m*), Phineus.

5   *****caecus, -a, -um**, blind.

    hunc (virum) . . . esse . . . afficī: *indirect statement* with *infinitive*.

9   **virginum capita, corpora volucrum**: *chiasmus*, cf. paragraph 57, lines 1–2, and paragraph 61, line 3.

    *****volucris, volucris** (*f*), bird.

10   *****Harpyiae, -ārum** (*f pl*), Harpies.

11   **Quotiēns . . . accubuerat, . . . veniēbant . . . auferēbant**: *past general* (see grammar note with paragraph 19).

12   **accubuerat**: the Greeks and Romans reclined at dinner on couches, propped up on their left arm; they naturally represented others as eating in the same way.

    *****appōnō** (ad- + pōnō), **appōnere** (3), **apposuī**, **appositum**, to put to *or* near, set before, serve.

    appositum: "that had been set before (him)."

13   *****quīn** (*conj.*), that . . . not, but that, but, that.

    neque multum āfuit quīn . . . morerētur: **quīn** *clause* after a verb of *lacking*, "nor was much lacking but that he should die," better English, "and he was not far from death."

    *****famēs, famis**, (*abl.*) **famē** (*f*), hunger.

    famē: *ablative of cause;* note that **famēs** has a 5th declension ablative singular but is otherwise of the 3rd declension.

    morerētur: note the formation of the *imperfect subjunctive* of *deponent verbs.*

Quīn Clauses after Verbs of Lacking, Preventing, and Doubting

Quīn introduces *clauses* with their verbs in the *subjunctive* after verbs of *lacking, preventing,* and *doubting*, when they are *negatived*, e.g., **Neque multum āfuit quīn morerētur**, "Nor was much lacking but that he should die," better English, "And he was not far from death."

---

1. Not only the boy who had been seized, but Hercules and Polyphemus also were left behind.
2. Leaving them behind, the Argonauts went forward to the town of Salmydessus.
3. There they learned that Phineus, the king, would perish of hunger without the aid of the Argonauts.
4. For a god had sent monsters to prevent him from eating food.
5. And there was no doubt that these monsters had the bodies of birds.

64. DIFFICULT DINING

Ab eō locō Argonautae ad Thrāciam nāvigāvērunt. 1
Postquam ad oppidum Salmydēssum nāvem appulērunt, in 2
terram ēgressī sunt. Ibi cum ab incolīs quaesīssent quis 3
rēgnum eius regiōnis obtinēret, certiōrēs factī sunt Phīneum 4
quendam tum rēgem esse. Cognōvērunt etiam hunc caecum 5
esse et gravissimō suppliciō afficī, quod quondam sē 6
crūdēlissimum in fīliōs suōs praebuisset. Cuius supplicī 7
hoc erat genus. Missa erant ā Iove mōnstra quaedam 8
speciē horribilī, quae virginum capita, corpora volucrum 9
habēbant. Hae volucrēs, quae Harpyiae appellābantur, 10
Phīneō summum timōrem afferēbant. Quotiēns enim ille 11
accubuerat, statim veniēbant cibumque appositum aufe- 12
rēbant; neque multum āfuit quīn Phīneus famē morerētur. 13

Cum Inversum *(with paragraph 65)*

We have seen examples of **cum** *circumstantial clauses*
in which the subordinate clause describes the circumstances or the situation prior to or simultaneous with
the action of the main clause, e.g., <u>Cum reliquī</u>
fūgissent, Pholus ex spēluncā ēgressus est,
"<u>When</u> (<u>After</u>) the others <u>had fled</u>, Pholus went out of
the cave" (see grammar note with paragraph 27). In
these **cum** circumstantial clauses the pluperfect or
imperfect *subjunctive* is used if the verb of the main
clause is in a past tense (secondary sequence).

The *indicative* instead is used with **cum** if the **cum**
clause *follows* the main clause and expresses a *fact*,
while the main clause describes the circumstances or
the situation, e.g., **Male rēs sē habēbat** <u>cum</u> **Argonautae nāvem** <u>appulērunt</u>, "Things were in a bad
shape <u>when</u> the Argonauts <u>put in</u>." Since the logical relationship between the two clauses is, in a sense, in-
verted, this usage of **cum** with the indicative is called
cum inversum.

Helpful Hints
2. Use an ablative absolute.
4. For "eating food," use a deponent verb and a noun in the ablative case.
5. Use the dative of possession.

1   **Male . . . rēs sē habēbat:** "Things were in bad shape."
     cum . . . appulērunt: the *indicative* is used with **cum** "when" in *sec-
         ondary sequence* if the **cum** clause *follows* the main clause and ex-
         presses a *fact*, while the *main clause* describes the *circumstances* or *sit-
         uation.* So here the meaning is that the Argonauts came when things
         were in a desperate situation. This is called **cum inversum**; see
         grammar note on page 133.
3   **gaudeō, gaudēre** (2 *semideponent*), **gāvīsus sum**, to be glad, rejoice.
4   **opīniōnem virtūtis:** "reputation for bravery."
     *dubitō (1), to doubt, hesitate.
     nec dubitābat quīn . . . auxilium ferrent: quīn *clause* after a
         verb of *doubting* (see grammar note with paragraph 64); when the
         main verbal idea is negatived (**nec dubitābat,** "and he did not
         doubt"), what is not doubted is expressed by **quīn** and the *subjunctive,*
         "and he did not doubt (but) that they were bringing help."
6   **quī . . . vocāret:** *relative clause of purpose.*
9   **remedium, -ī** (*n*), remedy.
     sī illī remedium repperissent: *pluperfect subjunctive* replacing a *fu-
         ture perfect indicative* in what would have been the direct statement.
         Translate "if they found (should have found) a remedy for him."
13   **nihil prōdesse:** "availed nothing"; in this use, **nihil** is equivalent to an
         adverb and is stronger than **nōn.**
     prōdesse: from **prōsum.**
14   **Zētēs, Zētae** (*m*), Zetes.
     Calais, Calais (*m*), Calais.
     āla, -ae (*f*), wing.
15   **Quod:** "This"; **quod** summarizes the previous sentence.

Cum Inversum *(see note on page 133)*

Pluperfect Subjunctive Replacing a Future Perfect Indicative

A *future perfect indicative* in a *subordinate clause* in a
direct statement is changed to a *pluperfect subjunctive*
when the statement is reported indirectly in secondary
sequence, e.g., the statement **Magna praemia dabō,
sī remedium reppereritis** "I will give great rewards, if you find (will have found) a remedy," becomes
the following when stated indirectly: **Pollicitus est
sē magna praemia datūrum esse, sī illī remedium repperissent,** "He promised that he would give
great rewards, if they found (should have found) a remedy." This is a future more vivid condition (see
grammar note with paragraph 25) in indirect statement. The future perfect in the if-clause becomes a
pluperfect subjunctive, indicating prior time according to
the sequence of tenses, and the future indicative of the
main clause becomes a future infinitive.

65. THE DELIVERANCE OF PHINEUS

Male igitur rēs sē habēbat cum Argonautae nāvem ap- 1
pulērunt. Phīneus autem simul atque audīvit eōs per- 2
vēnisse, magnopere gāvīsus est. Sciēbat enim quantam 3
opīniōnem virtūtis Argonautae habērent, nec dubitābat 4
quīn sibi auxilium ferrent. Itaque nūntium ad nāvem 5
mīsit, quī Iāsonem sociōsque ad rēgiam vocāret. Eō cum 6
vēnissent, Phīneus dēmōnstrāvit quantō in perīculō suae 7
rēs essent, et pollicitus est sē magna praemia datūrum 8
esse, sī illī remedium repperissent. Argonautae negōtium 9
libenter suscēpērunt; et ubi hōra vēnit, cum rēge ac- 10
cubuērunt. Simul atque cēna apposita est, Harpyiae in- 11
trāvērunt et cibum auferre cōnābantur. Argonautae prī- 12
mum gladiīs volucrēs petiērunt; ubi vērō vīdērunt hoc nihil 13
prōdesse, Zētēs et Calais, quī ālīs erant īnstrūctī, in āera 14
sē sustulērunt, ut dēsuper impetum facerent. Quod cum 15
Harpyiae sēnsissent, reī novitāte perterritae statim 16
fūgērunt, neque posteā umquam rediērunt. 17

1. Phineus was in the greatest danger when the Argonauts put in.
2. Having learned this, they promised that they would not desert
   him, if the birds attacked him.
3. For they did not doubt that they could kill the birds.
4. Their reputation for bravery was so great that the king hoped that
   they would save him.
5. Having tried in vain to wound the birds, they adopted another
   plan.

Helpful Hints
1. See lines 1–2 of paragraph 65 above and the grammar note on page 133.
2. For "Having learned this," use an ablative absolute with linking **quī**.
   For the future more vivid condition in indirect statement, see lines 8–9 of
   paragraph 65 above and the grammar note on page 134.
3. Use **neque enim** at the beginning of this sentence to connect it with the
   previous sentence.
4. For "Their," use a form of linking **quī**.
   Find a model for "reputation for bravery" in paragraph 65 above.

2   **īnfestus, -a, -um,** unsafe, dangerous.

4   **eō cōnsiliō:** *ablative of manner,* "in accordance with this purpose."

5   **nē quis ad Colchida pervenīret:** *negative purpose clause,* "in order that no one."

6   **sī . . . vēnerat, . . . concurrēbant:** a *past general condition* with *pluperfect indicative* in the if-clause and *imperfect indicative* in the main clause, "if anything (ever) came in between, they (always) ran together. . . . "

     ***spatium, -ī** (n),* space, interval, space of time, time.

8   **quā ratiōne Symplēgadēs vītāre posset:** what kind of clause?

9   **sublātīs ancorīs:** *ablative absolute.*

     lēnis, -is, -e, gentle.

10   **prōra, -ae** (f), prow, bow.

     stāns: *nominative masculine singular present participle* of **stō, stāre,** modifying the subject of **ēmīsit.**

     columba, -ae (f), pigeon, dove.

12   **cōnflīgō, cōnflīgere** (3), **cōnflīxī, cōnflīctum,** to dash together.

     caudā sōlā āmissā: *ablative absolute.*

13   **utrimque** (*adv.*), on either side *or* both sides.

14   **priusquam . . . concurrerent: priusquam** with the *subjunctive* in past time to indicate *anticipation* or *expectancy,* "before they could run together"; contrast this with the *perfect indicative* with **priusquam** (line 12), which is used to represent a past action as a *fact.*

     intellegentēs: *present active participle,* modifying **Argonautae,** "since they understood."

15   **positus esse** (with **in** + *abl.*), to be placed in, rest *or* depend on.

16   ***rēmus, -ī** (m),* oar.

17   **dīs:** *alternate form of* **deīs.**

     quod . . . ēreptī essent: quod *causal clause* with the *subjunctive* indicating that the reason given is not guaranteed to be a fact by the author but is someone else's alleged reason. The subjunctive implies that the reason given here is that of the Argonauts. The effect of the subjunctive may be reproduced in English by adding "as they felt" or "as they said." See grammar note on page 138.

     auxiliō: *ablative of cause,* "with the help."

19   ***ēveniō, ēvenīre** (4), **ēvēnī, ēventum,** to come out, turn out, happen, befall.

Past General Conditions

Conditional sentences with the *pluperfect indicative* in the if-clause and the *imperfect indicative* in the main clause describe general situations in past time and are called *past general conditions,* e.g., **Sī quid in medium spatium vēnerat, incrēdibilī celeritāte concurrēbant,** "If anything (ever) came in the space between, they (always) ran together with incredible speed." See the grammar note on past general with paragraph 19. *Continued on next page*

66. THE SYMPLEGADES

Hōc factō Phīneus, ut prō tantō beneficiō meritam grā- 1
tiam referret, Iāsonī dēmōnstrāvit quam īnfestae Symplē- 2
gadēs essent. Symplēgadēs autem duo erant saxa ingentī 3
magnitūdine, quae ā Iove in marī posita erant eō cōnsiliō, 4
nē quis ad Colchida pervenīret. Haec parvō intervāllō in 5
marī natābant, et sī quid in medium spatium vēnerat, in- 6
crēdibilī celeritāte concurrēbant. Postquam igitur ā Phīneō 7
doctus est quā ratiōne Symplēgadēs vītāre posset, Iāsōn 8
sublātīs ancorīs lēnī ventō prōvectus brevī tempore illīs 9
saxīs appropinquāvit. Tum in prōrā stāns columbam quam 10
in manū tenēbat ēmīsit. Illa per medium spatium volāvit, 11
et priusquam saxa cōnflīxērunt, incolumis caudā sōlā 12
āmissā ēvāsit. Tum saxa utrimque discessērunt; itaque 13
priusquam rūrsus concurrerent, Argonautae, intellegentēs 14
omnem spem salūtis in celeritāte positam esse, summā vī 15
rēmīs contendērunt ac nāvem incolumem perdūxērunt. Hōc 16
factō dīs grātiās maximās ēgērunt, quod eōrum auxiliō ē 17
tantō perīculō ēreptī essent; omnēs enim sciēbant nōn sine 18
auxiliō deōrum rem tam fēlīciter ēvēnisse. 19

> Note that in translating general conditions the word
> *ever* may be inserted in the if-clause and the word *al-*
> *ways* in the main clause, thus reinforcing the generality
> or universality of the conditional statement.

Quod Causal Clauses with the Subjunctive
(see page 138)

1. When the birds had been overcome, the king thanked the Argonauts, because they had saved his life.
2. If the Argonauts (ever) came into new dangers, they (always)
   adopted a suitable plan.
3. It was necessary to sail between the two rocks before they could
   dash together.
4. Before the Argonauts departed, Jason urged that no one should
   fear.
5. They said that they had not given up hope of safety.

Helpful Hints
1. Use an ablative absolute.
   For the mood of the verb in the causal clause, see lines 17–18 of
   paragraph 66 above, and see the grammar note on page 138.
2. See lines 6–7 of paragraph 66 above and see the grammar note on page 136.

1   **intermittō, intermittere** (3), **intermīsī, intermissum,** to leave
     off, interrupt, let pass; (*passive*) to be left between, intervene, elapse.
     Phāsis, Phāsidis (*m*), Phasis.
2   *__**Colchī, -ōrum** (*m pl*), Colchians.
5   **audīsset:** = **audīvisset.**
8   **mūtō** (1), to change.
9   **trāditūrum:** supply **esse** (cf. lines 6–7) = *future active infinitive* (**esse** is
     often omitted with perfect passive and future active infinitives).
     sī . . . perfēcisset: *pluperfect subjunctive* replacing a *future perfect
     indicative* in the original direct statement (*future more vivid condition*).
     See grammar note with paragraph 65.
10   *__**prius** (*comparative adverb*), before, first.
12   *__**iungō, iungere** (3), **iūnxī, iūnctum,** to join, yoke, harness.
     iungendī erant: *passive periphrastic* expressing *obligation* or *necessity.*
13   **hīs iūnctīs:** *ablative absolute.*
14   *__**arō** (1), to plow.
     arandus erat: *passive periphrastic.*
     *__**dēns, dentis** (*m*), tooth.
     serō, serere (3), **sēvī, satum,** to sow, plant.
     serendī (supply **erant**): *passive periphrastic,* **dentēs** is subject.
16   **reī bene gerendae:** "of doing a thing well."

Quod Causal Clauses with the Subjunctive
(with paragraph 66)

When **quod** "because" gives a reason for which the
writer takes full responsibility, the *indicative* is used,
and the reason is being stated as a fact; when **quod** is
used with the *subjunctive*, the implication is that the
reason being stated is that of someone other than the
author and that the author does not take responsibility
for it, e.g., **Hōc factō dīs grātiās maximās
ēgērunt, quod eōrum auxiliō ē tantō perīculō
ēreptī essent,** "With this done, they gave the greatest
thanks to the gods, <u>because</u> (as they felt) they had been
rescued from such great danger with their help." The
words "as they felt" have been added to the translation
to indicate that the reason given is that of the
Argonauts and not of the author.

Helpful Hints
2. For "held the throne of that country," see paragraph 64, line 4.
3. Use a future active participle to express the idea of "intending" (see grammar note with paragraph 58).
5. Be sure that the tense of the verb in the "When. . . . " clause indicates time
    before that of the main verb.
    For "what was to be done," use a passive periphrastic as an indirect
    question.

67. A HEAVY TASK

Brevī intermissō spatiō Argonautae ad flūmen Phāsim 1
vēnērunt, quod in fīnibus Colchōrum erat. Cum nāvem ap- 2
pulissent atque ēgressī essent, statim ad rēgem Aeētam sē 3
contulērunt, et ab eō postulāvērunt ut vellus aureum sibi 4
trāderētur. Ille cum audīsset quam ob causam Argonautae 5
vēnissent, īrā commōtus diū negāvit sē vellus trāditūrum 6
esse. Tandem tamen, quod sciēbat Iāsonem nōn sine aux- 7
iliō deōrum hoc negōtium suscēpisse, mūtātā sententiā pol- 8
licitus est sē vellus trāditūrum, sī Iāsōn labōrēs duōs diffi- 9
cillimōs prius perfēcisset; et cum Iāsōn dīxisset sē ad om- 10
nia perīcula subeunda parātum esse, quid fierī vellet os- 11
tendit. Prīmum iungendī erant duo taurī speciē horribilī, 12
quī flammam ex ōre efflābant; deinde hīs iūnctīs ager quī- 13
dam arandus erat et dentēs dracōnis serendī. Hāc rē 14
audītā Iāsōn etsī rem esse summī perīculī intellegēbat, 15
tamen, nē hanc occāsiōnem reī bene gerendae āmitteret, 16
negōtium suscēpit. 17

Passive Periphrastic Conjugation

The *gerundive* or *future passive participle* (ending in
-ndus, -nda, -ndum) can be used with any form of
the verb **sum** to form a *passive periphrastic*; the meaning is "am to be," "should be," or "must be," expressing
obligation or *necessity*, e.g., **iungendī erant duo
taurī**, "two bulls had to be yoked," **ager arandus
erat**, "a field had to be plowed," and **dentēs dracōnis serendī (erant)**, "dragon's teeth had to be sown."

Continued on page 142

---

1. They brought the ship through and came to the land where the fleece was.
2. Aeetes held the throne of that country when they came.
3. He did not doubt that they were intending to demand the fleece from him.
4. He had adopted a disgraceful plan so that no one might get possession of this.
5. When Jason asked him what was to be done, the king informed him of this plan.

1   *Mēdēa, -ae (f), Medea.
     adamō (1) (+ acc.), to fall in love with.
2   *aegrē (adv.), ill, with difficulty.
     rem aegrē ferre, idiom, to take it badly, be upset.
4   Quae cum ita essent: "Since these things were so."
6   *īnsciēns, īnscientis, unknowing, unaware.
     īnsciente patre: ablative absolute. Note that the ablative singular of
        the present participle (see grammar note with paragraph 26) usually
        ends in -e when used in an ablative absolute and in -ī when used as a
        simple adjective.
7   *herba, -ae (f) herb, plant.
     carpō, carpere (3), carpsī, carptum, to pluck.
8   sūcus, -ī (m), juice.
     exprimō (ex- + premō), exprimere (3), expressī, expressum, to
        press out.
        sūcō expressō: ablative absolute.
     *unguentum, -ī (n), ointment.
     quod . . . aleret . . . cōnfīrmāret: relative clause of characteristic,
        describing or characterizing the general group of which the antecedent
        is a particular example, "which (was the sort that) would nourish and
        strengthen."
9   alō, alere (3), aluī, altum, to nourish.
     nervus, -ī (m), sinew, muscle.
10 cōnficiendī essent: subjunctive by attraction.
11 māne, in the morning.
     Distinguish this adverb carefully from the verb maneō, manēre (2),
        mānsī, to remain (particularly from the imperative, manē).
     oblinō, oblinere (3), oblēvī, oblitum, to daub over, smear.
12 omnibus hominibus: dative with the compound verb praestābat,
     "surpassed all men."
     magnitūdine et vīribus: ablative of respect, "in size and strength."
13 *praestō, praestāre (1), praestitī, praestitum, (trans.) to show;
        (intrans. + dative with the intransitive compound verb and ablative of
        respect) to stand before, surpass, excel.
     vēnātiō, vēnātiōnis (f), hunting, hunt.
15 neglegō, neglegere (3), neglēxī, neglēctum, to disregard, neglect.
     hoc cōnsilium nōn neglegendum: supply esse, which is often
        omitted with the passive periphrastic in indirect statement, "that this
        plan was not to be neglected."
     *putō (1), to think.

1. Jason surpassed all men in bravery when he said he would un-
     dergo these dangers.
2. He did not doubt that the gods were going to bring him help.
3. Medea, moreover, deserting her father, came to his aid.
4. She hurried into the mountains adjacent to the city in the middle of
     the night, so that no one might see her.
5. She knew that Jason's body must be strengthened, because he had
     undertaken a most difficult labor.

68. THE MAGIC OINTMENT

At Mēdēa, rēgis fīlia, Iāsonem adamāverat; et ubi audīvit 1
eum tantum perīculum subitūrum esse, rem aegrē tulit. In- 2
tellegēbat enim patrem suum hunc labōrem prōposuisse eō 3
cōnsiliō, ut Iāsōn morerētur. Quae cum ita essent, Mēdēa, 4
quae summam scientiam artis magicae habēbat, hoc cōnsi- 5
lium iniit. Mediā nocte īnsciente patre ex urbe ēvāsit. 6
Postquam in fīnitimōs montēs vēnit, herbās quāsdam carp- 7
sit; tum sūcō expressō unguentum parāvit, quod vī suā cor- 8
pus aleret nervōsque cōnfīrmāret. Hōc factō Iāsonī unguen- 9
tum dedit; praecēpit autem ut eō diē quō istī labōrēs cōnfi- 10
ciendī essent corpus suum et arma māne oblineret. Iāsōn 11
etsī paene omnibus hominibus magnitūdine et vīribus cor- 12
poris praestābat (vīta enim omnis in vēnātiōnibus atque in 13
studiō reī mīlitāris cōnsistēbat), tamen hoc cōnsilium nōn 14
neglegendum putābat. 15

> **Relative Clauses of Characteristic**
>
> When a *relative clause* has its verb in the *indicative*, it states a *fact* about the antecedent. When the verb of a relative clause is in the *subjunctive*, it may *describe* or *characterize* the general group of which the antecedent is a particular example, e.g., **Unguentum parāvit, quod vī suā corpus aleret nervōsque cōnfīrmāret**, "She prepared an ointment, <u>which</u> (was the sort that) <u>would nourish</u> the body and <u>strengthen</u> the muscles by its potency." Rather than stating a fact about the antecedent, the relative clause here characterizes the antecedent by describing the general sort of thing that it is.
>
> Another type of relative clause that takes the subjunctive is the *relative clause of purpose* (see grammar note with paragraph 33); there are also *relative clauses of result*, which also take the subjunctive (see grammar note with paragraph 74).

Helpful Hints
1. See lines 2 and 11–13 of paragraph 68 above.
2. For the nominative plural of the word for "god," see the Latin to English vocabulary at the end of this book.
   For "him," use **ad** + *acc.* of the pronoun.
3. For "deserting her father," use an ablative absolute with a perfect participle.
   For "to his aid," use the double dative construction.

2   *orior, orīrī (4), ortus sum, to arise, rise, come forth, spring up.
      *ortā lūce, idiom, at dawn.
3   ingēns, ingentis, huge. Note that the form ingēns can be *masculine,
      feminine,* or *neuter.*
5   iugum, -ī (n), yoke.
6   *valeō, valēre (2), valuī, valītum, to be strong *or* effective, have ef-
      fect, prevail.
        Distinguish this verb carefully from the verbs volō (1), to fly, and
          volō, velle (*irreg.*), voluī, to be willing, wish.
8   omnibus īnspectantibus: *ablative absolute.*
9   *merīdiēs, -ēī (m), midday, noon, south.
12   *spargō, spargere (3), sparsī, sparsum, to scatter, sprinkle.
13   sēmentis, sēmentis (f), seeding, sowing.
      sēmentēs: English uses the singular.
    factae essent: *subjunctive by attraction.*
14   mīrō quōdam modō: "in a certain strange manner."
    *gignō, gignere (3), genuī, genitum, to produce, bring forth.

Passive Periphrastic Conjugation (continued from paragraph 67)

Indicative

Present	amandus sum	I am to be, must be, loved
Imperfect	amandus eram	I was to be, had to be, loved
Future	amandus erō	I will have to be loved
Perfect	amandus fuī	I was to be, had to be, loved
Pluperfect	amandus fueram	I had had to be loved
Future Perfect	amandus fuerō	I will have had to be loved

Subjunctive

Present	amandus sim
Imperfect	amandus essem
Perfect	amandus fuerim
Pluperfect	amandus fuissem

Infinitive

Present	amandus esse	to have to be loved
Perfect	amandus fuisse	to have had to be loved

69. THE SOWING OF THE DRAGON'S TEETH

Ubi ea diēs vēnit quam rēx ad arandum agrum dīxerat, 1
Iāsōn ortā lūce cum sociīs ad locum cōnstitūtum sē contulit. 2
Ibi stabulum ingēns repperit, in quō taurī erant inclūsī; 3
tum ōstiō apertō taurōs in lūcem trāxit, et summā cum dif- 4
ficultāte eīs iugum imposuit. At Aeētēs cum vidēret taurōs 5
nihil contrā Iāsonem valēre, magnopere mīrātus est; 6
nesciēbat enim fīliam suam auxilium eī dedisse. Tum 7
Iāsōn omnibus īnspectantibus agrum arāre coepit, quā in rē 8
tantam dīligentiam adhibuit ut ante merīdiem tōtum opus 9
cōnficeret. Hōc factō ad locum ubi rēx sedēbat adiit, et den- 10
tēs dracōnis postulāvit; quōs ubi accēpit, in agrum quem 11
arāverat magnā cum dīligentiā sparsit. Hōrum autem den- 12
tium nātūra erat tālis ut in eō locō ubi sēmentēs factae 13
essent virī armātī mīrō quōdam modō gignerentur. 14

1. At dawn the king sent Jason to yoke the two bulls.
2. He hoped that their fire would consume him.
3. While all wondered, Jason accomplished the labor that the king
   had imposed upon him.
4. Having yoked the bulls, he did not fear that he would be compelled
   to desist from his attempt.
5. He saw that the king himself was terrified, because the bulls had
   not prevailed against him.

Helpful Hints
1. For "At dawn," find a model in line 2 of paragraph 69 above.
2. For "that . . . ," use accusative and infinitive.
3. For "upon him," use the dative.
4. Use an ablative absolute.
5. For the negative, use **nihil**; see lines 5–6 of paragraph 69 above.

4   *lassitūdō, lassitūdinis (f), weariness, fatigue.

5   **dum virī istī gignerentur**: **dum** with *imperfect subjunctive* in *secondary sequence*, meaning "until" and denoting *expectancy*, "until those men might be produced."

       sub vesperum: "toward evening."

7   **ut praedictum esset**: *subjunctive* in a *subordinate clause* in *indirect statement*; the original thought would have been **ut praedictum est**, "as it was predicted."

       praedīcō, praedīcere (3), **praedīxī, praedictum**, to say beforehand, foretell, predict.

9   **mīrum in modum**: = **mīrō modō**. The word **modus** is sometimes used in the accusative in phrases with **in** where we would expect an *ablative of manner*.

10   **quod Mēdēa dedisset**: why subjunctive?

      omittendum esse: *passive periphrastic* in *indirect statement*. What would the words have been in direct statement?

13   **sibi**: *dative of reference*, "for himself."

14   *contrōversia, -ae (f), quarrel, dispute, debate.

15   **dēstringō, dēstringere** (3), **dēstrīnxī, dēstrictum**, to draw, unsheathe.

Dum + Subjunctive = "until"

Dum with the *subjunctive* means "until" and suggests *expectancy* or *anticipation*, e.g., **Iāsōn quiētī sē trādidit, dum virī istī gignerentur**, "Jason rested until those men might be produced." The present subjunctive is used in primary sequence and the imperfect subjunctive in secondary sequence (see grammar note with paragraph 24). Contrast this with the use of **dum** with the indicative meaning "while" or "as long as" (see grammar notes with paragraphs 5 and 8). Compare the use here of **dum** with the subjunctive with the use of **antequam** or **priusquam** with the subjunctive (see grammar note with paragraph 50).

70. A STRANGE CROP

Nōndum tamen Iāsōn hunc labōrem cōnfēcerat; im- 1
perāverat enim eī Aeētēs ut armātōs virōs quī ē dentibus 2
gignerentur sōlus interficeret. Postquam omnēs dentēs in 3
agrum sparsit, Iāsōn lassitūdine exanimātus quiētī sē trā- 4
didit, dum virī istī gignerentur. Paucās hōrās dormiēbat, 5
sed sub vesperum ē somnō subitō excitātus rem ita 6
ēvēnisse ut praedictum esset cognōvit; nam in omnibus agrī 7
partibus virī ingentī magnitūdine corporum gladiīs 8
galeīsque armātī mīrum in modum ē terrā oriēbantur. Hāc 9
rē cognitā Iāsōn cōnsilium quod Mēdēa dedisset nōn omit- 10
tendum esse putābat. Itaque saxum ingēns, ut Mēdēa 11
praecēperat, in mediōs virōs coniēcit. Illī undique ad eum 12
locum concurrērunt; et cum sibi quisque id saxum habēre 13
vellet, magna contrōversia orta est. Brevī tempore gladiīs 14
dēstrictīs inter sē pugnāre coepērunt; et cum plūrimī hōc 15
modō occīsī essent, reliquī vulneribus cōnfectī ā Iāsone 16
nūllō negōtiō interfectī sunt. 17

1. And so he was waiting until the armed (men) might be produced
   from the earth.
2. While Jason waited, Medea prepared everything for flight.
3. She feared for herself, because she had brought aid to Jason without her father's knowledge.
4. Toward evening Jason, seeing that the men were rising, followed
   Medea's plan.
5. Hurling a stone, he killed them while they were fighting among
   themselves.

Helpful Hints
2. For "while," use **dum**.
3. Find the Latin for "without her father's knowledge" in paragraph 68.
4. Find a model for "toward evening" in paragraph 70 above.
5. Use an ablative absolute.

2   **id**: *indirect statement*, "this," "it," with **factum esse**.
     ***dolus, -ī** (m)*, trick, craft.
3   **quīn . . . tulisset**: **quīn** clause after verb of *doubting*.
5   **fore**: alternative *future active infinitive* of **sum** = **futūram esse**.
     sī in rēgiā manēret: *imperfect subjunctive* replacing a *future indicative* in the implied direct statement of this *future more vivid condition*. What would the direct statement have been?
7   ***Absyrtus, -ī** (m)*, Absyrtus.
8   ***subdūcō, subdūcere** (3), **subdūxī, subductum**, to draw up, beach.
10   **nē . . . dēsereret**: what kind of clause?
     ***discrīmen, discrīminis** (n)*, crisis, peril, danger.
     dēserō, dēserere (3), **dēseruī, dēsertum**, to desert.
11   **prōsum, prōdesse** (*irreg.*), **prōfuī** (+ *dat.*), to be of advantage, profit, assist.
     ***memoriā tenēre**, *idiom*, to hold by memory, remember.
14   **sē . . . avectūrum** (supply **esse**): *indirect statement*.
15   **āvehō, āvehere** (3), **āvexī, āvectum**, to carry away.

> ### Imperfect Subjunctive Replacing a Future Indicative
>
> A *future indicative* in a *subordinate clause* in a direct statement is changed to an *imperfect subjunctive* when the statement is reported indirectly in secondary sequence, e.g., the statement **In magnō perīculō erō, sī in rēgiā <u>manēbō</u>** "I will be in great danger, if I <u>remain</u> in the palace" becomes the following when stated indirectly: **Mēdēa intellegēbat sē in magnō fore perīculō sī in rēgiā <u>manēret</u>**, "Medea understood that she would be in great danger if she <u>stayed</u> in the palace." (Compare the grammar note with paragraph 65 on the pluperfect subjunctive replacing a future perfect indicative.)

> ### Perfect Subjunctive
>
> The perfect subjunctive will be required in some of the English to Latin translation exercises. It is used in subordinate clauses in primary sequence to indicate action completed prior to the time of the action of the verb of the main clause. See the grammar note with paragraph 24. For the forms of the perfect subjunctive, see the charts at the end of this book.

71. THE FLIGHT OF MEDEA

At rēx Aeētēs ubi Iāsonem labōrem prōpositum cōnfē- 1
cisse cognōvit, graviter commōtus est; id enim per dolum 2
factum esse intellegēbat, nec dubitābat quīn Mēdēa eī aux- 3
ilium tulisset. Mēdēa autem cum intellegeret sē in magnō 4
fore perīculō sī in rēgiā manēret, fugā salūtem petere cōn- 5
stituit. Omnibus rēbus ad fugam parātīs mediā nocte īn- 6
sciente patre cum frātre Absyrtō ēvāsit, et quam celerrimē 7
ad locum ubi Argō subducta erat sē contulit. Eō cum vēnis- 8
set, sē ad pedēs Iāsonis prōiēcit, ac multīs cum lacrimīs 9
eum obsecrāvit nē in tantō discrīmine mulierem dēsereret 10
quae eī tantum prōfuisset. Ille quod memoriā tenēbat sē 11
eius auxiliō ē magnō perīculō ēvāsisse, libenter eam excēpit; 12
et postquam causam veniendī repperit, hortātus est nē pa- 13
tris īram timēret. Pollicitus est autem sē quam prīmum 14
eam nāvī suā āvectūrum. 15

1. Jason was now permitted to go to that place where the fleece was
   to be found.
2. He desired to do this as soon as possible, but decided to delay until Medea should lead him.
3. While Jason was delaying, Medea fled to the ship.
4. She urged Jason to rescue her from danger, if he could.
5. We cannot doubt that he remembered that she had come to his
   aid.

Helpful Hints

1. For "was to be found," use a passive periphrastic.
5. For "remembered," see line 11 of paragraph 71 above and the vocabulary
   note.
       Primary sequence requires the perfect subjunctive in the subordinate
   clause here to indicate time before the main verb.

3   **rēmīs**: this shows that they were truly in a hurry, for otherwise they
     would have relied on sails.
     quō in locō: translate "in which"; the antecedent is repeated in the rela-
     tive clause and need not be translated.

5   **quī . . . essent**: *relative clause of purpose.*
     *praesidium, -ī (*n*), protection, guard, escort.
     praesidiō nāvī: *double dative.*

7   **suspendō** (subs- = sub- + pōnō), **suspendere** (3), **suspendī**,
     suspēnsum, to hang up, hang.

8   **Id . . . auferre**: **auferre** is subject of **erat**, and **id** is the direct object of
     auferre. **Auferre** could be translated by an infinitive or a gerund, but
     Latin has no nominative gerund.

9   **ēgregiē** (*adv.*), excellently, splendidly, admirably.
     et . . . et: "both . . . and."
     *mūniō (4), to fortify.

13   *dēripiō** (dē- + rapiō), **dēripere** (3), **dēripuī**, **dēreptum**, to snatch
     down from *or* away, tear off, pull down.

14   **faucēs, faucium** (*f pl*), throat, jaws, mouth.

15   **illum**: not with **venēnum**.

17   **pedem referre**, *idiom*, to draw back, retire, retreat.

72. THE SEIZURE OF THE FLEECE

Postrīdiē eius diēī Iāsōn cum sociīs suīs ortā lūce nāvem 1
dēdūxit, et idōneam tempestātem nactus ad eum locum 2
rēmīs contendit, quō in locō Mēdēa vellus abditum esse dē- 3
mōnstrāverat. Cum eō vēnissent, Iāsōn ēgressus est; et so- 4
ciīs ad mare relictīs, quī praesidiō nāvī essent, ipse cum 5
Mēdēā in silvās sē contulit. Pauca mīlia passuum per sil- 6
vās prōgressus vellus quod quaerēbat in arbore suspēnsum 7
vīdit. Id tamen auferre erat summae difficultātis; namque 8
nōn sōlum locus ipse ēgregiē et nātūrā et arte erat mūnītus, 9
sed etiam dracō quīdam horribilī speciē arborem custōdiē- 10
bat. At Mēdēa, quae, ut suprā dēmōnstrāvimus, magicae 11
artis summam scientiam habēbat, rāmum quem dē arbore 12
proximā dēripuerat venēnō imbuit. Hōc factō dracōnī ap- 13
propinquāvit, quī faucibus apertīs eius adventum exspectā- 14
bat, atque in illum venēnum sparsit; deinde, dum dracō 15
somnō oppressus dormit, Iāsōn vellus aureum dē arbore 16
dēripuit, et cum Mēdēā quam celerrimē pedem rettulit. 17

1. Having launched his ship, Jason set out with Medea as soon as possible.
2. He wished not only to guard her, but also to use her help.
3. He was unwilling to wait until Aeetes should be prepared to follow.
4. When he had gone into the forest in which the fleece was hidden, he seized it and departed.
5. Since this had been accomplished by her help, Medea urged him to remember those things that he had promised.

Helpful Hints
1. Use an ablative absolute.
4. For "had gone," use the same idiom as in line 6 of paragraph 72 above.
5. Use a **cum** circumstantial clause.

2   *ānxius, -a, -um, anxious.
3   summī . . . perīculī: *predicate genitive of description* in an *indirect statement*, "for they understood that that task was (one) of the greatest danger."
    ad occāsum sōlis, *idiom*, until sunset.
5   aliquī: *adjective*, "some," corresponding to the *pronoun* aliquis, "someone," "anyone."
6   mātūrandum sibi (supply esse): *passive periphrastic* in *indirect statement*; mātūrandum is an *impersonal passive*, "it must be hurried," and sibi is *dative of agent* with the *passive periphrastic*, "by themselves" = "they must hurry."
7   *dux, ducis (*m/f*), leader, commander.
8   cōnspiciunt and concurrunt (line 10): *vivid or historic present* (see grammar note with paragraph 7).
9   ēlūceō, ēlūcēre (2), ēlūxī, to shine out, shine.
    ēlūcēns: *present participle* modifying lūmen. Remember that for a neuter noun the accusative is the same as the nominative and that the rule is the same for the present participle.
10 Quō: *linking* quī = Et eō, "And . . . to that place."
11 Iāsonī et Mēdēae advenientibus: *dative* with the *compound verb* occurrērunt.
14 dīs: *dative plural* of deus.
    quod . . . ēvēnisset: quod *causal clause* with the *subjunctive*, indicating that the reason given is not guaranteed to be a fact by the author but is someone else's alleged reason.

Dative of Agent with the Passive Periphrastic

With the *passive periphrastic conjugation*, the *person by whom* the thing is to be done is regularly denoted by the *dative*, not by a b and the ablative, e.g., Mātūrandum sibi putāvērunt, "They thought that it must be hurried by themselves," better English, "They thought that they must hurry." This is called the *dative of agent*.

73. THE RETURN OF THE ARGO

Dum autem ea geruntur, Argonautae, quī ad mare relictī 1
erant, ānxiō animō reditum Iāsonis exspectābant; id enim 2
negōtium summī esse perīculī intellegēbant. Cum iam ad 3
occāsum sōlis frūstrā exspectāvissent, dē eius salūte 4
dēspērāre coepērunt, nec dubitābant quīn aliquī cāsus ac- 5
cidisset. Quae cum ita essent, mātūrandum sibi 6
putāvērunt, ut ducī auxilium ferrent; sed dum proficīscī 7
parant, lūmen quoddam subitō cōnspiciunt mīrum in 8
modum intrā silvās ēlūcēns, et magnopere mīrātī quae 9
causa esset eius reī ad locum concurrunt. Quō cum vēnis- 10
sent, Iāsonī et Mēdēae advenientibus occurrērunt, vel- 11
lusque aureum eius lūminis causam esse cognōvērunt. 12
Omnī timōre sublātō ducem suum magnō cum gaudiō ex- 13
cēpērunt, ac dīs grātiās maximās ēgērunt, quod rēs tam 14
fēlīciter ēvēnisset. 15

1. Since his companions had been left on the shore, Jason thought that he ought to return as soon as possible.
2. While they were awaiting his return, a certain fear seized them.
3. For they understood that he had undertaken a very difficult task.
4. They remembered also all the dangers into which they had come before.
5. And so, when Jason brought the fleece back, they thanked the gods, because they had preserved him.

Helpful Hints

1. Use a passive periphrastic with the dative of agent.
4. Place the word for "all" first in your translation and the word for "also" second.
5. Be sure that the tense of the verb in the temporal clause indicates time before that of the main verb.
   Use the subjunctive in the **quod** causal clause (see grammar note on page 138).

2   **vigilia, -ae** (*f*), watch (the Romans divided the day, from sunrise to sunset, into twelve hours, **hōrae**, and the night, from sunset to sunrise, into four watches, **vigiliae**).

4   **ante:** *adverb.*

     inimīcō . . . animō: *ablative of description,* "of hostile mind."

     in eōs: "against them."

5   **sē . . . recipere,** *idiom,* to betake oneself, go.

     sē . . . recēpisse . . . iūvisse (line 6): *indirect statement.*

6   **iuvō, iuvāre** (1), **iūvī, iūtum,** to help.

     gravius: *comparative adverb.*

7   **exārdēscō, exārdēscere,** (3), **exārsī, exārsum,** to blaze out, be inflamed, rage.

     nāvis longa, *idiom,* warship (the adjective contrasts the shape of a warship with that of a merchantman).

8   **fugientēs:** *participle* used as a *substantive,* "the fugitives."

     īnsequor, īnsequī (3), **īnsecūtus sum,** to follow upon *or* up, pursue.

11   **nōn eādem celeritāte** (supply **prōgredī poterant**) **quā Colchī prōgredī poterant.**

     eādem celeritāte quā: "with the same speed as," literally, "with the same speed with which."

12   **neque multum āfuit quīn . . . caperentur: quīn** *clause* after a verb of *lacking,* "nor was much lacking but that they should be caught," better English, "and they were not far from being caught" (see grammar note with paragraph 64).

14   **quam quō . . . posset:** *result clause* introduced by a *relative adverb,* **quō** (**ut eō**), "than that a spear could be thrown to that place," better English, "than to where a spear could be thrown."

     adiciō (ad- + iaciō), **adicere** (3), **adiēcī, adiectum,** to throw to, throw, hurl.

     at, but (introducing a strong change in situation).

Relative Clauses of Result

Relative pronouns or *relative adverbs* such as **quō** may introduce *result clauses,* with their verbs in the *subjunctive,* e.g., **Nāvis Aeētae nōn longius aberat quam quō tēlum adicī posset,** "The ship of Aeetes was no further away than to where a spear could be thrown." The idea of result may be clearer if we rephrase the translation: "The ship was so close that (as a result) a spear could be thrown to it." The relative adverb **quō** here = **ut eō,** "that (as a result) . . . to that place."

74. THE PURSUIT

Hīs rēbus gestīs omnēs sine morā nāvem rūrsus cōn- 1
scendērunt, et prīmā vigiliā solvērunt; neque enim satis tū- 2
tum esse arbitrābantur in eō locō manēre. At rēx Aeētēs, 3
quī iam ante inimīcō in eōs animō fuerat, ubi cognōvit 4
fīliam suam nōn sōlum sē ad Argonautās recēpisse, sed 5
etiam eōs ad vellus auferendum iūvisse, hōc dolōre gravius 6
exārsit. Nāvem longam quam celerrimē dēdūcī iussit, et 7
mīlitibus impositīs fugientēs īnsecūtus est. Argonautae, 8
quī rem in discrīmine esse bene sciēbant, omnibus vīribus 9
rēmīs contendēbant. Cum tamen nāvis quā vehēbantur in- 10
gentī esset magnitūdine, nōn eādem celeritāte quā Colchī 11
prōgredī poterant; neque multum āfuit quīn ā Colchīs se- 12
quentibus caperentur. Iam nāvis Aeētae nōn longius 13
aberat quam quō tēlum adicī posset. At Mēdēa cum vīdis- 14
set quō in locō rēs esset, paene omnī spē salūtis dēpositā 15
hoc crūdēle cōnsilium cēpit. 16

1. Although all the Argonauts were brave men, nevertheless none of
   them except Jason was of such great courage that he dared to take
   the fleece.
2. They departed from that country not because of fear, but that they
   might not lose the fleece, which they were guarding.
3. Since they understood that they ought to hurry, they embarked in
   the first watch.
4. Launching a warship, Aeetes began to pursue the fleeing Argonauts.
5. Since a smaller ship had been launched, he advanced with greater
   speed.

Helpful Hints
1. Use a **cum** clause, a partitive genitive, a genitive of description, and a relative clause of result.
3. Use a passive periphrastic and dative of agent. For "in the first watch," find a model in paragraph 74 above.
4. Use an ablative absolute.
5. Use an ablative absolute.

3   **fugiēns**: *present participle*, modifying **Mēdēa**. This is an especially good example of how the present participle shows *same* time as that of the main verb.

   abdūcō, abdūcere (3), **abdūxī, abductum**, to lead *or* take away.

4   *****membrum, -ī** (*n*), limb, member.

5   *****exīstimō** (1), to consider, believe, think.

6   **Aeētam, cum membra fīlī vīdisset, non longius prōsecūtū-rum esse**: what would the original thought have been, of which this is an indirect statement? What tense and mood of the original thought does **vīdisset** replace in the indirect statement?

   prōsequor, prōsequī (3), **prōsecūtus sum**, to follow forward, follow.

7   **fallō, fallere** (3), **fefellī, falsum**, to deceive.

   Neque opīniō eam fefellit: "And the opinion did not deceive her," better English, "And she was not mistaken."

8   **ubi prīmum**, *idiom*, when first, as soon as.

9   **colligō** (com- + legō), **colligere** (3), **collēgī, collēctum**, to gather together, collect.

10   **rēmigō** (rēmus + agō) (1), to row.

11   **prius**: not to be translated until **quam** is reached; the two parts of **priusquam** are often separated, **prius** standing in the main clause.

12   **Ēridanus, -ī** (*m*), Eridanus, Po.

13   **animō dēmissō**: "with a downcast mind (spirit)."

75. A FEARFUL EXPEDIENT

Erat in nāvī Argonautārum fīlius quīdam rēgis Aeētae, 1
nōmine Absyrtus, quem, ut suprā dēmōnstrāvimus, Mēdēa 2
ex urbe fugiēns sēcum abdūxerat. Hunc puerum Mēdēa in- 3
terficere cōnstituit eō cōnsiliō, ut membrīs eius in mare 4
coniectīs cursum Colchōrum impedīret; exīstimābat enim 5
Aeētam, cum membra fīlī vīdisset, nōn longius prō- 6
secūtūrum esse. Neque opīniō eam fefellit; nam omnia ita 7
ēvēnērunt ut spērāverat. Aeētēs ubi prīmum membra 8
vīdit, ad ea colligenda nāvem tenērī iussit. Dum ea gerun- 9
tur, Argonautae nōn intermissō rēmigandī labōre ē cōn- 10
spectū hostium effūgērunt, neque prius fugere dēstitērunt 11
quam ad flūmen Ēridanum pervēnērunt. At Aeētēs nihil 12
sibi prōfutūrum esse arbitrātus longius prōgredī, animō 13
dēmissō domum revertit, ut fīlium suum sepelīret. 14

1. The Argonauts had Medea's brother with them when they embarked.
2. You cannot doubt that they were intending to protect him.
3. As soon, however, as the king had approached their ship, Medea
   not only killed the boy, but even cast his body into the water.
4. She did it for this purpose, that grief might prevent the king from
   following.
5. Since his course had been impeded in this manner, the Argonauts
   thought they ought to flee as far as possible.

Helpful Hints
2. For "were intending," use the perfect subjunctive of an active periphrastic.
4. To translate "for this purpose, that," see line 4 of paragraph 75 above.
5. Use a passive periphrastic and a dative of agent.

2   **etiam tum**, *idiom*, even then, still.
5   **sī Iāsōn vellus rettulisset, sē rēgnum eī trāditūrum**: what was
     the original, direct statement?
6   ***ostendō, ostendere** (3), **ostendī, ostentum**, to stretch out before,
     show, explain.
7   **trīstitia, -ae** (*f*), sadness.
8   **permaneō, permanēre** (2), **permānsī, permānsum**, to remain
     through, remain.
     aetāte: *ablative of respect.*
9   **dubius, -a, -um**, doubtful, uncertain.
     suprēmus, -a, -um, highest, last.
10   **Quā rē**: literally, "On account of which thing," better English, "Therefore."
     mihi liceat: *jussive subjunctive*, "let it be allowed to me," "let me be
     allowed."
     vīvō, vīvere (3), **vīxī, vīctum**, to live.
     dum vīvam: **dum** with *future indicative*, "as long as I (will) live."
11   **cum . . . dēcesserō**: **cum** *circumstantial* or *temporal* with *future perfect
     indicative*, "when I will have died," "when I die." See grammar note on
     page 158.
     tū: the *nominative personal pronoun* used for emphasis or contrast; here
     tū makes the promise more definite.
     succēdō (sub- + cēdō), **succēdere** (3), **successī, successum**, to go *or*
     come under, follow after, succeed.
12   ***ōrātiō, ōrātiōnis** (*f*), speech.
13   **rogāsset**: = **rogāvisset**: why subjunctive?

Hortatory and Jussive Subjunctives

The *present subjunctive* may be used in *main clauses*
for a variety of purposes. One is to issue commands.
   When commands in the subjunctive are addressed by
speakers *to themselves and those with them* (1st
person plural, "Let us . . . !"), we call them exhortations,
and we label the subjunctives *hortatory*. As an
example of the hortatory subjunctive (1st person
plural), we could say **Rēgnum occupēmus!** "Let us
seize the throne!"
   When commands in the subjunctive are addressed *to
others* (2nd or 3rd persons), we call them *jussive*. A
jussive subjunctive in the 3rd person may be
impersonal, e.g., **Mihi liceat rēgnum obtinēre!**
"Let it be allowed to me to hold the throne!" better
English, "Let me be allowed to hold the throne!"
Further examples of the jussive subjunctive would be
Rēgnum occupēs! "Seize the throne!" and **Rēgnum
occupet!** "Let him seize the throne!"
   The negative is introduced by **nē**: **Nē rēgnum occupet!** "Don't let him seize the throne!"

76. THE BARGAIN WITH PELIAS

Tandem Iāsōn ad eundem locum pervēnit unde erat pro- 1
fectus. Tum ē nāvī ēgressus ad Peliam, quī rēgnum etiam 2
tum obtinēbat, statim sē contulit, et vellere aureō dēmōn- 3
strātō ab eō postulāvit ut rēgnum sibi trāderētur; Peliās 4
enim pollicitus erat, sī Iāsōn vellus rettulisset, sē rēgnum 5
eī trāditūrum. Postquam Iāsōn quid fierī vellet ostendit, 6
Peliās prīmō nihil respondit, sed diū in eādem trīstitiā ta- 7
citus permānsit; tandem ita locūtus est: "Vidēs mē aetāte 8
iam esse cōnfectum, neque dubium est quīn suprēmus diēs 9
mihi appropinquet. Quā rē mihi liceat, dum vīvam, rēgnum 10
obtinēre; cum tandem dēcesserō, tū mihi succēdēs." Hāc 11
ōrātiōne adductus Iāsōn respondit sē id factūrum quod ille 12
rogāsset. 13

Dum + Future Indicative = "as long as"

Dum with the *future indicative* means "as long as,"
e.g., **dum vīvam**, "as long as I will live," better
English, "as long as I live." For **dum** with the imperfect indicative with this same meaning, see grammar
note with paragraph 8; contrast **dum** = "while" (see
grammar note with paragraph 5) and **dum** = "until"
(see grammar note with paragraph 70).

---

1. Since he was bringing back the fleece, Jason expected a certain reward.
2. Honor was given to him, but Pelias was unwilling to give up the
   throne.
3. "I," he said, "will depart from life in a short time; as long as I live,
   let us be friends."
4. "After my death you will be permitted to hold the throne; therefore,
   you ought to wait until that time comes."
5. "There is no doubt that the citizens are intending to make you
   their king."

Helpful Hints
4. "You will be permitted" = "it will be permitted to you."
   To translate "you ought," use the verb **dēbeō**.
   "Until" requires the subjunctive (see grammar note with paragraph 70).
5. Begin your translation with **neque** to connect this sentence with the previous one.
   For "there is no doubt" = "it is not doubtful," find a model in paragraph 76
   above.
   For "are intending to," use the active periphrastic.

5   **Vultisne: -ne** (*enclitic*), used to introduce a *question* to which either a *negative* or *positive* answer could be expected.

7   **num** (*adv.*), used to introduce a *question* to which a *negative* answer is expected.

8   **senex, senis** (*m*), old man.

11   *****aries, arietis** (*m*), ram.

12   *****vas, vāsis** (*n*), vessel.

13   **dum . . . effervēsceret: dum** with the *subjunctive* meaning "until" and denoting *expectancy*.

14   **effervēscō** (ex- + fervēscō), **effervēscere** (3), **efferbuī**, to boil up *or* over, boil.

    *****carmen, carminis** (*n*), song, charm.

    canō, canere (3), **cecinī, cantum**, to sing.

15   **exsiliō** (ex- + saliō), **exsilīre** (4), **exsiluī**, to leap out *or* forth.

Cum Temporal or Circumstantial Clauses with the Indicative *(with paragraph 76)*

When **cum** is used with the *indicative* in <u>primary or secondary sequence</u>, it may introduce a clause that is strictly *temporal* (i.e., that designates a specific point of time) in the past, present, or future.

We have already seen that when **cum** is used with the *subjunctive* in <u>secondary sequence</u>, it introduces a *circumstantial* clause referring to past time (see grammar note with paragraph 27). In <u>primary sequence</u> **cum** with the *indicative* may introduce a *circumstantial* clause referring to present or future time.

Note the following sentence: **Cum dēcesserō, tū mihi succēdēs**, "<u>When I will have died</u>, you will succeed me," better English, "<u>When I die</u>, you will succeed me." Here the **cum** clause in <u>primary sequence</u> with the future perfect *indicative* may be labeled either *circumstantial* or *temporal*.

Remember that **cum** may also introduce a *causal* clause with its verb in the *subjunctive* in <u>primary or secondary sequence</u> (see grammar note with paragraph 25).

77. MAGIC ARTS

Hīs rēbus cognitīs Mēdēa rem aegrē tulit, et rēgnī cupi- 1
ditāte adducta mortem rēgī per dolum īnferre cōnstituit. 2
Eā rē cōnstitūtā ad fīliās rēgis vēnit atque ita locūta est: 3
"Vidētis patrem vestrum aetāte iam esse cōnfectum, neque 4
ad labōrem rēgnandī perferendum satis valēre. Vultisne 5
eum rūrsus iuvenem fierī?" Tum fīliae rēgis ita re- 6
spondērunt: "Num hoc fierī potest? Quis enim umquam ē 7
sene iuvenis factus est?" At Mēdēa respondit: "Mē sum- 8
mam scientiam artis magicae habēre scītis. Nunc igitur 9
vōbīs dēmōnstrābō quō modō haec rēs fierī possit." 10
Postquam fīnem loquendī fēcit, arietem aetāte iam cōnfec- 11
tum interfēcit et membra eius in vāse aēneō posuit, atque 12
ignī subditō in aquam herbās quāsdam coniēcit. Tum, dum 13
aqua effervēsceret, carmen magicum cecinit. Brevī tempore 14
ariēs ē vāse exsiluit, et vīribus refectīs per agrōs currēbat. 15

1. Since Medea desired to seize the royal power as soon as possible, she adopted the plan of killing the king.
2. Having adopted this plan, she spoke thus to his daughters.
3. "When your father dies, you will be alone without aid."
4. "Shall I show you in what way his strength can be renewed?"
5. "There is no doubt that this can be done, if a certain plan is pleasing to you."

Helpful Hints
1. Use a gerundive in translating "of killing the king."
2. Use an ablative absolute and linking quī.
   For "to . . . daughters," use the dative case, which has the special feminine form filiābus to distinguish "daughters" from "sons" (filiīs).
5. The conditional clause will be in the subjunctive by attraction.

1   **mīrāculum, -ī** (*n*), wonder, marvel, miracle.
    intueor, intuērī (2), **intuitus sum**, to look upon, behold.
2   **quantum valeat:** *indirect question* with *present subjunctive* in *primary
    sequence*, "how strong is. . . . "
4   *****restituō** (re- + statuō), **restituere** (3), **restituī, restitūtum**, to set up
    again, put back, restore.
    ipsae: *modifying* the *subject* of **faciētis.** Why is it feminine plural?
    Vōs: *subject* of the *imperative* **conicite** and contrasted with **ego** below.
10 **aliter . . . ac:** "otherwise than."
11 **quibus:** *ablative* with **ūsa erat.**
13 **coniūnx, coniugis** (*m/f*), spouse, husband, wife.
14 **acceptūrum** (supply **esse**): *indirect statement* with **spērābat.**
15 **pereō, perīre** (*irreg.*), **periī, peritum**, to pass away, perish.
    Distinguish this verb carefully from **parō** (1), to make ready, prepare,
    and from **pāreō, pārēre** (2), **pāruī** (+ *dat.*), to obey.
    perīsset: = **periisset.**
16 **Iāsone et Mēdēā . . . expulsīs:** *ablative absolute.* Cf. **Iāsonī et
    Mēdēae advenientibus** (*dative*) in paragraph 73, lines 10–11.
    Acastus, -ī (*m*), Acastus.

78. A DANGEROUS EXPERIMENT

Dum fīliae rēgis hoc mīrāculum stupentēs intuentur, 1
Mēdēa ita locūta est: "Vidētis quantum valeat ars magica. 2
Vōs igitur, sī vultis patrem vestrum in adulēscentiam 3
restituere, id quod ego fēcī ipsae faciētis. Vōs patris mem- 4
bra in vās conicite; ego herbās magicās praebēbō." Quod 5
ubi audītum est, fīliae rēgis cōnsilium quod dedisset 6
Mēdēa nōn omittendum putāvērunt. Itaque patrem Peliam 7
necāvērunt et membra eius in vās aēneum coniēcērunt; nōn 8
enim dubitābant quīn hoc eī maximē prōfutūrum esset. At 9
rēs omnīnō aliter ēvēnit ac spērāverant; nam Mēdēa nōn 10
eāsdem herbās dedit quibus ipsa ūsa erat. Postquam diū 11
frūstrā exspectāvērunt, patrem suum rē vērā mortuum esse 12
intellēxērunt. Hīs rēbus gestīs Mēdēa coniugem suum 13
rēgnum acceptūrum spērābat; sed cīvēs cum intellegerent 14
quō modō Peliās perīsset, tantum scelus aegrē tulērunt. 15
Itaque Iāsone et Mēdēā ē rēgnō expulsīs Acastum rēgem 16
creāvērunt. 17

1. The daughters of the king saw that Medea could bring back to life those whom she had killed.
2. Therefore they wondered at her daring and skill and asked her to help their father.
3. "Do you wish," she said, "to use the same plan that I myself used?"
4. When this had been done and the king's life could not be restored, Medea said that she had not been the cause of his death.
5. "There is no doubt," she said, "that some accident happened."

Helpful Hints

2. Instead of "they wondered at . . . and asked," write the Latin for "having wondered at . . . , they asked."
   For "asked," use **ōrō** + a direct object.
4. Use a circumstantial **cum** clause with linking **quī**.
5. For "some," see paragraph 73, line 5.
   The subordinate clause will require the perfect subjunctive to indicate time before the main verb in primary sequence.

1   **Thessaliā:** *ablative of separation* with the *participle* **expulsī.**
   expulsī: *modifying* **Iāsōn et Mēdēa.** Cf. the *ablative absolute* at the
   end of paragraph 78.
3   ***Glaucē, Glaucēs,** (*acc.*) **Glaucēn** (*f*), Glauce.
5   **remittō, remittere** (3), **remīsī, remissum,** to send back, send.
   Mēdēae . . . nūntium remittere: "to give Medea notice of divorce,"
   "to divorce Medea."
7   **iūs iūrandum, iūris iūrandī** (*n*), oath.
   sē . . . ultūram (supply **esse**): *indirect statement* with **cōnfīrmāvit.**
   ultūram: from **ulcīscor.**
   *iniūria, -ae (*f*), injury, wrong, hurt, harm.
9   **texō, texere** (3), **texuī, textum,** to weave.
   Distinguish this verb carefully from **tegō, tegere** (3), **tēxī, tēctum,**
   to cover, conceal.
   color, colōris (*m*), color.
10   **sī . . . induisset:** *pluperfect subjunctive* replacing a *future perfect*
   indicative by *attraction.*
11   **ūrō, ūrere** (3), **ussī, ustum,** to burn.
13   **mōre suō:** *ablative of manner,* "according to her own custom," "in her
   (usual) way."

79. A FATAL GIFT

Iāsōn et Mēdēa Thessaliā expulsī ad urbem Corinthum 1
vēnērunt, cuius urbis rēgnum Creōn quīdam tum obtinēbat. 2
Erat autem Creontī fīlia ūna, nōmine Glaucē. Quam cum 3
vīdisset, Iāsōn cōnstituit Mēdēae uxōrī suae nūntium 4
remittere eō cōnsiliō, ut Glaucēn in mātrimōnium dūceret. 5
At Mēdēa ubi intellēxit quid ille in animō habēret, graviter 6
commōta iūre iūrandō cōnfīrmāvit sē tantam iniūriam 7
ultūram. Itaque hoc cōnsilium cēpit. Vestem parāvit 8
summā arte textam et variīs colōribus īnfectam; hanc mor- 9
tiferō quōdam venēnō imbuit, cuius vīs tālis erat ut sī quis 10
eam vestem induisset, corpus eius quasi ignī ūrerētur. Hōc 11
factō vestem ad Glaucēn mīsit; illa autem nihil malī sus- 12
picāns dōnum libenter accēpit, et novam vestem mōre suō 13
statim induit. 14

1. Jason did not get possession of the kingdom after the king had been killed, did he?
2. The citizens, changing their opinion, drove both Jason and Medea out of the state.
3. And so they determined to make their way to Corinth, a city that was many miles distant.
4. Those who inhabited that city received the fugitives, according to their custom.
5. Did Medea remain in that place many years?

Helpful Hints
1. Remember that questions that expect the answer "no" are introduced by **num**.
   Use an ablative absolute.
2. Use an ablative absolute.
3. In translating "a city that," translate as if "which city"; see line 2 of paragraph 79 above.
4. For "fugitives," use the present participle of the verb for "to flee" as a substantive, i.e., "(the ones) fleeing"; see paragraph 74, line 8.

3 *āmentia, -ae (*f*), madness. Compare the English word *dementia*.

4 **tum magnum sibi fore perīculum arbitrāta sī Corinthī**
manēret: *future more vivid condition* reported in *indirect statement* introduced by **arbitrāta**; what would the direct statement have been?

5 **Corinthī**: *locative case.*

7 ***currus, -ūs** (*m*), chariot.

8 **āla, -ae** (*f*), wing.
Distinguish this noun carefully from the adjective **alius, -a, -ud**, another, other.
alīs: *ablative* with **īnstrūctī**.

9 **ēscendō** (ē- + scandō), **ēscendere** (3), **ēscendī**, **ēscēnsum**, to climb up.

10 **itaque** (ita + -que), and thus.
vecta: from **vehō**.

11 **ut . . . dormīret**: *substantive clause* of *result, subject* of **Accidit**, "It happened that he was sleeping."

13 **ad id tempus**: "up to that time."
ērēctus, -a, -um, upright, erect.

14 **pars, partis, partium** (*f*), part, side, direction.
iaceō, iacēre (2), **iacuī**, to lie, be prostrate.
Distinguish this verb carefully from **iaciō, iacere** (3), **iēcī, iactum**, to throw, cast, hurl.
dēlābor, dēlābī (3), **dēlāpsus sum**, to slip or fall down.

80. MEDEA KILLS HER SONS

Cum vestem induisset Glaucē, gravem dolōrem sēnsit, et 1
paulō post crūdēlī cruciātū affecta ē vītā excessit. Hīs rēbus 2
gestīs Mēdēa furōre atque āmentiā impulsa fīliōs suōs 3
necāvit; tum magnum sibi fore perīculum arbitrāta sī 4
Corinthī manēret, ex eā regiōne fugere cōnstituit. Eā rē 5
cōnstitūtā sōlem ōrāvit ut in tantō perīculō auxilium sibi 6
ferret. Sōl autem eius precibus commōtus currum mīsit, 7
quem dūcēbant dracōnēs ālīs īnstrūctī. Mēdēa nōn omit- 8
tendam tantam occāsiōnem arbitrāta in currum ēscendit, 9
itaque per āera vecta incolumis ad urbem Athēnās pervēnit. 10
Iāsōn ipse brevī tempore interfectus est. Accidit, sīve cāsū 11
sīve cōnsiliō deōrum, ut in umbrā nāvis suae, quae sub- 12
ducta erat, dormīret. At nāvis, quae ad id tempus ērēcta 13
steterat, in eam partem ubi Iāsōn iacēbat subitō dēlāpsa 14
virum īnfēlīcem oppressit. 15

1. Do you remember that clothing sent by his wife brought death to
   Hercules?
2. While Medea was at Corinth, she killed the king's daughter in the
   same way.
3. Then, slaying her own sons, she fled to Athens as quickly as possible.
4. You have not heard what she did in Athens, have you?
5. If anyone inquires, you must answer according to your custom.

Helpful Hints

3. Use an ablative absolute.
4. The English *present* perfect "you have heard" is translated with the perfect
   tense in Latin, but it establishes *primary* sequence, so that the verb in the
   subordinate clause will be a perfect subjunctive.
5. Use a future perfect in the if-clause and the present tense of **dēbeō** in the
   main clause.

Ulysses

Ulysses offering wine to Polyphemus

Ulysses, a famous Greek hero, took a prominent part in the long siege of Troy. After the fall of the city, he set out with his followers on his homeward voyage to Ithaca, an island of which he was king, but his ship was driven out off its course to the country of the lotus-eaters, who are supposed to have lived on the north coast of Africa. Some of his comrades were so delighted with the fruit of the lotus that they wished to remain in the country, but Ulysses compelled them to embark again and continue their voyage.

He next came to the island of Sicily and fell into the hands of the giant Polyphemus, one of the Cyclopes. After several of his comrades had been killed by this monster, Ulysses made his escape by stratagem and sailed onward to the country of the winds. Here he received the help of Aeolus, king of the winds, and setting sail once more, arrived within sight of Ithaca, but through the folly of his companions the winds became suddenly adverse, and Ulysses was again driven back.

Ulysses then arrived at an island that was the home of Circe, a powerful enchantress, who exercised her charms on his companions and turned them into swine. By the help of the god Mercury, Ulysses not only escaped this fate himself but forced Circe to restore her victims to human shape. After staying a year with Circe, he again set out and eventually reached his home.

2 ***cōnstō, cōnstāre** (1), **cōnstitī, cōnstātum**, to stand together, agree, consist.

    cōnstat (*impersonal*), it is agreed, is established, is well-known.

    Homērus, -ī (*m*), Homer.

3 **Īlias, Īliadis**, *acc.* **Īliada** (*f*), the *Iliad*.

4 ***īnsidiae, -ārum** (*f pl*), ambush, plot, stratagem.

    īnsidiās: referring to the story of the wooden horse; concealed in the horse, Greek warriors entered Troy and opened the gates to their comrades.

5 ***profectiō, profectiōnis** (*f*), departure, start.

8 **prūdentia, -ae** (*f*), prudence.

    ***nōn nūllī**, some. This is an instance of the use of two negative words to express an affirmative idea.

9 **excōgitō** (1), to think out, contrive, devise, invent.

    excōgitāsse: = **excōgitāvisse**.

10 ***Ithaca, -ae** (*f*), Ithaca.

12 **Pēnelopē, Pēnelopēs**, *acc.* **Pēnelopēn** (*f*), Penelope.

14 ***patria, -ae** (*f*), fatherland, country.

    patriae uxōrisque videndae: "of seeing his country and wife."

        videndae: *genitive singular feminine*, agreeing with **uxōris**, the noun closer to it, but also is to be taken with **patriae**.

Review Questions:

1. What construction is **decem annōs**? (1)
2. What type of genitive is **poētārum**? (3)
3. What construction is **Troiā . . . captā**? (4)
4. How else could **Troiā . . . captā** be written? (4)
5. Why isn't an ablative absolute used for **tempestātem idōneam nactī**? (6)
6. What type of genitive is the phrase **summae virtūtis ac prūdentiae**? (8)
7. What type of ablative is **nōmine**? (12)

81. HOMEWARD BOUND

Urbem Troiam ā Graecīs decem annōs obsessam esse 1
satis cōnstat; dē hōc enim bellō Homērus, maximus 2
poētārum Graecōrum, Īliada opus nōtissimum scrīpsit. 3
Troiā tandem per īnsidiās captā, Graecī bellō fessī domum 4
redīre mātūrāvērunt. Omnibus rēbus ad profectiōnem 5
parātīs nāvēs dēdūxērunt, et tempestātem idōneam nactī 6
magnō cum gaudiō solvērunt. Erat inter Graecōs Ulixēs 7
quīdam, vir summae virtūtis ac prūdentiae, quem nōn nūllī 8
dīcunt dolum istum excōgitāsse quō Troiam captam esse 9
cōnstat. Hic rēgnum īnsulae Ithacae obtinuerat, et paulō 10
priusquam ad bellum cum reliquīs Graecīs profectus est, 11
puellam fōrmōsissimam, nōmine Pēnelopēn, in mātri- 12
mōnium dūxerat. Nunc igitur cum iam decem annōs quasi 13
in exsiliō cōnsūmpsisset, magnā cupiditāte patriae uxōris- 14
que videndae ārdēbat. 15

Content Questions:

1. How was Troy finally captured?
2. What is our ancient source of information about Troy?
3. What sort of person was Ulysses?
4. Where was Ulysses the ruler?
5. Why was he so eager to get home?

1. When the city of Troy had been besieged for ten years, Ulysses de-
   vised a trick, according to his custom.
2. The Greeks got possession of the city by means of the horse and cut
   down their foes.
3. However, some part of those who were then living in the city (of)
   Troy escaped.
4. About these there was written a work so famous that it was handed
   down to us.
5. Ulysses, to whom we must return, surpassed the other Greeks in
   prudence.

2   **ut nūlla**: note the negative used in introducing a result clause.
3   **aliae aliam in partem**: "some in one direction, others in another."
     Two forms of **alius** are often used together to express a distributive
     idea, the full expression of which would require the repetition of both.
4   **disiciō** (dis- + iaciō), **disicere** (3), **disiēcī, disiectum**, to throw apart,
     scatter.
5   *__dēferō__, **dēferre** (*irreg.*), **dētulī, dēlātum**, to bear *or* carry away *or*
     off.
6   **nōn nūllōs ē sociīs**: note the use of the preposition to express the parti-
     tive idea with **nōn nūllī** (cf. **nūlla nāvium**, lines 2–3).
11   **vīctus, -ūs** (*m*), living, sustenance, food.
     This noun is related to the participial stem of **vīvō, vīvere** (3), **vīxī,
     vīctum**, to live. Distinguish this verb carefully from **vincō,
     vincere** (3), **vīcī, victum**, to conquer, and **vinciō, vincīre** (4),
     vīnxī, vīnctum, to bind.
12   **in . . . cōnsisteret**: we say "consisted *of*," rather than "consisted *in.*"
     frūctus, -ūs (*m*), enjoyment, fruit.
     lōtus, -ī (*m*), lotus.
14   *__gustō__ (1), to taste.
     gustāssent: = **gustāvissent**.
     patriae . . . et sociōrum: *genitive* with the verb of *forgetting,* **oblītī**.
     oblīvīscor, oblīvīscī (3), **oblītus sum** (+ *gen.* or *acc.*), to forget,
     disregard, dismiss.
         oblītī: "dismissing . . . from their minds."
15   *__dulcis__, **-is, -e**, sweet.
16   **perpetuus, -a, -um**, continuous.
     in perpetuum, *idiom*, for all time, forever.

Review Questions:

1. What type of genitive is **passuum**? (1)
2. What kind of clause is **ut . . . posset**? (2–3)
3. What construction is **Ancorīs iactīs**? (6)
4. What kind of clause is **quī . . . referrent et . . .
    cognōscerent**? (7–8)?
5. What kind of clause is **quālis esset nātūra**? (8)
6. What case are the words **dulcī illō cibō**? Why? (15–16)
7. What form is **vēscerentur**? (16)

> ### Genitive with Verbs of Remembering and Forgetting
>
> Either the *genitive* or the *accusative* case may be used
> with verbs of *remembering* and *forgetting.* When
> **oblīvīscor** means simply "to forget," it is used with an
> accusative object; when it means "to disregard" or "to
> dismiss from the mind," it takes the genitive, e.g., __pa-
> triae et sociōrum__ **oblītī**, "dismissing their <u>father-
> land</u> and <u>companions</u> from their minds."

82. THE LOTUS-EATERS

Postquam Graecī pauca mīlia passuum ā lītore Troiae 1
prōgressī sunt, tanta tempestās subitō coorta est ut nūlla 2
nāvium cursum tenēre posset, sed aliae aliam in partem 3
disicerentur. Nāvis autem quā ipse Ulixēs vehēbātur vī 4
tempestātis ad merīdiem dēlāta decimō diē ad lītus Āfricae 5
appulsa est. Ancorīs iactīs Ulixēs cōnstituit nōn nūllōs ē 6
sociīs in terram expōnere, quī aquam ad nāvem referrent et 7
quālis esset nātūra eius regiōnis cognōscerent. Hī ē nāvī 8
ēgressī imperāta facere parābant. Sed dum fontem 9
quaerunt, quōsdam ex incolīs invēnērunt atque ab eīs hos- 10
pitiō acceptī sunt. Accidit autem ut maior pars vīctūs 11
eōrum hominum in mīrō quōdam frūctū, quem lōtum appel- 12
lābant, cōnsisteret. Cum Graecī paulum huius frūctūs 13
gustāssent, patriae tamen et sociōrum statim oblītī cōn- 14
firmāvērunt sē semper in illā terrā mānsūrōs, ut dulcī illō 15
cibō in perpetuum vēscerentur. 16

Content Questions:

1. How were Ulysses' ships driven off course?
2. In what direction was Ulysses' ship driven in the storm?
3. Why did Ulysses send some of his men out onto land?
4. On what sort of food did the natives of the area exist?
5. Why did the sailors want to stay in Africa?

1. After taking Troy, the Greeks, desiring to return home as quickly
   as possible, weighed anchor at once.
2. Some were carried in one ship, others in another.
3. The ship of Ulysses, who was a man of great prudence, a storm
   carried away to Africa.
4. Since the supply of water had begun to fail, some of his companions went ashore.
5. When they had taken food, they seemed to dismiss their leader
   and companions from their minds.

1 **hōrā septimā**: see the note on the word **vigilia** in line 2 of paragraph 74. The seventh hour would be a little after noon.

2 *****versor, versārī** (1), **versātus sum**, to turn often, be busy *or* employed, be involved, be.

  ē reliquīs: **ē** (**ex**) + *ablative* used with **nūllōs** instead of the *partitive genitive*.

4 **vīcus, -ī** (*m*), village.

5 **quō**: "to which place," "and . . . to this place."

8 **manū**: "by force."

10 **īnfectus, -a, -um**, not done, undone, unaccomplished.

12 **suā sponte**, *idiom*, voluntarily, of their own accord.

13 **vīnctīs**: from **vinciō**.

Review Questions:

What types of constructions are the following?

1. **nē . . . versārentur** (2)
2. **ut . . . cognōscerent** (3)
3. **quae causa esset morae** (3)
4. **causam veniendī** (6)
5. **ut . . . redīrent** (7)
6. **dēfendere coēpērunt** (8)
7. **sē . . . abitūrōs** (9)
8. **Hīs rēbus cognitīs** (10–11)
9. **ut . . . redīrent** (12–13)

83. THE RESCUE

Ulixēs cum ab hōrā septimā ad vesperum exspectāsset, 1
veritus nē sociī suī in perīculō versārentur, nōn nūllōs ē 2
reliquīs mīsit, ut quae causa esset morae cognōscerent. 3
Itaque hī in terram expositī ad vīcum quī nōn longē aberat 4
sē contulērunt; quō cum vēnissent, sociōs suōs quasi ēbriōs 5
repperērunt. Tum causam veniendī docuērunt, atque eīs 6
persuādēre cōnātī sunt ut sēcum ad nāvem redīrent. Illī 7
autem resistere ac sē manū dēfendere coepērunt, saepe 8
clāmitantēs sē numquam ex illō locō abitūrōs. Quae cum 9
ita essent, nūntiī rē īnfectā ad Ulixem rediērunt. Hīs rēbus 10
cognitīs ipse cum reliquīs quī in nāvī relictī erant ad eum 11
locum vēnit; sociōs suōs frūstrā hortātus ut suā sponte 12
redīrent, manibus vīnctīs invītōs ad nāvem trāxit. Tum 13
quam celerrimē ex portū solvit. 14

Content Questions:

1. Approximately how long did Ulysses wait before sending out a search party?
2. What did the search party discover?
3. What tactic did the search party try first to get their companions to leave this paradise?
4. What did those who resisted leaving shout at their friends?
5. How did Ulysses finally get his men back?

1. Ulysses was unwilling to weigh anchor until those whom he had landed should return with water.
2. When he wondered what the reason for the delay was, some kept saying one thing, others another.
3. Toward evening, those left to guard the ship went ashore, with Ulysses as leader.
4. Some thought that they could persuade their companions to embark of their own accord.
5. Since these resisted, they had to be dragged from that place by force.

Helpful Hints
1. Use the indicative in the relative clause, since it is not essential to the thought of the subjunctive clause within which it is contained (see grammar note with paragraph 34).

1   **ignōtus, -a, -um**, unknown.

4   *****explōrō** (1), to search out, explore.

6   **incolī**: *present passive infinitive.* Compare the noun **incola, -ae** (*m/f*), inhabitant.

9   **quod**: "this," i.e., entered the cave.

10   **lac, lactis** (*n*), milk.

      condō, condere (3), **condidī, conditum**, to put together, found, build, store away.

12   **torqueō, torquēre** (2), **torsī, tortum**, to turn.

13   *****hūmānus, -a, -um**, of man, human.

      quidem: regularly following the word it emphasizes, often with concessive force, as here.

      figūra, -ae (*f*), form, shape, figure.

16   *****Cyclōps, Cyclōpis** (*m*), Cyclops.

Review Questions:

What type of constructions are the following?

1. **explōrāre cōnstituit** (4)
2. **quam incolī** (6)
3. **introitum . . . mūnītum esse** (6–7)
4. **sē . . . factūrōs** (8)
5. **quis . . . habitāret** (11)
6. **oculīs . . . tortīs** (12)
7. **hūmānā . . . speciē et figūrā** (13)
8. **hunc esse ūnum** (16)

84. THE ONE-EYED GIANT

Eā tōtā nocte rēmīs contendērunt, et postrīdiē ad ignō- 1
tam terram nāvem appulērunt. Tum, quod nātūram eius 2
regiōnis ignōrābat, ipse Ulixēs cum duodecim sociīs in ter- 3
ram ēgressus locum explōrāre cōnstituit. Explōrātōrēs 4
paulum ā lītore prōgressī ad spēluncam ingentem per- 5
vēnērunt, quam incolī sēnsērunt; eius enim introitum et 6
nātūrā locī et manū mūnītum esse animadvertērunt. Etsī 7
intellegēbant sē nōn sine perīculō hoc factūrōs, tamen 8
spēluncam intrāvērunt; quod cum fēcissent, magnam 9
cōpiam lactis in vāsīs ingentibus conditam invēnērunt. 10
Dum mīrantur quis in eā sēde habitāret, sonitum terri- 11
bilem audīvērunt, et oculīs ad ōstium tortīs mōnstrum hor- 12
ribile vīdērunt, hūmānā quidem speciē et figūrā, sed in- 13
gentī magnitūdine corporis. Cum autem animadvertissent 14
mōnstrum ūnum modo oculum habēre in mediā fronte posi- 15
tum, intellēxērunt hunc esse ūnum ē Cyclōpibus, dē quibus 16
iam audīverant. 17

Content Questions:

1. Why did Ulysses and his men set out onto land this time?
2. How did they know that the cave was inhabited?
3. What did Ulysses and his men find in the cave?
4. What was the appearance of the giant who lived in the cave?
5. How did they know this was the monster about whom they had heard?

1. A little later it happened that Ulysses reached a land that was an island.
2. This was inhabited by many great monsters.
3. They had the bodies of men, but no one could approach them without danger.
4. While Ulysses was exploring the island with his companions, he came by chance to a cave.
5. This was the home of Polyphemus, one of these monsters.

2　**Aetna, -ae** (*f*), Etna.
3　**praeses, praesidis** (*m*) protector.
　　inventor, inventōris (*m*), finder, discoverer.
4　**officīna, -ae** (*f*), workshop, smithy.
5　*****interior, interius**, interior, inner.
8　**pecus, pecoris** (*n*), cattle, herd, flock.
　　　Distinguish this noun carefully from **pecus, pecudis** (*f*), head of cattle, beast, sheep, goat.
10　*****perlūstrō** (1), to look over, examine, survey.
12　**Quī:** "What?"
　　latrō, latrōnis (*m*), robber.
13　**sē:** "they," i.e., he and his companions.
14　**praedor, praedārī** (1), **praedātus sum**, to plunder, rob.
　　causa, -ae (*f*), cause, reason.
　　　causā (*ablative of cause* + preceding *genitive*), for the sake of, for the purpose of.
　　　praedandī causā: *gerund with* **causā** *to express purpose*, "for the purpose of robbing," "to rob."
　　redeuntēs: *participle of the compound verb* **redeō, redīre** (*irreg.*), **rediī, reditum.** Remember that the participle of **eō, īre** is **iēns, euntis**, etc.
18　**praecaveō, praecavēre** (2), **praecāvī, praecautum**, to beware beforehand, beware, be on one's guard.
　　　praecavendum (supply **esse**): *passive periphrastic infinitive in indirect statement; impersonal passive of intransitive verb with* **sibi** (*dative of agent*), "that he should be on his guard beforehand."
19　**frangō, frangere** (3), **frēgī, frāctum**, to break, dash to pieces, wreck.
21　**dīvellō, dīvellere** (3), **dīvellī, dīvulsum**, to tear apart, rend asunder, tear in pieces.

> ### *Gerund or Gerundive with* **causā** *to Express Purpose*
>
> A *gerund* or a *gerundive phrase* in the *genitive case* may be used with **causā** "for the sake of" to express purpose, e.g., **praedandī causā**, "for the sake of plundering," "to plunder." Note that **causā** always follows the gerund or gerundive phrase.

1.　While the Greeks were lingering for the sake of exploring the cave, Polyphemus approached that place with his flock.
2.　He placed a large stone in the entrance before they could flee.
3.　The Greeks understood that they must show courage; some, nevertheless, hid themselves in one part of the cave, others in another.
4.　They said that they ought not to take a stand, and therefore they fled.
5.　As soon as Polyphemus saw them, he gave them an opportunity of speaking.

85. THE GIANT'S DINNER

Cyclōpēs autem pāstōrēs erant, quī īnsulam Siciliam 1
praecipuēque montem Aetnam incolēbant; ibi enim Vol- 2
cānus, praeses fabrōrum ignisque inventor, cuius servī Cy- 3
clōpēs erant, officīnam suam habēbat. Graecī igitur simul 4
ac mōnstrum vīdērunt, terrōre paene exanimātī in inter- 5
iōrem spēluncae partem refūgērunt, et sē abdere cōnāban- 6
tur. Polyphēmus autem (sīc enim Cyclōps appellābātur) 7
pecus suum in spēluncam compulit; deinde, cum saxō in- 8
gentī ōstium obstrūxisset, ignem in mediā spēluncā fēcit. 9
Hōc factō omnia oculō perlūstrābat. Cum sēnsisset ho- 10
minēs in interiōre spēluncae parte esse abditōs, magnā 11
vōce exclāmāvit; "Quī hominēs estis? Mercātōrēs an la- 12
trōnēs?" Tum Ulixēs respondit sē neque mercātōrēs esse 13
neque praedandī causā vēnisse, sed Troiā captā domum re- 14
deuntēs vī tempestātum ā cursū dēlātōs esse. Ōrāvit 15
etiam ut sibi sine iniūriā abīre licēret. Tum Polyphēmus 16
quaesīvit ubi esset nāvis quā vectī essent. Ulixēs cum 17
magnopere sibi praecavendum exīstimāret, respondit 18
nāvem suam in saxa coniectam omnīnō frāctam esse. Ille 19
autem nūllō respōnsō datō duōs ē sociīs eius manū cor- 20
ripuit, et membrīs eōrum dīvulsīs carne vēscī coepit. 21

Impersonal Passive of Intransitive Verbs

A verb such as **praecaveō** in its *intransitive* sense, "I
am on my guard beforehand," cannot logically be put
into the passive voice. However, such intransitive verbs
can be used in the *gerundive*, which is passive in meaning; the gerundive must then be used in an *impersonal*
construction, e.g., **Mihi praecavendum est**, literally,
"It is necessary that it be guarded beforehand by me,"
better English, "I must be on my guard beforehand." In
indirect statement this becomes **Ulixēs cum magnopere sibi praecavendum (esse) exīstimā-
ret.** . . . "Since Ulysses was thinking that he should
be very much on his guard beforehand. . . . "

Helpful Hints
3. Translate as if the English said "that courage must be shown by them," using
a gerundive.
For "some . . . others," see paragraph 82, line 3, and vocabulary note.
4. For "said . . . not," use **negō**.

2   nē . . . quidem: *emphasizing* vōcem.
3   praesēns, praesentis, present, immediate, imminent.
5   *dēpellō, dēpellere (3), dēpulī, dēpulsum, to drive off *or* away.
    humī: *locative case,* "on the ground."
    prōstrātus: "throwing himself down."
    Quod: summarizing the previous idea, "This."
8   nihil: here used as a *pronoun,* the *subject* of agendum (esse).
    temere (*adv.*), rashly.
9   priusquam . . . faceret: priusquam with the *subjunctive* in *secondary
    sequence* in a clause expressing a possibility, "before he would do this."
10 animadvertō (animus + ad- + vertō), animadvertere (3), animad-
    vertī, animadversum, to turn the mind to, observe, notice.
11 introitus, -ūs (*m*), entrance (place of entering *or* act of entering).
    This noun is related to the verb introeō, introīre, to enter; cf. exitus,
       -ūs, which is related to the verb exeō, exīre, to go out.
    nihil sibi prōfutūrum (supply esse): *indirect statement* with intel-
    lēxit. Nihil is here used as a strong *negative.*
14 hōc cōnātū: *ablative of separation* with dēstitit.
19 dī: = deī.
20 lātūrī essent: "were going to bring," "would bring"; since the subjunctive
    has no future tense, the *active periphrastic conjugation* (see grammar
    note with paragraph 58) must be used to indicate *future time* clearly in
    some subjunctive constructions.

Review Questions:

1. What kind of clause is ut . . . ēdere possent? (2)
2. What case are the words hāc . . . horribilī cēnā? Why? (4)
3. Is gerendae a gerund or a gerundive? How can you tell? (6)
4. Is agendum a gerund or a gerundive? How can you tell? (8)
5. What kind of clause is quā ratiōne . . . ēvādere posset? (9–10)
6. What kind of clause is nē animōs dēmitterent? (17)
7. What construction is sē . . . ēvāsisse? (18–19)

86. A DESPERATE SITUATION

Dum haec geruntur, Graecōrum animōs tantus terror oc- 1
cupāvit ut nē vōcem quidem ēdere possent, sed omnī spē 2
salūtis dēpositā praesentem mortem exspectārent. At 3
Polyphēmus, postquam famēs hāc tam horribilī cēnā 4
dēpulsa est, humī prōstrātus somnō sē dedit. Quod cum 5
vīdisset Ulixēs, tantam occāsiōnem reī bene gerendae nōn 6
omittendam arbitrātus, pectus mōnstrī gladiō trānfīgere 7
voluit. Cum tamen nihil temere agendum exīstimāret, cōn- 8
stituit explōrāre, priusquam hoc faceret, quā ratiōne ē 9
spēluncā ēvādere posset. Cum saxum animadvertisset quō 10
introitus obstrūctus erat, nihil sibi prōfutūrum intellēxit 11
Polyphēmum interficere. Tanta enim erat eius saxī mag- 12
nitūdō ut nē ā decem quidem hominibus āmovērī posset. 13
Quae cum ita essent, Ulixēs hōc cōnātū dēstitit et ad sociōs 14
rediit; quī cum intellēxissent quō in locō rēs esset, nūllā spē 15
salūtis oblātā dē fortūnīs suīs dēspērāre coepērunt. Ille 16
tamen vehementer hortātus est nē animōs dēmitterent; 17
dēmōnstrāvit sē iam anteā ē multīs et magnīs perīculīs 18
ēvāsisse, neque dubium esse quīn in tantō discrīmine dī 19
auxilium lātūrī essent. 20

Content Questions:

1. What were the immediate results of the Greeks' fears?
2. Why didn't Ulysses and his men kill the Cyclops?
3. How large was the rock by which the entrance was blocked?
4. Why did the surviving men begin to despair?
5. How did Ulysses encourage his men?

1. The Greeks declared that they had not sailed there for the purpose of seeking plunder, but they were not permitted to depart.
2. Polyphemus did not even inform them what he was intending to do.
3. He suddenly seized and killed two of them.
4. As the stone prevented entrance, he did not fear that anyone would bring help to the Greeks.
5. Ulysses, however, kept urging his companions to remember the many serious dangers from which they had been rescued.

1   **quod prīdiē** (supply **fēcerat**): "that he had done the day before," "as on
     the day before."
7   *ovis, **ovis, ovium** (*f*), sheep.
8   **lāmenta, -ōrum** (*n pl*), lamentation.
     *dēdō, **dēdere** (3), **dēdidī, dēditum**, to give away *or* up.
14   **praeacūtus, -a, -um**, sharpened at the end, pointed, sharp.

Review Questions:

1. What form is **carne**? Why? (2)
2. What could you substitute for **magnam in spem vēnērunt**? (5)
3. What construction is **sē . . . ēvāsūrōs**? (5)
4. What could you substitute for **ab hāc spē repulsī sunt**? (6)
5. What case are **lamentīs** and **lacrimīs**? Why? (8)
6. What type of genitive is **magnī . . . cōnsilī**? (9–10)
7. What type of ablative is **summā cum dīligentiā**? (14)
8. From what verb does **fierī** come? (15)

87. A PLAN FOR VENGEANCE

Ortā lūce Polyphēmus iam ē somnō excitātus idem quod 1
prīdiē fēcit; nam correptīs duōbus virīs carne eōrum sine 2
morā vēscī coepit. Deinde, cum saxum āmōvisset, ipse cum 3
pecore suō ē spēluncā prōgressus est; quod cum Graecī 4
vīdērunt, magnam in spem vēnērunt sē paulō post ēvāsūrōs. 5
Statim ab hāc spē repulsī sunt; nam Polyphēmus, 6
postquam omnēs ovēs exiērunt, saxum reposuit. Reliquī 7
omnī spē salūtis dēpositā sē lāmentīs lacrimīsque dē- 8
didērunt; Ulixēs vērō, quī, ut suprā dēmōnstrāvimus, magnī 9
fuit cōnsilī, etsī intellegēbat rem in discrīmine esse, tamen 10
nōndum omnīnō dēspērābat. Tandem, cum diū haec tōtō 11
animō cōgitāvisset, hoc cōnsilium cēpit. Ē lignīs quae in 12
spēluncā reposita erant magnam clāvem dēlēgit. Hanc 13
summā cum dīligentiā praeacūtam fēcit; tum, postquam 14
sociīs quid fierī vellet ostendit, reditum Polyphēmī exspec- 15
tābat. 16

Content Questions:

1. What did Polyphemus do as soon as he awoke the next day?
2. Why did the Greeks momentarily regain their hope?
3. What happened when their hopes were dashed?
4. How and why was Ulysses able to come up with a plan?
5. What were the first four steps in Ulysses' plan?

1. The next day Polyphemus killed the same number of the Greeks as before.
2. Having done this, he moved the stone away, for the purpose of leading out his flock.
3. This he was accustomed to do daily with the greatest diligence.
4. Before he departed, he put the stone back, that the Greeks might not escape.
5. Ulysses, a man of the greatest knowledge, understood that he must adopt a new plan.

Helpful Hints
1. For "as," find a model in line 1 of paragraph 87 above.
5. Translate as if the English said "that a new plan must be adopted by himself," using a passive periphrastic.

2   quō: "as," cf. quod in line 1 of paragraph 87.

       *ūter, ūtris (m), skin, bag (used for holding wine).

       prōmō, prōmere (3), prōmpsī, prōmptum, to take or bring out, produce.

5   prōvocō (1), to call forth or out, challenge.

7   tertium: adverb.

8   *compleō, complēre (2), complēvī, complētum, to fill full, fill up.

11   postrēmus, -a, -um, last.

14   quam . . . facultātem: for facultātem quam (the antecedent is often put in the relative clause in Latin).

       nē . . . omittāmus: hortatory subjunctive (negative introduced by nē), "let us not lose" (see grammar note with paragraph 76).

Content Questions:

1. What had Ulysses brought with him to the cave?
2. What is the meaning of the fictitious name given by Ulysses?
3. What grand favor did Polyphemus grant to Ulysses?
4. What happened to Polyphemus after eating and drinking?
5. Why was **Nēmō** a good name for Ulysses to give Polyphemus? You will find out in the next paragraph.

Review Questions:

1. What type of construction is **eī . . . salūtī**? (3)
2. From what verb does **attulerat** come? (3)
3. What type of construction is **ad bibendum**? (4–5)
4. What is the function of **quod** in **quod cum fēcisset**? (6–7)
5. What type of clause is **ut . . . iubēret**? (7–8)
6. What form is **appellārī**? How is it used? (9)
7. In what case are **cibī** and **vīnī**? Why? (12)
8. What type of ablative is **brevī tempore**? (13)

88. A FICTITIOUS NAME

Sub vesperum Polyphēmus in spēluncam rediit, et eōdem 1
modō quō anteā cēnāvit. Tum Ulixēs ūtrem vīnī prōmpsit, 2
quem forte (id quod eī erat salūtī) sēcum attulerat; et 3
postquam magnum pōculum vīnō complēvit, mōnstrum ad 4
bibendum prōvocāvit. Polyphēmus, quī numquam anteā 5
vīnum gustāverat, pōculum statim exhausit; quod cum fē- 6
cisset, tantam voluptātem percēpit ut iterum ac tertium 7
pōculum complērī iubēret. Cum quaesīvisset quō nōmine 8
Ulixēs appellārētur, ille respondit sē Nēminem appellārī; 9
quod cum audīvisset, Polyphēmus ita locūtus est: "Hanc 10
tibi grātiam prō tantō beneficiō referam; tē postrēmum om- 11
nium dēvorābō." Hoc cum dīxisset, cibī vīnīque plēnus humī 12
recubuit, et brevī tempore somnō oppressus est. Tum 13
Ulixēs sociīs convocātīs, "Habēmus," inquit, "quam 14
petīvimus facultātem; nē tantam occāsiōnem reī bene 15
gerendae omittāmus." 16

1. "Will you," he said, "use the opportunity that will be offered?"
2. "Will you obey me if I command you to make an attack on
   Polyphemus?"
3. "There is no doubt that my plan is going to be our salvation."
4. "We must prepare everything that will be useful to us for overpow-
   ering Polyphemus."
5. "He will use the same food as before, but we will have an opportunity of doing the thing well."

Helpful Hints
1. "You" in sentences 1 and 2 is plural.
    The "opportunity" will have been "offered" *before* the men will "use" it;
    therefore use the future perfect (for completed action) to translate "will be
    offered."
2. The same considerations as in translating sentence 1 apply to the choice of
    tenses in sentence 2.
3. Use an active periphrastic and a double dative.
4. Use a passive periphrastic, a dative of purpose, and a gerundive of purpose.
5. Find models for both parts of this sentence in paragraph 88 above.
    Use a dative of possession in the second part of the sentence.

1   **Hāc ōrātiōne habitā**: *ablative absolute*. Note the idiom; the Romans *had* speeches; we *give* them.
     extrēmam clāvam: "the end of the stick."
     calefaciō, calefacere (3), **calefēcī, calefactum**, to make hot, heat.

2   **perfodiō, perfodere** (3), **perfōdī, perfossum**, to dig *or* pierce through, transfix.

8   **adstō, adstāre** (1), **adstitī**, to stand at *or* near.
     adstantēs: *modifying* the *subject*.

15   **quibus**: *dative* with **resistere**.
     resistere: *complementary infinitive* with both **possumus** and **volumus**.

16   **affectus sīs**: *perfect passive subjunctive* in a **quīn** *clause* after an expression of *doubt* in *primary sequence*, "you have been afflicted."

17   **īnsānia, -ae** (*f*), madness, insanity.

Review Questions:

1. What form is **dormientis**? What does it modify? (2)
2. Why are the words **hōc dolōre** ablative? (4)
3. From what verb does **sustulit** come? (4–5)
4. From what verb does **errābat** come? (5)
5. What form is **adstantēs**? (8–9)
6. What construction is **eum . . . incidisse**? (17)
7. What form is **arbitrātī**? What does it modify? (17)

89. THE BLINDING OF POLYPHEMUS

Hāc ōrātiōne habitā extrēmam clāvam ignī calefēcit, 1
atque hāc oculum Polyphēmī dormientis perfōdit; quō factō 2
omnēs in dīversās spēluncae partēs sē abdidērunt. At ille 3
hōc dolōre oculī ē somnō excitātus clāmōrem terribilem sus- 4
tulit, et dum in spēluncā errābat, Ulixem manū prehendere 5
cōnābātur; tamen cum iam omnīnō caecus esset, nūllō modō 6
id efficere potuit. Intereā reliquī Cyclōpēs clāmōre audītō 7
undique ad spēluncam convēnerant; et ad introitum ad- 8
stantēs quid Polyphēmus ageret quaesīvērunt, et quam ob 9
causam tantum clāmōrem sustulisset. Ille respondit sē 10
graviter vulnerātum esse ac magnō dolōre afficī. Cum 11
posteā quaesīvissent quis eī vim intulisset, respondit 12
Nēminem id fēcisse. Quibus rēbus audītīs ūnus ē Cy- 13
clōpibus, "At sī nēmō," inquit, "tē vulnerāvit, nōn dubium 14
est quīn cōnsiliō deōrum, quibus resistere nec possumus nec 15
volumus, hōc suppliciō affectus sīs." Hoc cum dīxisset, 16
abiērunt Cyclōpēs, eum in īnsāniam incidisse arbitrātī. 17

Content Questions:

1. What did the Greeks do after they had blinded Polyphemus?
2. What did Polyphemus do after he was blinded?
3. Why did the other Cyclopes come to the cave?
4. Who did Polyphemus say had blinded him?
5. What was the reaction of the other Cyclopes to Polyphemus' statements?

1. When Polyphemus had again led his flock back from the fields, he filled himself up with so much food that he was overpowered.
2. For this reason he was unable to resist the enemy.
3. Now he is said to have had only one eye, which was placed in the middle of his forehead.
4. When he had lost (his) eye, he could not find Ulysses and the other Greeks.
5. They had hidden themselves in the inner part of the cave.

Helpful Hints
2. Use linking **quī** and find a model for "for this reason" in paragraph 89 above.
3. For "Now," use **autem**.
4. Use an ablative absolute.

1   abīsse: = abīvisse or abiisse.
4   ut . . . vēnerat: "as," or "when" with the *indicative* verb.
5.   vēnerat . . . tractābat: *past general* (see grammar note with
       paragraph 19).
6   *tractō (1), to handle, touch, feel.
10   vīmen, vīminis (*n*), osier.
11   venter, ventris (*m*), belly.
       ventribus: *dative* with the *compound verb* subiēcit.
       subiciō (sub- + iaciō), subicere (3), subiēcī, subiectum (+ *acc.* and
         dat.), to throw *or* place something under something.
      *lateō (2), to lie hidden, be concealed.
12   fore: = futūrum esse.
14   patior, patī (3), passus sum, to bear, suffer, allow.
15   ōrdō, ōrdinis (*m*), arrangement, order, rank.
       ex ōrdine, *idiom*, in order.
16   novus, -a, -um, new.
       novissimus, -a, -um, last.

Review Questions:

1. In what case are **furōre** and **āmentiā**? (1–2)
2. What form is **possent** in **nē hominēs . . . exīre possent**? (6)
3. What construction is **omnem spem . . . positam esse**? (7–8)
4. How is **quam** translated with **māgis**? (7–8)
5. What form is **pinguissimās**? (9)
6. What form is **ferentēs**? What does it modify? (12)
7. What construction is **quō factō**? (16)

90. THE ESCAPE

Polyphēmus ubi sociōs suōs abīsse sēnsit, furōre atque 1
āmentiā impulsus Ulixem iterum quaerere coepit; tandem, 2
cum ōstium invēnisset, saxum quō obstrūctum erat āmōvit, 3
ut pecus in agrōs exīret. Tum ipse in introitū cōnsēdit; et ut 4
quaeque ovis ad hunc locum vēnerat, eius tergum manibus 5
tractābat, nē hominēs inter ovēs exīre possent. Quod cum 6
animadvertisset Ulixēs, omnem spem salūtis in dolō magis 7
quam in virtūte positam esse intellēxit. Itaque hoc cōnsi- 8
lium iniit. Prīmum ex ovibus trēs pinguissimās dēlēgit, 9
quās cum inter sē vīminibus coniūnxisset, ūnum ex sociīs 10
suīs ventribus eārum ita subiēcit ut omnīnō latēret; deinde 11
ovēs hominem ferentēs ad ōstium ēgit. Id accidit quod fore 12
suspicātus erat. Polyphēmus enim postquam terga ovium 13
manibus tractāvit, eās praeterīre passus est. Ulixēs ubi 14
rem tam fēlīciter ēvēnisse vīdit, omnēs sociōs suōs ex ōrdi- 15
ne eōdem modō ēmīsit; quō factō ipse novissimus ēvāsit. 16

Content Questions:

1. Why did Polyphemus open the doorway of the cave?
2. What did Polyphemus do after opening the doorway?
3. What did Ulysses realize at this time?
4. What was Ulysses' plan of escape for his men?
5. When did Ulysses himself escape?

1. Ulysses thought that Polyphemus would do the same thing as on the day before.
2. He did indeed allow the flock to go out, but he tried to prevent the men from escaping at the same time.
3. For he suspected that that would happen that did happen.
4. He was of so great strength that the Greeks could not resist him.
5. Yet, although they were at the end of hope, Ulysses nevertheless gave them safety through a trick.

Helpful Hints	
2.	Begin your translation with a pronoun to indicate the change of subject from that of the first sentence.
5.	Use an adjective to translate "end of."
	For "at," use **in**.

 3   nāvī praesidiō: *double dative.*
 6   id quidem quod erat: "that indeed that was," "as was indeed the case."
      aliquod: *adjective* "some," corresponding to the *pronoun* aliquid,
          "something."
 7   auxilior, auxiliārī (1), auxiliātus sum, to help.
      auxiliandī causā: *gerund* in the *genitive* with causā to express
          purpose.
 8   nōn satis tūtum esse: *indirect statement* with arbitrātus.
12   violō (1), to outrage, violate.
      iūstus, -a, -um, just.
    *dēbitus, -a, -um, owed, due.
13   immānitās, immānitātis (*f*), cruelty, barbarity.
16   ingēns: *accusative singular neuter,* modifying saxum.
      sublātum: *perfect passive participle* of tollō, modifying saxum.
17   nōn multum āfuit quīn: "it was not lacking much but that" = "it
          nearly. . . . "
18   damnum, -ī (*n*), harm, injury.

Review Questions:

1. How is quam translated with celerrimē? (2)
2. What type of ablative is magnā cum laetitiā? (4)
3. What construction is diēs trēs continuōs? (4–5)
4. What case is ipsī? What does it modify? (7)
5. What is an alternative for auxiliandī causā? (7)
6. What form is Polyphēme? (12)
7. What is an alternative for sublātum? (16)

91. OUT OF DANGER

Hīs rēbus ita cōnfectīs Ulixēs, veritus nē Polyphēmus 1
dolum cognōsceret, cum sociīs quam celerrimē ad lītus con- 2
tendit; quō cum vēnissent, ab eīs quī nāvī praesidiō relictī 3
erant magnā cum laetitiā exceptī sunt. Hī cum iam diēs 4
trēs continuōs reditum eōrum ānxiō animō exspectāvissent, 5
suspicātī (id quidem quod erat) eōs in aliquod grave perīcu- 6
lum incidisse, ipsī auxiliandī causā ēgredī parābant. Tum 7
Ulixēs nōn satis tūtum esse arbitrātus in eō locō manēre, 8
quam celerrimē proficīscī cōnstituit. Itaque omnēs nāvem 9
cōnscendere iussit, et sublātīs ancorīs paulum ā lītore in 10
altum prōvectus est. Tum magnā vōce exclāmāvit: "Tū, 11
Polyphēme, quī iūra hospitī violās, iūstam et dēbitam poe- 12
nam immānitātis tuae solvistī." Hāc vōce audītā 13
Polyphēmus vehementer commōtus ad mare sē contulit. 14
Ubi nāvem paulum ā lītore remōtam esse intellēxit, saxum 15
ingēns sublātum in eam partem coniēcit unde vōcem 16
vēnisse sēnsit. Graecī autem, etsī nōn multum āfuit quīn 17
nāvis eōrum mergerētur, tamen nūllō damnō acceptō cur- 18
sum tenuērunt. 19

Content Questions:

1. Why had some of the men been left with the ship?
2. How long had these men waited for Ulysses and the others to return?
3. Why did Ulysses decide to leave this area?
4. What mistake did Ulysses make at this time?
5. What did Polyphemus do after he heard Ulysses' voice?

1. Some god seems to have protected Ulysses.
2. Even to the end of his life, he was defended by the gods.
3. When the Greeks had snatched themselves out of his hands, Polyphemus thought that he ought to attempt something.
4. Pursuing them to the shore, he hurled a stone to wreck their ship.
5. The Greeks, however, having suspected that this would happen, were so far away that he accomplished nothing.

Helpful Hints
2. For the ablative plural of the word for "god," see the Latin to English Vocabulary.
3. Use a passive periphrastic, "that something ought to be attempted by him."
4. For "would happen," use an active periphrastic of **ēveniō**.

2 *Aeolia, -ae (f), Aeolia.
3 Hīc . . . frēnat: quoted from Vergil, *Aeneid* I.52–54.
  vāstus, -a, -um, waste, huge, enormous, vast.
  vāstō . . . antrō: the omission of in is *poetic*.
  *Aeolus, -ī (m), Aeolus.
  antrum, -ī (n), cave.
4 luctor, luctārī (1), luctātus sum, to wrestle, struggle.
  ventus, -ī (m), wind.
  sonōrus, -a, -um, sounding, loud, noisy, howling.
5 imperiō . . . vinclīs . . . carcere: *ablative of means*.
  premō, premere (3), pressī, pressum, to press, check, restrain.
  vinclīs: = vinculīs.
  carcer, carceris (m), prison.
  frēnō (1), to bridle, restrain.
7 reficiō, reficere (3), refēcī, refectum, to make again, renew, refresh.
9 *nāvigātiō, nāvigātiōnis (f), sailing, navigation, voyage.
  *exclūdō (ex- + claudō), exclūdere (3), exclūsī, exclūsum, to shut out,
  hinder, prevent.
    nē annī tempore ā nāvigātiōne exclūderētur: the Greeks
    were wary of sailing during the stormy weather.
  sibi: *dative of agent* with the *passive periphrastic*.
  *statuō, statuere (3), statuī, statūtum, to set up, decide, resolve.
10 cupidus, -a, -um, desirous, eager.
12 Favōnius, -ī (m), Favonius.
13 nāvigantī: *dative singular* of *present participle* used as a noun, "for one
  who is sailing."
  Ithacam: *accusative* of name of small island *without a preposition* to express *place to which*.
  *secundus, -a, -um, following, favorable.
15 mālus, -ī (m), mast.
  Distinguish this noun carefully from the noun mālum, -ī (n), apple, and
  from the adjective malus, -a, -um, bad.
16 merīdiānus, -a, -um, *idiom*, midday, noonday.
  merīdiānum tempus, *idiom*, midday, noon.
  ferē (*adv.*), nearly, about, almost, for the most part.

Review Questions:

1. What construction is **Pauca mīlia passuum**? (1)
2. What form is **eīs**? Why? (6)
3. What type of ablative is **Septimō diē**? (7–8)
4. What construction is **patriae videndae**? (10–11)
5. What would be an alternative for **nāvigantī**? (13)
6. What would be an alternative for **grātiīs . . . āctīs**? (14–15)
7. What would be an alternative for **ad profectiōnem**? (16)

92. THE COUNTRY OF THE WINDS

Pauca mīlia passuum ab eō locō prōgressus Ulixēs ad īn- 1
sulam Aeoliam nāvem appulit. Haec patria erat ventōrum. 2

Hīc vāstō rēx Aeolus antrō 3
luctantēs ventōs tempestātēsque sonōrās 4
imperiō premit ac vinclīs et carcere frēnat. 5

Ibi rēx ipse Graecōs hospitiō accēpit, atque eīs persuāsit ut 6
ad reficiendās vīrēs paucōs diēs commorārentur. Septimō 7
diē, cum sē ē labōribus refēcissent, Ulixēs, nē annī tempore 8
ā nāvigātiōne exclūderētur, sibi proficīscendum statuit. 9
Tum Aeolus, quī sciēbat Ulixem cupidissimum esse patriae 10
videndae, eī magnum ūtrem dedit, in quō omnēs ventōs 11
praeter ūnum inclūserat. Favōnium modo solverat, quod 12
ille ventus nāvigantī ab īnsulā Aeoliā Ithacam est secun- 13
dus. Ulixēs hoc dōnum libenter accēpit, et grātiīs prō tantō 14
beneficiō āctīs ūtrem ad mālum alligāvit. Omnibus rēbus 15
ad profectiōnem parātīs merīdiānō ferē tempore ē portū 16
solvit. 17

Content Questions:

1. Aeolus was the king of what island?
2. What did King Aeolus persuade the Greeks to do?
3. Why did Aeolus help Ulysses?
4. What did Ulysses do before he set sail again?
5. At what time of day did Ulysses set sail?

1. Ulysses, desirous of returning home, urged his companions to
   hurry to the island of Ithaca.
2. Because of (his) eagerness, he was unwilling to spend time in re-
   freshing (his) strength.
3. Therefore, when he had come to Aeolia, he said that he would not
   stay there long.
4. Others were eager for rest and spoke to one another in this manner (thus).
5. "With Ulysses as our leader, we will again fall into some danger."

Helpful Hints
4. For "to one another," Latin would say "among themselves"; see line 5 of
   paragraph 38.

1   **Novem diēs**: *accusative of duration of time.*
     Distinguish the adjective **novem** carefully from the adjective **novus,
     -a, -um,** new.
3   **gubernō** (1), to steer.
4   **iam diū mīrābantur**: "had already been wondering for a long time"; see
     grammar note below.
7   **aurum et argentum ibi latēre**: *indirect statement.* Note that **lateō,
     latēre** means "to be hidden."
     argentum, -ī (*n*), silver.
9   **ventī**: *subject* of **ruunt** and **perflant** in the quotation from Vergil's
     Aeneid I.82–83.
10   **velut**, even *or* just as, as.
     agmen, agminis (*n*), column.
       velut agmine factō: "as if a column had been formed," "as if formed
       in column."
11   **quā data porta**: i.e., **quā** (*adverb*) **porta data est.**
     porta, -ae (*f*), door, opening.
     *****ruō, ruere** (3), **ruī, ruitum,** to rush.
     turbō, turbinis (*m*), whirlwind.
     perflō (1), to blow through *or* over.
17   **pecūniae**: what kind of genitive?
18   **abiēcissent**: why subjunctive?

Literary Note

During the reign of the Emperor Caesar Augustus,
Publius Vergilius Maro, 70–19 B.C. (known to us as
Vergil) wrote an epic poem called the *Aeneid*. In it he
tells of the adventures of Aeneas as he travels with the
Trojans, who had survived the Trojan War, to their new
home in Italy. One of the places Aeneas visited was
Aeolia, the home of the king of the winds.

Iam diū + Imperfect Indicative

With **iam diū** and similar expressions of duration of
time, the *imperfect indicative* is used to represent an
action or state that began *prior* to a given past time
and was *still continuing* at that time, e.g., **At sociī,
quī** iam diū mīrābantur **. . . , tantam occāsiōnem nōn omittendam arbitrātī sunt,** "But
his companions, who had already been wondering for a
long time . . . , thought that such a great opportunity
should not be lost." Compare the grammar note on
iam diū + present indicative with paragraph 3.

93. THE WIND-BAG

Novem diēs Graecī secundissimō ventō cursum   1
tenuērunt; iamque in cōnspectum patriae suae vēnerant,   2
cum Ulixēs lassitūdine cōnfectus (ipse enim gubernābat) ad   3
quiētem capiendam recubuit.   At sociī, quī iam diū   4
mīrābantur quid in illō ūtre inclūsum esset, cum ducem   5
somnō oppressum vidērent, tantam occāsiōnem nōn omit-   6
tendam arbitrātī sunt; crēdēbant enim aurum et argentum   7
ibi latēre.   Itaque spē praedae adductī ūtrem sine morā   8
solvērunt; quō factō ventī,   9

velut agmine factō,   10
quā data porta, ruunt et terrās turbine perflant.   11

Hīc tanta tempestās subitō coorta est ut illī cursum tenēre   12
nōn possent, sed in eandem partem unde erant profectī re-   13
ferrentur.   Ulixēs ē somnō excitātus quō in locō rēs esset   14
statim intellēxit; ūtrem solūtum, Ithacam post tergum re-   15
lictam vīdit.   Tum vērō vehementer exārsit sociōsque   16
obiūrgāvit, quod cupiditāte pecūniae adductī spem patriae   17
videndae abiēcissent.   18

Content Questions:

1. Why was Ulysses so tired that he fell asleep?
2. Why did the men open the bag?
3. How great a storm arose after the bag was opened?
4. What did Ulysses see when he awoke?
5. Why did Ulysses scold his men?

1. Ulysses wished to cross the sea where the difficulty of navigation was smallest.
2. After he had stayed a few days on the island of Aeolia, finding the weather suitable for sailing, he ordered his companions to embark.
3. Setting out from the harbor, they advanced many miles with a favorable wind.
4. Ithaca indeed had already been in sight for a long time when the ship was carried back by a change of wind.
5. Ulysses saw at once that his companions had done some mischief.

Helpful Hints
1. Use the subjunctive in the subordinate clause (see grammar note with paragraph 47).
4. For "by a change of wind," translate as if "by a changed wind."
5. For "some mischief," translate as if "something of mischief."

2 *Circē, Circēs (f), Circe.
3 in terram . . . ēgregiendum esse: "that he must disembark."
   frūmentor, frūmentārī (1), frūmentātus sum, to fetch grain, forage.
7 quam: adverb.
   quam crūdēlī: "how cruel," "what a cruel."
8 eī quī . . . ēgressī essent: subject of affectī essent.
   quī . . . ēgressī essent: subjunctive by attraction.
   nūper (adv.), newly, lately, recently.
9 quī . . . vellet: relative clause of characteristic with a negative antecedent (nēmō), "no one (who was) willing to undertake this task."
10 dēducta est: "came."
   cōnsēnsus, -ūs (m), agreement, consent.
11 alterī . . . alterī: datives with the compound verb praeesset, "was to
   command," subjunctive in a relative clause of characteristic.
   *Eurylochus, -ī (m), Eurylochus.
13 sortior, sortīrī (4), sortītus sum, to cast or draw lots.
   uter, utra, utrum, which? (of two).
   Eurylochō: dative with the compound verb ēvēnit.
14 ut . . . susciperet: substantive clause of result serving as the subject of
   ēvēnit.

Review Questions:

1. What construction is **Brevī spatiō intermissō**? (1)
2. What would be an alternative for **frūmentandī causā**? (3)
3. What construction is **quid fierī vellet**? (6)
4. What type of genitive is **summae virtūtis**? (12)
5. What form is **ēgrederētur**? (13)

Relative Clauses of Characteristic with Negative or Indefinite Antecedents

Relative clauses of characteristic with their verbs in the subjunctive (see grammar note with paragraph 68) are regularly used after negative or indefinite antecedents, e.g., **Nēmō repertus est quī hoc negōtium suscipere vellet**, "No one was found who was willing to undertake this task," better English, "No one willing to undertake this task was found." The relative clause characterizes or defines the general group referred to in the negative antecedent **nēmō**.

   Relative clauses of characteristic can also be used after indefinite phrases such as **est quī, sunt quī, ūnus est quī, sōlus est quī**, and **quis est quī**.

94. A DRAWING OF LOTS

Brevī spatiō intermissō Graecī īnsulae cuidam appropin- 1
quāvērunt, in quā Circē, fīlia Sōlis, habitābat. Quō cum 2
Ulixēs nāvem appulisset, in terram frūmentandī causā 3
ēgrediendum esse statuit; nam cognōverat frūmentum quod 4
in nāvī habēret iam dēficere. Itaque sociīs ad sē convocātīs, 5
quō in locō rēs esset et quid fierī vellet ostendit. Cum ta- 6
men omnēs memoriā tenērent quam crūdēlī morte affectī 7
essent eī quī nūper ē nāvī ēgressī essent, nēmō repertus est 8
quī hoc negōtium suscipere vellet. Quae cum ita essent, rēs 9
in contrōversiam dēducta est. Tandem Ulixēs omnium cōn- 10
sēnsū sociōs in duās partēs dīvīsit, quārum alterī Eury- 11
lochus, vir summae virtūtis, alterī ipse praeesset. Tum hī 12
duo inter sē sortītī sunt uter in terram ēgrederētur. Eury- 13
lochō sorte ēvēnit ut cum duōbus et vīgintī sociīs rem 14
susciperet. 15

Content Questions:

1. Why did Ulysses' men disembark from his ship at this island?
2. Why did Ulysses have trouble getting men to go on the errand?
3. Into how many groups did Ulysses divide the men?
4. What sort of man was Eurylochus?
5. How did Ulysses decide which group would set out from the ship?

1. After many days they brought their ship to another island, where there was an approach from the sea.
2. Ulysses asked that part of his companions should go ashore, because he did not have a large supply of grain in the ship.
3. At first there was no one who was willing to do this.
4. All suspected that something serious would happen, if they met other monsters.
5. Afterwards certain of them were chosen to explore the place.

Helpful Hints
1. For "from," use ē.
4. For the tense and mood of the verb in the if-clause, see the grammar note with paragraph 65.
5. Use a relative clause of purpose.

6 *aliquantum, -ī (n), somewhat.
> aliquantum itineris: *accusative of extent of space* and *partitive genitive*, "some distance on (their) journey."

8 adīssent: = adīvissent or adiissent.
> cantus, -ūs (m), singing, song.

9 dulcēdō, dulcēdinis (f), sweetness.

10 quīn . . . pulsārent: quīn *clause* after a *negative* expression of *preventing* or *hindering*, "from knocking on."
> *pulsō (1), to push *or* strike against, knock, knock at.
> forās (*adv. used with verbs of motion*), out of doors, forth, out.

11 benignitās, benignitātis (f), kindness.

12 sibi: *dative of reference*, "against them."
> forīs (*adv. used to indicate place where*), out of doors, without, outside. Cf. forās above.

15 iussus, -ūs (m), bidding, command.

16 medicāmentum, -ī (n), drug, poison, potion.

Review Questions:

1. What type of clause is **ut nōn dubitārent**? (3)
2. What is an alternative for **ad mortem īrent**? (3–4)
3. What form is **vīsūrōs**? (6)
4. What form is **dulcissimum**? (8)
5. What construction is **Hōc factō**? (10)
6. What form is **libentissimē**? (15)
7. What form is **bibissent**? (17)
8. What form is **quod** in **quod cum Graecī bibissent**? (17)

95. THE HOUSE OF THE ENCHANTRESS

Hīs rēbus ita cōnstitūtīs eī quī sorte ductī erant in inter- 1
iōrem partem īnsulae profectī sunt. Tantus tamen timor 2
animōs eōrum occupāverat ut nōn dubitārent quīn ad 3
mortem īrent. Vix quidem poterant eī quī in nāvī relictī e- 4
rant lacrimās tenēre; crēdēbant enim sē sociōs suōs 5
numquam posteā vīsūrōs. Illī autem aliquantum itineris 6
prōgressī ad vīllam magnificam pervēnērunt, cuius ad 7
ōstium cum adīssent, cantum dulcissimum audīvērunt. 8
Tanta autem fuit eius vōcis dulcēdō ut nūllō modō retinērī 9
possent quīn iānuam pulsārent. Hōc factō ipsa Circē forās 10
exiit, et summā cum benignitāte omnēs in hospitium in- 11
vītāvit. Eurylochus īnsidiās sibi comparārī suspicātus forīs 12
exspectāre cōnstituit; at reliquī reī novitāte adductī vīllam 13
intrāvērunt. Cēnam omnibus rēbus īnstrūctam invēnērunt, 14
et iussū dominae libentissimē accubuērunt. At Circē vīnum 15
quod servī apposuērunt medicāmentō quōdam miscuerat; 16
quod cum Graecī bibissent, somnō oppressī sunt. 17

Content Questions:

1. Why was the group who were left at the ship so sad?
2. What did Eurylochus and his companions find?
3. Why did Eurylochus not enter the house with his companions?
4. Why were the men so deceived by Circe?
5. What sort of banquet was served to these guests?

1. Those who had been selected advanced from the shore, where the road was deserted.
2. There was nothing that would warn them of unbelievable danger.
3. In the inner part of the island they came upon a house adjacent to the road.
4. Circe, who had furnished this house for herself, urged them to remain there a few hours.
5. Although Eurylochus himself desired to take food, he tried to persuade the rest to resist her.

Helpful Hints
2. Use a relative clause of characteristic.

2   *tangō, tangere (3), tetigī, tāctum, to touch.
4   ignārus, -a, -um, ignorant of, not knowing.
       quid . . . agerētur: *indirect question* with ignārus.
       aedēs, aedis, aedium (*f*), (*sing.*) temple; (*pl.*) house.
6   regredī: *infinitive* of regredior.
7   sollicitūdō, sollicitūdinis (*f*), anxiety, care, apprehension.
9   Eurylochō: *dative* with imperāvit.
11   complexus: *participle* of complector.
12   sī quid gravius . . . futūram (line 14): *indirect statement* dependent
       on the idea of saying implied in obsecrāre coepit. What would the
       direct statement have been?
13   eī: *dative* with the *compound verb* accidisset.
14   sē nēminem . . . rem susceptūrum (line 16): what would the direct
       statement have been?
15   illī: *dative* with licēre, *indirect statement*, "that it was allowed to him."
       mālō, mālle (*irreg.*), māluī, to wish rather, prefer.
16   ūllus, -a, -um, any.
       cum: "when."
17   nūllō: *pronoun* (used instead of the ablative of nēmō).
       sōlus, -a, -um, alone.

Irregular Verb Review

The verbs nōlō, nōlle, nōluī, to not wish, be unwilling, and mālō, mālle, māluī, to wish rather, prefer,
are compounds of volō, velle, voluī, to be willing,
wish: nōlō = nōn volō, and mālō = magis volō.

Present

volō	nōlō	mālō
vīs	nōn vīs	māvīs
vult	nōn vult	māvult
volumus	nōlumus	mālumus
vultis	nōn vultis	māvultis
volunt	nōlunt	mālunt

Imperfect

volēbam	nōlēbam	mālēbam
volēbās	nōlēbās	mālēbās
volēbat, etc.	nōlēbat, etc.	mālēbat, etc.

Future

volam	nōlam	mālam
volēs	nōlēs	mālēs
volet, etc.	nōlet, etc.	mālet, etc.

   The perfect, pluperfect, and future perfect indicative
forms of these verbs are regular.

(Continued on page 200)

96. THE CHARM

Tum Circē, quae artis magicae summam scientiam 1
habēbat, virgā aureā quam gerēbat capita eōrum tetigit; 2
quō factō omnēs in porcōs subitō conversī sunt. Intereā 3
Eurylochus ignārus quid in aedibus agerētur ad ōstium 4
sedēbat. Postquam ad sōlis occāsum ānxiō animō et solli- 5
citō exspectāvit, sōlus ad nāvem regredī cōnstituit. Eō cum 6
vēnisset, sollicitūdine ac timōre ita perturbātus fuit ut 7
quae vīdisset vix nārrāre posset. At Ulixēs satis intellēxit 8
sociōs suōs in perīculō versārī, et gladiō arreptō Eurylochō 9
imperāvit ut sine morā viam ad istam domum dēmōn- 10
strāret. Ille tamen multīs cum lacrimīs Ulixem complexus 11
obsecrāre coepit nē in tantum perīculum sē committeret; sī 12
quid gravius eī accidisset, omnium salūtem in summō dis- 13
crīmine futūram. Ulixēs respondit sē nēminem invītum 14
adductūrum; illī licēre, sī māllet, in nāvī manēre; sē ipsum 15
sine ūllō praesidiō rem susceptūrum. Hoc cum magnā vōce 16
dīxisset, ē nāvī dēsiluit et nūllō sequente sōlus in viam sē 17
dedit. 18

Content Questions:

1. How did Circe turn the men into pigs?
2. How long did Eurylochus wait before returning to the ship?
3. Why was it difficult for Eurylochus to tell Ulysses what had happened?
4. How was Eurylochus finally forced to inform Ulysses fully?
5. Why did Eurylochus beg Ulysses not to go in search of the others?

1. Who is there who wants to know who Circe was?
2. Some say that the sun-god was her father, others assert that she was a daughter of that king who imposed the labors upon Jason.
3. Do you prefer to believe that she touched the heads of the Greeks with her hand?
4. We have informed you that she did not do this.
5. There is no doubt that she turned the Greeks into swine, according to her custom.

Helpful Hints

1. Use a relative clause of characteristic after the indefinite antecedent ("Who is there . . . ?").

    Remember to use the perfect subjunctive for prior time in primary sequence.

4   **līmen, līminis** (*n*), threshold, door.
7   **Circēs:** Greek *genitive singular*.
9   **calamitās, calamitātis** (*f*), misfortune, calamity, disaster.
11   *****prex, precis** (*used chiefly in the plural*) (*f*), prayer, entreaty.
12   **dēterreō** (2), to frighten off, deter.
13   **multum:** *adverbial* with **valēre.**
15   *****dēstringō, dēstringere** (3), **dēstrīnxī, dēstrictum,** to draw, un-
         sheathe.
       ut faciās: *indirect command* with *present subjunctive* in *primary
         sequence* after **vidē,** "see to it that you make."
17   **mortālēs . . . auram:** quoted from Vergil's *Aeneid* IV.277–278.
       mortālis, -is, -e, mortal.
       vīsus, -ūs (*m*), sight.
         vīsūs: "sight"; the use of the *plural* is *poetic*.
       mediō sermōne: "in the middle of their conversation."
18   **tenuis, -is, -e,** thin.
       ēvānēscō, ēvānēscere (3), **ēvānuī,** to vanish away, vanish.
       aura, -ae (*f*), air, breeze.

Content Questions:

1. Why did Ulysses decide to enter the house immediately?
2. In what form did the god Mercury appear to Ulysses?
3. How did Ulysses recognize Mercury?
4. What special gift did the god Mercury give to Ulysses?
5. Where did Mercury go after he helped Ulysses?

Irregular Verb Review (*continued*)

Present Subjunctive

velim	nōlim	mālim
velīs	nōlīs	mālīs
velit	nōlit	mālit

   The imperfect, perfect, and pluperfect subjunctives of
these verbs are regular.

Review Questions:

1. Why is **fēcisset** subjunctive in **mentiōrem fēcisset**? (4)
2. What is a good English translation of **sē ostendit**? (5)
3. What is a good English translation of **conversī**? (9)
4. What kind of answer is expected after a question introduced by
     num? (9)
5. What form is **tetigerit**? (15)
6. What kind of clause is **cum . . . tetigerit**? (14–15)

97. THE COUNTERCHARM

Aliquantum itineris prōgressus ad vīllam magnificam   1
pervēnit, quam cum oculīs perlūstrāsset, statim intrāre   2
statuit; intellēxit enim hanc esse eandem domum dē quā   3
Eurylochus mentiōnem fēcisset. At cum līmen intrāret,   4
subitō sē ostendit adulēscēns fōrmā pulcherrimā auream   5
virgam gerēns. Hic Ulixem iam domum intrantem manū   6
prehendit. "Quō," inquit, "ruis?" "Nōnne scīs hanc esse Cir-   7
cēs domum? Hīc inclūsī sunt amīcī tuī ex hūmānā speciē in   8
porcōs conversī. Num vīs ipse in eandem calamitātem   9
venīre?" Ulixēs simul atque vōcem audīvit, deum Mer-   10
curium agnōvit; nūllīs tamen precibus ab īnstitūtō cōnsiliō   11
dēterrērī potuit. Quod cum Mercurius sēnsisset, herbam   12
quandam eī dedit, quam contrā carmina multum valēre   13
dīcēbat. "Hanc cape," inquit, "et cum Circē tē virgā   14
tetigerit, tū gladiō dēstrictō impetum in eam vidē ut   15
faciās." Deinde subitō   16

    mortālēs vīsūs mediō sermōne relīquit,   17
    et procul in tenuem ex oculīs ēvānuit auram.   18

1. In the meantime, Eurylochus, not daring to follow his companions, was waiting until they should be ready to depart.
2. Since he had seen that he must not delay longer, he set out alone at sunset.
3. When he had arrived at the ship, he was so terrified that he seemed to be unable to speak.
4. Ulysses, however, fearing that his companions were in great peril, urged him to come to their help.
5. "Won't you," he said, "show me the place where your friends are?"

Helpful Hints
1.   Use a perfect participle to translate "daring."
2.   Use an impersonal passive periphrastic.
     For "he set out," find a model in paragraph 96, lines 17–18.
4.   For "fearing," use a perfect participle of a deponent verb.
5.   Use a pronoun to emphasize the subject of the main verb.

 2 **foris, foris, forum** (*f*), door.
    foribus: the word is usually plural, denoting the two leaves of a double
    door.
 3 **Circē**: *ablative singular.*
    *atque (*after words of comparison*), as, than.
13 **ut erat eī praeceptum**: **erat praeceptum**, *impersonal passive* of *in-
    transitive verb* (see grammar note with paragraph 85), "it had been
    ordered"; **eī**, *dative* with the *compound intransitive verb* **erat prae-
    ceptum**, literally, "it had been ordered to him," better English, "he had
    been ordered." Intransitive verbs in Latin, as here, can only be used im-
    personally in the passive; when such verbs take the dative in the active
    construction, they retain it in the passive.
14 **minitor, minitārī** (1), **minitātus sum**, to threaten. Note that Latin
    threatens *something*, whereas English threatens *someone with
    something.*
16 **sibi vītam adimeret**: "take her life"; the *dative of reference* may be
    used with certain verbs to denote the *person from whom a thing is taken.*
    This is called the *dative of separation.*

Review Questions:

1. What construction is **ad omnia perīcula subeunda**? (1–2)
2. Why does **īnstrūctam** end in -am? (4)
3. Why is **vīnī** genitive in **vīnī plēnum**? (6)
4. What kind of clause is **ut neque . . . neque . . . possent**?
   (11–12)
5. What construction is **gladiō dēstrictō**? (13)
6. What type of ablative is **multīs cum lacrimīs**? (15)
7. What type of infinitive is **obsecrāre**? (15)

98. THE ENCHANTRESS IS FOILED

Brevī intermissō spatiō Ulixēs ad omnia perīcula sube- 1
unda parātus iānuam pulsāvit, et foribus apertīs ab ipsā 2
Circē benignē exceptus est. Omnia eōdem modō atque an- 3
teā facta sunt. Cēnam magnificē īnstrūctam vīdit, et ac- 4
cumbere iussus est. Ubi famēs cibō dēpulsa est, Circē pōcu- 5
lum aureum vīnī plēnum Ulixī dedit. Ille etsī suspicābātur 6
venēnum sibi parātum esse, tamen pōculum exhausit; quō 7
factō Circē caput eius virgā tetigit, atque ea verba dīxit 8
quibus sociōs eius anteā in porcōs converterat. Rēs tamen 9
omnīnō aliter ēvēnit atque illa spērāverat. Tanta enim vīs 10
erat eius herbae quam Ulixī Mercurius dederat ut neque 11
venēnum neque verba quicquam efficere possent. Ulixēs 12
autem, ut erat eī praeceptum, gladiō dēstrictō impetum in 13
eam fēcit mortemque minitābātur. Circē cum artem suam 14
nihil valēre sēnsisset, multīs cum lacrimīs eum obsecrāre 15
coepit nē sibi vītam adimeret. 16

Content Questions:

1. What was Ulysses prepared to do when he knocked on the door?
2. What did Ulysses find in the house of Circe?
3. In what way did all things work out just as Mercury had said?
4. What did Ulysses do when Circe's tricks had no effect on him?
5. What did Circe do when her plans didn't work?

1. When Ulysses came upon the house that was nearest to the sea, he understood that he had finished his journey.
2. Did he not learn from a god that his companions had there been turned into swine?
3. He was also ordered to make an attack upon her who had done this.
4. The god, moreover, showed him in what way he could defend himself from the disaster that the others had suffered.
5. And so Circe accomplished nothing.

Helpful Hints
3. For "he was ordered," Latin must use an impersonal passive with the dative: "it was ordered to him." This is then followed by an indirect command.

---

4   sē ... sumptūrum (supply esse): *indirect statement* with ostendit.
6   sēsē: = sē.
      eī: *dative of reference*, literally, "with reference to him," almost
        equivalent to a *possessive adjective*, "his feet."
7   imperāsset: = imperāvisset.
8   immittī: *present passive infinitive* of immittō.
9   irruō (in- + ruō), irruere (3), irruī, to rush in.
12   unguō, unguere (3), ūnxī, ūnctum, to smear, annoint.
      sunt: with restitūtī.
16   in domum: when domus does not mean "home" but refers to the physical
        entity, "house," it is used with a preposition to indicate *place to which* or
        into which (ad or in + acc.) and *place where* (in + abl.).
      Circēs: *Greek genitive singular.*

Review Questions:

1. What type of clause is ut ... restitueret? (2–3)
2. How would certior enim factus erat ā deō Mercuriō be writ-
    ten with an active verb and with Mercury as the subject? (3)
3. Why is imperāsset subjunctive? (7)
4. Why does factūram end in -am in omnia quae ille imperās-
    set sē factūram? (7–8)
5. What construction is datō signō? (8)
6. What type of ablative is Magnō cum gaudiō? (13)
7. What type of clause is quī ... dīceret? (14–15)

Helpful Hints
1. In paragraph 98, line 16, find a model for "not to take her life."

2. For "She was commanded," use an impersonal passive of imperō.
    Find a model for translating the remainder of this sentence in lines 2–3 of
    paragraph 99 above.

3. For "If ... not," use nisi.

99. MEN ONCE MORE

Ulixēs ubi sēnsit eam timōre perterritam esse, pos- 1
tulāvit ut sociōs suōs sine morā in hūmānam speciem 2
restitueret (certior enim factus erat ā deō Mercuriō eōs in 3
porcōs conversōs esse); nisi id factum esset, sē dēbita sup- 4
plicia sūmptūrum ostendit. Circē hīs rēbus graviter com- 5
mōta sēsē eī ad pedēs prōiēcit, et multīs cum lacrimīs iūre 6
iūrandō cōnfīrmāvit omnia quae ille imperāsset sē fac- 7
tūram. Tum porcōs in ātrium immittī iussit. Illī datō signō 8
irruērunt. Cum ducem suum agnōvissent, magnō tamen 9
dolōre affectī sunt, quod nūllō modō eum dē rēbus suīs cer- 10
tiōrem facere poterant. Circē tamen unguentō quōdam cor- 11
pora eōrum ūnxit; quō factō sunt omnēs statim in hū- 12
mānum speciem restitūtī. Magnō cum gaudiō Ulixēs 13
amīcōs suōs agnōvit, et nūntium ad lītus mīsit, quī reliquīs 14
Graecīs sociōs receptōs esse dīceret. Illī autem hīs rēbus 15
cognitīs celeriter in domum Circēs sē contulērunt; quō cum 16
vēnissent ūniversī laetitiae sē dēdidērunt. 17

Content Questions:

1. How did Ulysses know that his men had been turned into pigs?
2. What was Circe's reaction when she recognized the special powers of Ulysses?
3. What were the emotions of Ulysses' men (pigs) when they recognized their leader?
4. How did Circe change the men back into human form?
5. How did the men left at the ship find out what happened?

1. Circe, having been overcome by Ulysses, asked him not to take her life.
2. She was commanded to restore the swine into human shape.
3. "If you do not do this," he said, "I will inflict the severest punishment."
4. "Is not a god helping me, so that you cannot resist me?"
5. When she had learned this, Circe obeyed him, and did everything that he had commanded.

3   **odium, -ī** (*n*), hatred.
4   **obtestor, obtestārī** (1), **obtestātus sum**, to call to witness, beseech,
     implore.
5   **impetrō** (1), to gain one's end, obtain (a request).
     ut facile eī persuādērētur: *result clause* with *impersonal passive of
     intransitive verb* taking the *dative case,* "so that it was easily persuaded
     to him," better English, "so that he was easily persuaded."
6   **ut diūtius manēret**: *substantive clause of result* serving as the *subject*
     of **persuādērētur**.
     diūtius (*comparative of* **diū**), longer.
7   **apud** (+ *acc.*), among, with, at the house of.
     dēsīderium, -ī (*n*), desire, longing.
10   **afflīgō** (ad- + flīgō), **afflīgere** (3), **afflīxī, afflīctum**, to dash to
     pieces, shatter.
11   **inūtilis, -is, -e**, not useful, useless.

Content Questions:

1. What did Ulysses intend to do at first?
2. How did Circe convince Ulysses to stay for a while with her?
3. What did Ulysses discover a year later?
4. How much time did it take for Ulysses to prepare to leave?
5. Why was Ulysses in such a hurry to leave?

Review Questions:

1. What would be another way to express **discēdere in animō
   habēbat**? (2)
2. What construction are the words **ōrāre et obtestārī**? (4)
3. What construction is **paucōs diēs**? (4)
4. What construction is **quā rē impetrātā**? (5)
5. What kind of genitive is **patriae suae**? (7–8)
6. What kind of dative is **ūsuī**? (12)
7. What kind of clause is **ut . . . perficerent**? (13–14)
8. What kind of clause is **ut . . . dēsisteret**? (15–16)
9. What kind of clause is **nē . . . exclūderētur**? (16–17)
10. What form is **Ulixī**? Why? (19)
11. Why is **pervenīret** subjunctive? (19–20)

1. Because of his longing for rest, Ulysses was persuaded to spend a
   whole year in that place.
2. When he had decided to depart, he began to collect those things that
   he thought would be useful.
3. He had to repair his ship before he could set out.
4. When this had been done, his companions were ordered to embark.
5. As the time of the year was suitable for sailing and the wind favorable, they hoped that they would quickly return home.

100. AFLOAT AGAIN

Postrīdiē eius diēī Ulixēs ex hāc īnsulā quam celerrimē 1
discēdere in animō habēbat. Circē tamen cum id cognōvis- 2
set, ab odiō ad amōrem conversa omnibus precibus eum 3
ōrāre et obtestārī coepit ut paucōs diēs apud sē morārētur; 4
quā rē impetrātā tanta beneficia in eum contulit ut facile eī 5
persuādērētur ut diūtius manēret. Postquam tōtum annum 6
apud Circēn cōnsūmpsit, Ulixēs magnō dēsīderiō patriae 7
suae mōtus est. Itaque sociīs ad sē convocātīs quid in ani- 8
mō habēret ostendit. Sed ubi ad lītus dēscendit, nāvem 9
suam tempestātibus ita afflīctam invēnit ut ad nāvigan- 10
dum paene inūtilis esset. Quō cognitō omnia quae ad nāvēs 11
reficiendās ūsuī erant comparārī iussit; quā in rē tantam 12
dīligentiam omnēs adhibēbant ut tertiō diē opus perfice- 13
rent. At Circē ubi omnia ad profectiōnem parāta vīdit, rem 14
aegrē tulit, atque Ulixem vehementer obsecrāvit ut cōnsiliō 15
dēsisteret. Ille tamen, nē annī tempore ā nāvigātiōne ex- 16
clūderētur, mātūrandum sibi exīstimāvit, et idōneam tem- 17
pestātem nactus nāvem solvit. Multa quidem perīcula 18
Ulixī subeunda erant priusquam in patriam suam per- 19
venīret, quae tamen hōc locō perscrībere longum est. 20

Literary Note

Ulysses told these long tales at a banquet, at which
he was a guest in the land of the Phaeacians. King
Alcinous and Queen Arete were entertaining this heroic-
looking stranger and thought he might be a good
husband for their beautiful daughter Nausicaa.
Ulysses, however, was still insistent on getting back to
Ithaca and his beloved Penelope. The Phaeacians took
him home, where he was reunited with Penelope and
his son, Telemachus, who by this time was a handsome
young man. So ends what we know about the heroic
Ulysses from the story told by Homer in the *Odyssey.*

Helpful Hints

1. For "Ulysses was persuaded," use an impersonal passive with the dative: "it
   was persuaded to Ulysses." This is then followed by an indirect command.
3. Use a passive periphrastic.
4. Use linking **quī**.
5. For "as . . . ," use **ut** and the indicative.

Grammatical Notes

(in Alphabetical Order)

Grammatical Notes

(in Sequence by Paragraph)

Ablative of Agent (1)
Complementary Infinitive (1)
Double or Predicate Accusative (2)
Ablative of Means, Instrument, or Cause with Verbs (2)
Ablative of Time When or Within Which (2)
Accusative of Duration of Time (3)
Dative with Adjectives (3)
Infinitive as Subject or Predicate Nominative (3)
Iam diū + Present Indicative (3)
Ablative of Description (4)
Ablative of Means, Instrument, or Cause with Adjectives or Participles
    (4)
Ablative of Manner (5)
Dum + Present Indicative = "while" (5)
Third Declension I-stem Nouns (6)
Ablative of Respect (6)
Vivid or Historic Present (7)
Dative with Compound Verbs (7)
Neuter I-stem Nouns of the Third Declension (7)
Dum + Imperfect Indicative = "while," "as long as" (8)
Genitive of Description (9)
Adverbs of Place (10)
Ablative of Manner (11)
Perfect Infinitives, Active and Passive (12)
Partitive Genitive with Superlative Adjectives (12)
Partitive Genitive (14)
Dative with Special Intransitive Verbs (14)
Ablative of Degree of Difference (14)
Dative of Purpose (15)
Locative Case (16)
Accusative of Place to Which (16)
Ablative of Separation (16)
Ablative of Accompaniment (17)
Deponent Verbs (17)
Reflexive Adjective (18)
Intensive Adjective (18)
Relative Pronouns (19)
Past General (19)
Present Active and Passive Infinitives (20)
Gerund or Verbal Noun (21)

Forms

I. Nouns

Number / Case	1st Declension — Fem.	2nd Declension — Masc.	2nd Declension — Masc.	2nd Declension — Neut.	3rd Declension — Masc.	3rd Declension — Fem.	3rd Declension — Neut.	4th Declension — Fem.	4th Declension — Neut.	5th Declension — Masc.
Singular										
Nom.	puélla	sérvus	púer	báculum	páter	vōx	nōmen	mánus	génū	diēs
Gen.	puéllae	sérvī	púerī	báculī	pátris	vōcis	nŏminis	mánūs	génūs	diḗī
Dat.	puéllae	sérvō	púerō	báculō	pátrī	vōcī	nŏminī	mánuī	génū	diḗī
Acc.	puéllam	sérvum	púerum	báculum	pátrem	vōcem	nōmen	mánum	génū	diem
Abl.	puéllā	sérvō	púerō	báculō	pátre	vōce	nŏmine	mánū	génū	diē
Plural										
Nom.	puéllae	sérvī	púerī	bácula	pátrēs	vōcēs	nŏmina	mánūs	génua	diēs
Gen.	puellárum	servórum	puerórum	baculórum	pátrum	vōcum	nŏminum	mánuum	génuum	diḗrum
Dat.	puéllīs	sérvīs	púerīs	báculīs	pátribus	vōcibus	nŏminibus	mánibus	génibus	diḗbus
Acc.	puéllās	sérvōs	púerōs	bácula	pátrēs	vōcēs	nŏmina	mánūs	génua	diēs
Abl.	puéllīs	sérvīs	púerīs	báculīs	pátribus	vōcibus	nŏminibus	mánibus	génibus	diḗbus

II. Adjectives

Number / Case	1st and 2nd Declension			3rd Declension		
	Masc.	*Fem.*	*Neut.*	*Masc.*	*Fem.*	*Neut.*
Singular						
Nominative	mágnus	mágna	mágnum	ómnis	ómnis	ómne
Genitive	mágnī	mágnae	mágnī	ómnis	ómnis	ómnis
Dative	mágnō	mágnae	mágnō	ómnī	ómnī	ómnī
Accusative	mágnum	mágnam	mágnum	ómnem	ómnem	ómne
Ablative	mágnō	mágnā	mágnō	ómnī	ómnī	ómnī
Plural						
Nominative	mágnī	mágnae	mágna	ómnēs	ómnēs	ómnia
Genitive	magnórum	magnárum	magnórum	ómnium	ómnium	ómnium
Dative	mágnīs	mágnīs	mágnīs	ómnibus	ómnibus	ómnibus
Accusative	mágnōs	mágnās	mágna	ómnēs	ómnēs	ómnia
Ablative	mágnīs	mágnīs	mágnīs	ómnibus	ómnibus	ómnibus

III. Numerical Adjectives or Numbers

Case	Masc.	Fem.	Neut.	Masc.	Fem.	Neut.	Masc.	Fem.	Neut.
Nom.	únus	úna	únum	dúo	dúae	dúo	trēs	trēs	tría
Gen.	únïus	únïus	únïus	duórum	duárum	duórum	tríum	tríum	tríum
Dat.	únï	únï	únï	duóbus	duábus	duóbus	tríbus	tríbus	tríbus
Acc.	únum	únam	únum	dúōs	dúās	dúo	trēs	trēs	tría
Abl.	únō	únā	únō	duóbus	duábus	duóbus	tríbus	tríbus	tríbus

Cardinal

I	ūnus, -a, -um, one
II	duo, -ae, -o, two
III	trēs, trēs, tria, three
IV	quattuor, four
V	quīnque, five
VI	sex, six
VII	septem, seven
VIII	octō, eight
IX	novem, nine
X	decem, ten
XI	ūndecim, eleven
XII	duodecim, twelve
XX	vīgintī, twenty
L	quīnquāgintā, fifty
C	centum, a hundred
D	quīngentī, -ae, -a, five hundred
M	mīlle, a thousand

Ordinal

prīmus, -a, -um, first
secundus, -a, -um, second
tertius, -a, -um, third
quārtus, -a, -um
quīntus, -a, -um
sextus, -a, -um
septimus, -a, -um
octāvus, -a, -um
nōnus, -a, -um
decimus, -a, -um
ūndecimus, -a, -um
duodecimus, -a, -um
vīcēsimus, -a, -um
quīnquāgēsimus, -a, -um
centēsimus, -a, -um
quīngentēsimus, -a, -um
mīllēsimus, -a, -um

N.B. The cardinal numbers from **quattuor** to **centum** do not change their form to indicate case and gender.

IV. Comparative Adjectives

Number Case	Masculine	Feminine	Neuter
Singular			
Nom.	púlchrior	púlchrior	púlchrius
Gen.	pulchrióris	pulchrióris	pulchrióris
Dat.	pulchriórī	pulchriórī	pulchriórī
Acc.	pulchriórem	pulchriórem	púlchrius
Abl.	pulchrióre	pulchrióre	pulchrióre
Plural			
Nom.	pulchriórēs	pulchriórēs	pulchrióra
Gen.	pulchriórum	pulchriórum	pulchriórum
Dat.	pulchrióribus	pulchrióribus	pulchrióribus
Acc.	pulchriórēs	pulchriórēs	pulchrióra
Abl.	pulchrióribus	pulchrióribus	pulchrióribus

Adjectives have *positive, comparative,* and *superlative* forms. You can recognize the comparative by the letters *-ior/-ius/-iōr-* and the superlative by the letters *-issimus, -errimus,* or *-illimus,* e.g.:

ignavus, *lazy*	ignāvior	ignāvissimus, -a, -um
pulcher, *beautiful*	pulchrior	pulcherrimus, -a, -um
facilis, *easy*	facilior	facillimus, -a, -um

Some adjectives are irregular in the comparative and superlative, e.g.:

bonus, *good*	melior, *better*	optimus, *best*
malus, *bad*	peior, *worse*	pessimus, *worst*
magnus, *big*	maior, *bigger*	maximus, *biggest*
parvus, *small*	minor, *smaller*	minimus, *smallest*
multus, *much*	plūs, *more*	plūrimus, *most, very much*
multī, *many*	plūrēs, *more*	plūrimī, *most, very many*

Note that comparative adjectives are declined like 3rd declension nouns and not like 3rd declension adjectives; that is, they are not i-stems.

V. Present Active Participles

Number Case	Masculine	Feminine	Neuter
Singular			
Nom.	párāns	párāns	párāns
Gen.	parántis	parántis	parántis
Dat.	parántī	parántī	parántī
Acc.	parántem	parántem	párāns
Abl.	paránte	paránte	paránte
Plural			
Nom.	parántēs	parántēs	parántia
Gen.	parántium	parántium	parántium
Dat.	parántibus	parántibus	parántibus
Acc.	parántēs	parántēs	parántia
Abl.	parántibus	parántibus	parántibus

Present active participles are i-stems, but they may have either **-e** (as above) or **-ī** in the ablative singular.

Summary:

    3rd declension adjectives (i-stems):
        ablative singular: **-ī**
        genitive plural: **-ium**
        neuter nominative/accusative plural: **-ia**

    Comparative adjectives (not i-stems):
        ablative singular: **-e**
        genitive plural: **-um**
        neuter nominative/accusative plural: **-a**

    Present active participles (i-stems)
        ablative singular: **-e** or **-ī**
        genitive plural: **-ium**
        neuter nominative/accusative plural: **-ia**

VI. Demonstrative Adjectives and Pronouns

Number Case	Masc.	Fem.	Neut.	Masc.	Fem.	Neut.
Singular						
Nom.	is	éa	id	ídem	éadem	ídem
Gen.	éius	éius	éius	eiúsdem	eiúsdem	eiúsdem
Dat.	éī	éī	éī	eídem	eídem	eídem
Acc.	éum	éam	id	eúndem	eándem	ídem
Abl.	éō	éā	éō	eódem	eádem	eódem
Plural						
Nom.	éī	éae	éa	eídem	eaédem	éadem
Gen.	eórum	eárum	eórum	eōrúndem	eārúndem	eōrúndem
Dat.	éīs	éīs	éīs	eísdem	eísdem	eísdem
Acc.	éōs	éās	éa	eósdem	eásdem	éadem
Abl.	éīs	éīs	éīs	eísdem	eísdem	eísdem

Number Case	Masc.	Fem.	Neut.	Masc.	Fem.	Neut.
Singular						
Nom.	hic	haec	hoc	ílle	ílla	íllud
Gen.	húius	húius	húius	illíus	illíus	illíus
Dat.	húic	húic	húic	íllī	íllī	íllī
Acc.	hunc	hanc	hoc	íllum	íllam	íllud
Abl.	hōc	hāc	hōc	íllō	íllā	íllō
Plural						
Nom.	hī	hae	haec	íllī	íllae	ílla
Gen.	hórum	hárum	hórum	illórum	illárum	illórum
Dat.	hīs	hīs	hīs	íllīs	íllīs	íllīs
Acc.	hōs	hās	haec	íllōs	íllās	ílla
Abl.	hīs	hīs	hīs	íllīs	íllīs	íllīs

The intensive adjective **ipse, ipsa, ipsum** has the same endings as **ille, illa, illud** except for **ipsum** in the neuter nominative and accusative singular.

The demonstrative **iste, ista, istud** has the same endings as **ille, illa, illud**.

VII. Intensive Adjective

Number Case	Masc.	Fem.	Neut.
Singular			
Nom.	ípse	ípsa	ípsum
Gen.	ipsíus	ipsíus	ipsíus
Dat.	ípsī	ípsī	ípsī
Acc.	ípsum	ípsam	ípsum
Abl.	ípsō	ípsā	ípsō
Plural			
Nom.	ípsī	ípsae	ípsa
Gen.	ipsórum	ipsárum	ipsórum
Dat.	ípsīs	ípsīs	ípsīs
Acc.	ípsōs	ípsās	ípsa
Abl.	ípsīs	ípsīs	ípsīs

The demonstrative adjectives and pronouns and the intensive adjective are irregular, but many endings are those of the 1st and 2nd declensions, and the genitive and dative singulars show similarities:

hic, haec, hoc:	huius	huic
ille, illa, illud:	illīus	illī
is, ea, id:	eius	eī
ipse, ipsa, ipsum:	ipsīus	ipsī

VIII. Relative and Interrogative Pronouns and Adjectives

	Singular			Plural		
	Masc.	Fem.	Neut.	Masc.	Fem.	Neut.
Nom.	quī	quae	quod	quī	quae	quae
Gen.	cúius	cúius	cúius	quórum	quárum	quórum
Dat.	cúi	cúi	cúi	quíbus	quíbus	quíbus
Acc.	quem	quam	quod	quōs	quās	quae
Abl.	quō	quā	quō	quíbus	quíbus	quíbus

The interrogative pronoun **quis, quid**, "who?" "what?" has the same forms as the relative pronoun, except for the nominative masculine/feminine singular **quis** and the nominative and accusative neuter singular **quid**. In the singular, the feminine has the same forms as the masculine. In the plural, all forms are the same as those of the relative pronoun. The interrogative adjective **quī, quae, quod,** "which?" "what?" has the same forms as the relative pronoun.

IX. Indefinite Adjectives and Pronouns

Number / Case	Masc.	Fem.	Neut.	Masc.	Fem.	Neut.
Singular						
Nom.	quídam	quaédam	quóddam	áliquī	áliqua	áliquod
Gen.	cuiúsdam	cuiúsdam	cuiúsdam	alicuíus	alicuíus	alicuíus
Dat.	cuídam	cuídam	cuídam	alicuí	alicuí	alicuí
Acc.	quéndam	quándam	quóddam	aliquem	aliquam	áliquod
Abl.	quódam	quádam	quódam	áliquō	áliquā	áliquō
Plural						
Nom.	quídam	quaédam	quaédam	áliquī	áliquae	áliqua
Gen.	quōrúndam	quārúndam	quōrúndam	aliquōrum	aliquārum	aliquōrum
Dat.	quibúsdam	quibúsdam	quibúsdam	aliquibus	aliquibus	aliquibus
Acc.	quōsdam	quásdam	quaédam	aliquōs	aliquās	áliqua
Abl.	quibúsdam	quibúsdam	quibúsdam	aliquibus	aliquibus	aliquibus

The indefinite pronoun **quidam, quaedam, quiddam** "a certain one," "a certain thing," has the same forms as the indefinite adjective given above ("a certain," "certain"), except for **quiddam** in the neuter nominative and accusative singular. The indefinite pronoun **aliquis, aliquid,** "someone," "anyone," "something," "anything," has the forms of the interrogative pronoun **quis, quid,** "who?" "what?" as do the pronouns **quisque, quidque,** "each," and **quisquam, quidquam (quicquam),** "anyone," "anything."

X. Personal and Demonstrative Pronouns

	Singular					Plural				
Case	1st	2nd	3rd			1st	2nd	3rd		
			Masc.	Fem.	Neut.			Masc.	Fem.	Neut.
Nom.	égo	tū	is	éa	id	nōs	vōs	éī	éae	éa
Gen.	méī	túī	éius	éius	éius	nóstrī	véstrī	eórum	eárum	eórum
Dat.	míhi	tíbi	éī	éī	éī	nṓbīs	vṓbīs	éīs	éīs	éīs
Acc.	mē	tē	éum	éam	id	nōs	vōs	éōs	éās	éa
Abl.	mē	tē	éō	éā	éō	nṓbīs	vṓbīs	éīs	éīs	éīs

XI. Reflexive Pronoun

Case	Singular	Plural
Nom.	—	—
Gen.	súī	súī
Dat.	síbi	síbi
Acc.	sē	sē
Abl.	sē	sē

The reflexive pronoun given above is that of the third person, "of him-self/herself," "of themselves," etc. For the first and second persons, the personal pronouns may be used as reflexives, e.g., **meī, mihi.**

XII. Adverbs

Latin adverbs may be formed from adjectives of the 1st and 2nd
declensions by adding *-ē* to the base of the adjective, e.g., **strēnuē,**
"strenuously," from **strēnuus, -a, -um.** To form an adverb from a
3rd declension adjective, add *-iter* to the base of the adjective or *-ter*
to bases ending in -nt-, e.g., **breviter,** "briefly," from **brevis, -is, -e,**
and **prūdenter,** "wisely," from **prūdēns, prūdentis.**

The comparative ends in *-ius*.

The superlative ends in *-issimē, -errimē,* or *-illimē,* e.g.:

lentē, *slowly*	lentius	lentissimē
fēlīciter, *luckily*	fēlīcius	fēlīcissimē
dīligenter, *carefully*	dīligentius	dīligentissimē
celeriter, *quickly*	celerius	celerrimē
facile, *easily*	facilius	facillimē

Some adverbs are irregular:

bene, *well*	melius, *better*	optimē, *best*
male, *badly*	peius, *worse*	pessimē, *worst*
magnopere, *greatly*	magis, *more*	maximē, *most*
paulum, *little*	minus, *less*	minimē, *least*
multum, *much*	plūs, *more*	plūrimum, *most*

Some adverbs are not formed from adjectives:

diū, *for a long time*	diūtius	diūtissimē
saepe, *often*	saepius	saepissimē
sērō, *late*	sērius	sērissimē

XIII. Regular Verbs Active:
Infinitive, Imperative, Indicative

			1st Conjugation	2nd Conjugation	3rd Conjugation		4th Conjugation
Present Infinitive			paráre	habére	mittere	iácere (-iō)	audíre
Imperative	Present	Singular	párā	hábē	mitte	iáce	aúdī
		Plural	paráte	habéte	míttite	iácite	audíte
Present	Singular	1	párō	hábeō	míttō	iáciō	aúdiō
		2	páras	hábēs	míttis	iácis	aúdīs
		3	párat	hábet	míttit	iácit	aúdit
	Plural	1	parámus	habémus	míttimus	iácimus	audímus
		2	parátis	habétis	míttitis	iácitis	audítis
		3	párant	hábent	míttunt	iáciunt	aúdiunt
Imperfect	Singular	1	parábam	habébam	mittébam	iaciébam	audiébam
		2	parábās	habébās	mittébās	iaciébās	audiébās
		3	parábat	habébat	mittébat	iaciébat	audiébat
	Plural	1	parābámus	habēbámus	mittēbámus	iaciēbámus	audiēbámus
		2	parābátis	habēbátis	mittēbátis	iaciēbátis	audiēbátis
		3	parábant	habébant	mittébant	iaciébant	audiébant

XIV. Regular Verbs Active:
Indicative, Infinitive (continued)

Future	*Singular*	1	parābō	habēbō	mittam	iaciam	audiam
		2	parābis	habēbis	mittēs	iaciēs	audiēs
		3	parābit	habēbit	mittet	iaciet	audiet
	Plural	1	parābimus	habēbimus	mittēmus	iaciēmus	audiēmus
		2	parābitis	habēbitis	mittētis	iaciētis	audiētis
		3	parābunt	habēbunt	mittent	iacient	audient
Perfect Infinitive			parāvisse	habuisse	mīsisse	iēcisse	audīvisse
Perfect	*Singular*	1	parāvī	hābuī	mīsī	iēcī	audīvī
		2	parāvistī	habuistī	mīsistī	iēcistī	audīvistī
		3	parāvit	hābuit	mīsit	iēcit	audīvit
	Plural	1	parāvimus	habuimus	mīsimus	iēcimus	audīvimus
		2	parāvistis	habuistis	mīsistis	iēcistis	audīvistis
		3	parāvērunt	habuērunt	mīsērunt	iēcērunt	audīvērunt

XV. Regular Verbs Active:
Indicative (continued)

			parāv-	habu-	mīs-	iēc-	audīv-
Pluperfect	*Singular*	1	paráveram	habúeram	míseram	iéceram	audíveram
		2	paráverās	habúerās	míserās	iécerās	audíverās
		3	paráverat	habúerat	míserat	iécerat	audíverat
	Plural	1	parāverámus	habuerámus	mīserámus	iēcerámus	audīverámus
		2	parāverátis	habuerátis	miserátis	iēcerátis	audīverátis
		3	paráverant	habúerant	míserant	iécerant	audíverant
Future Perfect	*Singular*	1	paráverō	habúerō	míserō	iécerō	audíverō
		2	paráveris	habúeris	míseris	iéceris	audíveris
		3	paráverit	habúerit	míserit	iécerit	audíverit
	Plural	1	parāvérimus	habuérimus	mīsérimus	iēcérimus	audīvérimus
		2	parāvéritis	habuéritis	miséritis	iēcéritis	audīvéritis
		3	paráverint	habúerint	míserint	iécerint	audíverint

XVI. Regular Verbs Passive:
Indicative

			1st Conjugation	2nd Conjugation	3rd Conjugation		4th Conjugation
Present	Singular	1	pórtor	móveor	míttor	iácior	aúdior
		2	portáris	movéris	mítteris	iáceris	audíris
		3	portátur	movétur	míttitur	iácitur	audítur
	Plural	1	portámur	movémur	míttimur	iácimur	audímur
		2	portáminī	movéminī	míttíminī	iacíminī	audíminī
		3	portántur	movéntur	míttúntur	iaciúntur	audiúntur
Imperfect	Singular	1	portábar	movébar	mittébar	iaciébar	audiébar
		2	portābáris	movēbáris	mittēbáris	iaciēbáris	audiēbáris
		3	portābátur	movēbátur	mittēbátur	iaciēbátur	audiēbátur
	Plural	1	portābámur	movēbámur	mittēbámur	iaciēbámur	audiēbámur
		2	portābáminī	movēbáminī	mittēbáminī	iaciēbáminī	audiēbáminī
		3	portābántur	movēbántur	mittēbántur	iaciēbántur	audiēbántur

XVII. Regular Verbs Passive:
Indicative (continued)

Future

Singular	1	portābor	movēbor	míttar	iáciar	aúdiar
	2	portāberis	movēberis	mittéris	iaciéris	audiéris
	3	portābitur	movēbitur	mittétur	iaciétur	audiétur
Plural	1	portābimur	movēbimur	mittémur	iaciémur	audiémur
	2	portābíminī	movēbíminī	mittémini	iaciémini	audiémini
	3	portābúntur	movēbúntur	mitténtur	iaciéntur	audiéntur

		PERFECT PASSIVE		PLUPERFECT PASSIVE		FUTURE PERFECT PASSIVE	
Singular	1	portátus, -a	sum	portátus, -a	éram	portátus, -a	érō
	2	portátus, -a	es	portátus, -a	érās	portátus, -a	éris
	3	portátus, -a, -um	est	portátus, -a, -um	érat	portátus, -a, -um	érit
Plural	1	portátī, -ae	súmus	portátī, -ae	erámus	portátī, -ae	érimus
	2	portátī, -ae	éstis	portátī, -ae	erátis	portátī, -ae	éritis
	3	portátī, -ae, -a	sunt	portátī, -ae, -a	érant	portátī, -ae, -a	érunt

XVIII. Regular Verbs Active: Subjunctive

			1st Conjugation	2nd Conjugation	3rd Conjugation		4th Conjugation
Present	*Singular*	1	párem	hábeam	míttam	iáciam	aúdiam
		2	párēs	hábeās	míttās	iáciās	aúdiās
		3	páret	hábeat	míttat	iáciat	aúdiat
	Plural	1	parēmus	habeāmus	mittāmus	iaciāmus	audiāmus
		2	parētis	habeātis	mittātis	iaciātis	audiātis
		3	párent	hábeant	míttant	iáciant	aúdiant
Imperfect	*Singular*	1	parārem	habērem	mítterem	iácerem	audīrem
		2	parārēs	habērēs	mítterēs	iácerēs	audīrēs
		3	parāret	habēret	mítteret	iáceret	audīret
	Plural	1	parārēmus	habērēmus	mitterēmus	iacerēmus	audīrēmus
		2	parārētis	habērētis	mitterētis	iacerētis	audīrētis
		3	parārent	habērent	mítterent	iácerent	audīrent

XIX. Regular Verbs Active:
Subjunctive (continued)

			1st Conjugation	2nd Conjugation	3rd Conjugation		4th Conjugation
Perfect	Singular	1	parâverim	habúerim	míserim	iécerim	audíverim
		2	parâveris	habúeris	míseris	iéceris	audíveris
		3	parâverit	habúerit	míserit	iécerit	audíverit
	Plural	1	parāvérimus	habuérimus	mīsérimus	iēcérimus	audivérimus
		2	parāvéritis	habuéritis	mīséritis	iēcéritis	audivéritis
		3	parâverint	habúerint	míserint	iécerint	audíverint
Pluperfect	Singular	1	parâvíssem	habuíssem	mīsíssem	iēcíssem	audivíssem
		2	parāvissēs	habuissēs	mīsissēs	iēcissēs	audivíssēs
		3	parâvísset	habuísset	mīsísset	iēcísset	audivísset
	Plural	1	parāvissēmus	habuissēmus	mīsissēmus	iēcissēmus	audivissēmus
		2	parāvissétis	habuissétis	mīsissétis	iēcissétis	audivissétis
		3	parâvíssent	habuíssent	mīsíssent	iēcíssent	audivíssent

XX. Regular Verbs Passive: Subjunctive

			1st Conjugation	2nd Conjugation	3rd Conjugation		4th Conjugation
Present	Singular	1	párer	hábear	míttar	iáciar	aúdiar
		2	parēris	habeáris	mittáris	iaciáris	audiáris
		3	parētur	habeátur	mittátur	iaciátur	audiátur
	Plural	1	parēmur	habeámur	mittámur	iaciámur	audiámur
		2	parēmini	habeámini	mittámini	iaciámini	audiámini
		3	parēntur	habeántur	mittántur	iaciántur	audiántur
Imperfect	Singular	1	parárer	habérer	mitterer	iácerer	audírer
		2	pararéris	habēréris	mitteréris	iaceréris	audīréris
		3	pararétur	habērétur	mitterétur	iacerétur	audīrétur
	Plural	1	pararémur	habērémur	mitterémur	iacerémur	audīrémur
		2	pararémini	habērémini	mitterémini	iacerémini	audīrémini
		3	pararéntur	habēréntur	mitteréntur	iaceréntur	audīréntur

The perfect passive subjunctive consists of the perfect passive participle plus the present subjunctive of the verb **esse** (see p. 234), e.g., **parātus sim**. The pluperfect passive subjunctive consists of the perfect passive participle plus the imperfect subjunctive of the verb **esse** (see page 234), e.g., **parātus essem**.

XXI. Irregular Verbs:
Infinitive, Imperative, Indicative

Infinitive			ésse	pósse	vélle	nólle
Imperative			es	—	—	nólī
			éste	—	—	nōlíte
Present	Singular	1	sum	póssum	vólō	nólō
		2	es	pótes	vīs	nōn vīs
		3	est	pótest	vult	nōn vult
	Plural	1	súmus	póssumus	vólumus	nólumus
		2	éstis	potéstis	vúltis	nōn vúltis
		3	sunt	póssunt	vólunt	nólunt
Imperfect	Singular	1	éram	póteram	volébam	nōlébam
		2	érās	póterās	volébās	nōlébās
		3	érat	póterat	volébat	nōlébat
	Plural	1	erámus	poterámus	volēbámus	nōlēbámus
		2	erátis	poterátis	volēbátis	nōlēbátis
		3	érant	póterant	volébant	nōlébant
Future	Singular	1	érō	póterō	vólam	nólam
		2	éris	póteris	vólēs	nólēs
		3	érit	póterit	vólet	nólet
	Plural	1	érimus	potérimus	volémus	nōlémus
		2	éritis	potéritis	volétis	nōlétis
		3	érunt	póterunt	vólent	nólent

XXII. Irregular Verbs:
Infinitive, Imperative, Indicative (cont.)

			Infinitive	mālle	íre	férre	férrī	fíerī
			Imperative	—	ī	fer	férre	—
				—	íte	férte	ferímini	—
Present	*Singular*	1		mālō	éō	férō	féror	fíō
		2		mávīs	īs	fers	férris	fís
		3		mávult	it	fert	fértur	fit
	Plural	1		málumus	ímus	férimus	férimur	fímus
		2		māvúltis	ítis	fértis	ferímini	fítis
		3		málunt	éunt	férunt	ferúntur	fíunt
Imperfect	*Singular*	1		mālébam	íbam	ferébam	ferébar	fiébam
		2		mālébās	íbās	ferébās	ferēbáris	fiébās
		3		mālébat	íbat	ferébat	ferēbátur	fiébat
	Plural	1		mālēbámus	ībámus	ferēbámus	ferēbámur	fiēbámus
		2		mālēbátis	ībátis	ferēbátis	ferēbáminī	fiēbátis
		3		mālébant	íbant	ferébant	ferēbántur	fiébant
Future	*Singular*	1		málam	íbō	féram	férar	fíam
		2		málēs	íbis	férēs	feréris	fíēs
		3		málet	íbit	féret	ferétur	fíet
	Plural	1		mālémus	íbimus	ferémus	ferémur	fiémus
		2		mālétis	íbitis	ferétis	ferémini	fiétis
		3		málent	íbunt	férent	feréntur	fíent

Note: perfect, pluperfect, and future perfect tenses are formed regularly from the perfect stem plus the regular endings for each tense. These tenses of **fīō** are made up of the participle **factus, -a, -um** plus **sum, eram**, and **erō** respectively.

XXIII. Irregular Verbs:
Subjunctive

Present	*Singular*	1	sim	póssim	vélim	nólim
		2	sīs	póssīs	vélīs	nólīs
		3	sit	póssit	vélit	nólit
	Plural	1	sīmus	possímus	velímus	nōlímus
		2	sítis	possítis	velítis	nōlítis
		3	sint	póssint	vélint	nólint
Imperfect	*Singular*	1	éssem	póssem	véllem	nóllem
		2	éssēs	póssēs	véllēs	nóllēs
		3	ésset	pósset	véllet	nóllet
	Plural	1	essémus	possémus	vellémus	nōllémus
		2	essétis	possétis	vellétis	nōllétis
		3	éssent	póssent	véllent	nóllent
Perfect	*Singular*	1	fúerim	potúerim	volúerim	nōlúerim
		2	fúeris	potúeris	volúeris	nōlúeris
		3	fúerit	potúerit	volúerit	nōlúerit
	Plural	1	fuérimus	potuérimus	voluérimus	nōluérimus
		2	fuéritis	potuéritis	voluéritis	nōluéritis
		3	fúerint	potúerint	volúerint	nōlúerint
Pluperfect	*Singular*	1	fuíssem	potuíssem	voluíssem	nōluíssem
		2	fuíssēs	potuíssēs	voluíssēs	nōluíssēs
		3	fuísset	potuísset	voluísset	nōluísset
	Plural	1	fuissémus	potuissémus	voluissémus	nōluissémus
		2	fuissétis	potuissétis	voluissétis	nōluissétis
		3	fuíssent	potuíssent	voluíssent	nōluíssent

XXIV. Irregular Verbs:
Subjunctive (continued)

Present	**Singular**	1	málim	éam	féram	férar	fíam
		2	málīs	éās	férās	feráris	fíās
		3	málit	éat	férat	ferátur	fíat
	Plural	1	mālímus	eámus	ferámus	ferámur	fiámus
		2	mālítis	eátis	ferátis	feráminī	fiátis
		3	málint	éant	férant	ferántur	fíant
Imperfect	**Singular**	1	mállem	írem	férrem	férrer	fíerem
		2	mállēs	írēs	férrēs	ferréris	fíerēs
		3	mállet	íret	férret	ferrétur	fíeret
	Plural	1	mállémus	īrémus	ferrémus	ferrémur	fierémus
		2	mállétis	īrétis	ferrétis	ferréminī	fierétis
		3	mállent	írent	férrent	ferréntur	fíerent
Perfect	**Singular**	1	mālúerim	íverim	túlerim	látus sim	fáctus sim
		2	mālúeris	íveris	túleris	látus sīs	fáctus sīs
		3	mālúerit	íverit	túlerit	látus sit	fáctus sit
	Plural	1	māluérimus	īvérimus	tulérimus	látī símus	fáctī símus
		2	māluéritis	īvéritis	tuléritis	látī sítis	fáctī sítis
		3	mālúerint	íverint	túlerint	látī sint	fáctī sint
Pluperfect	**Singular**	1	māluíssem	īvíssem	tulíssem	látus éssem	fáctus éssem
		2	māluíssēs	īvíssēs	tulíssēs	látus éssēs	fáctus éssēs
		3	māluísset	īvísset	tulísset	látus ésset	fáctus ésset
	Plural	1	māluissémus	īvissémus	tulissémus	látī essémus	fáctī essémus
		2	māluissétis	īvissétis	tulissétis	látī essétis	fáctī essétis
		3	māluíssent	īvíssent	tulíssent	látī éssent	fáctī éssent

Note: the perfect active infinitive of **eō, īre, īvī** or **iī, itum** is often syncopated or shortened to **īsse**. The pluperfect subjunctive of this verb and its compounds may also present this shortened form, e.g., **redīsset, perīsset**, and **adīsset**.

XXV. Infinitives

Present		Perfect	
Active	Passive	Active	Passive
1 paráre	parárī	parāvísse	parátus, -a, -um ésse
2 habére	habérī	habuísse	hábitus, -a, -um ésse
3 míttere	míttī	mīsísse	míssus, -a, -um ésse
4 audíre	audírī	audīvísse	audítus, -a, -um ésse
Future			
Active			
1 parātúrus, -a, -um ésse			
2 habitúrus, -a, -um ésse			
3 missúrus, -a, -um ésse			
4 audītúrus, -a, -um ésse			

XXVI. Participles

Present		Perfect	
Active	Passive	Active	Passive
1 párāns, parántis			parátus, -a, -um
2 hábēns, habéntis			hábitus, -a, -um
3 míttēns, mitténtis			míssus, -a, -um
4 aúdiēns, audiéntis			audítus, -a, -um
Future			
Active			
1 parātúrus, -a, -um			
2 habitúrus, -a, -um			
3 missúrus, -a, -um			
4 audītúrus, -a, -um			

Latin to English Vocabulary

The numbers in parentheses at the end of entries indicate the paragraph in which the word appears for the first time.

A

ā, ab (+ *abl.*), away from, from, of, by (1)

abditus, -a, -um, hidden, concealed (42)

abdō, abdere (3), **abdidī, abditum**, to put away, hide, conceal (42)

abdūcō, abdūcere (3), **abdūxī, abductum**, to lead *or* take away (75)

abeō, abīre (*irreg.*), **abiī, abitum** (*intrans.*), to go away, depart

abiciō (ab- + iaciō), **abicere** (3), **abiēcī, abiectum**, to throw away (62)

abripiō (ab- + rapiō), **abripere** (3), **abripuī, abreptum**, to snatch away, carry off (42)

abscīdō (abs- = ab- + caedō), **abscīdere** (3), **abscīdī, abscīsum**, to cut away *or* off (5)

absum, abesse (*irreg.*), **āfuī, āfutūrus** (*intrans.*), to be away, be absent, be far, be distant, be wanting, be lacking (47)

absūmō, absūmere (3), **absūmpsī, absūmptum**, to take away, consume, destroy (26)

Absyrtus, -ī (*m*), Absyrtus (71)

ac, see **atque** (3)

Acastus, -ī (*m*), Acastus (78)

accendō, accendere (3), **accendī, accēnsum** (*trans.*), to kindle, light (13)

accidō (ad- + cadō), **accidere** (3), **accidī** (*intrans.* + **ut** + *subjunctive*), to fall to *or* upon, befall, happen (40)

accipiō (ad- + capiō), **accipere** (3), **accēpī, acceptum**, to take to oneself, receive, accept, hear, suffer (2)

accumbō, accumbere (3), **accubuī, accubitum** (*intrans.*), to lie down (at table), recline (to eat) (64)

accurrō (ad- + currō), **accurrere** (3), **accucurrī** *or* **accurrī, accursum** (*intrans.*), to run to, come up (7)

ācer, ācris, ācre, sharp, shrill (29)

aciēs, -ēī (*f*), line of battle (17)

Acrisius, -ī (*m*), Acrisius (1)

ācriter, sharply, fiercely (35)

ad (+ *acc.*), to, toward, at, near, for (2)

ūsque ad, up to, even to, until, till

adamō (1) (*trans.* + *acc.*), to fall in love with (68)

addūcō, addūcere (3), **addūxī, adductum**, to lead to, bring, take, induce, influence

adeō, adīre (*irreg.*), **adiī, aditum**, to go to, approach (9)

adhibeō (ad- + habeō) (2), to hold to, employ, show, exhibit (32)

adiciō (ad- + iaciō), **adicere** (3), **adiēcī, adiectum**, to throw to, throw, hurl (74)

adimō (ad- + emō), **adimere** (3), **adēmī, adēmptum** (+ *acc.* and *dat.* or *ab.* + *abl.*), to take to oneself, take away, take (98)

aditus, -ūs (*m*), approach, entrance (26)

adiungō, adiungere (3), **adiūnxī, adiūnctum** (+ *acc.* and *dat.*), to join to, join (52)

Admētē, Admētēs (*f*), Admete (32)

admīror, admīrārī (1), **admīrātus sum**, to wonder at, admire (39)

admittō, admittere (3), **admīsī, admissum**, to send to, admit, allow (34)

adstō, adstāre (1), **adstitī** (*intrans.*), to stand at *or* near (89)

adsum, adesse (*irreg.*), **adfuī, adfutūrus** (*intrans.*), to be present

adulēscēns, adulēscentis, adulēscentium (*m*), youth, young man (16)

adulēscentia, -ae (*f*), youth (78)

adūrō, adūrere (3), **adussī, adustum**, to set fire to, burn, scorch, sear (22)

adveniō, advenīre (4), **advēnī, adventum** (*intrans.*), to come to *or* toward, approach, arrive

adventus, -ūs (*m*), approach, arrival (17)

Aeacus, -ī (*m*), Aeacus (51)

aedēs, aedis, aedium (*f*), (*sing.*) temple; (*pl.*) house (96)

aedificō (aedēs + faciō) (1), to make a building, build (60)

Aeētēs, Aeētae (m), Aeetes (59)

aegrē, ill, with difficulty (68)

Aegyptiī, -ōrum (m pl), Egyptians (15)

aēneus, -a, -um, of copper or bronze (29)

Aeolia, -ae (f), Aeolia (92)

Aeolus, -ī (m), Aeolus, king of the winds (92)

āēr, āeris (m), air (4)

aes, aeris (n), copper, bronze (29)

Aesōn, Aesonis (m), Aeson (57)

aestās, aestātis (f), summer (35)

aetās, aetātis (f), age (54)

Aethiopēs, -um (m pl), Ethiopians (6)

Aetna, -ae (f), Etna (85)

afferō (ad- + ferō), afferre (irreg.), attulī, adlātum, to bear to, bring (33)

afficiō (ad- + faciō), afficere (3), affēcī, affectum, to do to, move, affect, visit, afflict (9)

afflīgō (ad- + flīgō), afflīgere (3), afflīxī, afflīctum, to dash to pieces, shatter (100)

Āfrica, -ae (f), Africa (38)

ager, agrī (m), field, land (24)

agmen, agminis (n), column (93)

agnōscō (ad- + gnōscō, to learn), agnōscere (3), agnōvī, agnitum, to recognize (62)

agō, agere (3), ēgī, āctum, to drive, do, pass, lead
    grātiās agere, to give thanks, thank (66)
    vītam agere, to live, to live a . . . life (3)

āla, -ae (f), wing (65)

albus, -a, -um, white (55)

Alcmēna, -ae (f), Alcmena (12)

aliēnus, -a, -um, belonging to another, out of place (49)

aliquandō, at some time or other, finally, at length (48)

aliquantum, -ī (n), somewhat (95)

aliquī, aliqua, aliquod (adj.), some, any (49)

aliquis, aliquid (pronoun), someone, anyone, something, anything

aliter, in another way, otherwise, differently (47)

alius, alia, aliud, another, other (61)
    aliī . . . aliī, some . . . others

alligō (ad- + ligō) (1), to bind to, bind, tie (7)

alō, alere (3), aluī, altum, to nourish (68)

Alpēs, -ium (f pl), Alps (41)

alter, altera, alterum, one or the other (of two), another, second (15)

altum, -ī (n), the deep, the sea

altus, -a, -um, high, deep (24)

Amāzonēs, -um (f pl), Amazons (32)

āmentia, -ae (f), madness (80)

amīcus, -a, -um (+ dat.), friendly (to)

amīcus, -ī (m), friend (22)

āmittō, āmittere (3), āmīsī, āmissum, to send away, lose (43)
    vītam āmittere, to lose one's life, die

amō (1), to love

amor, amōris (m), love (55)

āmoveō, āmovēre (2), āmōvī, āmōtum (trans.), to move away (44)

amphora, -ae (f), jar, bottle (25)

an, or (in questions)

ancora, -ae (f), anchor
    ancorās tollere, to weigh anchor (63)
    in ancorīs, at anchor

Andromeda, -ae (f), Andromeda (6)

anguis, anguis, anguium (m/f), serpent, snake (4)

anima, -ae (f), breath, soul, life (55)

animadvertō (animus + ad- + vertō), animadvertere (3), animadvertī, animadversum (trans.), to turn the mind to, observe, notice (43)

animus, -ī (m), mind, disposition, heart, spirit, courage (6)
    animum dēmittere, to lose courage
    in animō habēre, to have in mind, intend

annus, -ī (m), year (3)

ante, (+ acc.) before; (adv.) before (48)

anteā, before this, before (31)

antīquus, -a, -um, ancient
    antīquī, -ōrum (m pl), the ancients (15)

antrum, -ī (n), cave (92)

ānxius, -a, -um, anxious (73)

aper, aprī (m), wild boar (24)

aperiō, aperīre (4), aperuī, apertum (trans.), to open (26)

apertus, -a, -um, open (26)

Apollō, Apollinis (m), Apollo (a god) (4)

appellō (1), to call, name (1)

appellō (ad- + pellō), appellere (3), appulī, appulsum, to drive to, bring to (2)
    (with or without nāvem), to put in

appetō (ad- + petō), appetere (3),

appetīvī, appetītum (*intrans.*), to
draw near, approach (15)
appōnō (ad- + pōnō), appōnere (3),
apposuī, appositum, to put to *or* near,
set before, serve (64)
appropinquō (ad- + propinquō) (1) (+
dat.), to approach to, approach (7)
apud (+ *acc.*), among, with, at the house of
(9)
aqua, -ae (*f*), water (8)
āra, -ae (*f*), altar (15)
arbitror, arbitrārī (1), arbritrātus
sum (+ *indirect statement*), to consider,
think, judge (61)
arbor, arboris (*f*), tree (72)
arca, -ae (*f*), chest, box, ark (1)
Arcadia, -ae (*f*), Arcadia (a country) (24)
accessō, arcessere (3), arcessīvī,
arcessītum, to call, summon, fetch (38)
arcus, -ūs (*m*), bow (14)
ārdeō, ārdēre (2), ārsī, ārsūrus
(*intrans.*), to be on fire, burn (22)
argentum, -ī (*n*), silver (92)
Argō, Argōnis (*f*), the Argo (71)
Argolicus, -a, -um, of Argolis, Argolic
(31)
Argonautae (Argō + nauta), -ārum, (*m
pl*), the Argonauts (62)
Argus, -ī (*m*), Argus (60)
ariēs, arietis (*m*), ram (77)
arma, -ōrum (*n pl*), arms, weapons (3)
armātus, -a, -um, armed (69)
armō (1), to arm, equip (60)
arō (1), to plow (67)
arripiō (ad- + rapiō), arripere (3),
arripuī, arreptum, to snatch to
oneself, snatch up, seize (13)
ars, artis (*f*), art, skill (14)
ascendō (ad- + scandō), ascendere (3),
ascendī, ascēnsum, to climb to,
ascend, mount (4)
at, but (68)
Athēnae, -ārum (*f pl*), Athens (80)
Atlās, Atlantis (*m*), Atlas (46)
atque *or* ac, and; (*after words of
comparison*) as, than (16)
simul atque *or* ac, as soon as (10)
ātrium, -ī (*n*), hall (10)
attingō (ad- + tangō), attingere (3),
attigī, attāctum (+ *acc.*), to touch at,
arrive at, reach (37)
audācia, -ae (*f*), daring, boldness,
audacity (23)
audeō, audēre (2), ausus sum

(*semideponent*), to dare (32)
audiō (4), to hear, listen, attend to (4)
auferō (ab- + ferō), auferre (*irreg.*),
abstulī, ablātum, to bear away, carry
off (57)
Augēās, Augēae (*m*), Augeas (28)
aura, -ae (*f*), air, breeze (92)
aureus, -a, -um, of gold, golden (39)
auris, auris, aurium (*f*), ear (16)
aurum, -ī (*n*), gold (45)
aut, or
aut . . . aut, either . . . or
autem (*postpositive*), moreover, but,
however, now, and indeed (1)
auxilior, auxiliārī (1), auxiliātus
sum (*intrans.*), to help (91)
auxilium, -ī (*n*), help, aid (22)
āvehō, āvehere (3), āvexī, āvectum,
to carry away (71)
avis, avis, avium (*f*), bird (29)
āvolō (1) (*intrans.*), to fly away (29)
avus, -ī (*m*), grandfather (1)

B

balteus, -ī (*m*), belt, girdle (32)
barbarus, -ī (*m*), barbarian (40)
beātus, -a, -um, happy, blessed (3)
bellicōsus, -a, -um, warlike (16)
bellum, -ī (*n*), war (32)
bēlua, -ae (*f*), beast, monster (8)
bene, well, successfully (67)
beneficium (bene + faciō), -ī (*n*), well-
doing, kindness, service, benefit (2)
benignē, kindly (2)
benignitās, benignitātis (*f*), kindness
(95)
bibō, bibere (3), bibī, to drink (26)
biceps, bicipitis, two-headed (38)
bonus, -a, -um, good (51)
bōs, bovis, gen. pl. boum, dat. and abl. pl.
būbus (*m/f*), ox, bull, cow (43)
bracchium, -ī (*n*), arm (21)
brevis, -is, -e, short (2)
Būsīris, Būsīridis (*m*), Busiris (15)

C

Cācus, -ī (*m*), Cacus (42)
cadāver, cadāveris (*n*), dead body,
corpse, carcass (21)
cadō, cadere (3), cecidī, cāsum
(*intrans.*), to fall (40)
caecus, -a, -um, blind (64)
caedēs, caedis, caedium (*f*), cutting
down, killing, slaughter (23)
caelum, -ī (*n*), heaven, sky (40)

Calais, Calais (m), Calais (65)

calamitās, calamitātis (f), misfortune,
    calamity, disaster (97)

calceus, -ī (m), shoe (58)

calefaciō, calefacere (3), calefēcī,
    calefactum, to make hot, heat (89)

calor, calōris (m), heat (39)

campus, -ī (m), plain, field (51)

cancer, cancrī (m), crab (22)

canis, canis, canum (m/f), dog

canō, canere (3), cecinī, cantum
    (trans.), to sing (77)

cantus, -ūs (m), singing, song (95)

capiō, capere (3), cēpī, captum, to
    take, catch, seize, receive, suffer, adopt
    (2)
        cōnsilium capere, to think up a
        plan
        dolōrem capere, to suffer grief (6)

captīva, -ae (f), captive, prisoner (35)

caput, capitis (n), head (3)

carcer, carceris (m), prison (92)

careō (2) (+ abl.), to lack

carmen, carminis (n), song, charm (77)

carō, carnis (f), flesh (29)

carpō, carpere (3), carpsī, carptum,
    to pluck (68)

Castor, Castoris (m), Castor (61)

castra, -ōrum (n pl), camp (33)

cāsus, -ūs (m), fall, chance, accident,
    emergency (11)

catēna, -ae (f), chain (15)

cauda, -ae (f), tail (42)

causa, -ae (f), cause, reason (27)
        causā (+ preceding gen.), for the sake of,
        for the purpose of (85)

caveō, cavēre (2), cāvī, cautum (+
    acc.), to beware, take care, beware of, be
    on one's guard against (58)

celeritās, celeritātis (f), swiftness,
    quickness, speed (7)

celeriter, swiftly, quickly (22)

cēlō (1) (trans.), to hide, conceal (19)

cēna, -ae (f), dinner (25)

Cēnaeum, -ī (n), Cenaeum (a
    promontory) (55)

cēnō (1) (intrans.), to dine (88)

centaurus, -ī (m), centaur (25)

centum (indecl. adj.), one hundred (16)

Cēpheus, -ī (m), Cepheus (6)

Cerberus, -ī (m), Cerberus (49)

Cerēs, Cereris (f), Ceres (a goddess)
    (50)

cernō, cernere (3), crēvī, crētum, to

discern, perceive, make out (44)

certāmen, certāminis (n), struggle,
    contest (11)

certus, -a, -um, determined, fixed,
    definite, certain (7)
        certiōrem facere, to make more
        certain, inform

cervus, -ī (m), stag (23)

cēterī, -ae, -a (pl. adj.), the other, the
    remaining, the rest of (4)

Charōn, Charontis (m), Charon (50)

cibus, -ī (m), food (64)

cingō, cingere (3), cīnxī, cīnctum, to
    surround, gird (49)

Circē, Circēs (f), Circe (94)

circiter, (+ acc.) about; (adv.) about (60)

circum (+ acc.), about, around, round (8)

circumdō, circumdare (1),
    circumdedī, circumdatum, to put
    around, surround (45)

circumstō, circumstāre (1),
    circumstetī, to stand around (56)

cithara, -ae (f), cithara, lyre (14)

cīvis, cīvis, cīvium (m/f), citizen, fellow-
    citizen, subject (6)

cīvitās, cīvitātis (f), state (54)

clāmitō (1) (+ indirect statement), to shout
    repeatedly, call out (83)

clāmor, clāmōris (m), shout, cry (13)

clārus, -a, -um, famous

clāva, -ae (f), stick, club (21)

clēmentia, -ae (f), mercy, kindness (35)

co-, see com-

coēgī, see cōgō

coepī, coepisse, coeptum (used in
    forms of the perfect system), have begun,
    began (22)

cōgitō (1), to consider, think over (87)

cognōscō (co- + gnōscō, to learn),
    cognōscere (3), cognōvī, cognitum
    (+ acc. or indirect statement or indirect
    question), to find out, learn of, learn;
    (perfect) to have found out, have learned
    of, be aware of, know (10)

cōgō (co- + agō), cōgere (3), coēgī,
    coāctum, to drive together, collect,
    compel, force (17)

cohortor, cohortārī (1), cohortātus
    sum, to encourage, exhort (34)

Colchī, -ōrum (m pl), Colchians (67)

Colchis, Colchidis (f), Colchis (59)

colligō (com- + legō), colligere (3),
    collēgī, collēctum, to gather
    together, collect (75)

collum, -ī (*n*), neck (8)

colō, colere (3), coluī, cultum, to till, cultivate, inhabit, worship (29)

color, colōris (*m*), color (79)

columba, -ae (*f*), pigeon, dove (66)

columna, -ae (*f*), column, pillar (38)

com-, con-, co- (*forms of* cum *used in compounds*), with, together, entirely, thoroughly

comes (com- + eō), comitis (*m/f*), companion (55)

commeātus, -ūs (*m*), supplies, provisions (41)

commemorō (1), to bring to memory, recount, mention (45)

committō, committere (3), commīsī, commissum, to send together, commit, entrust, expose (25)
    proelium committere, to join battle

commoror, commorārī (1), commorātus sum (*intrans.*), to delay, linger, stay, tarry (61)

commoveō, commovēre (2), commōvī, commōtum, to move, rouse, disturb (5)

commūtātiō (com- + mūtō), commūtātiōnis (*f*), change (31)

comparō (1), to prepare, collect (41)

compellō, compellere (3), compulī, compulsum, to drive together, drive (36)

complector, complectī (3), complexus sum, to embrace, grasp (21)

compleō, complēre (2), complēvī, complētum, to fill full, fill up (88)

complūrēs, complūra (*pl. adj.*), several, many (47)

comportō (1), to carry *or* bring together, collect (60)

comprehendō, comprehendere (3), comprehendī, comprehēnsum, to seize, catch (1)

comprimō (com- + premō), comprimere (3), compressī, compressum, to press together, squeeze, compress (13)

con-, see com-

cōnātus, -ūs (*m*), attempt, effort (15)

concēdō, concēdere (3), concessī, concessum (+ *dat.* + ut + *subjunctive*), to grant, yield, permit (37)

concurrō, concurrere (3), concucurrī *or* concurrī, concursum (*intrans.*), to run, come, rush *or* dash together (66)

condō, condere (3), condidī, conditum, to put together, found, build, store away (84)

cōnferō, cōnferre (*irreg.*), contulī, collātum, to bring together, grant, confer
    sē cōnferre, to betake oneself, make one's way, go (10)

cōnficiō (con- + facio), cōnficere (3), cōnfēcī, cōnfectum, to make *or* do completely, complete, finish, accomplish, wear out (20)

cōnfirmō (1), to strengthen, establish, declare, assert (14)

cōnflīgō, cōnflīgere (3), cōnflīxī, cōnflīctum (*intrans.*), to dash together (66)

coniciō (con- + iaciō), conicere (3), coniēcī, cōniectum, to throw together, throw, cast, hurl (11)

coniungō, coniungere (3), coniūnxī, coniūnctum (*trans.*), to join together, join (38)

coniūnx, coniugis (*m/f*), spouse, husband, wife (78)

conlocō (1), to put, place (31)

conloquium, -ī (*n*), conversation (46)

cōnor, cōnārī (1), cōnātus sum, to try, attempt (44)

cōnscendō (con- + scandō), cōnscendere (3), cōnscendī, cōnscēnsum, to climb (*with or without* nāvem), to go on board, embark (30)

cōnsēnsus (con- + sentiō), -ūs (*m*), agreement, consent (94)

cōnsequor, cōnsequī (3), cōnsecūtus sum, to follow up, follow, overtake (23)

cōnservō (1), to preserve, keep (55)

cōnsīdō, cōnsīdere (3), cōnsēdī, cōnsessum, to sit down (90)

cōnsilium, -ī (*n*), advice, plan, design, purpose, prudence (3)
    cōnsilium capere, to think up a plan

cōnsistō, cōnsistere (3), cōnstitī, to station oneself, take one's stand, consist (26)

cōnspectus, -ūs (*m*), sight (5)

cōnspiciō (con- + speciō), cōnspicere (3), cōnspexī, cōnspectum, to behold, perceive, see (7)

cōnstituō (con- + statuō), cōnstituere
(3), cōnstituī, cōnstitūtum, to set up,
appoint, determine, decide (2)

cōnstō, cōnstāre (1), constitī,
constātūrus, to stand together, agree,
consist
cōnstat (*impersonal* + *indirect
statement*), it is agreed, is
established, is well-known (81)

cōnsuēscō, cōnsuēscere (3),
cōnsuēvī, cōnsuētum, to become
accustomed; (*perfect*) to have become
accustomed, be accustomed (15)

cōnsulō, cōnsulere (3), cōnsuluī,
cōnsultum, to consult (6)

cōnsūmō, cōnsūmere (3), cōnsūmpsī,
cōnsūmptum, to take completely, use
up, consume, spend (14)

contegō, contegere (3), contēxī,
contēctum, to cover (4)

contendō, contendere (3), contendī,
contentum (*intrans.*), to stretch, exert
oneself, hurry, rush (7)

continēns, continentis (*f*), mainland,
continent (4)

contineō (con- + teneō), continēre (2),
continuī, contentum, to hold
together, keep within, shut up, bound (36)

continuus, -a, -um, continuous,
successive, in succession (47)

contrā (+ *acc.*), against, contrary to (28)

contrōversia, -ae (*f*), quarrel, dispute,
debate (70)

conveniō, convenīre (4), convēnī,
conventum (*intrans.*), to come together,
assemble, gather (58)

convertō, convertere (3), convertī,
conversum (*trans.*), to turn around,
turn, change
in fugam convertere, to put to
flight (17)

convocō (1), to call together, summon,
assemble (88)

coorior, coorīrī (4), coortus sum, to
arise (30)

cōpia, -ae (*f*), supply, abundance; (*pl.*)
forces, troops (17)

Corinthus, -ī (*f*), Corinth (79)

cornū, -ūs (*n*), horn (23)

corpus, corporis (*n*), body (8)

corripiō (com- + rapiō), corripere (3),
corripuī, correptum, to snatch up,
seize (15)

cottīdiē, daily, every day (36)

crēdibilis, -is, -e, believable, credible
(20)

crēdō, crēdere (3), crēdidī, crēditum
(+ *dat.* + *indirect statement*), to believe
(93)

creō (1) (+ *double acc.*), to elect, appoint,
make (71)

Creōn, Creontis (*m*), Creon (16)

crepitus, -ūs (*m*), rattle, clatter, noise
(29)

Crēta, -ae (*f*), Crete (30)

crotalum, -ī (*n*), clapper, rattle (29)

cruciātus, -ūs (*m*), torture (31)

crūdēlis, crūdēle (+ in + *acc.*), cruel
(15)

crūs, crūris (*n*), leg (22)

cubiculum, -ī (*n*), bedroom (12)

cubō, cubāre (1), cubuī, cubitum
(*intrans.*), to lie down, lie, recline (12)

culter, cultrī (*m*), knife (15)

cum (+ *abl.*), with (1)

cum, when, while, after, since, although
(25)

cūnae, -ārum (*f pl*), cradle (12)

cupiditās, cupiditātis (*f*), desire,
longing, eagerness (45)

cupidus, -a, -um (+ *gen.*), desirous, eager
(92)

cupiō, cupere (3), cupīvī, cupītum, to
desire, long for, wish (9)

currō, currere (3), cucurrī, cursum
(*intrans.*), to run (7)

currus, -ūs (*m*), chariot (80)

cursus, -ūs (*m*), running, course (23)

custōdiō (4), to guard (38)

Cyclōps, Cyclōpis (*m*), Cyclops (84)

Cyzicus, -ī (*f*), Cyzicus (62)

D

damnum, -ī (*n*), harm, injury (91)

Danaē, Danaēs (*f*), Danaë (1)

dē (+ *abl.*), down from, from, out of, about,
concerning, of (1)

dēbeō (2), to owe; (+ *inf.*) ought (1)

dēbitus, -a, -um, owed, due (91)

dēcēdō, dēcēdere (3), dēcessī,
dēcessum (*intrans.*), to go from *or*
away, depart (50)

decem (*indecl. adj.*), ten (60)

dēcidō (dē- + cadō), dēcidere (3), dēcidī
(*intrans.*), to fall down (46)

decimus, -a, -um, tenth (82)

dēcipiō (dē + capiō), dēcipere (3),
dēcēpī, dēceptum, to catch, deceive
(43)

decorō (1), to adorn, distinguish (18)

dēcurrō, dēcurrere (3), dēcucurrī or
dēcurrī, dēcursum (intrans.), to run
down (62)

dēdecus, dēdecoris (n), dishonor,
disgrace (34)

dēdō, dēdere (3), dēdidī, dēditum
(+ acc. + dat.), to give away or up (87)

dēdūcō, dēdūcere (3), dēdūxī,
dēductum, to lead down or away, bring
(7)
    nāvem dēdūcere, to draw down or
    launch a ship

dēfendō, dēfendere (3), dēfendī,
dēfēnsum, to defend, protect (83)

dēferō, dēferre (irreg.), dētulī,
dēlātum, to bear or carry away or off
(82)

dēfessus, -a, -um (+ abl.), worn out,
exhausted (35)

dēficiō (dē- + faciō), dēficere (3),
dēfēcī, dēfectum (intrans.), to fail, run
short (35)

Dēianīra, -ae (f), Dejanira (54)

dēiciō (dē- + iaciō), dēicere (3), dēiēcī,
dēiectum, to throw down (43)

deinde, then, next (22)

dēlābor, dēlābī (3), dēlāpsus sum
(intrans.), to slip or fall down (80)

dēligō (dē- + legō), dēligere (3), dēlēgī,
dēlēctum, to choose out, choose, select
(17)

Delphī, -ōrum (m pl), Delphi (a town)
(58)

Delphicus, -a, -um, of Delphi, Delphic,
Delphian (19)

dēmissus, -a, -um, downcast, dejected
(75)

dēmittō, dēmittere (3), dēmīsī,
dēmissum, to send down, let fall (40)
    animum dēmittere, to lose courage

dēmōnstrō (1), to point out, show, make
known (4)

dēmum, at last (21)

dēnique, lastly, finally (51)

dēns, dentis (m), tooth (67)

dēnsus, -a, -um, thick (21)

dēpellō, dēpellere (3), dēpulī,
dēpulsum, to drive off or away (86)

dēplōrō (1), to lament (7)

dēpōnō, dēpōnere (3), dēposuī,
dēpositum, to put down, deposit, lay
aside, give up (9)
    ex memoriā dēpōnere, to forget

    spem dēpōnere, to despair

dēripiō (dē- + rapiō), dēripere (3),
dēripuī, dēreptum, to snatch down
from or away, tear off, pull down (72)

dēscendō (dē- + scandō), dēscendere
(3), dēscendī, dēscēnsum (intrans.),
to climb down, descend (9)

dēserō, dēserere (3), dēseruī,
dēsertum, to desert (71)

dēsertus, -a, -um, deserted (10)

dēsīderium, -ī (n), desire, longing (100)

dēsiliō (dē- + saliō), dēsilīre (4),
dēsiluī, dēsultum (intrans.), to leap
down (96)

dēsistō, dēsistere (3), dēstitī,
dēstitum (+ abl. or ab + abl. or inf.), to
leave off, desist, cease, stop (22)

dēspērō (1) (intrans.), to despair (34)

dēstringō, dēstringere (3), dēstrīnxī,
dēstrictum, to draw, unsheathe (70)

dēsuper, down from above (8)

dēterreō (2), to frighten off, deter (97)

dētrahō, dētrahere (3), dētrāxī,
dētractum, to draw or pull off (21)

deus, -ī, (nom. pl.) dī, (dat. and abl. pl.) dīs
(m), god (1)

dēvertō, dēvertere (3), dēvertī,
dēversum (intrans.), to turn away or
aside

dēvorō (1), to swallow down, swallow,
devour (6)

dexter, dextra, dextrum, right

dextra, -ae (f), right hand (22)

dī-, see dis-

Diāna, -ae (f), Diana (a goddess) (10)

dīcō, dīcere (3), dīxī, dictum, to say,
speak, tell (3)
    diem dīcere, to appoint or set a day
    (7)

didicī, see discō

diēs, -ēī (m/f), day (7)

difficilis (dis- + facilis), -is, -e, not easy,
difficult (5)

difficultās, difficultātis (f), difficulty
(24)

diffundō (dis- + fundō), diffundere (3),
diffūdī, diffūsum, to pour forth,
spread or shed abroad, diffuse (26)

dīligenter, carefully, diligently (14)

dīligentia, -ae (f), care, diligence,
industry (60)

dīlūcēscō, dīlūcēscere (3), dīlūxī
(intrans.), to grow light, dawn (62)

dīmittō, dīmittere (3), dīmīsī,

dīmissum, to send different ways, send
forth *or* away, dispatch, let slip, lose (3)
Diomēdēs, Diomēdis (*m*), Diomedes
(30)
dis- or dī- (*prefix*), apart (*sometimes has a
negative force*)
discēdō, discēdere (3), discessī,
discessum (*intrans.*), to go apart,
withdraw, depart, wander (away) (63)
discō, discere (3), didicī, to learn (11)
discrīmen, discrīminis (*n*), crisis, peril,
danger (71)
discus, -ī (*m*), discus (11)
disiciō (dis- + iaciō), disicere (3),
disiēcī, disiectum, to throw apart,
scatter (82)
diū, for a long time, a long time *or* while,
long (4)
    comp., diūtius, longer
dīvellō, dīvellere (3), dīvellī,
dīvulsum, to tear apart, rend asunder,
tear in pieces (85)
dīversus, -a, -um, turned different ways,
opposite, contrary, different (89)
dīvidō, dīvidere (3), dīvīsī, dīvīsum,
to divide, separate (38)
dō, dare (1), dedī, datum, to give, put
(2)
doceō, docēre (2), docuī, doctum, to
teach, explain (46)
dolor, dolōris (*m*), pain, grief, grievance
(6)
    dolōrem capere, to suffer grief (6)
dolus, -ī (*m*), trick, craft (71)
domina, -ae (*f*), mistress (95)
domus, -ūs (*f*), house, home (2)
dōnum, -ī (*n*), gift (2)
dormiō (4) (*intrans.*), to sleep (1)
dracō, dracōnis (*m*), dragon, serpent
(45)
dubitō (1), to doubt (+ quīn); to hesitate (+
inf.) (65)
dubius, -a, -um, doubtful, uncertain (76)
dūcō, dūcere (3), dūxī, ductum, to lead,
draw, bring, make, dig (3)
    (*with or without* in mātrimōnium),
    to marry (3)
dulcēdō, dulcēdinis (*f*), sweetness (95)
dulcis, -is, -e, sweet (82)
dum, while, as, as long as, until (3)
duo, duae, duo (*pl. adj.*), two (57)
duodecim (duo + decem) (*indecl. adj.*),
twelve (20)
duodēvīgintī (*indecl. adj.*), eighteen (28)

dux, ducis (*m/f*), leader, commander (73)

E

ē, see ex
ēbrius, -a, -um, drunk (83)
ēdō, ēdere (3), ēdidī, ēditum, to put
forth, give out, utter (8)
ēdūcō, ēdūcere (3), ēdūxī, ēductum,
to lead out, draw (8)
effervēscō (ex- + fervēscō), effervēscere (3), efferbuī (*intrans.*), to boil up
or over, boil (77)
efficiō (ex- + faciō), efficere (3), effēcī,
effectum, to make *or* work out,
accomplish, effect (44)
efflō (ex- + flō) (1) (*trans.*), to breathe out
(42)
effugiō (ex- + fugiō), effugere (3),
effūgī (*intrans.*), to flee out *or* away,
escape (73)
effundō (ex- + fundō), effundere (3),
effūdī, effūsum (*intrans.*), to pour out
(55)
ego, meī (*pers. pron.*), I (78)
ēgredior (ē- + gradior), ēgredī (3),
ēgressus sum (*intrans.*), to go out *or*
forth (27)
    (*with or without* ē nāvī), to go ashore,
    disembark
ēgregiē, excellently, splendidly,
admirably (72)
ēlābor, ēlābī (3), ēlāpsus sum
(*intrans.*), to slip out, slip (27)
Ēlis, Ēlidis (*f*), Elis (28)
ēlūceō, ēlūcēre (2), ēlūxī (*intrans.*), to
shine out, shine (73)
Ēlysius, -a, -um, Elysian (51)
ēmittō, ēmittere (3), ēmīsī,
ēmissum, to send out *or* forth (66)
enim (*postpositive*), for (1)
    neque enim, for . . . not
ēnūntiō (1), to speak out, announce, make
known (19)
eō, īre (*irreg.*), iī *or* īvī, itum (*intrans.*),
to go
eō, to that place, there (10)
equus, -ī (*m*), horse (25)
ērēctus, -a, -um, upright, erect (80)
ergā (+ *acc.*), toward, for (55)
Ergīnus, -ī (*m*), Erginus (17)
Ēridanus, -ī (*m*), Eridanus, Po (75)
ēripiō (ē- + rapiō), ēripere (3), ēripuī,
ēreptum (+ *abl.* or ab or ex + *abl.*), to
snatch out *or* away, rescue (57)
errō (1) (*intrans.*), to wander, stray, be

mistaken (62)

ērudiō (4), to instruct (14)

Erymanthius, -a, -um, of Erymanthus, Erymanthian (24)

Erythēa, -ae (f), Erythea (38)

ēscendō (ē- + scandō), ēscendere (3), ēscendī, ēscēnsum (intrans.), to climb up (80)

et, and (1)

et . . . et, both . . . and

etiam (et + iam) (postpositive), and now, also, too, even, in addition (1)

etiam tum, even then, still

etsī, even if, although (24)

Eunomus, -ī (m), Eunomus (54)

Eurōpa, -ae (f), Europe (38)

Eurylochus, -ī (m), Eurylochus (94)

Eurystheus, -ī (m), Eurystheus (20)

Eurytiōn, Eurytiōnis (m), Eurytion (38)

Eurytus, -ī (m), Eurytus (55)

ēvādō, ēvādere (3), ēvāsī, ēvāsum (intrans.), to go forth, get away, escape (5)

ēvānēscō, ēvānēscere (3), ēvānuī (intrans.), to vanish away, vanish (97)

ēveniō, ēvenīre (4), ēvēnī, ēventum (intrans.), to come out, turn out, happen, befall (66)

ēvocō (1), to call out, challenge (33)

ex or ē (+ abl.), out of, from, of (4)

ex ōrdine, in order (90)

exanimō (ex- + anima) (1), to put out of breath, fatigue, tire, exhaust, kill, agitate, stupefy (9)

exārdēscō, exārdēscere (3), exārsī, exārsum, to blaze out, be inflamed, rage (74)

excēdō, excēdere (3), excessī, excessum (intrans.), to go out or forth, depart (14)

excipiō (ex- + capiō), excipere (3), excēpī, exceptum, to take out or up, receive, welcome, entertain (2)

excitō (1), to call out, rouse, arouse (5)

exclāmō (1), to shout or cry out, exclaim (13)

exclūdō (ex- + claudō), exclūdere (3), exclūsī, exclūsum, to shut out, hinder, prevent (92)

excōgitō (1), to think out, contrive, devise, invent (81)

excruciō (1), to torture (51)

exeō, exīre (irreg.), exiī, exitum (intrans.), to go out

exerceō (2), to exercise (14)

exercitātiō, exercitātiōnis (f), exercise (14)

exeritus, -ūs (m), army (17)

exhauriō, exhaurīre (4), exhausī, exhaustum, to drink up or off, drain (27)

exīstimō (1), to consider, believe, think (75)

exorior, exorīrī (4), exortus sum (intrans.), to arise from, spring up, rise (22)

expellō, expellere (3), expulī, expulsum, to drive out, expel

expiō (1), to expiate (19)

explōrātor, explōrātōris (m), explorer, scout, spy (17)

explōrō (1), to search out, explore (84)

expōnō, expōnere (3), exposuī, expositum, to put out, set forth, put on shore, land, explain (7)

exprimō (ex- + premō), exprimere (3), expressī, expressum, to press out (68)

exsiliō (ex- + saliō), exsilīre (4), exsiluī (intrans.), to leap out or forth (77)

exsilium, -ī (n), exile (54)

exspectō (1), to look out for, wait for, await, expect, wait (7)

exstruō, exstruere (3), exstrūxī, exstrūctum, to pile or heap up, build, erect (56)

extrahō, extrahere (3), extrāxī, extractum (+ ab or ex + abl.), to draw or drag out, release, rescue (6)

extrēmus, -a, -um, last, extreme, furthest, the end of (46)

exuō, exuere (3), exuī, exūtum, to put or take off (9)

F

faber, fabrī (m), smith (29)

fābula, -ae (f), story (57)

facile, easily (100)

facinus, facinoris (n), deed, crime (18)

faciō, facere (3), fēcī, factum, to make, do (2)

impetum facere, to make an attack, charge (against or upon + in + acc.) (8)

iter facere, to journey, march

facultās, facultātis (f), possibility, opportunity, chance, means (21)

fallō, fallere (3), fefellī, falsum, to

deceive (75)

falsus, -a, -um, feigned, pretended, false (43)

falx, falcis, falcium (*f*), sickle, curved sword (4)

fāma, -ae (*f*), report, rumor (21)

famēs, famis, (*abl.*) **famē** (*f*), hunger (64)

far, farris (*n*), spelt, wheat, meal (15)

fātum, -ī (*n*), destiny, fate (7)

faucēs, faucium (*f pl*), throat, jaws, mouth (21)

Favōnius, -ī (*m*), Favonius (92)

fax, facis (*f*), torch, firebrand (22)

fēlīciter, happily, fortunately, successfully (66)

fēmina, -ae (*f*), woman (19)

fera, -ae (*f*), wild animal, beast (21)

ferē, nearly, about, almost, for the most part (92)

ferō, ferre (*irreg.*), **tulī, lātum**, to bear, bring

ferōx, ferōcis, fierce, savage (30)

ferreus, -a, -um, of iron, iron (15)

fessus, -a, -um, worn out, exhausted, weary (42)

figūra, -ae (*f*), form, shape, figure (84)

fīlia, -ae (*f*), daughter (6)

fīlius, -ī (*m*), son (1)

fingō, fingere (3), **fīnxī, fictum**, to invent, make up (57)

fīnis, fīnis, fīnium (*m*), end, boundary; (*pl.*) borders, territory, country (2)

fīnitimus, -a, -um (+ *dat.*), neighboring, adjoining, adjacent (16)

fīō, fierī (*irreg.*), **factus sum**, to be done *or* made, become, come about (4)

flamma, -ae (*f*), flame, fire (67)

flūmen, flūminis (*n*), river (28)

fōns, fontis, fontium (*m*), fountain, spring (63)

forās, out of doors, forth, out (95)

forīs, out of doors, without, outside (95)

foris, foris, forum (*f*), door (98)

fōrma, -ae (*f*), form, appearance, beauty (45)

fōrmōsus, -a, -um, beautiful (6)

forte (*abl.* of **fors**), by chance, accidentally (11)

fortis, -is, -e, brave (13)

fortiter, bravely (24)

fortūna, -ae (*f*), fortune (33)

fossa, -ae (*f*), ditch, trench (24)

frangō, frangere (3), **frēgī, frāctum**, to break, dash to pieces, wreck (85)

frāter, frātris (*m*), brother (12)

fraus, fraudis (*f*), deception, fraud (58)

fremitus, -ūs (*m*), roaring, roar (7)

frēnō (1), to bridle, restrain (92)

fretum, -ī (*n*), strait (38)

frōns, frontis (*f*), forehead (84)

frūctus, -ūs (*m*), enjoyment, fruit (82)

frūmentor, frūmentārī (1), **frūmentātus sum**, to fetch grain, forage (94)

frūmentum, -ī (*n*), grain (35)

frūstrā, in vain, vainly (4)

fuga, -ae (*f*), flight

   in fugam convertere, to put to flight (17)

fugiō, fugere (3), **fūgī, fugitum** (*intrans.*), to flee, run away (5)

fūmus, -ī (*m*), smoke (44)

furor, furōris (*m*), rage, fury, frenzy, madness (18)

fūrtum, -ī (*n*), theft (43)

G

galea, -ae (*f*), helmet (4)

Gallia, -ae (*f*), Gaul (41)

gaudeō, gaudēre (2 *semideponent*), **gāvīsus sum** (*intrans.* + *abl.*), to be glad, rejoice (18)

gaudium, -ī (*n*), gladness, joy (9)

gēns, gentis, gentium (*f*), race, nation, people (16)

genus, generis (*n*), kind, nature (34)

gerō, gerere (3), **gessī, gestum**, to carry, wear, carry on, do (7)

Gēryōn, Gēryonis (*m*), Geryon (38)

gignō, gignere (3), **genuī, genitum**, to produce, bring forth (69)

gladius, -ī (*m*), sword (8)

Glaucē, Glaucēs (*f*), Glauce (79)

glōria, -ae (*f*), glory (61)

Gorgōn, Gorgonis (*f*), Gorgon (4)

Graeae, -ārum (*f pl*), the Graeae (4)

Graecia, -ae (*f*), Greece (11)

Graecus, -a, -um, Greek (81)

grātia, -ae (*f*), favor, gratitude, thanks; (*pl.*) thanks

   grātiās agere, to give thanks, thank (9)

   grātiam referre, to return a favor, show gratitude, requite

grātus, -a, -um (+ *dat.*), pleasing (to), grateful (to) (3)

gravis, -is, -e, heavy, severe, grievous, serious (8)

graviter, severely, seriously (8)

gubernō (1), to steer (92)
gustō (1), to taste (82)

H

habeō (2), to have, hold, consider (16)
  in animō habēre, to have in mind,
  intend
  ōrātiōnem habēre, to give *or* deliver
  a speech, speak
habitō (1) (*intrans.*), to dwell, live (3)
haereō, haerēre (2), haesī, haesum
  (*intrans.*), to stick, hesitate (48)
haesitō (1) (*intrans.*), to hesitate (44)
Hammōn, Hammōnis (*m*), Ammon (6)
harēna, -ae (*f*), sand, shore (2)
Harpyiae, -ārum (*f pl*), Harpies (64)
hauriō, haurīre (4), hausī, haustum,
  to draw (25)
herba, -ae (*f*), herb, plant (68)
Herculēs, Herculis (*m*), Hercules (12)
Hēsionē, Hēsionēs (*f*), Hesione (36)
Hesperidēs, -um (*f pl*), the Hesperides
  (45)
hīc, here, hereupon (3)
hic, haec, hoc, this, he, she, it, they
hinc, from this place, hence (3)
Hippolytē, Hippolytēs (*f*), Hippolyte
  (32)
Hispānia, -ae (*f*), Spain (40)
Homērus, -ī (*m*), Homer (32)
homō, hominis (*m/f*), human being,
  human, man (5)
honor, honōris (*m*), honor (9)
hōra, -ae (*f*), hour (62)
horribilis, -is, -e, dreadful, terrible,
  horrible (4)
hortor, hortārī (1), hortātus sum, to
  exhort, encourage, urge (48)
hortus, -ī (*m*), garden (45)
hospitium, -ī (*n*), hospitality (62)
hostis, hostis, hostium (*m/f*), enemy,
  foe (17)
hūc, to this place, hither (10)
hūmānus, -a, -um, of man, human (84)
humī (*locative of* humus), on the ground
  (55)
Hydra, -ae (*f*), the Hydra (22)
Hylās, Hylae (*m*), Hylas (63)

I

iaceō, iacēre (2), iacuī (*intrans.*), to lie,
  be prostrate (27)
iaciō, iacere (3), iēcī, iactum, to throw,
  cast, hurl (82)
iam, already, now (5)

iānua, -ae (*f*), door (95)
  iānuam pulsāre, to knock on the door
Iāsōn, Iāsonis (*m*), Jason (66)
ibi, in that place, there (3)
ictus, -ūs (*m*), blow (5)
īdem, eadem, idem, the same;
  (*sometimes translated*) likewise, also
  (31)
idōneus, -a, -um (+ ad + *acc.*), suitable,
  fit, favorable (17)
igitur (*usually postpositive*), therefore (3)
ignārus, -a, -um, ignorant of, not
  knowing (96)
ignāvus, -a, -um, lazy, cowardly (3)
ignis, ignis, ignium (*m*), fire (22)
ignōrō (1), to be ignorant of, not know (4)
ignōtus (in- + nōtus), -a, -um , unknown
  (84)
Īlias, Īliadis (*f*), the *Iliad* (81)
ille, illa, illud, that, he, she, it, they (2)
imber, imbris, imbrium (*m*), rain,
  shower (40)
imbuō, imbuere (3), imbuī, imbūtum,
  to wet, soak, dip (22)
immānitās, immānitātis (*f*), cruelty,
  barbarity (91)
immittō (in- + mittō), immittere (3),
  immīsī, immissum, to send *or* let in
  (28)
immolō (in- + mola) (1), to sacrifice (15)
impediō (in- + pēs) (4), to hinder, prevent,
  impede (75)
impellō (in- + pellō), impellere (3),
  impulī, impulsum, to drive *or* urge
  on, incite, urge (56)
imperātor, imperātōris (*m*),
  commander, general (17)
imperātum, -ī (*n*), command, order (82)
imperītus (in- + perītus), -a, -um (+
  gen.), inexperienced, unskilled, ignorant
  (30)
imperium, -ī (*n*), command, sway, rule
  (52)
imperō (1) (+ *dat.* + ut + *subjunctive*), to
  command, order, enjoin (20)
impetrō (1), to gain one's end, obtain (a
  request) (100)
impetus (in- + petō), -ūs (*m*), attack (8)
  impetum facere, to make an attack,
  charge (against *or* upon + in + *acc.*) (8)
impōnō (in- + pōnō), impōnere (3),
  imposuī, impositum, to place *or* lay
  upon, impose, embark (15)
improbus, -a, -um, wicked (51)

in, (+ *acc.*) into, in, to, upon, towards; (+ *abl.*)
in, on, among (1)
  in perpetuum, for all time, forever
  (82)
in- (*prefix*), not, in-, un-
incidō (in- + cadō), incidere (3), incidī
  (*intrans.*), to fall into *or* upon (18)
inclūdō (in- + claudō), inclūdere (3),
  inclūsī, inclūsum, to shut up in,
  enclose, imprison (1)
incola (in- + colō), -ae, (*m/f*), inhabitant
  (24)
incolō, incolere (3), incoluī, to inhabit
  (21)
incolumis, -is, -e, unhurt, safe (30)
incommodum, -ī (*n*), inconvenience,
  harm (39)
incrēdibilis, -is, -e, unbelievable,
  incredible (23)
indūcō, indūcere (3), indūxī,
  inductum, to lead in *or* on, move, excite
induō, induere (3), induī, indūtum, to
  put on, clothe, dress (4)
ineō, inīre (*irreg.*), iniī, initum (*trans.*),
  to go into, enter, adopt
īnfāns, īnfantis, īnfantum *or*
  īnfantium (*m/f*), infant, babe (1)
īnfectus, -a, -um, not done, undone,
  unaccomplished (83)
īnfēlīx, īnfēlīcis, unhappy, unfortunate
  (14)
īnferī, -ōrum (*m pl*), the inhabitants of
  the underworld, the dead, the shades (51)
īnferō, īnferre (*irreg.*), intulī,
  illātum, to bring in *or* against, wage
  against, inflict (32)
īnfestus, -a, -um, unsafe, dangerous (21)
īnficiō (in- + faciō), īnficere (3), īnfēcī,
  īnfectum, to stain, dye (8)
ingēns, ingentis, huge, vast (22)
iniciō (in- + iaciō), inicere (3), iniēcī,
  iniectum, to throw in *or* upon *or* onto,
  cause, inspire (7)
inimīcus (in- + amīcus), -a, -um (+ *dat.* or
  + in + *acc.*), unfriendly, hostile (62)
initium, -ī (*n*), beginning (34)
iniūria (in- + iūs), -ae (*f*), injury, wrong,
  hurt, harm (79)
inquit, he says, he said (25)
īnsānia, -ae (*f*), madness, insanity (89)
īnsciēns, īnscientis, unknowing,
  unaware (68)
īnsequor, īnsequī (3), īnsecūtus sum,
  to follow upon *or* up, pursue (74)

īnsidiae, -ārum, (*f pl*), ambush, plot,
  stratagem (81)
īnspectō (1), to look on, watch (69))
īnspiciō (in- + speciō), īnspicere (3),
  īnspexī, īnspectum (+ in + *acc.*), to
  look into *or* upon (5)
īnstituō (in- + statuō), īnstituere (3),
  īnstituī, īnstitūtum, to decide upon,
  determine
īnstruō, īnstruere (3), īnstrūxī,
  īnstrūctum, to build in *or* into, draw up,
  equip, furnish (33)
īnsula, -ae (*f*), island (2)
intellegō, intellegere (3), intellēxī,
  intellēctum, to perceive, understand
  (38)
intendō, intendere (3), intendī,
  intentum, to stretch out, stretch, draw,
  aim (14)
inter (+ *acc.*), between, among (11)
intereā (inter- + is), in the meantime,
  meanwhile (8)
interficiō (inter- + faciō), interficere
  (3), interfēcī, interfectum, to put out
  of the way, kill (13)
interior, -ius (*comp. of* inter), interior,
  inner (85)
intermittō, intermittere (3),
  intermīsī, intermissum, to leave off,
  interrupt, let pass; (*passive*) to be left
  between, intervene, elapse (60)
intervāllum, -ī (*n*), interval, space,
  distance (33)
intrā (+ *acc.*), within (36)
intrō (1), to go within *or* into, enter (65)
introitus, -ūs (*m*), entrance (44)
intueor, intuērī (2), intuitus sum to
  look upon, behold (78)
inūsitātus, -a, -um, unusual,
  extraordinary (44)
inūtilis, -is, -e (+ *dat.* or ad + *acc.*), not
  useful, useless (100)
inveniō, invenīre (4), invēnī,
  inventum, to come upon, find (10)
inventor, inventōris (*m*), finder,
  discoverer (85)
invītō (1), to invite (95)
invītus, -a, -um, unwilling, against one's
  will (83)
Iolāus, -ī (*m*), Iolaus (22)
Iolē, Iolēs (*f*), Iole (55)
Iovis, *gen. of* Iuppiter (1)
Iphiclēs, Iphiclis (*m*), Iphicles (13)
ipse, ipsa, ipsum, -self, himself, herself,

itself, themselves; (*often translated*) very (1)

īra, -ae (*f*), anger, wrath (67)

īrāscor, īrāscī (3), īrātus sum (*intrans.*), to be angry

īrātus, -a, -um, angered, enraged, angry, furious (14)

irrīdeō (in- + rīdeō), irrīdēre (2), irrīsī, irrīsum, to laugh at, mock (25)

irrumpō (in- + rumpō), irrumpere (3), irrūpī, irruptum (*intrans.* + *dat.* or in + *acc./trans.* + *acc.*), to burst in or into (10)

irruō (in- + ruō), irruere (3), irruī (*intrans.*), to rush in (99)

is, ea, id, this, that, he, she, it, they

iste, ista, istud, that of yours, that (11)

ita, in this manner or way, thus, in such a way, so (12)

    ita ut, as, just as

Italia, -ae (*f*), Italy (41)

itaque, and so, accordingly, therefore, thus (2)

iter, itineris (*n*), a going, journey, march (15)

    iter facere, to journey, march (15)

iterum, a second time, again (8)

Ithaca, -ae (*f*), Ithaca (81)

iubeō, iubēre (2), iussī, iussum, to bid, order, command (6)

iūcundus, -a, -um, pleasant, sweet (26)

iūdex (iūs + dīcō), iūdicis (*m*), judge (51)

iugum, -ī (*n*), yoke (69)

iungō, iungere (3), iūnxī, iūnctum, to join, yoke, harness (67)

Iūnō, Iūnōnis (*f*), Juno (12)

Iuppiter, Iovis (*m*), Jupiter or Jove (1)

iūrandum, see iūs

iūs, iūris, iūrum or iūrium (*n*), right, justice, law

    iūs dīcere, to pronounce judgment (51)

    iūs iūrandum, iūris iūrandī, oath

iussum, -ī (*n*), order, command (6)

iussus, -ūs (*m*), bidding, command (95)

iūstus, -a, -um, just (91)

iuvenis, iuvenis (*m*), young man, youth (3)

iuvō, iuvāre (1), iūvī, iūtum, to help (74)

L

labor, labōris (*m*), labor, toil, effort, task (20)

labōrō (1), to labor, toil (22)

lac, lactis (*n*), milk (84)

Lacōnia, -ae (*f*), Laconia (a country) (52)

lacrima, -ae (*f*), tear (7)

lacus, -ūs (*m*), lake (29)

laetitia, -ae (*f*), joy (31)

lāmenta, -ōrum (*n pl*), lamentation (87)

Lāomedōn, Lāomedontis (*m*), Laomedon (36)

lapis, lapidis (*m*), stone (40)

laqueus, -ī (*m*), noose (24)

Lārīsa, -ae (*f*), Larissa (11)

lassitūdō, lassitūdinis (*f*), weariness, fatigue (70)

lateō (2), to lie hidden, be concealed (90)

latrō, latrōnis (*m*), robber (85)

lātus, -a, -um, broad, wide (60)

lēgātus, -ī (*m*), ambassador (16)

lēnis, -is, -e, gentle (66)

leō, leōnis (*m*), lion (21)

Lernaeus, -a, -um, of Lerna, Lernean (22)

Lēthē, Lēthēs (*f*), Lethe (51)

levis, -is, -e, light, slight (27)

leviter, slightly (27)

libenter, willingly, gladly (2)

līberī, -ōrum (*m pl*), children (18)

līberō (1) (+ *abl.* or rarely ab or ex + *abl.*), to set free, free, liberate, release (16)

lībertās, lībertātis (*f*), freedom, liberty (35)

licet, licēre (2), licuit or licitum est (*inf. as subject* + *dat.*), it is allowed or permitted (50)

Lichās, Lichae (*m*), Lichas (55)

ligna, -ōrum (*n pl*), wood (22)

ligneus, -a, -um, of wood, wooden (1)

Ligurēs, -um (*m pl*), Ligurians (40)

Liguria, -ae (*f*), Liguria (46)

līmen, līminis (*n*), threshold, door (97)

līmus, -ī (*m*), mud (29)

linter, lintris (*f*), boat, skiff (29)

Linus, -ī (*m*), Linus (14)

lītus, lītoris (*n*), shore (2)

locus, -ī (*m*); (*pl.*) loca, -ōrum (*n*), place, situation (4)

longē, far

longinquus, -a, -um, distant, remote (45)

longius, farther (40)

longus, -a, -um, long, tedious (54)

    longē, far

    longius, farther (40)

loquor, loquī (3), locūtus sum, to speak (55)

lōtus, -ī (m), lotus (82)
luctor, luctārī (1), luctātus sum, to
    wrestle, struggle (92)
lūdus, -ī (m), game, sport (11)
lūmen, lūminis (n), light (13)
lūx, lūcis (f), light (49)
    ortā lūce, at dawn (69)

M

magicus, -a, -um, of magic, magic (4)
magis, more, rather
magister, magistrī (m), master, teacher
    (14)
magnificē, splendidly (98)
magnificus (magnus + faciō), -a, -um,
    splendid, magnificent (95)
magnitūdō, magnitūdinis (f),
    greatness, size (28)
magnopere (abl. of magnum opus),
    greatly, very much, exceedingly,
    earnestly (1)
magnus, -a, -um, large, big, great,
    mighty, loud (1)
maior, maius, comp. of magnus (82)
male, badly, ill (65)
mālō, mālle (irreg.), māluī (magis +
    volō), to wish rather, prefer (96)
mālum, -ī (n), apple (45)
malum, -ī (n), evil, mischief (55)
mālus, -ī (m), mast (92)
malus, -a, -um, bad
    male, badly, ill
mandō (manus + dō) (1) (+ dat. + ut +
    subjunctive), to put into one's hands,
    entrust, commit, charge, command (32)
māne, in the morning, early in the morning
    (68)
maneō, manēre (2), mānsī, mānsum
    (intrans.), to remain, wait (3)
mānēs, mānium (m pl), spirit, shade (50)
manus, -ūs (f), hand (4)
mare, maris, marium (n), sea (1)
marītus, -ī (m), husband (13)
Mārs, Mārtis (m), Mars (a god) (32)
māter, mātris (f), mother (1)
mātrimōnium, -ī (n), marriage (3)
    in mātrimōnium dūcere, to marry
    (3)
mātūrō (1) (intrans.), to hurry (35)
maximē, very greatly, exceedingly,
    especially (18)
maximus, -a, -um, supl. of magnus (1)
Mēdēa, -ae (f), Medea (68)
medicāmentum, -ī (n), drug, poison,
    potion (95)

medius, -a, -um, mid, middle, the middle
    of (12)
Medūsa, -ae (f), Medusa (3)
membrum, -ī (n), limb, member (75)
memoria, -ae (f), memory (34)
    ē memoriā dēpōnere, to forget
    memoriā tenēre, to remember
mentiō, mentiōnis (f), mention (49)
mercātor, mercātōris (m), trader,
    merchant (46)
mercēs, mercēdis (f), pay, reward,
    wages (50)
Mercurius, -ī (m), Mercury (50)
mergō, mergere (3), mersī, mersum
    (trans.), to dip, plunge, sink; (passive,
    intrans.) to sink (8)
merīdiānus, -a, -um, midday, noonday
    (92)
        merīdiānum tempus, midday, noon
        (92)
merīdiēs (medius + diēs), -ēī (m),
    midday, noon, south (69)
meritus, -a, -um, deserved, due, just (9)
meus, -a, -um, my, mine
mīles, mīlitis (m), soldier (34)
mīlitāris, -is, -e, military, warlike (32)
    rēs mīlitāris, art of war, warfare (32)
mīlle (indecl. adj.), a thousand; mīlia,
    mīlium (n pl), thousands (28)
        mīlia passuum, thousands of paces,
        miles (48)
minae, -ārum (f pl), threats (52)
Minerva, -ae (f), Minerva (a goddess) (4)
minimē, least, very little, by no means, not
    at all (3)
minitor, minitārī (1), minitātus sum,
    to threaten (98)
Mīnōs, Mīnōis (m), Minos (51)
minus, less (14)
Minyae, -ārum (m pl), Minyae (16)
mīrāculum, -ī (n), wonder, marvel,
    miracle (78)
mīror, mīrārī (1), mīrātus sum, to
    wonder, wonder at (27)
mīrus, -a, -um, wonderful, strange (13)
misceō, miscēre (2), miscuī, mixtum
    (trans.), to mix, mingle (95)
miser, misera, miserum, miserable
misericordia, -ae (f), pity, compassion
    (56)
mittō, mittere (3), mīsī, missum, to
    send (6)
modo, only, just now, lately (31)
modus, -ī (m), way, manner (5)

moenia, -ium (*n pl*), walls (36)

mola, -ae (*f*), meal (15)

moneō (2), to warn (58)

mōns, montis, montium (*m*), mountain (28)

mōnstrum, -ī (*n*), wonder, monster (4)

mora, -ae (*f*), delay (8)

mordeō, mordēre (2), momordī, morsum, to bite (22)

morior, morī (3), mortuus sum (*intrans.*), to die, lose one's life (55)

moror, morārī (1), morātus sum (*intrans.*), to delay, linger, stay (39)

mors, mortis, mortium (*f*), death (21)

mortālis, -is, -e, mortal (97)

mortifer (mors + ferō), mortifera, mortiferum, death-bringing, deadly (22)

mortuus, -a, -um, dead (13)

mōs, mōris (*m*), way, manner, habit, custom (15)

moveō, movēre (2), mōvī, mōtum (*trans.*), to move (12)

mūgiō (4) (*intrans.*), to low, bellow (43)

mūgītus, -ūs (*m*), lowing, bellowing (43)

mulier, mulieris (*f*), woman (32)

multitūdō, multitūdinis (*f*), multitude (32)

multus, -a, -um, much, great; (*pl.*) many (3)

    multō, by much *or* far, much, far (62)

    multum, much, greatly, far

mūniō (4), to fortify (72)

mūnus, mūneris (*n*), service, office, duty, present, gift (48)

mūrus, -ī (*m*), wall (28)

mūsica, -ae (*f*), music (14)

mūtō (1), to change (67)

Mȳsia, -ae (*f*), Mysia (a country) (63)

N

nactus, *part. of* nancīscor

nam, for (1)

namque, for (45)

nancīscor, nancīscī (3), nactus sum, to get, obtain, find (31)

nārrō (1), to tell, relate, narrate (1)

natō (1) (*intrans.*), to swim, float (66)

nātūra, -ae (*f*), nature, character (4)

nauta, -ae (*m*), sailor (30)

nauticus, -a, -um, naval, nautical (60)

nāvigātiō, nāvigātiōnis (*f*), sailing, navigation, voyage (92)

nāvigō (nāvis + agō) (1) (*intrans.*), to sail (30)

nāvis, nāvis, nāvium (*f*), ship

    ē nāvī ēgredī, to go ashore, disembark

    nāvem appellere, to put in (10)

    nāvem cōnscendere, to go on board, embark (30)

    nāvem dēdūcere, to draw down *or* launch a ship

    nāvem solvere, to cast off, set sail, put to sea

    nāvis longa, warship

ne- (*prefix*), not

-ne (*enclitic*), used to denote a question

nē, not, that not, lest (42)

    nē . . . quidem (*emphasizing the word in between*), not even

nec, see neque (7)

necesse (*indecl. adj.*), necessary (41)

necō (1), to put to death, slay, kill (1)

neglegō, neglegere (3), neglēxī, neglēctum, to disregard, neglect (68)

negō (1), to say no *or* not, deny, refuse (33)

negōtium, -ī (*n*), business, matter, task, trouble, difficulty (28)

Nemeaeus, -a, -um, of Nemea, Nemean (21)

nēmō, *dat.* nēminī, *acc.* nēminem, (*m/f*), no one, nobody (49)

nepōs, nepōtis (*m*), grandson (1)

Neptūnus, -ī (*m*), Neptune (6)

neque *or* nec, and not, nor (8)

    neque enim, for . . . not

    neque . . . neque, neither . . . nor

    neque quisquam, and no one

nervus, -ī (*m*), sinew, muscle (68)

nesciō (4), to not know, be ignorant (57)

    nesciō quis, I know not who, some one or other (nesciō *is thus used with other interrogative words also*) (57)

Nessus, -ī (*m*), Nessus (54)

neu, see nēve (34)

neuter, neutra, neutrum, neither (34)

nēve (nē + -ve) or neu, or not, and that not, and not, nor (34)

niger, nigra, nigrum, black (51)

nihil (*indecl.*) (*n*), nothing (40)

nisi (ne- + sī), if not, unless (50)

nix, nivis (*f*), snow (41)

noctū, at *or* by night (42)

nocturnus, -a, -um, of night, nocturnal (23)

    nocturnum tempus, nighttime (23)

nōlō (ne + volō), nōlle (*irreg.*), nōluī (+ *inf.*), to not wish, be unwilling (17)

nōmen, nōminis (*n*), name (6)

nōn, not (14)

nōndum, not yet (36)

nōnne (*used to introduce a question to which an affirmative answer is expected*) not? (97)

nonnūllī, -ae, -a, some (81)

nōs, *pl. of* ego

noster, nostra, nostrum, our (60)

nōtus, -a, -um (+ *dat.*), known, well-known, famous (19)

novem (*indecl. adj.*), nine (22)

novitās, novitātis (*f*), newness, novelty (61)

novus, -a, -um, new (22)

  novissimus, -a, -um, last (90)

nox, noctis, noctium (*f*), night (12)

nūbēs, nūbis, nūbium (*f*), cloud (56)

nūdus, -a, -um (+ *gen.*), naked, bare (59)

nūllus (ne- + ūllus), **-a, -um**, not any, none, no (13)

num (*used to introduce a question to which a negative answer is expected*) (77)

numerus, -ī (*m*), number (29)

nummus, -ī (*m*), coin (50)

numquam (ne- + umquam), never (49)

nunc, now (55)

nūntiō (1) (+ *dat.*), to report, announce (23)

nūntius, -ī (*m*), messenger, message (11)

nūper, newly, lately, recently (94)

nusquam (ne- + usquam), nowhere (43)

nympha, -ae (*f*), nymph (45)

O

ob, (+ *acc.*) on account of, for; (*as a prefix*) toward, to, against (6)

obiciō (ob- + iaciō), **obicere** (3), **obiēcī, obiectum** (+ *dat.*), to throw in the way *or* to (31)

obiūrgō (1), to chide, scold, reproach (14)

oblinō, oblinere (3), **oblēvī, oblitum**, to daub over, smear (68)

oblīvīscor, oblīvīscī (3), **oblītus sum** (+ *gen.* or *acc.*), to forget, disregard, dismiss from the mind (82)

obscūrō (1), to darken, hide, conceal (56)

obscūrus, -a, -um, dark (62)

obsecrō (1), to beseech, entreat (53)

obserō, obserere (3), **obsēvī, obsitum**, to sow, plant, cover, fill (28)

obsideō (ob- + sedeō), **obsidēre** (2), **obsēdī, obsessum**, to beset, besiege

obstruō, obstruere (3), **obstrūxī, obstrūctum**, to build against, block up (43)

obtestor, obtestārī (1), **obtestātus sum**, to call to witness, beseech, implore (100)

obtineō (ob- + teneō), **obtinēre** (2), **obtinuī, obtentum**, to hold against, hold (28)

occāsiō (ob- + cadō), **occāsiōnis** (*f*), chance, opportunity (55)

occāsus, -ūs (*m*), setting (35)

  occāsus sōlis, sunset (35)

occīdō (ob- + caedō), **occīdere** (3), **occīdī, occīsum**, to cut down, kill (5)

occupō (1), to seize, fill (6)

occurrō (ob- + currō), **occurrere** (3), **occucurrī** *or* **occurrī, occursum** (+ *dat.*), to run against, meet (24)

Ōceanus, -ī (*m*), Oceanus, the ocean (46)

oculus, -ī (*m*), eye (84)

ōdī, ōdisse (*irreg.*), **ōsum** (*used in forms of the perfect system, with the force of forms in the present system*), to hate (12)

odium, -ī (*n*), hatred (100)

odor, odōris (*m*), smell, odor (26)

Oechalia, -ae (*f*), Oechalia (55)

Oeneus, -ī (*m*), Oeneus (54)

Oeta, -ae (*f*), Oeta (56)

offendō, offendere (3), **offendī, offēnsum**, to offend (6)

offerō (ob- + ferō), **offerre** (*irreg.*), **obtulī, oblātum** (+ *acc.* + *dat.*), to bear to, proffer, offer (36)

officīna, -ae (*f*), workshop, smithy (85)

officium, -ī (*n*), service, duty (14)

Olympus, -ī (*m*), Olympus (56)

omittō (ob- + mittō), **omittere** (3), **omīsī, omissum**, to let go, neglect, disregard, throw away, lose (70)

omnīnō, altogether, wholly, entirely, completely, at all, (4)

omnis, -is, -e, all, every, whole (2)

onerō (1), to load, burden (41)

opera, -ae (*f*), work, effort, labor (28)

opīniō, opīniōnis (*f*), opinion, expectation, reputation (28)

oppidum, -ī (*n*), town (21)

opportūnus, -a, -um (+ *dat.*), suitable, seasonable, convenient, opportune (37)

opprimō (ob- + premō), **opprimere** (3), **oppressī, oppressum**, to press against, overpower, crush (72)

optimus, -a, -um, *supl. of* bonus (26)

opus, operis (*n*), work, task (28)

ōrāculum, -ī (*n*), oracle (1)

ōrātiō, ōrātiōnis (*f*), speech (76)

  ōrātiōnem habēre, to give *or* deliver

a speech, speak

orbis, orbis, orbium (*m*), circle (46)

> **orbis terrārum**, circle of the lands, earth, world (46)

Orcus, -ī (*m*), Orcus, the underworld (49)

ōrdō, ōrdinis (*m*), arrangement, order, rank (90)

> **ex ōrdine**, in order (90)

orior, orīrī (4), **ortus sum** (*intrans.*), to arise, rise, come forth, spring up (69)

> **ortā lūce**, at dawn (69)

ōrnō (1), to equip, adorn (19)

ōrō (1), to speak, beg, pray (31)

Orpheus, -ī (*m*), Orpheus (61)

ōs, ōris (*n*), mouth (42)

ostendō, ostendere (3), **ostendī, ostentum** (+ *dat.*), to stretch out before, show, explain (10)

ōstium, -ī (*n*), mouth, doorway, door (33)

ovis, ovis, ovium (*f*), sheep (87)

P

pābulum, -ī (*n*), food, fodder (41)

paene, almost, nearly (9)

palaestra, -ae (*f*), palestra, wrestling-place (14)

palūs, palūdis (*f*), swamp, marsh (22)

parātus, -a, -um, prepared, equipped, ready (15)

pāreō (2) (+ *dat.*), to obey (37)

parō (1), to make ready, prepare (7)

pars, partis, partium (*f*), part, side, group, direction (11)

parvus, -a, -um, little, small (13)

pāscō, pāscere (3), **pāvī, pāstum**, to feed (42)

passus, -ūs (*m*), pace (48)

> **mīlia passuum**, thousands of paces, miles (48)

pāstor, pāstōris (*m*), shepherd (56)

patefaciō, patefacere (3), **patefēcī, patefactum** (+ *dat.*), to throw *or* lay open, open (44)

pater, patris (*m*), father (9)

patior, patī (3), **passus sum**, to bear, suffer, allow, permit (90)

patria, -ae (*f*), fatherland, country (81)

paucī, -ae, -a (*pl. adj.*), few (9)

paulisper, for a little while, for a short time

paulum, -ī (*n*), a little

> **paulō**, by a little, a little, somewhat (60)
> **paulum**, a little, somewhat (24)

pavor, pavōris (*m*), terror, panic (6)

pectus, pectoris (*n*), breast, chest (54)

pecūnia, -ae (*f*), money (93)

pecus, pecoris (*n*), cattle, herd, flock (36)

pecus, pecudis (*f*), head of cattle, beast, sheep, goat (36)

Peliās, Peliae (*m*), Pelias (57)

pellis, pellis, pellium (*f*), hide, skin, pelt (21)

pellō, pellere (3), **pepulī, pulsum**, to drive, drive away, beat, rout (17)

pendō, pendere (3), **pependī, pēnsum** (+ *dat.*), to weigh out, pay (16)

Pēnelopē, Pēnelopēs (*f*), Penelope (81)

per (+ *acc.*), through, by means of, during the whole of, throughout the (4)

percipiō (per- + capiō), **percipere** (3), **percēpī, perceptum**, to feel (37)

percutiō (per- + quatiō), **percutere** (3), **percussī, percussum**, to strike through, strike (14)

perdūcō, perdūcere (3), **perdūxī, perductum**, to lead *or* bring through, lead, bring (2)

peregrīnus, -ī (*m*), stranger, foreigner (31)

perennis (per- + annus), **-is, -e**, lasting throughout the year, perennial, perpetual (41)

pereō, perīre (*irreg.*), **periī, peritūrus** (*intrans.*), to pass away, perish (59)

perferō, perferre (*irreg.*), **pertulī, perlātum**, to bear through, endure, weather (60)

perficiō (per- + faciō), **perficere** (3), **perfēcī, perfectum**, to make *or* do thoroughly, accomplish (54)

perflō (1), to blow through *or* over (93)

perfodiō, perfodere (3), **perfōdī, perfossum**, to dig *or* pierce through, transfix (89)

perīculum, -ī (*n*), danger, peril, risk (6)

perlūstrō (1), to look over, examine, survey (85)

permaneō, permanēre (2), **permānsī, permānsum** (*intrans.*), to remain through, remain (76)

perpetuus, -a, -um, continuous, perpetual (82)

> **in perpetuum**, for all time, forever (82)

perrumpō, perrumpere (3), **perrūpī, perruptum**, to burst *or* break through, break (15)

perscrībō, perscrībere (3),

perscrīpsī, perscīptum, to write in full, describe fully, recount (54)

persequor, persequī (3), **persecūtus sum**, to follow up, pursue (23)

Perseus, -ī (*m*), Perseus (1)

persolvō, persolvere (3), **persolvī, persolūtum**, to pay completely, pay (36)

persuādeō, persuādēre (2), **persuāsī, persuāsum** (+ *dat.* + **ut** + *subjunctive*), to persuade, prevail upon, induce (33)

perterreō (2), to frighten thoroughly, terrify (24)

perturbō (1), to confuse thoroughly, throw into confusion, disturb, agitate (34)

perveniō, pervenīre (4), **pervēnī, perventum** (*intrans.*), to come through, come, arrive, reach (4)

pēs, pedis (*m*), foot (4)

pedem referre, to draw back, retire, retreat (72)

petō, petere (3), **petīvī** *or* **petiī, petītum**, to seek, ask, attack (26)

Phāsis, Phāsidis (*m*), Phasis (67)

Phīneus, -ī (*m*), Phineus (64)

Pholus, -ī (*m*), Pholus (25)

Phrixus, -ī (*m*), Phrixus (59)

pinguis, -is, -e, fat (90)

piscātor, piscātōris (*m*), fisherman (2)

plausus, -ūs (*m*), applause (61)

plēnus, -a, -um (+ *gen.*), full (of) (26)

plūrēs, plūra, plūrium (*comp. of* **multus**) (*pl. adj.*), more, many, several (48)

plūrimus, -a, -um (+ *gen.*), (*supl. of* **multus**), most (19)

Plūtōn, Plūtōnis (*m*), Pluto (50)

pōculum, -ī (*n*), cup (25)

poena, -ae (*f*), penalty, punishment (51)

poēta, -ae (*m*), poet (1)

polliceor, pollicērī (2), **pollicitus sum** (+ *dat.*), to promise (53)

Polydectēs, Polydectis (*m*), Polydectes (2)

Polyphēmus, -ī (*m*), Polyphemus (63)

pondus, ponderis (*n*), weight (47)

pōnō, pōnere (3), **posuī, positum**, to place, put

  positus esse, (*with* **in** *and abl.*), to be placed in, rest *or* depend on (50)

pōns, pontis (*m*), bridge (50)

porcus, -ī (*m*), pig

porta, -ae (*f*), gate (45)

portus, -ūs (*m*), harbor, haven, port (31)

poscō, poscere (3), **poposcī** (+ *double acc.*), to ask, ask for, demand (33)

possideō, possidēre (2), **possēdī, possessum**, to hold, possess (32)

possum (**potis** + **sum**), **posse** (*irreg.*), **potuī** (+ *inf.*), to be able, have power, can (30)

post, (*adv.* + *abl.*) after, later; (*prep.* + *acc.*) after, behind (8)

posteā (**post-** + **is**), after this, afterwards (14)

posterus, -a, -um, following, next (43)

postquam, later than, after, when (2)

postrēmus, -a, -um (*supl. of* **posterus**), last (88)

postrīdiē (**posterus** + **diēs**), on the following *or* next day (63)

postulō (1) (+ **ut** + *subjunctive*), to ask, request, demand (16)

potior, potīrī (4), **potītus sum** (+ *abl.*), to become master of, get possession of (59)

prae (+ *abl.*), before

praeacūtus, -a, -um, sharpened at the end, pointed, sharp (87)

praebeō (2) (+ *acc.* + *dat.*), to hold forth, supply, furnish, give, show, present, exhibit (38)

praecaveō, praecavēre (2), **praecāvī, praecautum**, to beware beforehand, beware, be on one's guard (85)

praecipiō (**prae-** + **capiō**), **praecipere** (3), **praecēpī, praeceptum** (+ *dat.* + **ut** + *subjunctive*), to take beforehand, anticipate, direct, order, charge (36)

praecipuē, especially (19)

praeclārus, -a, -um, very bright, splendid, remarkable, famous (54)

praeda, -ae (*f*), booty, spoil, plunder (30)

praedīcō, praedīcere (3), **praedīxī, praedictum** (+ *dat.*), to say beforehand, foretell, predict (70)

praedor, praedārī (1), **praedātus sum**, to plunder, rob (85)

praemium, -ī (*n*), reward (31)

praesēns, praesentis (+ *dat.*), present, immediate, imminent (86)

praesentia, -ae (*f*), the present (58)

praeses, praesidis (*m*), protector (85)

praesidium, -ī (*n*), protection, guard, escort (72)

praestāns, praestantis, surpassing, preeminent, remarkable (45)

praestō, praestāre (1), **praestitī,**

praestitum *or* praestātum (+ *dat.* and *abl.*), to stand before, surpass, excel, show (3)

praesum, praeesse (*irreg.*), praefuī (+ *dat.*), to be before, preside over, be in charge of, command (60)

praeter (+ *acc.*), past, by, besides, except (25)

praetereā (praeter- + is), besides this, besides, moreover (9)

praetereō, praeterīre (*irreg.*), prae-teriī, praeteritum, to go *or* pass by (90)

prehendō, prehendere (3), prehendī, prehēnsum, to seize (13)

premō, premere (3), pressī, pressum, to press, check, restrain (92)

pretium, -ī (*n*), price, charge (50)

prex, precis (*used chiefly in the plural*) (*f*), prayer, entreaty (97)

prīdiē, on the day before (87)

prīmō, at first (20)

prīmum, first, in the first place (4)
    quam prīmum, as soon as possible

prīmus, -a, -um, first (74)

prīstinus, -a, -um, former (34)

prius, before, first (67)

priusquam, before than, sooner than, before (35)

prō (+ *abl.*), before, in front of, for, in behalf of, for, as, in return for (2)

procul, at *or* from a distance, far off, in the distance (7)

proelium, -ī (*n*), battle, combat (18)
    proelium committere, to join battle

profectiō, profectiōnis (*f*), departure, start (81)

proficīscor, proficīscī (3), profectus sum (*intrans.*), to set out, depart, start (17)

prōgredior (prō- + gradior), prōgredī (3), prōgressus sum (*intrans.*), to go forward, advance (24)

prohibeō (prō- + habeō) (2) (+ *inf.*), to hold back, prevent, hinder (40)

prōiciō (prō- + iaciō), prōicere (3), prōiēcī, proiectum, to throw forth *or* down, throw (24)

prōmō, prōmere (3), prōmpsī, prōmptum, to take *or* bring out, produce (88)

properō (1) (*intrans.*), to hurry (13)

prōpōnō, prōpōnere (3), prōposuī, prōpositum, to put *or* set before, offer, propose, set forth, say (36)

propter (+ *acc.*), on account of, because of, for (1)

prōra, -ae (*f*), prow, bow (66)

prōsequor, prōsequī (3), prōsecūtus sum, to follow forward, follow (75)

Prōserpina, -ae (*f*), Proserpina, Proserpine (50)

prōsternō, prōsternere (3), prōstrāvī, prōstrātum, to strew *or* spread before, throw *or* knock down (14)

prōsum, prōdesse (*irreg.*), prōfuī (+ *dat.*), to be of advantage, profit, avail, assist (47)

prōvehō, prōvehere (3), prōvexī, prōvectum, to carry forward, advance (54)

prōvocō (1), to call forth *or* out, challenge (88)

proximus, -a, -um (+ *dat.*), nearest, next (17)

prūdentia, -ae (*f*), prudence (81)

puella, -ae (*f*), girl, maiden (7)

puer, puerī (*m*), boy (1)

pugna, -ae (*f*), fighting, battle, combat (33)

pugnō (1), to fight (17)

pulcher, pulchra, pulchrum, beautiful, handsome (42)

pulsō (1), to push *or* strike against, knock, knock at (95)

pūnctum, -ī (*n*), point, instant, moment (37)

pūrgō (1), to make clean, clean, cleanse (28)

putō (1), to think (68)

Pȳthia, -ae (*f*), Pythia (19)

Q

quā, in which place, where (22)

quaerō, quaerere (3), quaesīvī, quaesītum, to seek, ask, inquire (4)

quālis, -is, -e, of what sort? what kind of? (82)

quam, how, as, than; (*with supl.*) as . . . as possible
    quam prīmum, as soon as possible

quamquam, although (22)

quantum, how much? how?

quantus, -a, -um, how great *or* much? (38)

quārtus, -a, -um, fourth (10)

quasi (quam + sī), as if (56)

quattuor (*indecl. adj.*), four (42)

-que (*enclitic*), and

quī, quae, quod, who, which, that
quī, quae, quod (*inter. adj.*), which? what?
quīdam, quaedam, quoddam (*adj.; may either precede or follow the noun it modifies*), a certain, certain (2)
quidem (*postpositive*), in fact, indeed, certainly (40)
 nē . . . quidem (*emphasizing the word in between*), not even
quiēs, quiētis (*f*), rest, repose (2)
quīn, that . . . not, but that, but, that (64)
quīnquāgintā (*indecl. adj.*), fifty (61)
quīntus, -a, -um, fifth (48)
quis, quid (*inter. pronoun*), who? what?
quis, quae or **qua, quid** (*indef. adj. or pronoun after* **sī, nisi, num,** *or* **nē**), any, anyone, anybody, anything, some, someone, somebody, something (58)
quisquam, quidquam (quicquam) (*pronoun; postpositive*), anyone, anything (50)
quisque, quaeque, quidque (quodque) (*adj.*), each
quisque, quidque (*pronoun*), each (50)
quō, to what place? whither? to which place, whither (94)
 quō ūsque, till when? how long?
quod, that, in that, because (10)
quondam (*sometimes postpositive*), once upon a time, formerly, once (6)
quoniam, since (16)
quoque (*postpositive*), also (33)
quotannīs, every year, yearly, annually (16)
quotiēns, as often as (22)

R

rāmus, -ī (*m*), branch, bough (72)
ratiō, ratiōnis (*f*), plan, means, method, manner (66)
re- or **red-** (*prefix*), again, back, against
recipiō (re- + capiō), **recipere** (3), **recēpī, receptum**, to take or get back, recover (18)
 sē recipere, to betake oneself, withdraw, to collect oneself, recover (18)
recumbō, recumbere (3), **recubuī**, to lie back or down (88)
recuperō (1), to recover (59)
recūsō (1), to refuse (56)
red-, see **re-**
reddō, reddere (3), **reddidī, redditum** (+ *dat.*), to give back, return,

restore, render (9)
redeō, redīre (*irreg.*), **rediī, reditum** (*intrans.*), to go back, return (11)
redintegrō (1), to make whole again, renew (34)
reditus, -ūs (*m*), return (8)
redūcō, redūcere (3), **redūxī, reductum**, to lead or bring back, restore (18)
referō, referre (*irreg.*), **rettulī, relātum**, to bring or carry back, return, fetch (3)
 pedem referre, to draw back, retire, retreat (72)
 grātiam referre, to return a favor, show gratitude, requite
reficiō (re- + faciō), **reficere** (3), **refēcī, refectum**, to make again, renew, repair, refresh, recruit (42)
refugiō, refugere (3), **refūgī**, to flee back, run away, retreat (10)
rēgia, -ae (*f*), palace (10)
rēgīna, -ae (*f*), queen (12)
regiō, regiōnis (*f*), direction, country, region (9)
rēgnō (1) (*intrans.*), to reign, rule (6)
rēgnum, -ī (*n*), royal power, rule, throne, kingdom, realm (9)
regredior (re- + gradior), **regredī** (3), **regressus sum** (*intrans.*), to go back, return (96)
relinquō, relinquere (3), **relīquī, relictum**, to leave behind, leave (23)
reliquus, -a, -um, left, the remaining, the other, the rest of
remedium, -ī (*n*), remedy (65)
rēmigō (rēmus + agō) (1), to row (75)
remittō, remittere (3), **remīsī, remissum**, to send back, send (79)
removeō, removēre (2), **remōvī, remōtum** (*trans.*), to move back, remove (91)
rēmus, -ī (*m*), oar (66)
renūntiō (1) (+ *dat.*), to bring back word, report, announce (37)
repellō, repellere (3), **reppulī, repulsum**, to drive back or away, repulse, repel (87)
reperiō, reperīre (4), **repperī, repertum**, to find, discover (2)
repōnō, repōnere (3), **reposuī, repositum**, to put or set back, store up or away (55)
repugnō (1), to fight against, struggle,

resist (24)

rēs, reī (*f*), thing, matter, affair, circumstance, situation (5)

    rēs mīlitāris, art of war, warfare (32)

    rē vērā, in truth, in fact, really (57)

resistō, resistere (3), **restitī** (+ *dat.*), to stand against, resist (83)

respīrō (1) (*intrans.* or *trans.*), to breathe back *or* out, breathe (21)

respondeō, respondēre (2), **respondī, respōnsum** (+ *dat.*), to reply, answer (58)

respōnsum, -ī (*n*), reply, answer, response (37)

restituō (re- + statuō), **restituere** (3), **restituī, restitūtum** (+ *dat.*), to set up again, put back, restore (78)

retineō (re- + teneō), **retinēre** (2), **retinuī, retentum**, to hold *or* keep back, keep, restrain, hold fast (23)

revertor (re- + vertō), **revertī** (3), **revertī, reversum** (*the perfect is active in form*, **revertī**, *not* **reversus sum**) (*intrans.*), to turn back, return (54)

rēx, rēgis (*m*), king (2)

Rhadamanthus, -ī (*m*), Rhadamanthus (51)

rīdeō, rīdēre (2), **rīsī, rīsum** (*intrans.*), to laugh (13)

rīpa, -ae (*f*), bank (50)

rīte, duly, fitly (15)

rōbur, rōboris (*n*), oak (60)

rogō (1), to ask (76)

rogus, -ī (*m*), funeral pile, pyre (56)

Rōma, -ae (*f*), Rome (42)

rōstrum, -ī (*n*), beak (29)

ruō, ruere (3), **ruī, ruitum** (*intrans.*), to rush (93)

rūpēs, rūpis (*f*), rock, cliff (7)

rūrsus (for **reversus**, *part. of* **revertor**), again (8)

S

sacerdōs, sacerdōtis (*m/f*), priest, priestess (15)

sacrificium, -ī (*n*), sacrifice (15)

saepe, often, frequently

saevus, -a, -um, fierce, savage (6)

sagitta, -ae (*f*), arrow (22)

sāl, salis (*m*), salt (15)

Salmydēssus, -ī (*f*), Salmydessus (64)

salsus (sāl), **-a, -um**, salted, salt (15)

salūs, salūtis (*f*), safety, deliverance, escape (9)

sānctus, -a, -um, consecrated, sacred (16)

sanguis, sanguinis (*m*), blood (8)

sānitās (sānus, "sound"), **sānitātis** (*f*), soundness, right reason, sanity (18)

satis, enough, sufficiently (63)

saxum, -ī (*n*), rock, stone (43)

scelus, sceleris (*n*), wickedness, crime (19)

scēptrum, -ī (*n*), scepter

scientia, -ae (*f*), knowledge, skill (32)

sciō (4), to know (47)

scrībō, scrībere (3), **scrīpsī, scrīptum** (+ *dat.*), to write (20)

scūtum, -ī (*n*), shield (12)

secundus (sequor), **-a, -um** (+ *dat.*), following, favorable (92)

sed, but (10)

sedeō, sedēre (2), **sēdī, sessum** (*intrans.*), to sit (19)

sēdēs, sēdis, sēdum or **sēdium** (*f*), seat, abode, home (2)

sēmentis, sēmentis (*f*), seeding, sowing (69)

semper, always (21)

senex, senis (*m*), old man (77)

sententia, -ae (*f*), opinion, purpose (57)

sentiō, sentīre (4), **sēnsī, sēnsum**, to perceive, feel, realize, sense (8)

sepeliō, sepelīre (4), **sepelīvī, sepultum**, to bury (27)

septimus, -a, -um, seventh (83)

sequor, sequī (3), **secūtus sum**, to follow (27)

Serīphus, -ī (*f*), Seriphos (2)

sermō, sermōnis (*m*), conversation, talk, speech (18)

serō, serere (3), **sēvī, satum**, to sow, plant (67)

serpēns, serpentis, serpentium (*f*), serpent (12)

serviō (4) (+ *dat.*), to serve, be subject to (20)

servitūs, servitūtis (*f*), slavery, servitude, service (20)

servō (1), to save, preserve (2)

servus, -ī (*m*), slave, servant

sī, if (25)

sīc, so, thus (53)

Sicilia, -ae (*f*), Sicily (85)

signum, -ī (*n*), sign, signal (34)

silva, -ae (*f*), woods, forest (18)

simul, at the same time (7)

simul atque *or* **simul ac**, as soon as (10)

sine (+ *abl.*), without (8)

sinister, sinistra, sinistrum, left

sinistra, -ae (*f*), left hand (22)

sinus, -ūs (*m*), bosom, lap (1)

situs, -a, -um, placed, situated (45)

sīve (sī + -ve "or") *or* seu, or if (27)

  sīve . . . sīve, whether . . . or (27)

socius, -ī (*m*), companion, comrade, ally (35)

sōl, sōlis (*m*), sun, the sun-god (35)

  occāsus sōlis, sunset (35)

solium, -ī (*n*), seat, throne (51)

sollicitūdō, sollicitūdinis (*f*), anxiety, care, apprehension (96)

sollicitus, -a, -um, troubled, anxious (96)

sōlum, alone, only (72)

sōlus, -a, -um, alone, only (32)

solvō, solvere (3), solvī, solūtum, to loosen, unbind, release, open, pay (9)

  (*with or without* nāvem), to cast off, set sail, put to sea

  poenās solvere, to pay a penalty, be punished

somnus, -ī (*m*), sleep, drowsiness (5)

  sē somnō dare, to go to sleep

sonitus, -ūs (*m*), sound, noise (84)

sonōrus, -a, -um, sounding, loud, noisy, howling (92)

soror, sorōris (*f*), sister (4)

sors, sortis (*f*), lot (94)

sortior, sortīrī (4), sortītus sum, to cast *or* draw lots (94)

spargō, spargere (3), sparsī, sparsum, to scatter, sprinkle (69)

spatium, -ī (*n*), space, interval, space of time, time (66)

speciēs, -ēī (*f*), sight, appearance, shape (4)

spectātor, spectātōris (*m*), looker-on, spectator (11)

spectō (1), to look at *or* on

speculum, -ī (*n*), looking-glass, mirror (4)

spēlunca, -ae (*f*), cave, cavern (25)

spērō (spēs) (1), to hope (59)

spēs, speī (*f*), hope (9)

  spem dēpōnere, to despair

sponte *abl. sing.* (*f*), (with suā) of his (her, their) own accord, voluntarily (47)

squālor, squālōris (*m*), dirt, filth (28)

stabulum, -ī (*n*), standing-place, stall, stable, enclosure (28)

statim (stō), on the spot, forthwith, at once, immediately (5)

statuō, statuere (3), statuī, statūtum, to set up, decide, resolve (92)

stō, stāre (1), stetī, statum (*intrans.*), to stand (7)

studeō (2) (+ *dat.*), to be eager, give attention, apply oneself (14)

studiōsus, -a, -um (+ *gen.*), eager, diligent, studious (14)

studium, -ī (*n*), eagerness, zeal, study, pursuit (68)

stupeō (2) (*intrans.*), to be stunned, astounded, amazed at (+ *abl.*) (78)

Stymphālis, Stymphālidis, of Stymphalus, Stymphalian (29)

Stymphālus, -ī (*f*), Stymphalus (29)

Styx, Stygis, (*acc.*) Styga (*f*), Styx (50)

suāvis, -is, -e, sweet, pleasant (26)

sub (+ *acc.* or *abl.*), under (50)

  sub vesperum, toward evening

subdō, subdere (3), subdidī, subditum (+ *dat.*), to put under, apply (56)

subdūcō, subdūcere (3), subdūxī, subductum, to draw up, beach (71)

subeō, subīre (*irreg.*), subiī, subitum, to go under, undergo, submit to, sustain, bear, endure (46)

subiciō (sub- + iaciō), subicere (3), subiēcī, subiectum (+ *acc.* and *dat.*), to throw *or* place something under something (90)

subitō, unexpectedly, suddenly (7)

sublātus, see tollō

subsidium (sub- + sedeō), -ī (*n*), support, help, reserve, reinforcement (61)

succēdō (sub- + cēdō), succēdere (3), successī, successum (+ *dat.*), to go *or* come under, follow after, succeed (76)

succendō, succendere (3), succendī, succēnsum, to kindle beneath, set on fire (76)

succīdō (sub- + caedō), succīdere (3), succīdī, succīsum, to cut below *or* down, fell (22)

sūcus, -ī (*m*), juice (68)

suī, himself, herself, itself, themselves, him, her, it, them (55)

sum, esse (*irreg.*), fuī, futūrus (*intrans.*), to be (1)

summus (*supl. of* superus, upper), -a, -um, uppermost, highest, greatest (24)

sūmō, sūmere (3), sūmpsī, sūmptum, to take up, take (15)

to take up, take (15)
supplicium sūmere, to exact *or*
inflict punishment
superior (*comp. of* **superus**, upper), **-ius**,
higher, former, previous, preceding (36)
superō (1), to overcome, defeat, conquer,
surpass (16)
supersum, superesse (*irreg.*), **super-
fuī, superfutūrus** (*intrans.*), to be over
or left, remain (35)
supplicium, -ī (*n*), punishment, torture
(31)
supplicium sūmere, to exact *or*
inflict punishment
suprā (*adv.* and + *acc.*), above, before (25)
suprēmus (*supl. of* **superus**, upper), **-a,
-um**, highest, last (76)
suscipiō (sub- + capiō), **suscipere** (3),
suscēpī, susceptum, to undertake
(14)
suspendō (subs- = sub- + pendō),
suspendere (3), **suspendī,
suspēnsum**, to hang up, hang (72)
suspīciō (sub- + speciō), **suspīciōnis** (*f*),
suspicion (55)
suspicor (sub- + speciō), **suspicārī** (1),
suspicātus sum, to suspect (55)
sustineō (subs- = sub- + teneō),
sustinēre (2), **sustinuī, sustentum**,
to hold *or* bear up, sustain, withstand (26)
sustulī, see **tollō**
suus, -a, -um, his, her, its, *or* their own;
his, her, its, their (1)
Symplēgadēs, -um (*f pl*), the
Symplegades (29)

T

taceō (2) (*intrans.*), to be silent (20)
tacitus, -a, -um, silent (76)
Taenarus, -ī (*f*), Taenarus (a
promontory) (52)
tālāria, -ium (*n pl*), winged shoes (4)
tālis, -is, -e, such (13)
tam, so (27)
tamen (*sometimes postpositive*), however,
yet, nevertheless (2)
tandem (*sometimes postpositive*), at
length *or* last, finally (4)
tangō, tangere (3), **tetigī, tāctum**, to
touch (96)
tantum, so much *or* far (39)
tantus, -a, -um, so great *or* much (2)
Tartarus, -ī (*m*), Tartarus (51)
taurus, -ī (*m*), bull (30)
tegō, tegere (3), **tēxī, tēctum**, to cover,

conceal (41)
tēlum, -ī (*n*), missile, spear, weapon (14)
temere, rashly (86)
tempestās, tempestātis (*f*), weather,
storm, tempest (31)
templum, -ī (*n*), sanctuary, temple (10)
temptō (1), to try, attempt (33)
tempus, temporis (*n*), time, season (2)
merīdiānum tempus, midday, noon
(92)
nocturnum tempus, nighttime
teneō (2), to hold, keep, hold back, restrain,
stop (7)
memoriā tenēre, to remember
tenuis, -is, -e, thin (97)
tergum, -ī (*n*), back (5)
tergum vertere, to flee
terra, -ae (*f*), land, earth (38)
orbis terrārum, circle of the lands,
earth, world (46)
terreō (2), to frighten, terrify (1)
terribilis, -is, -e, terrible, dreadful (7)
terror, terrōris (*m*), fright, terror (9)
tertius, -a, -um, third (100)
tertium, the *or* a third time (88)
tetigī, see **tangō**
texō, texere (3), **texuī, textum**, to
weave (79)
Thēbae, -ārum (*f pl*), Thebes (16)
Thēbānī, -ōrum (*m pl*), Thebans (16)
Thermōdōn, Thermōdontis (*m*),
Thermodon (33)
Thēseus, -ī (*m*), Theseus (61)
Thessalia, -ae (*f*), Thessaly (a country)
(11)
Thrācia, -ae (*f*), Thrace (a country) (31)
Tiberis, Tiberis (*m*), Tiber (42)
timeō (2), to fear (1)
timor, timōris (*m*), fear (7)
tinguō, tinguere (3), **tīnxī, tīnctum**, to
wet, soak, dye (55)
Tīrȳns, Tīrynthis (*f*), Tiryns (22)
tollō, tollere (3), **sustulī, sublātum**,
to lift, raise, take away, remove (8)
ancorās tollere, to weigh anchor
torqueō, torquēre (2), **torsī, tortum**,
to turn (84)
tōtus, -a, -um, all the, whole, entire (7)
tractō (1), to handle, touch, feel (90)
trādō (trāns- + dō), **trādere** (3), **trādidī,
trāditum** (+ *dat.*), to give, give across,
over, *or* up, hand over, deliver, hand
down, relate, report (6)
trādūcō (trāns- + dūcō), **trādūcere** (3),

trādūxī, trāductum, to lead across (41)

trahō, trahere (3), trāxī, tractum, to draw, drag (30)

trāiciō (trāns- + iaciō), trāicere (3), trāiēcī, trāiectum, to throw across, strike through, pierce (21)

trāiectus, -ūs (m), crossing over, passage (50)

trānō (trāns- + nō, "swim") (1), to swim across or over (54)

tranquillitās, tranquillitātis (f), calm (30)

tranquillus, -a, -um, calm (2)

trāns (+ acc.), across, over

trānseō, trānsīre (irreg.), trānsiī, trānsitum, to go across or over, cross (34)

trānsfīgō, trānsfīgere (3), trānsfīxī, trānsfīxum, to thrust or pierce through, transfix (29)

trānsportō (1), to carry across or over, transport (40)

trānsvehō, trānsvehere (3), trānsvexī, trānsvectum, to carry across or over (50)

trēs, tria (pl. adj.), three (10)

tribūtum, -ī (n), contribution, tribute (16)

trīstitia, -ae (f), sadness (76)

Troia, -ae (f), Troy (35)

Troiānī, -ōrum (m pl), Trojans (36)

tū, tuī, you (sing.) (3)

tum, then, at that time (1)
    etiam tum, even then, still (1)

turbō (1), to confuse, throw into disorder, disturb, trouble (1)

turbō, turbinis (m), whirlwind, hurricane (93)

turpis, -is, -e, disgraceful (3)

tūtus, -a, -um, safe (2)

tuus, -a, -um, thy, thine, your

U

ubi, (adv.) where; (conj.) when (4)

ulcīscor, ulcīscī (3), ultus sum, to avenge, revenge (55)

Ulixēs, Ulixis (m), Ulysses (81)

ūllus, -a, -um, any (96)

ulterior, -ius (comp. adj.), farther (52)

umbra, -ae (f), shadow, shade (80)

umerus, -ī (m), shoulder (21)

umquam, ever (28)

unda, -ae (f), wave

unde, whence, from where (22)

ūndecimus, -a, -um, eleventh (45)

undique (unde + -que), from or on all sides (8)

unguentum, -ī (n), ointment (68)

unguō, unguere (3), ūnxī, ūnctum, to smear, anoint (99)

ūniversus (ūnus + vertō), -a, -um, all together, whole, entire, all (99)

ūnus, -a, -um, one, only one, only, alone (5)

urbs, urbis, urbium (f), city (11)

ūrō, ūrere (3), ussī, ustum, to burn (79)

ūsque, all the way or time
    ūsque ad, up to, even to, until, till
    quō ūsque, till when? how long?

ūsus, -ūs (m), use, experience (32)

ut, as, when, that (28)
    ita ut, as, just as

uter, utra, utrum, which? (of two) (94)

ūter, ūtris (m), skin, bag (88)

uterque, utraque, utrumque, each (of two), either, both (38)

ūtor, ūtī (3), ūsus sum (+ abl.), to use (60)

utrimque, on either side or both sides (66)

uxor, uxōris (f), wife (9)

V

vacuus, -a, -um (+ gen. or abl.), empty (10)

valeō, valēre (2), valuī, valitum (intrans.), to be strong or effective, have effect, prevail (69)

validus, -a, -um, strong (12)

vallēs, vallis, vallium (f), valley (21)

varius, -a, -um, various (51)

vās, vāsis (pl. vāsa, -ōrum) (n), vessel (77)

vāstō (1), to lay waste (24)

vāstus, -a, -um, waste, huge, enormous, vast (92)

vehementer, violently, vehemently, earnestly, exceedingly, greatly (17)

vehō, vehere (3), vexī, vectum, to carry (62)

vellus, velleris (n), fleece (59)

velut, even or just as, as (93)

vēnātiō, vēnātiōnis (f), hunting, hunt (68)

venēnum, -ī (n), poison (26)

veniō, venīre (4), vēnī, ventum (intrans.), to come (4)

venter, ventris (m), belly (90)

ventus, -ī (m), wind, breeze (92)

verbum, -ī (n), word (34)

vereor, vererī (2), veritus sum, to fear (52)

vērō, in truth, indeed, however (24)

versor, versārī (1), versātus sum, to turn often, be busy or employed, be involved, be (83)

vertō, vertere (3), vertī, versum, to turn (5)

    tergum vertere, to flee

vērus, -a, -um, true

    rē vērā, in truth, in fact, really (57)

vēscor, vēscī (3) (+ abl.), to feed on, eat (29)

vesper, vesperī (m), evening (23)

    sub vesperum, toward evening

vester, vestra, vestrum, your

vēstīgium, -ī (n), track, footprint (23)

vestis, vestis, vestium (f), clothing, dress, robe (21)

vestītus, -ūs (m), clothing (51)

via, -ae (f), road, way (4)

viātor, viātōris (m), wayfarer, traveler (54)

victima, -ae (f), victim (15)

victōria, -ae (f), victory (18)

vīctus, -ūs (m), living, sustenance, food (82)

vīcus, -ī (m), village (83)

videō, vidēre (2), vīdī, vīsum, to see; (pass.) to seem (2)

vigilia, -ae (f), watch (74)

vīgintī (indecl. adj.), twenty (94)

vīlla, -ae (f), country house, villa (95)

vīmen, vīminis (n), osier (90)

vinciō, vincīre (4), vīnxī, vīnctum, to bind (15)

vinculum, -ī (n), bond, chain (9)

vīnum, -ī (n), wine (25)

violō (1), to outrage, violate (91)

vir, virī (m), man (15)

virga, -ae (f), wand (96)

virgō, virginis (f), maiden (6)

virtūs, virtūtis (f), manliness, courage, bravery (3)

vīs, vīs (f), violence, force, virtue, potency, efficacy; (pl.) vīrēs, -ium, strength (13)

    omnibus vīribus, with all one's strength or might, with might and main

vīsus, -ūs (m), sight (97)

vīta, -ae (f), life (3)

    vītam agere, to live, to live a . . . life (3)

    vītam āmittere, to lose one's life, die

vītō (1), to avoid, escape (11)

vīvō, vīvere (3), vīxī, vīctum, to live (76)

vīvus, -a, -um, alive, living (23)

vix, with difficulty, scarcely, hardly, barely (44)

vocō (1), to call, summon (3)

Volcānus, -ī (m), Vulcan (29)

volō, velle (irreg.), voluī, to be willing, wish

volō (1) (intrans.), to fly (4)

volucris, volucris (f), bird (64)

voluntās, voluntātis (f), wish, will (19)

voluptās, voluptātis (f), pleasure (57)

vorō (1), to swallow whole, devour (36)

vōs (pl. of tū), you

vōx, vōcis (f), voice, word (13)

vulnerō (1), to wound (8)

vulnus, vulneris (n), wound (8)

Z

Zētēs, Zētae (m), Zetes (65)

Idioms

This is a list of idioms and special grammatical items that appear in the stories. They are grouped in useful categories, and it will be advantageous for you to pay special attention to them in your reading. Paragraph and line numbers are given so that you can find all the examples and study them in context.

Gerund/Gerundive Constructions

ad + gerund (*purpose*): 31.16, 61.11, 88.4, 100.10

causā + gerund (*purpose*): 85.14, 91.7, 94.3

ad + gerundive (*purpose*): 60.5, 60.10, 60.12, 61.7, 67.10, 74.6, 75.9, 77.5, 92.7, 93.3, 98.1, 100.11

passive periphrastic (nom.): 67.12, 67.14 (2), 68.10, 100.19

passive periphrastic (acc.): 68.15, 70.10, 78.7, 80.8, 86.7, 86.8, 93.6

passive periphrastic (acc., intrans. verb): 73.6, 85.18, 92.9, 94.4, 100.17

causam + gerund: 30.12, 33.6, 48.3, 53.2, 71.13, 83.6

diem conveniendī: 58.9, 60.4

facultās + gerund: 21.10, 29.6, 44.12

fīnem loquendī: 77.11

reī bene gerendae: 67.16, 86.6, 88.15

other: 30.7, 34.2, 55.2, 58.13, 75.10, 77.5, 81,15, 92.11, 93.18

Time Constructions

ā puerō: 14.1, 58.11

ad id tempus: 28.5, 80.13

ad sōlis occāsum: 35.1, 62.4, 73.3, 96.5

ad vesperum: 23.8, 83.1

annī tempore: 92.8, 100.16

brevī intermissō spatiō: 67.1, 98.1

brevī tempore: 2.5, 8.8, 18.8, 21.10, 22.4, 27.8, 30.14, 41.2, 42.1, 44.12, 48.11, 58.1, 70.14, 77.14, 80.11, 88.13

continuōs complūrēs diēs: 47.11; (**trēs**) 10.3, 41.10, 91.4; (**novem**) 93.1

diē: (**tertiō**) 100.13; (**quārtō**) 10.4, 41.10; (**quīntō**) 48.10; (**septimō**) 92.7; (**decimō**) 82.5; (**cōnstitūtā**) 58.9

diem dīcere: 7.1, 11.7, 15.5, 37.3, 58.9, 60.4

eā tōtā nocte: 84.1

etiam tum: 1.4, 12.3, 76.2

illō tempore: 6.2, 15.3, 21.2, 24.2, 28.2, 36.1, 59.6

magnam partem diēī: 14.1, 29.9, 43.5

mediā nocte: 12.5, 68.6, 71.6

neque posteā umquam: 65.17; **numquam posteā**: 95.6

ortā lūce: 69.2, 72.1, 87.1

paucās/ōs: (**annōs**) 9.9; (**hōrās**) 62.4, 63.4, 70.5; (**diēs**) 42.3, 61.9, 92.7, 100.4

paucīs post: (**annīs**) 58.7; (**diēbus**) 33.3, 39.7

paulō post: 14.9, 18.6, 22.1, 30.8, 31.19, 55.8, 56.2, 80.2, 87.5

posterō diē: 43.1, 57.8

postrīdiē eius diēī: 63.1, 72.1, 100.1; *without* eius diēī: 84.1

proximō diē: 17.6, 33.11

simul ac/atque: 10.10, 24.5, 26.1, 43.1, 46.2, 65.2, 65.11, 85.4, 97.10

sub vesperum: 70.6, 88.1

tandem tamen: 4.8, 20.1, 35.1, 44,4, 52.12, 56.10, 67.7

tempore opportūnissimō: 37.4, 40.9

tōtum annum: 23.11, 46.7, 100.6

Correlative and Related Constructions

aliae aliam in partem: 82.3

alter . . . alter: 57.1; **alterī . . . alterī**: 94.11

aut . . . aut: 61.2

eōdem modō atque anteā: 98.3

eōdem modō quō anteā: 88.1

et . . . et: 39.11, 72.9, 84.6

in utrōque lītore: 38.9

nē . . . quidem: 60.9, 86.2, 86.13

nec . . . nec: 89.15; **neque . . . neque**: 29.8, 41.6, 85.13, 98.11

nōn modo . . . sed etiam: 31.13, 57.3

nōn modo ob causās . . . sed etiam quod: 45.13

nōn modo quod . . . sed quod: 42.6, 43.3

nōn nūllī/nūllōs: 81.8, 82.6, 83.2

ob eam causam: 6.10, 63.6; **ob hanc causam**: 6.5, 36.6; **ob hanc rem**, 9.6

propter hanc causam: 5.2

quam ob causam: 41.6, 47.3, 50.13, 58.4, 67.5, 89.9

sīve cāsū sīve cōnsiliō deōrum: 27.6, 37.4, 80.11

utrimque: 66.13

Third Person Reflexive

suī: 55.2

sibi: *indirect object*, 23.8, 61.9, 80.6, 95.12, 98.7

sibi: *indirect reflexive*, 31.6, 39.10, 67.4, 76.4

sibi: *intransitive/impersonal verb*, 48.7, 53.3, 85.16

sibi: *agent with passive periphrastic*, 73.6, 85.18, 92.9, 100.17

sibi: *other*, 70.13, 75.13, 80.4, 86.11, 98.16

sē: *object of preposition* ad, 23.3, 59.10, 94.5, 100.8; apud, 63.12, 100.4; inter, 38.5, 70.15, 90.10, 94.13

sē cōnferre: 10.1, 21.3, 29.10, 37.8, 43.11, 48.2, 52.2, 56.6, 58.4, 67.3, 69.2, 71.8, 72.6, 76.3, 83.5, 91.14, 99.16

sē recipere: 18.8, 30.9, 53.12, 74.5

sē trādere: 20.4, 70.4

sē prōicere: 24.7, 71.9, 99.6

sē līberāre: 24.9, 44.11

sē reficere: 42.3, 92.8

sē dare: 27.13, 86.5, 96.17; abdere, 85.6, 89.3; dēdere, 87.8, 99.17

sē mergere: 8.9; adiungere, 52.7; impōnere, 56.8; habēre, 65.1; tollere, 65.15; dēfendere, 83.8; committere, 96.12; ostendere, 97.5

sē: *subject of infinitive*, 62.13, 63.12, 64.6, 65.8, 67.6, 67.10, 71.4, 71.11, 71.14, 76.5, 76.12, 79.7, 82.15, 83.9, 84.8, 85.13, 86.18, 87.5, 88.9, 89.10, 95.5, 96.14, 96.15, 99.4, 99.7

sēcum: 33.2, 35.12, 43.7, 55.11, 63.6, 83.7, 88.3

Thanks and Reasons for Thanks

grātiās agere: 2.9; maximās grātiās, 66.17, 73.14; meritās grātiās, 9.7

meritam grātiam referre: 31.13, 37.14, 66.1

prō tantō beneficiō: 2.9, 9.7, 37.13, 66.1, 88.11, 92.14

Description—Genitive and Ablative

ingentī magnitūdine: 66.3; (corporis) 39.12, 42.7, 46.9, 52.10, 84.13;

(corporum) 70.8; ingentis magnitūdinis: 28.4

rēs multae operae: 28.7; magnī perīculī, 22.5, 30.15, 59.9; maximī perīculī, 9.5; summī perīculī (*without* rēs), 73.3; summae difficultātis, 38.2, 41.4; summae difficultātis (*without* rēs), 45.13, 72.8; summī labōris, 47.11

speciē horribilī: 4.11, 7.8, 36.7, 49.8, 64.9, 67.12

summae virtūtis: 81.8, 94.12

tantae audāciae: 23.3

Hope and the Loss of Hope

dē eius salūte dēspērāre: 73.4

dē suīs fortūnīs dēspērāre: 34.9, 86.16

diū frūstrā: 4.2, 22.7, 44.3, 63.14

fugā salūtem petere: 26.12, 35.3, 71.5

frūstrā tamen: 11.5, 23.9

magnam in spem venīre: 87.5

omnī spē dēpositā: 74.15, 86.2, 87.8

spē praedae adductī: 93.8

spem patriae videndae: 93.17

spem salūtis dēpōnere: 9.3, 30.7, 37.11, 40.8, 86.2, 87.8; pōnere, 66.15, 90.7

Quīn Constructions

nec dubitābat/nt quīn: 65.4, 71.3, 73.5

nōn dubitārent quīn: 95.3

neque multum āfuit quīn: 64.13, 74.12, 91.17

neque dubium est quīn: 76.9, 86.19, 89.14

Infinitive Constructions

cōnstat: 81.2, 81.10

dīcitur: 12.2, 32.1, 50.4

cōnstituit: 2.2, 3.5, 6.11, 16.8, 19.2, 22.9, 33.10, 35.11, 37.3, 40.2, 42.3, 43.6, 46.2, 47.8, 52.6, 59.8, 71.5, 75.4, 77.2, 79.4, 80.5, 82.6, 84.4, 86.8, 91.9, 95.13, 96.6; (+ *direct object*) 38.10, 55.13;

cōnstituērunt, 57.7; (+ *direct object*) 51.10

fore: 71.5, 80.4, 90.12

iubeō: 6.7, 20.2, 20.3, 21.1, 22.1, 23.3, 24.1, 28.7, 31.8, 60.5, 74.7, 75.9, 88.8, 91.10, 98.5, 99.8, 100.12

licēbat: 50.18, 53.3, 76.10, 85.16

mōs erat: 15.8, 50.13, 55.15; (+ ut) 54.5

English to Latin Vocabulary

This English to Latin vocabulary is provided merely as a reminder of approximate Latin equivalents of English words. For further information about the Latin words, you must consult the Latin to English vocabulary and the readings and grammar notes.

A
a little, **paulō**
a second time, **iterum**
abode, **sēdēs**
about (*adv.*), **circiter, ferē**
about (*prep.*), **circum, dē**
above (*adv., prep.*), **suprā**
Absyrtus, **Absyrtus**
abundance, **cōpia**
Acastus, **Acastus**
accept, **accipiō**
accident, **cāsus**
accidentally, **forte**
accomplish, **cōnficiō, efficiō, perficiō**
accordingly, **itaque**
accustom, **cōnsuēscō**
Acrisius, **Acrisius**
across, **trāns**
adjacent, **fīnitimus**
adjoining, **fīnitimus**
Admete, **Admētē**
admirably, **ēgregiē**
admire, **admīror**
admit, **admittō**
adopt, **capiō, ineō**
adorn, **decorō, ōrnō**
advance, **prōgredior**
advice, **cōnsilium**
Aeacus, **Aeacus**
Aeetes, **Aeētēs**
Aeolia, **Aeolia**
Aeolus, **Aeolus**
Aeson, **Aesōn**
affair, **rēs**
affect, **afficiō**
afflict, **afficiō**
Africa, **Āfrica**
after (*adv.*), **post, posteā**
after (*conj.*), **cum, postquam**

after (*prep.*), **post**
after this (*adv.*), **posteā**
afterwards, **posteā**
again, **iterum, rūrsus**
against (*prep.*), **contrā**
against one's will, **invītus**
age, **aetās**
agitate, **exanimō, perturbō**
agree, **cōnstō**
agreement, **cōnsēnsus**
aid, **auxilium**
aim, **intendō**
air, **āēr, aura**
Alcmena, **Alcmēna**
alive, **vīvus**
all, **omnis, tōtus, ūniversus**
all the time, **ūsque**
all the way, **ūsque**
all together, **ūniversus**
allow, **admittō, patior**
allowed, it is, **licet**
ally, **socius**
almost, **ferē, paene**
alone (*adj.*), **sōlus, ūnus**
alone (*adv.*), **sōlum**
Alps, **Alpēs**
already, **iam**
also, **etiam, quoque**
also (*dem. pron.*), **īdem, eadem, idem**
altar, **āra**
although, **cum, etsī, quamquam**
altogether, **omnīnō**
always, **semper**
Amazons, **Amāzonēs**
ambassador, **lēgātus**
ambush, **īnsidiae**
Ammon, **Hammōn**

among, **apud, in, inter**
anchor, **ancora**
at anchor, **in ancorīs**
ancient, **antīquus**
Ancients, the, **antīquī**
and, **atque, ac, et, -que**
and not, **neque, nec, nēve, neu**
and now, **etiam**
and so, **itaque**
and that not, **nēve, neu**
Andromeda, **Andromeda**
anger, **īra**
angered, angry, **īrātus**
announce, **nūntiō, ēnūntiō,**
annually, **quotannīs**
anoint, **unguō**
another, **alius, alter**
answer, **respōnsum**
answer, to, **respondeō**
anticipate, **praecipiō**
anxiety, **sollicitūdō**
anxious, **ānxius, sollicitus**
any, -one, -thing, -body, **aliquis, quis, quisquam, ūllus**
apart (*prefix*), **dis-, dī-**
Apollo, **Apollō**
appearance, **fōrma, speciēs**
applause, **plausus**
apple, **mālum**
apply, **subdō**
apply oneself, **studeō**
appoint, **cōnstituō, creō**
appoint a day, **diem dīcere**
apprehension, **sollicitūdō**

approach, **aditus,**
 adventus
approach, to, **adeō,**
 adveniō,
 appropinquō
Arcadia, **Arcadia**
Argo, **Argō**
Argolic, of Argolis,
 Argolicus
Argonauts, **Argonautae**
Argus, **Argus**
arise, **coorior, exorior**
ark, **arca**
arm, **bracchium**
arm, to, **armō**
armed, **armātus**
arms, **arma**
army, **exercitus**
around, **circum**
arouse, **excitō**
arrangement, **ōrdō**
arrival, **adventus**
arrive, **adveniō,**
 perveniō
arrive at, **attingō**
arrow, **sagitta**
art, **ars**
art of warfare, **rēs**
 mīlitāris
as (*adv.*), **atque, ac,**
 quam
as (*after words of*
 comparison; conj.), **ut,**
 ita ut, velut
as (*prep.*), **prō**
as . . . as possible, **quam**
 (*with superl.*)
as if, **quasi**
as long as, **dum**
as often as, **quotiēns**
as soon as, **simul**
 atque/ac
as soon as possible,
 quam prīmum
ascend, **ascendō**
ask, **petō, poscō,**
 postulō, quaerō,
 rogō
ask for, **poscō**
assemble, (*intrans.*)
 conveniō; (*trans.*)
 convocō
assert, **cōnfīrmō**
assist, **prōsum**

at, **ad**
at a distance, **procul**
at all, **omnīnō**
at last, at length,
 aliquandō, dēmum,
 tandem
at once, **statim**
at some time or another,
 aliquandō
at that time, **tum**
at the same time, **simul**
Athens, **Athēnae**
Atlas, **Atlās**
attack, **impetus**
attack, to, **petō**
attempt, **cōnātus**
attempt, to, **cōnor,**
 temptō
attend, to, **audiō**
audacity, **audācia**
Augeas, **Augēās**
avail, **prōsum**
avenge, **ulcīscor**
avoid, **vītō**
await, **exspectō**
away from, **ā, ab**

B
babe, **īnfāns**
back, **tergum**
back (*prefix*), **re-, red-**
bad, **malus**
badly, **male**
bag, **ūter**
bank (of a river), **rīpa**
barbarian, **barbarus**
barbarity, **immānitās**
bare, **nūdus**
barely, **vix**
battle, **proelium,**
 pugna
be, **sum**
be able, **possum**
be absent, **absum**
be accustomed,
 cōnsuēscō
be amazed, **stupeō**
be angry, **īrāscor**
be astounded, **stupeō**
be away, **absum**
be before, **praesum**
be concealed, **lateō**
be distant, **absum**
be done, **fīō**
be eager, **studeō**

be effective, **valeō**
be glad, **gaudeō**
be ignorant of, **ignōrō**
be inflamed, **exārdēscō**
be lacking, **absum**
be left, **supersum**
be left between,
 intermittō
be made, **fīō**
be mistaken, **errō**
be of advantage, **prōsum**
be on fire, **ārdeō**
be on one's guard,
 praecaveō
be on one's guard against,
 caveō
be over, **supersum**
be present, **adsum**
be prostrate, **iaceō**
be silent, **taceō**
be strong, **valeō**
be stunned, **stupeō**
be subject to, **serviō**
be unwilling, **nōlō**
be wanting, **absum**
be willing, **volō**
beach, to, **subdūcō**
beak, **rōstrum**
bear, **ferō, patior,**
 subeō
bear away *or* off, **auferō,**
 dēferō
bear through, **perferō**
bear to, **adferō, offerō**
bear up, **sustineō**
beast, **bēlua, fera,**
 pecus
beat, **pellō**
beautiful, **fōrmōsus,**
 pulcher
beauty, **fōrma**
because of (*conj.*), **quod,**
 quia
because of (*prep.*),
 propter
become, **fīō**
become accustomed,
 cōnsuēscō
become master of,
 potior
bedroom, **cubiculum**
befall, **accidō, ēveniō**
before (*adv.*), **ante,**
 anteā, suprā

before (*comp. adv.*),
  prius
before (*conj.*),
  priusquam
before (*prep.*), **ante,**
  prae, prō, suprā
before this, **anteā**
beg, **ōrō**
began, **coepī**
beginning, **initium**
behind, **post**
behold, **cōnspiciō,**
  intueor
believable, **crēdibilis**
believe, **crēdō,**
  exīstimō
bellow, **mūgiō**
bellowing, **mūgītus**
belly, **venter**
belonging to another,
  aliēnus
belt, **balteus**
benefit, **benificium**
beseech, **obsecrō,**
  obtestator
beset, **obsideō**
besides (*prep.*), **praeter**
besides this (*adv.*),
  praetereā
besiege, **obsideō**
betake oneself, **sē**
  cōnferre, sē
  recipere
between, **inter**
beware, **caveō**
beware beforehand,
  praecaveō
beware of, **caveō**
bid, **iubeō**
bidding, **iussus**
big, **magnus**
bind, **adligō, contineō,**
  vinciō
bird, **avis, volucris**
bite, **mordeō**
black, **niger**
blaze out, **exārdēscō**
blessed, **beātus**
blind, **caecus**
block up, **obstruō**
blood, **sanguis**
blow, **ictus**
blow through *or* over,
  perflō

boat, **linter**
body, **corpus**
boil up *or* over,
  effervēscō
boldness, **audācia**
bond, **vinculum**
booty, **praeda**
borders, **fīnēs**
bosom, **sinus**
both, **uterque**
both . . . and, **et . . . et**
bottle, **amphora**
bough, **rāmus**
boundary, **fīnis**
bow, **arcus**
bow (of a ship), **prōra**
box, **arca**
boy, **puer**
branch, **rāmus**
brave, **fortis**
bravely, **fortiter**
bravery, **virtus**
break, **frangō**
break through,
  perrumpō
breast, **pectus**
breath, **anima**
breathe, **respīrō**
breathe back, **respīrō**
breathe out, **efflō,**
  respīrō
breeze, **aura**
bridge, **pōns**
bridle, **frēnō**
bright (very),
  praeclārus
bring, **dūcō, addūcō,**
  dēdūcō, ferō, afferō
bring against, **īnferō**
bring back, **redūcō,**
  referō
bring back to life, **excitō,**
  rūrsus ad vītam
  redūcere
bring back word,
  renūntiō
bring forth, **gignō**
bring in, **īnferō**
bring out, **prōmō**
bring through, **perdūcō**
bring to, **appellō**
bring together,
  comportō, cōnferō
bring to memory,

  commemorō
broad, **lātus**
bronze, **aes**
bronze (*adj.*), **aēneus**
brother, **frāter**
build, **aedificō, condō,**
  exstruō
build against, **obstruō**
build in *or* into, **īnstruō**
bull, **bōs, taurus**
burden, **onerō**
burn, **ārdeō, ūrō, adūrō**
burst in *or* into, **irrumpō**
burst through,
  perrumpō
bury, **sepeliō**
business, **negōtium**
Busiris, **Būsīris**
busy, be employed,
  involved, **versor**
but (*conj.*), at, **autem,**
  sed
but that, **quĭn**
by, **ā, ab, praeter**
by a little, **paulō**
by chance, **forte**
by far, **multō, multum**
by means of, **per**
by much, **multō**
by night, **noctū**
by no means, **minimē**

C
Cacus, **Cācus**
Calais, **Calais**
calamity, **calamitās**
call, **appellō, arcessō,**
  vocō
call forth, **prōvocō**
call out, **clāmitō,**
  excitō, ēvocō,
  prōvocō
call together, **convocō**
call to witness, **obtestor**
calm, **tranquillitās**
calm (*adj.*), **tranquillus**
camp, **castra**
can, **possum**
captive, **captīva**
carcass, **cadāver**
care, **dīligentia,**
  sollicitūdō
carefully, **dīligenter**
carry, **gerō, portō,**
  vehō

carry across, trānsportō
carry away, abripiō,
  auferō, dēferō,
  āvehō
carry back, referō
carry forward, prōvehō
carry off, abripiō,
  auferō, dēferō,
  āvehō
carry on, gerō
carry over, trānsportō,
  trānsvehō
carry together,
  comportō
cast, iaciō, coniciō
cast lots, sortior
cast off, solvō
Castor, Castor
catch, capiō, dēcipiō,
  comprehendō
cattle, pecus
cause, causa
cause, to, iniciō
cave or cavern, antrum,
  caverna, spēlunca
cease, dēsistō
Cenaeum, Cēnaeum
centaur, centaurus
Cepheus, Cēpheus
Cerberus, Cerberus
Ceres, Cerēs
certain, certus, quīdam
certainly, quidem
chain, catēna,
  vinculum
challenge, ēvocō,
  prōvocō
chance, cāsus, facultās,
  occāsiō; see also by
  chance
change, commūtātiō
change, to, convertō,
  mūtō
character, nātūra
charge, pretium
charge, to, mandō,
  praecipiō, impetum
  facere
chariot, currus
charm, carmen
Charon, Charōn,
check, premō
chest, arca
chide, obiūrgō

children, līberī
choose, choose out,
  dēligō
Circe, Circē
circle, orbis
circle of the lands, orbis
  terrārum
circumstance, rēs
cithara, cithara
citizen, cīvis
city, urbs
clapper, crotalum
clatter, crepitus
clean, cleanse, pūrgō
cliff, rūpēs
climb, cōnscendō
climb down, dēscendō
climb to, ascendō
climb up, ascendō
clothe, induō
clothing, vestis,
  vestītus
cloud, nūbēs
club, clāva
coin, nummus
Colchians, Colchī
Colchis, Colchis
collect, cōgō, colligō,
  comparō, comportō
collect oneself, sē
  recipere
color, color
column, columna
column (of march),
  agmen
combat, proelium,
  pugna
come, veniō
come about, fīō
come forth, orior
come out, ēveniō
come through, perveniō
come to, adveniō
come together,
  conveniō
come toward, adveniō
come under, succēdō
come up, accurrō
come upon, inveniō
commander, dux,
  imperātor
command, imperātum,
  imperium, iussum,
  iussus

command, to, imperō,
  iubeō, mandō,
  praesum
commit, committō,
  mandō
companion, comes,
  socius
compassion,
  misericordia
compel, cōgō
complete, cōnficiō
compress, comprimō
comrade, socius
conceal, abdō, cēlō,
  obscūrō, tegō
concealed, abditus
concerning, dē
confer, cōnferō
confuse, turbō
confuse thoroughly,
  perturbō
conquer, superō
consecrated, sānctus
consent, cōnsēnsus
consider, arbitror,
  cōgitō, exīstimō,
  habeō
consist, cōnsistō,
  cōnstō
consult, cōnsulō
consume, absūmō,
  cōnsūmō
contest, certāmen
continent, continēns
continuous, continuus,
  perpetuus
contrary, dīversus
contrary to, contrā
contribution, tribūtum
contrive, excōgitō
convenient, opportūnus
conversation,
  colloquium, sermō
copper, aes
copper (adj.), aēneus
Corinth, Corinthus
corpse, cadāver
country, fīnēs, patria,
  regiō
country house, vīlla
courage, animus, virtūs
course, cursus
cover, obserō, tegō,
  contegō

cow, bōs
cowardly, ignāvus
crab, cancer
cradle, cūnae
craft, dōlus
credible, crēdibilis
Creon, Creōn
Crete, Crēta
crime, facinus, scelus
crisis, discrīmen
cross, trānseō
crossing over, trāiectus
cruel, crūdēlis
cruelty, immānitās
crush, opprimō
cry, clāmor
cry, to, exclāmō
cry out, to, exclāmō
cultivate, colō
cup, pōculum
curved sword, falx
custom, mōs
cut away, abscīdō
cut below, succīdō
cut down, occīdō,
   succīdō
cut off, abscīdō
cutting down, caedēs
Cyclops, Cyclōps
Cyzicus, Cyzicus

D
daily, cottīdiē
Danae, Danaē
danger, discrīmen,
   perīculum
dangerous, īnfestus
dare, audeō
daring, audācia
dark, obscūrus
darken, obscūrō
dash to, afflīgō
dash together, concurrō,
   cōnflīgō
dash to pieces, frangō
daub over, oblinō
daughter, fīlia
dawn, dīlūcēscō
dawn, at, ortā lūce
day, diēs
   on the day before,
     prīdiē
   on the following or next
     day, postrīdiē
dead, mortuus

the dead, the, Īnferī
dead body, cadāver
deadly, death-bringing,
   mortifer
death, mōrs
debate, contrōversia
deceive, dēcipiō, fallō
deception, fraus
decide, statuō,
   cōnstituō
decide upon, īnstituō
declare, cōnfīrmō
deed, facinus
deep, altus
   deep, the, altum
defeat, superō
defend, dēfendō
definite, certus
Dejanira, Dēianīra
dejected, dēmissus
delay, mora
delay, to, moror,
   commoror
deliver, trādō
deliver a speech,
   ratiōnem habēre
deliverance, salūs
Delphi, Delphī
Delphic, Delphian, of
   Delphi, Delphicus
demand, poscō, postulō
deny, negō
depart, abeō, dēcēdō,
   discēdō, excēdō,
   proficīscor
departure, profectiō
depend on, pōnō (in
   passive)
deposit, dēpōnō
descend, dēscendō
describe fully,
   perscrībō
desert, dēserō
deserted, dēsertus
deserved, meritus
design, cōnsilium
desire, cupiditās,
   dēsīderium
desire, to, cupiō,
   dēsīderō
desirous, cupidus
desist, dēsistō
despair, dēspērō, spem
   dēpōnere

destiny, fātum
destroy, absūmō
deter, dēterreō
determine, īnstituō,
   cōnstituō
determined, certus
devise, excōgitō
devour, vorō, dēvorō
Diana, Diāna
die, morior
different, dīversus
differently, aliter
difficult, difficilis
difficulty, difficultās,
   negōtium
diffuse, diffundō
dig, dūcō
dig through, perfodiō
diligence, dīligentia
diligent, studiōsus
diligently, dīligenter
dine, cēnō
dinner, cēna
Diomedes, Diomēdēs
dip, imbuō, mergō
direct, praecipiō
direction, pars, regiō
dirt, squālor
disaster, calamitās
discern, cernō
discover, inveniō,
   reperiō
discoverer, inventor
discus, discus
disembark, ēgredior
disgrace, dēdecus
disgraceful, turpis
dishonor, dēdecus
dismiss from the mind,
   oblīvīscor
dispatch, dīmittō
disposition, animus
dispute, contrōversia
disregard, neglegō,
   omittō
distance, intervāllum
distant, longinquus
distant, to be, absum
distinguish, decorō
disturb, commoveō,
   turbō, perturbō
ditch, fossa
divide, dīvidō
do, agō, faciō, gerō

do completely, cōnficiō
do thoroughly, perficiō,
do to, afficiō
dog, canis
door, foris, iānua,
    līmen, ōstium
doors, out of, forīs
doorway, ōstium
doubt, *use the neuter of
    the adjective* dubius
doubt, to, dubitō
doubtful, dubius
dove, columba
downcast, dēmissus
down from, dē
down from above,
    dēsuper
drag, trahō
drag out, extrahō
dragon, dracō
drain, exhauriō
draw, dēstringō, dūcō,
    ēdūcō, hauriō,
    intendō, trahō
draw back, pedem
    referre
draw down (launch) a
    ship, nāvem
    dēdūcere
draw lots, sortior
draw near, appetō
draw off, dētrahō
draw out, extrahō
draw up, īnstruō,
    subdūcō
dreadful, horribilis
dress, vestis
drink, bibō
drink off, exhauriō
drink up, exhauriō
drive, agō, pellō,
    compellō
drive away, back, *or* off,
    dēpellō repellō
drive out, expellō
drive to, appellō
drive together, cōgō,
    compellō
drowsiness, somnus
drug, medicāmentum
drunk, ēbrius
due, dēbitus, meritus
duly, rīte
duty, officium

dwell, habitō
dye, īnficiō, tinguō

E

each, quisque
each (of two), uterque
eager, cupidus,
    studiōsus
eagerness, cupiditās,
    studium
ear, auris
earnestly, magnopere,
    vehementer
earth, orbis terrārum,
    terra
easily, facile
eat, vēscor
effect, efficiō
efficacy, vīs
effort, cōnātus, opera
Egyptians, Aegyptiī
eighteen, duōdēvīgintī
either (of two), uterque
either . . . or, aut . . . aut
elapse, intermittō (*in
    passive*)
elect, creō
eleventh, ūndecimus
Elis, Ēlis
Elysian, Ēlysius
embark, cōnscendō,
    impōnō
embrace, complector
employ, adhibeō
empty, vacuus
enclose, inclūdō
enclosure, stabulum
encourage, hortor,
    cohortor
end, fīnis
end of, extrēmus
endure, perferō, subeō
enemy, hostis
enjoin, imperō
enjoyment, frūctus
enormous, ingēns,
    vāstus
enough, satis
enraged, īrātus
enter, ineō, intrō
entertain, excipiō
entire, tōtus, ūniversus
entrance, aditus,
    introitus
entreat, obsecrō

entreaty, prex
equip, armō, īnstruō,
    ōrnō
equipped, parātus
erect, ērēctus
erect, to, exstruō
Erginus, Ergīnus
Eridanus, Ēridanus
Erymanthian, of
    Erymanthus,
    Erymanthius
Erythea, Erythēa
escape, salūs
escape, to, effugiō,
    ēvādō, vītō
escort, praesidium
especially, maximē,
    praecipuē
establish, cōnfīrmō
Ethiopians, Aethiopēs
Etna, Aetna
Eunomus, Eunomus
Europe, Eurōpa
Eurylochus, Eurylochus
Eurystheus, Eurystheus
Eurytion, Eurytiōn
Eurytus, Eurytus
even, etiam
even as, velut
even if, etsī
even then, etiam tum
even to, ūsque ad
evening, vesper
ever, umquam
every, omnis
every day, cottīdiē
every year, quotannīs
evil (*noun*), malum
exact punishment,
    supplicium sūmere
examine, perlūstrō
exceedingly,
    magnopere,
    maximē,
    vehementer
excel, praestō
excellently, ēgregiē
except, praeter
excite, indūcō
exclaim, exclāmō
exercise, exercitātiō
exercise, to, exerceō
exert oneself, contendō
exhaust, exanimō

exhausted, **fessus**,
dēfessus
exhibit, **praebeō**
exhort, **hortor**,
cohortor
exile, **exsilium**
expect, **exspectō**
expectation, **opīniō**
expel, **expellō**
experience, **ūsus**
expiate, **expiō**
explain, **doceō**, **expōnō**,
ostendō
explore, **explōrō**
explorer, **explōrātor**
expose, **committō**
extraordinary,
inūsitātus
extreme, **extrēmus**
eye, **oculus**

F
fail, **dēficiō**
falchion, **falx**
fall, **cāsus**
fall, to, **cadō**
fall down, **dēcidō**,
dēlābor
fall in love with, **adamō**
fall into, **incidō**
fall to, **accidō**
fall upon, **accidō**, **incidō**
false, **falsus**
famous, **clārus**,
praeclārus, **nōtus**
far, **procul**, **longē**
far, by far, **multō**,
multum
farther, **longius**,
ulterior
fat, **pinguis**
fate, **fātum**
father, **pater**
fatherland, **patria**
fatigue, **lassitūdō**
fatigue, to, **exanimō**
Favonius, **Favōnius**
favor, **grātia**
favorable, **idōneus**,
secundus
fear, **timor**
fear, to, **timeō**, **vereor**
feed (*trans.*), **pāscō**
feed on, **vēscor**
feel, **percipiō**, **sentiō**,

tractō
feigned, **falsus**
fell, cut down, **succīdō**
fellow-citizen, **cīvis**
fetch, **arcessō**, **referō**
fetch grain, **frūmentor**
few, **paucī**
field, **ager**, **campus**
fierce, **ferōx**, **saevus**
fiercely, **ācriter**
fifth, **quīntus**
fifty, **quīnquāgintā**
fight, **pugnō**
fight against, **repugnō**
fighting, **pugna**
figure, **figūra**
fill, **obserō**, **occupō**
fill up *or* full, **compleō**
filth, **squālor**
finally, **aliquandō**,
dēnique, **tandem**
find, **inveniō**,
nancīscor, **reperiō**
find out, **cōgnōscō**
finder, **inventor**
finish, **cōnficiō**
fire, **ignis**
firebrand, **fax**
first (*adj.*), **prīmus**
first (*adv.*), **prīmum**
first (*comp. adv.*), **prius**
first, at, **prīmō**
fisherman, **piscātor**
fit, **idōneus**
fitly, **rīte**
fixed, **certus**
flame, **flamma**
flee, **fugiō**, **tergum**
vertere
flee back, **refugiō**
flee out *or* away, **effugiō**
fleece, **vellus**
flesh, **carō**
flight, **fuga**
float, **natō**
flock, **pecus**
fly, **volō**
fly away, **āvolō**
fodder, **pābulum**
foe, **hostis**
follow, **sequor**,
cōnsequor,
prōsequor
follow after, **succēdō**

follow forward,
prōsequor
follow up *or* upon, **cōn-**,
in-, *or* **persequor**
following, **posterus**,
secundus
following day, on the,
postrīdiē
food, **cibus**, **pābulum**,
vīctus
foot, **pēs**
footprint, **vēstīgium**
for (*conj.*), **enim**, **nam**,
namque
for (*prep.*), **ad**, **ergā**, **ob**,
prō, **propter**
for a long time, **diū**
for a little while,
paulisper
for a short time,
paulisper
for all time, **in**
perpetuum
for . . . not, **neque enim**
for the most part, **ferē**
for the sake *or* purpose of,
causā
forage, **frūmentor**
force, **vīs**
force, to, **cōgō**
forces, **cōpīae**
forehead, **frōns**
foreigner, **peregrīnus**
forest, **silva**
foretell, **praedīcō**
forever, **in perpetuum**
forget, **ē memoriā**
dēpōnere,
oblīvīscor
form, **figūra**, **fōrma**
former, **prīstinus**,
superior
formerly, **quondam**
forth, **forās**
forthwith, **statim**
fortify, **mūniō**
fortunately, **fēlīciter**
fortune, **fortūna**
found, **condō**
fountain, **fōns**
four, **quattuor**
fourth, **quārtus**
fraud, **fraus**
free, **līberō**

freedom, lībertās

frenzy, furor

frequently, saepe

friend, amīcus

fright, terror

frighten, terreō

frighten off, dēterreō

frighten thoroughly,
  perterreō

from, ā, ab, dē, ē, ex

from a distance, procul

from all sides, undique

from this place, hinc

fruit, frūctus

full, plēnus

funeral pile or pyre,
  rogus

furious, īrātus

furnish, īnstruō,
  praebeō

furthest, extrēmus

fury, furor

G

gain one's end, impetrō

game, lūdus

garden, hortus

gate, porta

gather (intrans.),
  conveniō

gather together (trans.),
  colligō

Gaul, Gallia

general, imperātor

gentle, lēnis

Geryon, Gēryōn

get, nancīscor

get away, ēvādō

get back, recipiō

get possession of, potior

gift, dōnum, mūnus

gird, cingō

girdle, balteus

girl, puella

give, dō, trādō,
  praebeō,

give across or over,
  trādō

give attention, studeō

give away, dēdō

give back, reddō

give out, ēdō

give thanks, grātiās
  agere

give up, dēdō, dēpōnō,

trādō

gladly, libenter

gladness, gaudium

Glauce, Glaucē

glory, glōria

go, eō

go across or over,
  trānseō

go apart, discēdō

go ashore, ēgredior

go away, abeō, dēcēdō

go back, redeō,
  regredior

go by, praetereō

go forth, ēgredior,
  ēvādō, excēdō

go forward, prōgredior

go from, dēcēdō

go into, ineō, intrō

go on board, cōnscendō

go out, ēgredior

go to, adeō

go under, subeō,
  succēdō

go within, intrō

goat, pecus

god, deus

going, iter

gold, aurum

golden, of gold, aureus

good, bonus

Gorgon, Gorgōn

Graeae, Graeae

grain, frūmentum

grandfather, avus

grandson, nepōs

grant, concēdō,
  cōnferrō

grasp, complector

grateful, grātus

gratitude, grātia

great, magnus, multus

greatest, summus

greatly, magnopere,
  multum,
  vehementer

  very greatly,
    maximē

greatness, magnitūdō

Greece, Graecia

Greek, Graecus

grief, dolor

grievance, dolor

grievous, gravis

grow light, dīlūcēscō

guard, praesidium

guard, to, custōdiō

H

habit, mōs

hall, ātrium

hand, manus

hand down, trādō

hand over, trādō

handle, tractō

hang (up), suspendō

happen, accidō, ēveniō

happily, fēlīciter

happy, beātus

harbor, portus

hardly, vix

harm, damnum,
  incommodum,
  iniūria

harness, iungō

Harpies, Harpyiae

hasten, contendō,
  mātūrō, properō

hate, ōdī

hatred, odium

have, habeō

have become accustomed,
  cōnsuēscō

have begun, coepī

have charge of, praesum

have effect, valeō

have found out,
  cognōscō

have power, possum

haven, portus

head, caput

head (of cattle), pecus

heap up, exstruō

hear, audiō, accipiō

heart, animus

heat, calor

heaven, caelum

heavy, gravis

helmet, galea

help, auxilium,
  subsidium

help, to, auxilior, iuvō

hence, hinc

herb, herba

Hercules, Herculēs

herd, pecus

here, hīc

hereupon, hīc

her (own), suus

herself, **ipsa**
herself, her, **suī**
he says, **inquit**
Hesione, **Hēsionē**
hesitate, **dubitō, haerō,**
  haesitō
Hesperides,
  Hesperidēs
hidden, **abditus**
hide, **pellis**
hide, to, **abdō, cēlō,**
  obscūrō
high, **altus**
higher, **superior**
highest, **summus,**
  suprēmus
himself, **ipse**
himself, him, **suī**
hinder, **exclūdō,**
  impediō, prōhibeō
Hippolyte, **Hippolytē**
his (own), **suus**
hither, **hūc**
hog, **porcus**
hold, **habeō, possideō,**
  teneō, obtineō
hold against, **obtineō**
hold back, **prōhibeō,**
  teneō, retineō
hold fast, **retineō**
hold forth, **praebeō**
hold to, **adhibeō**
hold together, **contineō**
hold up, **sustineō**
home, **domus, sēdēs**
Homer, **Homērus**
honor, **honor**
hope, **spēs**
hope, to, **spērō**
horn, **cornū**
horrible, **horribilis**
horse, **equus**
hospitality, **hospitium**
hostile, **inimīcus**
hour, **hōra**
house, **aedēs, domus,**
how, **quam, quantum**
however, **autem,**
  tamen, vērō
how great, how much,
  quantus
how long, **quō ūsque**
how much, **quantum**
huge, **ingēns, vāstus**

human, **hūmānus**
human being, **homō**
hundred, **centum**
hunger, **famēs**
hunt, hunting, **vēnātiō**
hurl, **iaciō, adiciō,**
  coniciō
hurricane, **turbō**
hurry, **contendō,**
  matūrō, properō
hurt, **iniūria**
husband, **coniūnx,**
  maritus
Hydra, **Hydra**
Hylas, **Hylās**

I

I, **ego**
if, **sī**
if not, **nisi**
ignorant, **ignārus,**
  imperītus
ignorant, to be, **nesciō**
Iliad, **Īlias**
ill, **aegrē, male**
immediate, **praesēns**
immediately, **statim**
imminent, **praesēns**
impede, **impediō**
implore, **obtestor**
impose, **impōnō**
imprison, **inclūdō**
in, **in**
in another way, **aliter**
in behalf of, **prō**
in fact, **quidem, rē vērā**
in front of, **prō**
in order, **ex ōrdine**
in return for, **prō**
in succession, **continuus**
in that, **quod**
in that place, **ibi**
in the first place,
  prīmum
in the meantime,
  intereā
in this manner, **ita**
in truth, **rē vērā, vērō**
in vain, **frūstrā**
in which place, **quā**
incite, **impellō**
inclose, **inclūdō**
inclosure, **stabulum**
inconvenience,
  incommodum

incredible, **incrēdibilis**
indeed, **quidem, vērō**
induce, **addūcō,**
  persuādeō
industry, **dīligentia**
inexperienced,
  imperītus
infant, **īnfāns**
inflict, **īnferō**
inflict punishment,
  supplicium sūmere
influence, **addūcō**
inform, **certiōrem**
  facere
inhabit, **colō, incolō**
inhabitant, **incola**
inhabitants of the
  underworld, **īnferī**
injury, **damnum,**
  iniūria
inner, **interior**
inquire, **quaerō**
inquire of, **quaerere ex**
  + *abl.*
insanity, **īnsānia**
inspire, **iniciō**
instant, **pūnctum**
instruct, **ērudiō**
intend, **in animō**
  habēre
interior, **interior**
interrupt, **intermittō**
interval, **intervāllum,**
  spatium
intervene, **intermittō**
  (*passive*)
into, **in**
intrust, **committō**
invent, **excōgitō, fingō**
invite, **invītō**
Iolaus, **Iolāus**
Iole, **Iolē**
Iphicles, **Īphiclēs**
iron, of iron, **ferreus**
island, **īnsula**
it, **hoc, id, illud**
it is agreed, **cōnstat**
it is established, **cōnstat**
it is well-known, **cōnstat**
Italy, **Italia**
Ithaca, **Ithaca**
its (own), **suus**
itself, **ipsum**
itself *or* it, **suī**

J

jar, **amphora**
Jason, **Iāsōn**
jaws, **faucēs**
join, **iungō, coniungō**
join battle, **proelium committere**
join to, **adiungō**
join together, **coniungō**
journey, **iter**
journey, to, **iter facere**
Jove, **Iuppiter**
joy, **gaudium, laetitia**
judge, **iūdex**
judge, to, **arbitror**
juice, **sūcus**
Juno, **Iūnō**
Jupiter, **Iuppiter**
just, **iūstus, meritus**
just as, **velut**
just now, **modō**
justice, **iūs**

K

keep, **cōnservō, teneō, retineō**
keep back, **retineō**
keep within, **contineō**
kill, **exanimō, interficiō, necō, occīdō**
killing, **caedēs**
kind, **genus**
kindle, **accendō**
kindle beneath, **succendō**
kindly, **benignē**
kindness, **beneficium, benignitās, clēmentia**
king, **rēx**
kingdom, **rēgnum**
knife, **culter**
knock at, **pulsō**
knock down, **prōsternō**
know, **cognōscō, sciō**
knowledge, **scientia**
known, **nōtus**

L

labor, **labor, opera**
lack, **careō**
Laconia, **Lacōnia**
lake, **lacus**
lament, **dēplōrō**

lamentation, **lāmenta**
land, **ager, terra**
land, to, **expōnō**
Laomedon, **Lāomedōn**
lap, **sinus**
large, **magnus**
Larissa, **Lārīsa**
last, **extrēmus, nōvissimus, postrēmus, suprēmus**
lasting throughout the year, **perennis**
lastly, **dēnique**
lately, **modo, nūper**
later, **post**
later than, **postquam**
laugh, **rīdeō**
laugh at, **irrīdeō**
launch a ship, **nāvem dēdūcere**
law, **iūs**
lay aside, **dēpōnō**
lay open, **patefaciō**
lay upon, **impōnō**
lay waste, **vāstō**
lazy, **ignāvus**
lead, **agō, dūcō**
lead across, **trādūcō**
lead away, **abdūcō, dēdūcō**
lead back, **redūcō**
lead down, **dēdūcō**
lead in, **indūcō**
lead on, **indūcō**
lead out, **ēdūcō**
lead through, **perdūcō**
lead to, **addūcō**
leader, **dux**
leap down, **dēsiliō**
lead forth, **exsiliō**
leap out, **exsiliō**
learn (of), **cognōscō, discō**
least, **minimē**
leave, **relinquō**
leave behind, **relinquō**
leave off, **dēsistō, intermittō**
left, **reliquus**
left, **sinister**
left hand, **sinistra**
leg, **crūs**
Lernean, of Lerna,

Lernaeus
less, **minus**
lest, **nē**
let fall, **dēmittō**
let go, **omittō**
let in, **immittō**
let pass, **intermittō**
let slip, **dīmittō**
Lethe, **Lēthē**
liberate, **līberō**
liberty, **lībertās**
Lichas, **Lichās**
lie, **cubō, iaceō**
lie back, **recumbō**
lie down, **cubō, recumbō**
lie down (at the table), **accumbō**
lie hidden, **latēre**
life, **anima, vīta**
lift, **tollō**
light, **levis**
light, **lūmen**
light, to, **accendō**
Liguria, **Liguria**
Ligurians, **Ligurēs**
likewise, **īdem**
limb, **membrum**
line of battle, **aciēs**
linger, **moror, commoror**
Linus, **Linus**
lion, **leō**
listen to, **audiō**
little, **parvus**
little, a, **paulum**
little, very little, **minimē**
live, **habitō, vītam agere, vīvō**
living, **vīctus**
living, **vīvus**
load, **onerō**
long, **longus**
long (adv.), **diū**
long time (a), a long while, **diū**
longer, **diūtius**
long for, **cupiō**
longing, **cupiditās, dēsīderium**
look at, **spectō**
look into, **īnspiciō**
look on, **spectō, īnspectō**

look out for, **exspectō**
look over, **perlūstrō**
look upon, **īnspiciō,**
   intueor
looker-on, **spectātor**
looking glass, **speculum**
loosen, **solvō**
lose, **āmittō, dīmittō,**
   omittō
lose courage, **animum**
   dēmittere
lose life, **morior, vītam**
   āmittere
lot, **sors**
lotus, **lōtus**
loud, **magnus, sonōrus**
love, **amor**
love, to, **amō**
low, to, **mūgiō**
lowing, **mūgītus**
lyre, **cithara**

M

madness, **āmentia,**
   furor, īnsānia
magic, of magic,
   magicus
magnificent,
   magnificus
maiden, **puella, virgō**
mainland, **continēns**
make, **creō, dūcō, faciō**
make a building,
   aedificō
make again, **reficiō**
make an attack,
   impetum facere
make clean, **pūrgō**
make completely,
   cōnficiō
make hot, **calefaciō**
make known,
   dēmōnstrō, ēnūntiō
make more certain,
   certiōrem facere
make one's way, **sē**
   cōnferre
make out, **cernō, efficiō**
make ready, **parō**
make thoroughly,
   perficiō
make up, **fingō**
make whole again,
   redintegrō
man, **homō, vir**

manliness, **virtūs**
manner, **modus, mōs,**
   ratiō
many, **plūrēs,**
   complūrēs, multī
march, **iter**
march, to, **iter facere**
marriage,
   mātrimōnium
marry, **dūcō (in**
   mātrimōnium)
Mars, **Mārs**
marsh, **palūs**
marvel, **mīrāculum**
mast, **mālus**
master, **magister**
matter, **negōtium, rēs**
meal, **far, mola**
means, **facultās, ratiō**
means, by no, **minimē**
meanwhile, **intereā**
Medea, **Mēdēa**
Medusa, **Medūsa**
meet, **occurrō**
member, **membrum**
memory, **memoria**
mention, **mentiō**
mention, to,
   commemorō
merchant, **mercātor**
Mercury, **Mercurius**
mercy, **clēmentia**
message, **nūntius**
messenger, **nūntius**
method, **ratiō**
mid, **medius**
midday, **merīdiānus**
midday, **merīdiānum**
   tempus, merīdiēs
middle, in the middle of,
   medius
mighty, **magnus**
mile, **mīlia passuum**
military, **mīlitāris**
milk, **lac**
mind, **animus**
mine, **meus**
Minerva, **Minerva**
mingle, **misceō**
Minos, **Mīnōs**
Minyae, **Minyae**
miracle, **mīrāculum**
mirror, **speculum**
mischief, **malum**

miserable, **miser**
misfortune, **calamitās**
missile, **tēlum**
mistress, **domina**
mix, **misceō**
mock, **irrīdeō**
moment, **pūnctum**
money, **pecūnia**
monster, **bēlua,**
   mōnstrum
more (*adj.*), **plūrēs**
more (*adv.*), **magis**
moreover, **autem,**
   praetereā
morning, (early) in the,
   māne
mortal, **mortālis**
mother, **māter**
mount, **ascendō**
mountain, **mōns**
mouth, **ōs, ōstium**
move, **afficiō, indūcō,**
   moveō, commoveō
move away, **āmoveō**
move back, **removeō**
much, **multus**
much, **multum**
much, by much, **multō**
much, very much,
   magnopere
mud, **līmus**
multitude, **multitūdō**
muscle, **nervus**
music, **mūsica**
my, **meus**
Mysia, **Mȳsia**

N

naked, **nūdus**
name, **nōmen**
name, to, **appellō**
narrate, **nārrō**
nation, **gēns**
nature, **genus, nātūra**
nautical, **nauticus**
naval, **nauticus**
navigation, **nāvigātiō**
near, **ad**
nearest, **proximus**
nearly, **ferē, paene**
necessary, **necesse**
neck, **collum**
neglect, **neglegō,**
   omittō
neighboring, **fīnitimus**

neither, **neuter**
neither . . . nor,
  neque . . . neque,
  nec . . . nec
Nemean, of Nemea,
  Nemeaeus
Neptune, **Neptūnus**
Nessus, **Nessus**
never, **numquam**
nevertheless, **tamen**
new, **nŏvus**
newly, **nūper**
newness, **novitās**
next, **posterus,**
  proximus
next (*adv.*), **deinde**
next day, on the,
  postrīdiē
night, **nox**
night, at, by, **noctū**
night, of, **nocturnus**
nighttime, **nocturnum**
  tempus
nine, **novem**
no, **nūllus**
no one, **nēmō**
no one, and, **neque**
  quisquam
noise, **crepitus, sonitus**
noisy, **sonōrus**
none, **nūllus**
noon, **merīdiānum**
  tempus, merīdiēs
noonday, **merīdiānus**
noose, **laqueus**
nor, **nec, neque, nēve,**
  neu
not, **nē, nōn**
  that not, **nē**
not? **nōnne**
not any, **nūllus**
not at all, **minimē**
not done, **īnfectus**
not easy, **difficilis**
not even, **nē . . .**
  quidem
not know, **ignōrō,**
  nesciō
not useful, **inūtilis**
not wish, **nōlō**
not yet, **nōndum**
nothing, **nihil**
notice, **animadvertō**
nourish, **alō**

novelty, **novitās**
now, **autem, iam, nunc**
nowhere, **nusquam**
number, **numerus**
nymph, **nympha**

O

oak, **rōbur**
oar, **rēmus**
oath, **iūs iūrandum**
obey, **pāreō**
observe, **animadvertō**
obtain, **nancīscor**
obtain by request,
  impetrō
ocean, **ōceanus**
Oceanus, **Ōceanus**
odor, **odor**
Oechalia, **Oechalia**
Oeneus, **Oeneus**
Oeta, **Oeta**
of, **ab, dē, ex**
of his (her, their) own
  accord, **suā sponte**
of man, **hūmānus**
of what sort, **quālis**
offend, **offendō**
offer, **offerō, prōpōnō**
office, **mūnus**
often, **saepe**
ointment, **unguentum**
old man, **senex**
Olympus, **Olympus**
on, **in**
on account of, **ob,**
  propter
on all sides, **undique**
on both sides, **utrimque**
on either side, **utrimque**
on the day before, **prīdiē**
on the ground, **humī**
on the spot, **statim**
once, **ōlim**
once upon a time, **ōlim,**
  quondam,
one, **ūnus**
one (of two), **alter**
one hundred, **centum**
only, **sōlum, modo**
only one, **ūnus**
open, **apertus**
open, to, **aperiō,**
  patefaciō, solvō
opinion, **opīniō,**
  sententia

opportune, **opportūnus**
opportunity, **facultās,**
  occāsiō
opposite, **dīversus**
or, **aut**
or? **an**
or if, **sīve, seu**
or not, **nēve, neu**
oracle, **orāculum**
Orcus, **Orcus**
order, **imperātum,**
  iussum, ōrdō
order, to, **imperō,**
  iubeō, praecipiō
order, in, **ex ōrdine**
Orpheus, **Orpheus**
osier, **vīmen**
other, **alius, cēterī,**
  reliquus
other (of two), **alter**
otherwise, **aliter**
ought, **dēbeō**
our, **noster**
out of, **dē, ē, ex**
out of doors, **forās,**
  forīs,
out of place, **aliēnus**
outrage, **violō**
outside, **forīs**
over, **trāns**
overcome, **superō**
overpower, **opprimō**
overtake, **cōnsequor**
owe, **dēbeō**
owed, **dēbitus**
ox, **bōs**

P

pace, **passus**
pain, **dolor**
palace, **rēgia**
palestra, **palaestra**
panic, **pavor**
part, **pars**
pass, **agō**
pass away, **pereō**
pass by, **praetereō**
passage, **trāiectus**
past (*prep.*), **praeter**
pay, **mercēs**
pay, to, **pendō, solvō**
pay completely,
  persolvō
Pelias, **Peliās**
pelt, **pellis**

penalty, **poena**
Penelope, **Pēnelopē**
people, **gēns**
perceive, **cernō,**
   cōnspiciō,
   intellegō, sentiō
perennial, **perennis**
peril, **discrīmen,**
   perīculum
perish, **pereō**
permit, **patior**
permitted, it is, **licet**
perpetual, **perennis,**
   perpetuus
Perseus, **Perseus**
persuade, **persuādeō**
Phasis, **Phāsis**
Phineus, **Phīneus**
Pholus, **Pholus**
Phrixus, **Phrixus**
pierce, **trāiciō**
pierce through,
   perfodiō, trānsfīgō
pig, **porcus**
pigeon, **columba**
pile up, **exstruō**
pillar, **columna**
pity, **misericordia**
place, **locus**
place, to, **collocō, pōnō**
place under, **subiciō**
place upon, **impōnō**
placed, **situs**
plain, **campus**
plan, **cōnsilium, ratiō**
plant, **herba**
plant, to, **serō, obserō**
pleasant, **iūcundus,**
   suāvis,
pleasing, **grātus**
pleasure, **voluptās**
plot, **īnsidiae**
plow, **arō**
pluck, **carpō**
plunder, **praeda**
plunder, to, **praedor**
plunge, **mergō**
Pluto, **Plūtōn**
Po (River), **Ēridanus**
poet, **poēta**
point, **pūnctum**
point out, **dēmōnstrō**
pointed, **praeacūtus**
poison, **medicāmen-**

tum, **venēnum**
Polydectes, **Polydectēs**
Polyphemus,
   Polyphēmus
port, **portus**
possess, **possideō**
possibility, **facultās**
potency, **vīs**
potion, **medicāmentum**
pour forth, **diffundō**
pour out, **effundō**
pray, **ōrō**
prayer, **prex**
preceding, **superior**
predict, **praedīcō**
preeminent, **praestāns**
prefer, **mālō**
prepare, **parō, comparō**
prepared, **parātus**
present, **mūnus**
present (*adj.*), **praesēns**
present, to, **praebeō**
present (time),
   praesentia
preserve, **servō,**
   cōnservō
preside over, **praesum**
press, **premō**
press against, **opprimō**
press out, **exprimō**
press together,
   comprimō
pretended, **falsus**
prevail, **valeō**
prevail upon,
   persuādeō
prevent, **exclūdō,**
   impediō, prōhibeō
previous, **superior**
price, **pretium**
priest, priestess,
   sacerdōs
prison, **carcer**
prisoner, **captīva**
produce, **gignō, prōmō**
proffer, **offerō**
profit, **prōsum**
promise, **polliceor**
pronounce judgment, **iūs**
   dīcere
propose, **prōpōnō**
Proserpine, **Prōserpina**
protect, **dēfendō**
protection, **praesidium**

protector, **praeses**
provisions, **commeātus**
prow, **prōra**
prudence, **cōnsilium,**
   prūdentia
pull down, **dēripiō**
pull off, **dētrahō**
punish, **supplicium**
   sūmere
punishment, **poena,**
   supplicium
purpose, **cōnsilium,**
   sententia
pursue, **īnsequor,**
   persequor
pursuit, **studium**
push against, **pulsō**
put, **conlocō, dō, pōnō**
put around, **circumdō**
put away, **abdō**
put back, **repōnō,**
   restituō
put before, **prōpōnō**
put down, **dēpōnō**
put forth, **ēdō**
put in, **appellō**
put into one's hands,
   mandō
put near, **appōnō**
put off, **exuō**
put on, **induō**
put on shore, **expōnō**
put out, **expōnō**
put out of breath,
   exanimō
put out of the way,
   interficiō
put to, **appōnō**
put to death, **necō**
put to flight, **in fugam**
   convertere
put to sea, **solvō**
put together, **condō**
put under, **subdō**
pyre, **rogus**
Pythia, **Pȳthia**

Q

quarrel, **contrōversia**
queen, **rēgīna**
quickly, **celeriter**
quickness, **celeritās**

R

race, **gēns**
rage, **furor**
rage, to, **exārdēscō**
rain, **imber**
raise, **tollō**
ram, **ariēs**
rank, **ōrdō**
rashly, **temere**
rather, **magis**
rattle, **crepitus,
crotalum**
reach, **attingō,
perveniō**
ready, **parātus**
really, **rē vērā**
realm, **rēgnum**
reason, **causa**
receive, **capiō, accipiō,
excipiō**
recently, **nūper**
recline, **cubō**
recognize, **agnōscō**
recount, **commemorō,
perscrībō**
recover, **recipiō, sē
recipere, recuperō**
recruit, **reficiō,**
refresh, **reficiō**
refuse, **negō, recūsō**
region, **regiō**
reign, **rēgnō**
reinforcement,
subsidium
rejoice, **gaudeō**
relate, **nārrō, trādō**
release, **extrahō,
līberō, solvō**
remain, **maneō,
permaneō,
supersum**
remain through,
permaneō
remaining, **cēterī,
reliquus**
remarkable,
**praeclārus,
praestāns**
remedy, **remedium**
remember, **memoriā
tenēre**
remote, **longinquus**
remove, **removeō,
tollō**

rend asunder, **dīvellō**
render, **reddō**
renew, **redintegrō,
reficiō**
repair, **reficiō**
repel, **repellō**
reply, **respōnsum**
reply, to, **respondeō**
report, **fāma**
report, to, **nūntiō,
renūntiō, trādō**
repose, **quiēs**
reproach, **obiūrgō**
repulse, **repellō**
reputation, **opīniō**
request, **postulō**
requite, **grātiam
referre**
rescue, **ēripiō, extrahō**
reserve, **subsidium**
resist, **repugnō, resistō**
resolve, **statuō**
respond, **respondeō**
response, **respōnsum**
rest, **quiēs**
rest of, **cēterī, reliquus**
rest on, **positus esse**
restore, **reddō, reducō,
restituō**
restrain, **frēnō, premō,
teneō, retineō**
retire, **pedem referre**
retreat, **refugiō, pedem
referre**
return, **reditus**
return, to, (trans.) **reddō,
referō**; (intrans.)
**redeō, regredior,
revertor**
return a favor, **grātiam
referre**
revenge, **ulcīscor**
reward, **mercēs,
praemium**
Rhadamanthus,
Rhadamanthus
right, **dexter**
right, **iūs**
right hand, **dextra**
right reason, **sānitās**
rise, **orior**
risk, **perīculum**
river, **flūmen**
road, **via**

roar, roaring, **fremitus**
rob, **praedor**
robber, **latrō**
robe, **vestis**
rock, **rūpēs, saxum**
Rome, **Rōma**
round, **circum**
rouse, **commoveō,
excitō**
rout, **pellō**
row, **rēmigō**
royal power, **rēgnum**
rule, **imperium,
rēgnum**
rule, to, **rēgnō**
rumor, **fāma**
run, **currō**
run against, **occurrō**
run away, **fugiō,
refugiō**
run down, **dēcurrō**
run to, **accurrō**
run together, **concurrō**
running, **cursus**
rush, **ruō**
rush in, **inruō**
rush together, **concurrō**

S

sacred, **sānctus**
sacrifice, **sacrificium**
sacrifice, to, **immolō**
sadness, **trīstitia**
safe, **incolumis, tūtus**
safety, **salūs**
said, **inquit**
sail, **nāvigō**
sailing, **nāvigātiō**
sailor, **nauta**
Salmydessus,
Salmydēssus
salt, **sāl**
salted, **salsus**
same, **īdem**
sanctuary, **templum**
sand, **harēna**
sanity, **sānitās**
savage, **ferōx, saevus**
save, **servō**
say, **dīcō, prōpōnō**
say beforehand,
praedīcō
say no or not, **negō**
scarcely, **vix**
scatter, **disiciō, spargō**

scepter, scēptrum
scold, obiūrgō
scorch, adūrō
scout, explōrātor
sea, mare
sear, adūrō
search out, explōrō
season, tempus
seasonable, opportūnus
seat, sēdēs, solium
second, alter
see, cōnspiciō, videō
seeding, sēmentis
seek, petō, quaerō
seem, videor
seize, arripiō,
    corripiō, capiō,
    occupō, prehendō,
    comprehendō
select, dēligō
self, ipse
send, mittō
send away, āmittō,
    dīmittō
send back, remittō
send different ways,
    dīmittō
send down, dēmittō
send forth, dīmittō,
    ēmittō
send in, immittō
send out, ēmittō
send to, admittō
send together, committō
separate, dīvidō
serious, gravis
seriously, graviter
Seriphos, Serīphus
serpent, anguis, dracō,
    serpēns
servant, servus
serve, appōnō, serviō
service, beneficium,
    mūnus, officium,
    servitūs
servitude, servitūs
set a day, diem dīcere
set back, repōnō
set before, appōnō,
    prōpōnō
set fire to, adūrō
set forth, expōnō,
    prōpōnō
set free, līberō

set on fire, succendō
set out, proficīscor
set sail, solvō
set up, statuō,
    cōnstituō
set up again, restituō
setting, occāsus
seventh, septimus
several, plūrēs,
    cōmplūrēs
severe, gravis
severely, graviter
shade, mānēs, umbra
shades, īnferī, mānēs
shadow, umbra
shape, figūra, speciēs
sharp, ācer,
    praeacūtus
sharpened at the end,
    praeacūtus
sharply, ācriter
shatter, afflīgō
she, ea, haec, illa
shed abroad, diffundō
sheep, ovis, pecus
shepherd, pāstor
shield, scūtum
shine, ēlūceō
shine out, ēlūceō
ship, nāvis
shoe, calceus
shore, harēna, lītus
short, brevis
shoulder, umerus
shout, clāmor
shout out, exclāmō
shout repeatedly,
    clāmitō
show, adhibeō,
    demōnstrō,
    ostendō, praebeō,
    praestō
show gratitude, grātiam
    referre
shower, imber
shrill, ācer
shut out, exclūdō
shut up, contineō
shut up in, inclūdō
Sicily, Sicilia
sickle, falx
side, pars
sight, cōnspectus,
    speciēs, vīsus

sign, signum
signal, signum
silent, silentus
silver, argentum
since, cum, quoniam
sinew, nervus
sing, canō
singing, cantus
sink, mergō
sister, soror
sit, sedeō
sit down, cōnsīdō
situated, situs
situation, rēs
size, magnitūdō
skiff, linter
skill, scientia
skin, pellis, ūter
sky, caelum
slaughter, caedēs
slave, servus
slavery, servitūs
slay, necō
sleep, somnus
sleep, to, dormiō
slight, levis
slightly, leviter
slip, labor
slip down, dēlābor
slip out, ēlābor
small, parvus
smear, oblinō, unguō
smell, odor
smith, faber
smithy, officīna
smoke, fūmus
snake, anguis
snatch away, abripiō
snatch away from,
    dēripiō
snatch down from,
    dēripiō
snatch out, ēripiō
snatch to oneself,
    arripiō
snatch up, arripiō,
    corripiō
snow, nix
so, ita, sīc, tam
so far, tantum
so great, tantus
so much, tantus
soak, imbuō, tinguō
soldier, mīles

some, aliquī
some, someone,
  somebody, something,
  aliquis, quis
some . . . others, aliī . . .
  aliī
someone or other,
  nesciō quis
somewhat, aliquantum,
  paulō
son, fīlius
song, cantus, carmen
soon, see as soon
sooner than, priusquam
soul, anima
sound, sonitus
sounding, sonōrus
soundness, sānitās
south, merīdiēs
sow, serō, obserō
sowing, sēmentis
space, intervāllum,
  spatium
space of time, spatium
Spain, Hispānia
speak, dīcō, loquor,
  ōrātiōnem habēre,
  ōrō
speak out, ēnūntiō
spear, tēlum
spectator, spectātor
speech, ōrātiō, sermō
speed, celeritās
spelt, far
spend, cōnsūmō
spirit, animus, mānēs
splendid, ēgrēgius,
  magnificus,
  praeclārus
splendidly, ēgregiē,
  magnificē
spoil, praeda
sport, lūdus
spouse, coniūnx
spread abroad, diffundō
spread before,
  prōsternō
spring, fōns
spring up, orior,
  exorior
sprinkle, spargō
spy, explōrātor
squeeze, comprimō
stable, stabulum

stag, cervus
stain, īnficiō
stall, stabulum
stand, stō
stand against, resistō
stand around, circumstō
stand at, adstō
stand before, praestō
stand near, adstō
stand together, cōnstō
standing-place,
  stabulum
start, prōfectiō
start, to, prōficīscor
state, cīvitās
station oneself, cōnsistō
stay, moror, commoror
steer, gubernō
stick, clāva
stick, to, haerō
still, etiam tum
stone, lapis, saxum
stop, dēsistō, teneō
store away, condō,
  repōnō
store up, repōnō
storm, tempestās
story, fābula
strait, fretum
strange, mīrus
stranger, advena,
  peregrinus
stratagem, īnsidiae
stray, errō
strength, vīrēs
strengthen, cōnfīrmō
stretch, contendō,
  intendō
stretch out, intendō
stretch out before,
  ostendō
strew before, prōsternō
strike, percutiō
strike against, pulsō
strike through, percutiō,
  trāiciō
strong, validus
struggle, certāmen
struggle, to, luctor,
  repugnō
studious, studiōsus
study, studium
stupefy, exanimō
Stymphalian, of

Symphalus,
  Stymphālis
Stymphalus,
  Stymphālus
Styx, Styx
subject, cīvis
submit to, subeō
succeed, succēdō
successfully, bene,
  fēlīciter
successive, continuus
such, tālis
suddenly, subitō
suffer, capiō, accipiō,
  patior
sufficiently, satis
suitable, idōneus,
  opportūnus
summer, aestās
summon, arcessō, vocō,
  convocō
sun, sōl
sun-god, sōl
sunset, occāsus sōlis
supplies, commeātus
supply, cōpia
supply, to, praebeō
support, subsidium
surpass, praestō,
  superō
surpassing, praestāns
surround, cingō,
  circumdō
survey, perlūstrō
suspect, suspicor
suspicion, suspīciō
sustain, subeō,
  sustineō
sustenance, vīctus
swallow, dēvorō
swallow down, dēvorō
swallow whole, vorō
swamp, palūs
sway, imperium
sweet, dulcis,
  iūcundus, suāvis
sweetness, dulcēdō
swift, celer
swiftly, celeriter
swiftness, celeritās
swim, natō
swim across, trānō
swim over, trānō
swine, porcus

sword, **gladius**
Symplegades,
　Symplēgadēs

T
Taenarus, **Taenarus**
tail, **cauda**
take, **addūcō, adimō,**
　capiō, sūmō
take away, **abdūcō,**
　adimō, absūmō,
　tollō
take back, **recipiō**
take beforehand,
　praecipiō
take care, **caveō**
take completely,
　cōnsūmō
take off, **exuō**
take one's stand,
　cōnsistō
take out, **excipiō,**
　prōmō
take to oneself, **accipiō,**
　adimō
take up, **excipiō, sūmō**
talk, **sermō**
Tartarus, **Tartarus**
task, **negōtium, opus**
taste, **gustō**
teach, **doceō**
teacher, **magister**
tear, **lacrima**
tear apart, **dīvellō**
tear in pieces, **dīvellō**
tear off, **dēripiō**
tedious, **longus**
tell, **dīcō, nārrō**
tempest, **tempestās**
temple, **aedēs,**
　templum
ten, **decem**
tenth, **decimus**
terrible, **horribilis,**
　terribilis
terrify, **terreō,**
　perterreō
territory, **fīnēs**
terror, **pavor, terror**
than, **atque, ac, quam**
thank, **grātiās agere**
thanks, **grātiae**
that, is, **ille, quī**
that (*conj.*), **ut**
　that not, **nē, quīn**

that (of yours), **iste**
Thebans, **Thēbānī**
Thebes, **Thēbae**
theft, **fūrtum**
their own, **suus**
themselves (*intens.*), **ipsī**
themselves (*reflex.*), **suī**
then, **deinde, tum**
there, **ibi**
therefore, **igitur,**
　itaque
Thermodon,
　Thermōdōn
Theseus, **Thēseus**
Thessaly, **Thessalia**
they, **eī, hī, illī**
thick, **dēnsus**
thin, **tenuis**
thing, **rēs**
think, **arbitror,**
　exīstimō, putō
think out, **excōgitō**
think over, **cōgitō**
third, **tertius**
third time, **tertium**
this, **ea, hic, is**
thousand, **mīlle**
thousands, **mīlia**
thousands of paces, **mīlia**
　passuum
Thrace, **Thrācia**
threaten, **minitor**
threats, **minae**
three, **trēs**
threshold, **līmen**
throat, **faucēs**
throne, **rēgnum, solium**
through, **per**
throw, **iaciō, adiciō,**
　coniciō, prōiciō,
　prōsternō
throw across, **trāiciō**
throw apart, **disiciō**
throw away, **abiciō,**
　omittō
throw down, **dēiciō**
throw forth, **prōiciō**
throw in, **iniciō**
throw in the way, **obiciō**
throw into confusion,
　perturbō
throw into disorder,
　turbō
throw open, **patefaciō**

throw to, **adiciō, obiciō**
throw together, **coniciō**
throw under, **subiciō**
throw upon, **iniciō**
thrust through,
　trānsfīgō
thus, **ita, itaque, sīc**
Tiber, **Tiberis**
till, **colō**
till when, **quō ūsque**
time, **spatium, tempus**
tire, **exanimō**
Tiryns, **Tīrȳns**
to, **ad, in**
toil, **labor**
toil, to, **labōrō**
too, **etiam**
tooth, **dēns**
torch, **fax**
torture, **cruciātus,**
　supplicium
torture, to, **excruciō**
to that place, **eō**
to this place, **hūc**
to what place, **quō**
touch, **tangō, tractō**
touch at, **attingō**
toward, **ad, ergā, in**
toward evening, **sub**
　vesperum
town, **oppidum**
track, **vēstīgium**
trader, **mercātor**
transfix, **perfodiō,**
　trānsfīgō
transport, **trānsportō**
traveler, **viātor**
tree, **arbor**
trench, **fossa**
tribute, **tribūtum**
trick, **dolus**
Trojans, **Troiānī**
troops, **cōpiae**
trouble, **negōtium**
trouble, to, **turbō**
troubled, **sollicitus**
Troy, **Troia**
true, **vērus**
try, **conor, temptō**
turn, **torqueō, vertō,**
　convertō
turn around, **convertō**
turn aside, **dēvertō**
turn away, **dēvertō**

turn back, **revertor**
turn often, **versor**
turn out, **ēveniō**
turn the mind to,
   animadvertō
turned different ways,
   dīversus
twelve, **duodecim**
twenty, **vīgintī**
two, **duo**
two-headed, **biceps**

U

Ulysses, **Ulixēs**
unaccomplished,
   īnfectus
unaware, **īnsciēns**
unbelievable,
   incrēdibilis
unbind, **solvō**
uncertain, **dubius**
under, **sub**
undergo, **subeō**
understand, **intellegō**
undertake, **suscipiō**
undertaking, **rēs**
underworld, **Orcus**
undone, **īnfectus**
unexpectedly, **subitō**
unfortunate, **īnfēlix**
unfriendly, **inimīcus**
unhappy, **īnfēlix**
unhurt, **incolumis**
unknowing, **īnsciēns**
unknown, **ignōtus**
unless, **nisi**
unsafe, **īnfestus**
unsheathe, **dēstringō**
unskilled, **imperītus**
until, **dum, ūsque ad**
unusual, **inūsitātus**
unwilling, **invītus**
unwilling, to be, **nōlō**
upon, **in**
uppermost, **summus**
upright, **ērēctus**
up to, **ūsque ad**
urge, **hortor, impellō**
urge on, **impellō**
use, **ūsus**
use, to, **ūtor**
use up, **cōnsūmō**
useful, **ūsuī**
useless, **inūtilis**
utter, **ēdō**

V

vainly, **frūstrā**
valley, **vallēs**
vanish, **ēvānēscō**
vanish away, **ēvānēscō**
various, **varius**
vast, **ingēns, vāstus**
vehemently,
   vehementer
very, **ipse**
very greatly, **maximē**
very little, **mimimē**
very much, **magnopere**
vessel, **vās, vāsa**
victim, **victima**
victory, **victōria**
villa, **vīlla**
village, **vīcus**
violate, **violō**
violence, **vīs**
violently, **vehementer**
virtue, **vīs**
visit, **afficiō**
voice, **vōx**
voluntarily, **suā sponte**
voyage, **nāvigātiō**
Vulcan, **Volcānus**

W

wage against, **īnferō**
wages, **mercēs**
wait, **exspectō, maneō**
wait for, **exspectō**
walls, **moenia**
wand, **virga**
wander, **errō**
war, **bellum**
warfare, **rēs mīlitāris**
warlike, **bellicōsus,**
   mīlitāris
warn, **moneō**
warship, **nāvis longa**
waste, **vāstus**
watch, **vigilia**
watch, to, **īnspectō**
water, **aqua**
wave, **unda**
way, **modus, mōs, via**
wayfarer, **viātor**
weapon, **tēlum**
weapons, **arma**
wear, **gerō**
wear out, **cōnficiō**
weariness, **lassitūdō**
weary, **fessus**

weather, **tempestās**
weather, to, **perferō**
weave, **texō**
weigh anchor, **ancorās**
   tollere
weigh out, **pendō**
weight, **pondus**
welcome, **excipiō**
well, **bene**
well-doing, **beneficium**
well-known, **nōtus**
wet, **imbuō, tinguō**
what, **quis, quī**
what kind of, **quālis**
wheat, **far**
when, **cum, postquam,**
   ubi, ut
whence, **unde**
where, **quā, ubi**
whether . . . or, **sīve . . .**
   sīve
which, **quis, quī**
which (of two), **uter**
while, **cum, dum**
whirlwind, **turbō**
white, **albus**
whither, **quō**
who, **quī, quis**
whole, **omnis, tōtus,**
   ūniversus
wholly, **omnīnō**
wicked, **improbus**
wickedness, **scelus**
wide, **lātus**
wife, **coniūnx, uxor**
wild animal, **fera**
wild boar, **aper**
will, **voluntās**
willingly, **libenter**
wind, **ventus**
wine, **vīnum**
wing, **āla**
winged shoes, **tālāria**
wish, **voluntās**
wish, to, **cupiō, volō**
wish rather, **mālō**
with, **apud, cum**
with all one's might,
   omnibus vīribus
with difficulty, **aegrē,**
   vix
with might and main,
   omnibus vīribus
withdraw, **discēdō, sē**

recipere
within, **intrā**
without, **sine**
without (outside), **forīs**
withstand, **sustineō**
woman, **fēmina, mulier**
wonder, **mīrāculum,
  mōnstrum**
wonder, to, **mīror**
wonder at, **mīror,
  admīror**
wonderful, **mīrus**
wood, **ligna, silva**
wood, wooden, of wood,
  ligneus
word, **verbum, vōx**
work, **opera, opus**
work out, **efficiō**

workshop, **officīna**
world, **orbis terrārum**
worn out, **dēfessus**
worship, **colō**
wound, **vulnus**
wound, to, **vulnerō**
wrath, **īra**
wrathful, **īrātus**
wreck, **frangō**
wrestle, **luctor**
wrestling-place,
  palaestra
write, **scrībō**
write in full, **perscrībō**
wrong, **iniūria**

Y

year, **annus**

yearly, **quotannīs**
yet, **tamen**
yield, **concēdō**
yoke, **iugum**
yoke, to, **iungō**
you, (*sing.*) **tū**; (*pl.*) **vōs**
young man, **adulēscēns,
  iuvenis**
your, (*sing.*) **tuus**; (*pl.*)
  vester
youth, **adulēscēns,
  iuvenis**
youth, **adulēscentia**

Z

zeal, **studium**
Zetes, **Zētēs**